Ple
is p
one
by te

The Economics of Football

This book presents the first detailed economic analysis of professional football at club level, using a combination of economic reasoning and statistical and econometric analysis. Most of the original empirical research reported in the book is based on English club football. A wide range of international comparisons helps to emphasise the broader relevance as well as the unique characteristics of the English experience. Specific topics include: the links between football clubs' financial strength and competitive balance and uncertainty of outcome; the determinants of professional footballers' compensation; measuring the football manager's contribution to team performance; the determinants of managerial change and its effects on team performance; patterns of spectator demand for attendance; modelling and predicting match results; fixed-odds betting on football match results and the market in football clubs' company shares.

The book concludes with an extended discussion of the major economic policy issues currently facing football's legislators and administrators worldwide.

STEPHEN DOBSON is Senior Lecturer in Economics in the School of Management and Economics at The Queen's University of Belfast. He is the joint author of two books, *Introduction to Economics* (1999) and *Microeconomics* (1995). He has also published articles in journals including *The Statistician, Economic History Review* and *Scottish Journal of Political Economy.*

JOHN GODDARD is Senior Lecturer in the Department of Economics at University of Wales Swansea. He has published articles in journals including *International Journal of Industrial Organization, Economics Letters* and *Managerial and Decision Economics.* He is the joint author of a recent book, *European Banking: Efficiency, Technology, Growth.*

The Economics of Football

Stephen Dobson

School of Management and Economics,
The Queen's University of Belfast

and John Goddard

Department of Economics,
University of Wales Swansea

PUBLISHED BY THE PRESS SYNDICATE OF THE UNIVERSITY OF CAMBRIDGE
The Pitt Building, Trumpington Street, Cambridge, United Kingdom

CAMBRIDGE UNIVERSITY PRESS
The Edinburgh Building, Cambridge CB2 2RU, UK
40 West 20th Street, New York, NY 10011-4211, USA
477 Williamstown Road, Port Melbourne, VIC 3207, Australia
Ruiz de Alarcón 13, 28014 Madrid, Spain
Dock House, The Waterfront, Cape Town 8001, South Africa

http://www.cambridge.org

© Stephen Dobson and John Goddard 2001

First published 2001
Third printing 2004

Printed in the United Kingdom at the University Press, Cambridge

Typeface Plantin MT 10/13 pt   *System* QuarkXPress™   [SE]

A catalogue record for this book is available from the British Library

Library of Congress Cataloguing in Publication data

Dobson, Stephen.
The economics of football / Stephen Dobson, John Goddard.
   p.   cm.
Include bibliographical references and index.
ISBN 0 521 66158 7
1. Soccer – Economic aspects – Great Britain.   2. Soccer – Great Britain – France.
I. Goddard, John.   II. Title.
GV943.3.D63   2001
338.4'3796334'0941–dc21   2001018128

ISBN 0 521 66158 7 hardback

To Carlyn and Imogen   SD
To Les and Chris   JG

Contents

Figures

Tables

Preface

Only a few years ago professional football in England was in a state of serious decline. Attendances were falling, revenues were stagnant and the image of the game was marred by hooliganism. Academic economists and the business and finance community paid very little attention to the sector, and most of the publicity surrounding the sport was bad. Since the start of the 1990s, however, professional football in England and elsewhere has experienced an astonishing transformation. Player salaries have risen exponentially, television contracts yield revenues on a scale unimaginable only a few years ago, many football stadia have been completely rebuilt, the profile of commercial sponsorship and merchandising has increased beyond measure and a number of clubs are now floated on the stock market. The business side of football regularly makes headline news, and newspapers devote pages to coverage of financial aspects of the sport.

Football's importance, of course, is not only economic, but also social and cultural. The level of interest is reflected not only by the several million people who attend matches in person each season, but also by the millions more who watch matches on television and follow its fortunes through coverage in the media. The amount of welfare created by football is perhaps even larger than the revenues that are generated at the professional level would suggest. At grassroots level, for example, football's popularity as a participant sport generates benefits for the health of the population. At the highest level, international or European success generates intangible benefits for the nation in the form of prestige and goodwill. Despite football's prominent public profile, and despite the fact that its weekly or daily audiences (including television viewers) run into millions, academic economists have devoted relatively little attention to professional football. This study aims to rectify this situation, by presenting a research-driven economic appraisal of professional football at club level. The approach is based on a combination of economic reasoning and empirical analysis.

The application of economic analysis to the football industry (and to team sports in general) represents an important sub-field within economics. In the USA economists have been writing and publishing books and scholarly articles on baseball, basketball and (American) football since the mid-1950s. Consequently, the academic literature is dominated by studies of the economics of North American sports. These writings shed light on a wide range of important issues, including the determinants of the compensation received by professional sports players, the nature of joint production in team sports, competitive balance, uncertainty of outcome and the distribution of playing talent in sports leagues and the contribution of the coach or manager to team performance.

The common thread linking research into all of these topics is the development and testing of economic hypotheses, using sports as a laboratory within which suitable data can be collected. A major attraction of sports to empirical economists, indeed, is that the availability of data permits investigation of a large number of economic propositions that would be difficult to test in other areas, because of a lack of suitable data. The professional football sector therefore offers opportunities for empirical research in areas such as consumer behaviour, labour economics and industrial organisation, as well as more specialised topics of particular relevance to the economics of sports.

At this point, the reader's attention is drawn to a small number of stylistic conventions that are adopted throughout the present volume. Currently, the English league football season runs from August to May, although in the past there have been minor variations; for many years the league season was scheduled to finish at the end of April, but often overran owing to postponements caused by bad weather. Often the season which began in August 1998 and finished in May 1999 is referred to as the 1998–1999 season. In order to be concise, however, in this volume all football seasons are referred to by their end-year only. The season which ran from August 1998 to May 1999 is therefore known as the 1999 season.

Readers familiar with the recent history of English football will be aware that an important organisational change took place during the summer of 1992 (or, in present terminology, at the start of the 1993 season), with the creation of the Premier League. Previously, the Football League was responsible for the organisation of league competition involving all 92 professional clubs in England and Wales. The clubs were divided into four divisions, with promotion and relegation of a few clubs (usually between two and four) taking place between each division at the end of each season. Between the 1959 and 1992 seasons, the divisions had simply been numbered from 1 to 4. The decision of the Division 1 clubs to withdraw from the Football League resulted in the formation of their own organising body, the Premier League, which negotiates television contracts and takes decisions on behalf of its own clubs. The Football League responded by renumbering its three remaining divisions (previously 2 to 4) from One to Three. The league's competitive structure was not affected directly by these developments: promotion and relegation between the Premier League and Division One of the Football League were still automatic at the end of each season. But the renumbering of the divisions does create potential for confusion in a volume of this kind, which draws on both pre- and post-1992 data. To avoid confusion, the convention adopted throughout this volume is that *numbers* are used to refer to pre-1992 divisions (Divisions 1 to 4), while *words* refer to post-1992 divisions (the Premier League, and Divisions One, Two and Three of the Football League).

Acknowledgements

We would like to thank Ioannis Asimakopoulos, Rick Audas, Peter Dawson, Bill Gerrard, Angelos Kanas, Carlyn Ramlogan and John Wilson for many helpful comments and suggestions. We would also like to thank an anonymous referee for comments on an earlier draft of this manuscript, which have encouraged us to develop and extend the analysis in a number of directions. SD would like to thank Andy Tremayne and Stephen Trotter, former colleagues at Hull, for many interesting insights on football economics, and Eric Strobl and Lester Henry for conversations while SD was 'liming' at the St Augustine campus of the University of the West Indies. JG would like to thank Phil Molyneux, Jonathan Williams and Stephen Jones for their insights during discussions held in the Coffee Bar at Bangor, prior to its recent closure. Both authors would especially like to thank several generations of students at Abertay, Bangor, Hull and Swansea, particularly all those whose dissertations combined an enthusiasm for football with a tolerance of economics and statistics. There are too many of you to mention by name, but you know who you are, wherever you are.

We would also like to thank a number of staff at Cambridge University Press for their assistance during the development of this project. In particular we are grateful to Ashwin Rattan (Economics Editor) for his unfailing support, advice and encouragement throughout; Barbara Docherty (Copy Editor) for her meticulous efforts in checking and correcting our original manuscript; and Michelle Williams (Production Controller) for her guidance and assistance during the processes of proof reading and production.

1 Introduction

Academic interest in the economics of professional team sports dates back as far as the mid-1950s. Since then, many books and journal articles have been written on the subject. Much of the academic literature originates in the USA. In common with trends that are evident throughout the subject discipline of economics, research on the economics of sport has become increasingly sophisticated, both theoretically and in its use of econometric methodology, especially in recent times. Papers on the economics of sport now appear regularly in many of the leading economics journals, and most economists would agree that in view of its social, cultural and economic importance, professional sport is a legitimate area of interest for both theoretical and empirical researchers. Indeed, many would argue that the unique configurations of individual and team incentives, and the interactions between co-operative and competitive modes of behaviour that professional team sports tend to generate, make this particularly fertile territory in which to explore the perennial questions about incentives, effort, risk and reward which lie at the heart of all areas of economic inquiry.

This volume makes a contribution to the burgeoning literature on the economics of team sports by providing the first comprehensive survey of research that is focused on professional football at club level. A survey of the economics of professional football seems appropriate at the present time, if not long overdue. The spectacular recent increase in the size of football's audience is, of course, a strong motivating factor. Such a survey will recognise and reflect not only football's global popularity at the start of the twenty-first century, but also the special historical significance of England as the original birthplace of the sport. Club football played in the English Premier League and Football League provides the laboratory for most of the original, empirical research that is reported in this volume.

Each chapter of this volume concentrates on a particular aspect of the economics of professional football. The previous theoretical and empirical literature that is relevant to each topic is reviewed, and new and original empirical analyses are presented. The sections that describe the existing literature aim to convey an impression of the breadth and depth of previous academic research into the economics of professional team sports. Much has been written already about football, and very much more has been written about other sports, especially in the USA where attention naturally tends to focus on sports such as baseball, basketball and (American) football. Though football is the main subject of this volume, due attention and emphasis is devoted to insights that have been obtained from research into other sports, wherever these turn out to be of wider relevance.

As already emphasised, anyone who reads the academic literature on the economics of sport cannot fail to be struck by the sheer volume of column inches that has been devoted to this topic. Of all the articles that have been published, however, there are perhaps a few that have had a particularly important influence in shaping the research agenda for the economics of team sports in general, and for the economics of football in particular. Many of the ideas contained in these articles are as relevant to researchers today as they were when the articles concerned were originally published. In this introductory chapter, three such articles are highlighted and reviewed in some detail. There is, of course, an element of subjectivity in choosing such a small number of articles out of the many excellent ones that have been published. Even so, a consensus seems to have evolved that regards the articles by Simon Rottenberg (1956) and Walter Neale (1964) as fundamental to the subsequent development of research on team sports in general. Both articles address various economic implications of the structural features of the markets within which professional sports teams operate. The article by Peter Sloane (1971) has also had a major influence on the developing the research agenda, especially in respect of the economics of football. In section 1.1, the principal contributions of each of these articles are reviewed in turn, and the subsequent development of the economics of team sports as an academic discipline is outlined. The aim of section 1.1 is to place the research that is reported in the rest of this volume into its proper context. This is followed in section 1.2 by a summary of the contents of each of the following chapters, and in section 1.3 by an outline of the use of econometric methods in the empirical investigations that are reported in this volume.

1.1 The economics of team sports: three seminal contributions and the subsequent development of the subject

Rottenberg: 'The baseball players' labor market', Journal of Political Economy, *1956*

Rottenberg is widely credited with writing the first academic analysis of the economics of professional team sports. The paper was written at a time when US professional baseball players' contracts included a reserve clause. Once he signed his first one-year contract with a team in organised baseball, a player ceased to be a free agent. On expiry of his present contract, his team retained the option to renew his contract for another year.[1] This served to limit players' freedom of movement, by binding them to their present employers. Effectively, the reserve clause created a monopsony in the players' labour market: each contracted player could negotiate with only one potential buyer of his services. The baseball authorities defended the reserve clause on the grounds that it was necessary to ensure an equal distribution of playing talent among opposing teams. Without the reserve clause, the rich teams (with the largest potential markets) would outbid the poorer ones for the best available players. This would tend to reduce uncertainty of outcome and spectator interest in the league competition as a whole, and depress the attendances and revenues of all teams.

Rottenberg's contribution was to argue that free agency in the players' labour market would not necessarily lead to a concentration of the best players in the richest teams. In other words, a reserve clause was not a necessary condition to ensure competitive balance. Professional team sports are intrinsically different from other businesses, in which a firm is likely to prosper if it can eliminate competition and establish a position as a monopoly supplier. In sports, it does not pay a rich team to accumulate star players to the extent that (sporting) competition is greatly diminished, because of the joint nature of 'production' in sports. Consequently, a team that attempts to accumulate all of the best available playing talent will find at some stage that diminishing returns begin to set in: 'In baseball no team can be successful unless its competitors also survive and prosper sufficiently so that the differences in the quality of play among teams are not "too great." ... At some point, therefore, a first star player is worth more to poor team B than, say, a third star to rich team A. At this point, B is in a position to bid players away from A in the market' (Rottenberg, 1956, pp. 254, 255).

---

[1] This was subject only to a rule that prevented the wage being cut by more than 25 per cent in any one year if the team was in one of the major leagues.

If teams are rational profit maximisers, the distribution of playing talent among the teams should be reasonably even. Neither a reserve clause nor explicit collusion is necessary in order to bring about this result. It is in each team's self-interest to ensure that it does not become too strong relative to its competitors: 'It follows that players will be distributed among teams so that they are put to their most "productive" use; each will play for the team that is able to get the highest return from his services. But this is exactly the result which would be yielded by a free market' (Rottenberg, 1956, p. 256).

A reserve clause will therefore deliver roughly the same distribution of playing talent among teams as free agency. Whether players are free agents or not, the distribution of playing talent is determined by the incentive to maximise the capitalised value of the services supplied by individual players. If there is another team for which this capitalised value would be higher than it is for the player's present team, then there is a price at which it is advantageous for both teams to trade the player's contract.

Rottenberg also discusses the implications of the reserve clause, and the monopsony power it confers on teams as buyers of playing services, for players' salaries. Each player's reservation wage (the minimum wage he would accept to play baseball) is determined primarily by the next highest wage he could earn outside baseball adjusted to reflect his valuation of the non-pecuniary costs and benefits of playing baseball. Although theoretically the team has the contractual power to impose the reservation wage on all players, Rottenberg notes that in practice this does not seem to happen. Many players earn far more from baseball than they could in alternative employment. This is attributed to the fact that players as well as teams have bargaining power in wage negotiations: in an extreme case, a player can simply threaten to withdraw his services. If a player's reservation wage is $10,000, but he is worth $20,000 to his team, then a wage anywhere between $10,000 and $20,000 is possible, depending on the 'shrewdness and guile of the parties in devising their bargaining strategies' (Rottenberg, 1956, p. 253). Competition among sellers, however, imposes limitations on players' bargaining power. A star player worth $40,000 to his team cannot extract a wage beyond $30,000 if a lesser player worth $20,000 is willing to accept a wage of $10,000 to fill the same position.

The main effect of the reserve clause is that players receive salaries below their value to the team that employs them. In other words, it tends to direct rents away from players and towards teams. The reserve clause does not achieve its stated aim of influencing the allocation of playing talent between teams. Rottenberg concludes by considering several alternative regimes that might produce a more or less equal distribution of playing talent between teams with free agency in the players' labour market. These include:

- *Revenue pooling.* If all revenues are shared equally, teams have no pecuniary incentive to spend on players to enhance their own performance and revenue. An equal distribution of mediocre playing talent is the most likely outcome.
- *Salary capping.* The effect of a salary cap on the distribution of talent will depend on the extent to which teams can circumvent it by offering players non-pecuniary rewards.
- *Allocating multiple team franchises in large cities.* If reasonable equality between each team's potential market size can be achieved, this is expected to create a more equal distribution of playing talent.

Neale: 'The peculiar economics of professional sports', Quarterly Journal of Economics, *1964*

Neale's analysis begins by emphasising the joint nature of production in professional sports. Heavyweight boxing is used as an example to introduce what Neale calls the 'Louis Schmelling Paradox'. World champion Joe Louis' earnings were higher if there was an evenly matched contender available for him to fight than if the nearest contender was relatively weak. The same point applies also in baseball. 'Suppose the Yankees used their wealth to buy up not only all the good players but also all of the teams in the American League: no games, no receipts, no Yankees. When, for a brief period in the late fifties, the Yankees lost the championship and opened the possibility of a non-Yankee World Series they found themselves – anomalously – facing sporting disgrace and bigger crowds' (Neale, 1964, p. 2).

Does this imply that professional sport is an industry in which monopoly is less profitable than competition, contradicting what we teach students and what they can read in any Principles text? Neale addresses this paradox by distinguishing between 'sporting' and 'economic' competition. Sporting competition is more profitable than sporting monopoly for the reasons outlined above, but sporting competition is not the same as economic competition. Similarly, although in law the sports team is a firm (which may be motivated by profit), it is not a firm in the economist's sense. A single team cannot supply the entire market; if it did it would have no one to play. Teams must co-operate with each other to produce individual matches and a viable league competition, so there is joint production. The league's organising body exerts strict controls over a wide range of matters including competition rules and schedules, player mobility and the entry and exit of clubs. In short, the league rather than the individual team is the 'firm' in the economist's sense. A sports league should be regarded as analogous to a multi-plant firm, in which the individual teams are 'plants', subject to decisions which are taken and implemented collectively at league level.

If the sports league is the 'firm' in the economic sense, this raises the question as to why it is unusual to observe direct competition between rival leagues operating within the same sport. Although the National League and American League do operate simultaneously in baseball, analytically they should be regarded as one larger 'multi-league' firm, since they come together at the end of each season to produce the World Series. Geographical division is a more common form of segmentation though, according to Neale, one that is inherently unstable. Where direct competition is prevented by geography, profit incentives tend to promote enlargement and the elimination of geographical boundaries.[2] Competition between different sports is more common than competition between rival leagues within the same sport, though segmentation based on nation, region, season of the year or even social class are still common.[3] All such forms of segmentation tend to inhibit direct head-to-head competition.

Neale suggests that the general lack of competition between sports leagues arises because the cost and demand characteristics of the market for professional team sports tend to create conditions of natural monopoly, making it efficient for a single league to supply the entire market. On the cost side, Neale suggests that the long-run average cost curve is probably horizontal. Although an increase in the scale of production might entail the use of less efficient playing inputs, raising average costs, this tends to be offset by an 'enthusiasm effect'. If the sport operates on a larger scale, public enthusiasm encourages more people to take up playing, eventually raising the supply of players at the highest level. To some extent, the enthusiasm effect makes supply and demand interdependent: if more people play the sport, more will also want to attend matches at the professional level. Finally, the existence of rival leagues would effectively break the monopsony power of teams as buyers of

---

[2] This observation seems to be borne out by recent changes in the structure of competition in European football.

[3] Traditionally, English cricket and rugby union were upper- or middle-class sports, while football and rugby league were working-class sports. More recently, the class divisions may have become more blurred, but have not disappeared altogether. Cricket is played only in summer; rugby league switched from a winter to a summer calendar in the late 1990s; football and rugby union are still played in winter. Rugby league still has a strong regional identity centred on Lancashire and Yorkshire. Cricket is popular throughout England, but very much a minority sport in Scotland.

playing services, enhancing players' bargaining power in wage negotiations. This would tend to make costs higher than they are when one league operates as a monopoly supplier.

On the demand side, Neale suggests that baseball teams produce a number of streams of utility: directly for spectators who buy tickets for seats in the stadium and for television viewers who watch the match at home; and indirectly for everyone who enjoys following the championship race as it unfolds. The closer the competition, the greater is the indirect effect. For newspapers and television companies in particular, the indirect effect is a marketable commodity that helps sell more of their product. The size of the indirect effect depends on the scale and universality of the championship, and is therefore maximised when the league is a monopoly supplier. Overall 'it is clear that professional sports are a natural monopoly, marked by definite peculiarities both in the structure and in the functioning of their markets' (Neale, 1964, p. 14).

An important implication is that the peculiar economic characteristics of professional sports leagues and their constituent teams should be recognised by legislatures, by the courts and by the general public, whenever practices such as collective decision making or other (apparently) anticompetitive modes of behaviour come under scrutiny.

Sloane: 'The economics of professional football: the football club as a utility maximiser', Scottish Journal of Political Economy, 1971

Sloane's paper questions Neale's conclusion that the league rather than the individual team or club is the relevant 'firm' (or decision making unit) in professional team sports. In the case of English football, for example, the sport's governing bodies merely set the rules within which clubs can freely operate. Most economic decisions, such as how much money to spend on stadium development and how many players to employ, are made by the clubs. Although the total quantity of 'output' (the number of matches played by each club) is regulated, this clearly reflects the clubs' common interest. In cartels, it is not unusual for firms to reach joint decisions concerning price or production, but this does not imply that the cartel should be elevated to the theoretical status of a 'firm'. In short, Sloane suggests that Neale's argument tends to overemphasise mutual interdependence. 'The fact that clubs together produce a joint product is neither a necessary nor a sufficient condition for analysing the industry as though the league was a firm' (Sloane, 1971, p. 128).

Having argued that the club is the relevant economic decision maker, Sloane goes on to raise a number of important questions concerning the objectives of sports clubs. Implicit in the reasoning of both Rottenberg and Neale is an assumption of profit maximisation. Despite the 'peculiarities' of sports economics elucidated by Neale, the behaviour of professional sports teams is analysed within a very conventional analytical framework. While this may be reasonable in the case of US professional team sports, where many teams do have an established track record of profitability, Sloane suggests that it may not be universally applicable. Through most of the history of English football, profit making clubs have been very much the exception and not the rule. Chairmen and directors with a controlling interest in football clubs are usually individuals who have achieved success in business in other fields. Their motives for investing may include a desire for power or prestige, or simple sporting enthusiasm: a wish to see the local club succeed on the field of play. In many cases, profit or pecuniary gain seems unlikely to be a significant motivating factor. If so, it may be sensible to view the objective of the football club as one of utility maximisation subject to a financial solvency constraint. The financial solvency constraint recognises that the benevolence of any chairman or director must reach its limit at some point.

Non-profit maximising models of the firm had received considerable attention in the economics literature during the decade prior to the publication of Sloane's article. 'A major drawback to the general introduction of the utility maximisation assumption in the theory of the firm is that it may be rationalised so that it is consistent with almost any type of behaviour and therefore tends to lack operational significance' (Sloane, 1971, p. 133).

In the case of football clubs, however, it is not too difficult to identify several plausible and easily quantifiable objectives. Sloane suggests the following:
- *Profit*. Sloane's expectation that profit is not the sole or even the most important objective does not preclude its inclusion as one of a number of arguments in the utility function.
- *Security*. Simple survival may be a major objective for many clubs. Decisions (concerning, for example, sales of players) may aim more at ensuring security than at maximising playing success.
- *Attendance or revenue*. A capacity crowd enhances atmosphere and a sense of occasion, and may in itself be seen as a measure of success. Recently, an increasing willingness to charge whatever ticket prices the market will bear suggests that revenue (or profit) carry a heavier weight in the utility function than in earlier periods, when it was usual to charge the same price for all matches, irrespective of the level of demand.
- *Playing success*. This is probably the most important objective of all, and one to which chairmen, directors, managers, players and spectators can all subscribe.

- *Health of the league.* This enters the utility function in recognition of clubs' mutual interdependence.

Formally, the club's objective is to maximise:

$$U = u(P, A, X, \pi_R - \pi_0 - T) \qquad \text{subject to } \pi_R \geq \pi_0 + T \qquad (1.1)$$

where P = playing success; A = average attendance; X = health of the league; π_R = recorded profit; π_0 = minimum acceptable after-tax profit; and T = taxes.

It is important to note that the utility maximising model has implications very different to those which follow from the profit maximising assumptions of Rottenberg and Neale. In particular, if the weighting of P in the utility function is heavy relative to that of X and π_R, the argument that diminishing returns would prevent the accumulation of playing talent in the hands of a small number of rich clubs does not necessarily hold, unless there are binding financial constraints preventing expenditure on new players. The idea that profit incentives should help maintain a reasonably even allocation of playing talent between richer and poorer teams therefore breaks down. The case for regulation to over-ride the 'free market' outcome, whether in the form of a reserve clause, revenue sharing or the taxation of transfer fees, therefore seems to be enhanced if clubs are pursuing non-profit rather than profit objectives.

The economics of team sports since the 1970s

Since the appearance of the pioneering work of Rottenberg, Neale and Sloane, there has been a proliferation of published academic research on the economics of team sports, in the form of both journal articles and books. Many of these contributions will be reviewed in their proper place later in this volume. At this point, however, we shall highlight just a few of the main themes in the development of the economics of team sports literature over the last three decades, by identifying a handful of journal articles that seem to us to have been particularly influential. The ideas that were originally developed in these articles will figure prominently, and will be considered in greater detail, throughout this volume.

While Rottenberg and Neale both adopted a discursive style for the presentation of their insights, an article by El-Hodiri and Quirk (1971) demonstrated that these and other ideas could also be represented and developed within a more formal, mathematical framework. The kind of model developed by El-Hodiri and Quirk is now the standard apparatus for analysing questions about the implications for competitive balance within a sports league of institutional or policy changes, such as the introduction of free agency, salary caps or revenue sharing arrangements.

Nearly a quarter of a century later, and with the benefit of hindsight after witnessing a number of attempts at introducing such changes by the North American sports governing bodies in the interim, Fort and Quirk (1995) and Vrooman (1995) provided a compelling demonstration of the usefulness of this framework for policy analysis in team sports.

Sports economists have often claimed that an abundance of easily accessible data on the characteristics and performance of individual personnel makes professional team sports an ideal laboratory for the empirical scrutiny of economic theories and hypotheses that might prove difficult to test elsewhere. An article by Scully (1974), which investigated the relationship between the performance of individual players in US Major League Baseball and their compensation, provides a classic example of a contribution of this kind. Scully's motivation was to demonstrate that severe restrictions on the rights of the players to sell their services in the labour market (in the form of the reserve clause) led to exploitation perpetrated by the teams as employers, in the sense that individual players' wages were systematically below their contributions to their teams' revenue-earning capability. But the applicability of Scully's methods and the relevance of his findings went much further than this. Identifying the links between pay, productivity and human capital is a task of central importance towards achieving a much broader understanding of how labour markets work, as well as insights into specific issues such as inequality and discrimination in opportunity and compensation.

Developments elsewhere in the field of economics are also capable of providing valuable insights into the economics of sports. Two such examples are articles by Rosen (1981) on the economics of superstars, and by Lazear and Rosen (1981) on the earnings of chief executives in large corporations. Both provide insights into an issue of major controversy in the public debate about the economics of sports: the massively inflated earnings of the leading stars. Rosen demonstrated how in certain professions the technological conditions of supply create markets in which the top performers can service very large audiences at little or no incremental cost to themselves as the audience size increases. The outcome is that the extra compensation of the top performers (in comparison with slightly less talented rivals) is hugely disproportionate to their extra talent. Film stars and musicians are obvious examples, but the model is relevant to sports stars as well. Lazear and Rosen likened the high earnings of chief executives to a lavish first prize in a tournament. The possibility of emerging as a future prize winner provides incentives for others to strive for success early in their careers, with obvious benefits for the productivity of the workforce as a whole. The internal labour market of a sports team, with its squad of aspiring youngsters competing for first-team places that may eventually enable them to acquire superstar status, may resemble that of a corporation in this respect.

For most of the 1970s and 1980s, research into the economics of football specifically (as opposed to team sports in general) focused mainly on identifying the demand for attendance at football matches. An article by Hart, Hutton and Sharot (1975) was an early forerunner of a number of other UK demand studies that appeared over the course of the next two decades. For a broader perspective, one could also consult books and other works published by social historians (such as Walvin, 1975), sociologists (Dunning, Murphy and Williams, 1988; Guilianotti, 1999), or geographers (Bale, 1992). During the 1990s, however, the range of football-related issues attracting the interest of British and other European economists increased rapidly. Recent years have seen the publication of articles on topics as diverse as the settlement of transfer fees for football players moving between clubs; the implications of the creation of a European league for competitive balance in domestic and European football; the performance and job security of football managers; and discrimination against black players in football's labour market. If the present volume makes even a small contribution towards disseminating knowledge and stimulating interest in this relatively new, exciting and rapidly expanding area of theoretical and empirical research, then it will have achieved one of its most important objectives.

1.2 Outline of this volume

This section contains a brief outline of the contents of each of the following chapters of this volume. Chapter 2 provides an overview of the historical development of English football as a business, and looks in some detail at football's present-day commercial structure. The chapter also draws comparisons between the historical development and commercial structure of club football in England and in a number of other countries, including several in mainland Europe as well as Japan. Recent changes in the economic and financial structure of professional football in England and elsewhere have raised widespread concern about the implications of growing economic disparities between clubs operating at different levels within the league. As seen above, economists studying professional team sports have for many years been aware of the link between the distribution of resources among the members of sports leagues, and the degree of competitive balance. Explicit or implicit types of cross-subsidy and regulations restricting free economic competition in both the product and players' labour markets have been a pervasive feature of the history of English football. The retain-and-transfer system, the maximum wage, the minimum admission price and gate and television revenue sharing are some of the most prominent measures of this kind, all of which are described in chapter 2. The chapter concludes by reporting an empirical investigation in which a number of standard economic measures of convergence, divergence and inequality are applied to an English club-level league gate revenues data set.

Competitive balance and uncertainty of outcome are the main themes of chapter 3. Following Rottenberg, a number of US economists have developed theoretical models of competitive balance in sports league competition, which formalise some of Rottenberg's original insights, and permit exploration of a number of other policy issues. Naturally, the US literature on this topic has developed primarily with North American professional team sports in mind. Chapter 3 begins with a description of the North American model for the organisation and regulation of professional team sports. A number of features which differ significantly from their counterparts in the British or European model are highlighted. The chapter then reviews the main findings of the US literature, and considers their relevance for the case of English football. Two key assumptions of the US literature in particular seem questionable if these models are applied directly to European football. Following Sloane, the first is the assumption that team owners are motivated solely by profit. The second is the assumption that playing talent is drawn from a pool whose total size is fixed. Especially since the Bosman ruling in 1995 (see chapter 2), European football labour markets have been open rather than closed, with players frequently hired from outside the domestic league. In chapter 3 the competitive balance model is adapted for English football by introducing behavioural assumptions other than profit maximisation, and by treating the labour market as open.

Closely balanced competition is important because it maximises uncertainty of outcome or unpredictability: an essential characteristic of any sports contest. The empirical sections of chapter 3 examine the extent to which individual match results in English football are predictable or unpredictable. Patterns and trends in English league match results and goal scoring records since the 1970s are identified and compared with equivalent data from a number of other European leagues. The main long-term trend in the data is a progressive improvement in the performance of away teams, and a corresponding decline in the importance of home advantage. Analysis of sequences of match results reveals evidence of a negative 'persistence' effect: a recent run of good results appears to create either pressure or complacency, increasing the risk that the next result will be bad. Chapter 3 concludes by developing a statistical model that processes the patterns in sequences of past match results, in order to assess probable outcomes and provide forecasts for future results.

Professional football players are the main focus of attention in chapter 4. The chapter starts by presenting a descriptive profile of various personal and career characteristics of the players who turned out most regularly for their clubs in English league matches played during the 1979 and 1999 seasons. The analysis helps identify a number of significant changes to the composition of English football's regular labour force that have taken place over the last 20 years. This is followed by a more general investigation of patterns of international migration among professional footballers, which draws on the findings of previous sociological research.

Chapter 4 then goes on to consider the determinants of players' compensation. While the earnings of some superstar players are now a cause of major controversy, above-inflation increases in players' wages, especially at the highest level, have been a permanent feature of English football since the abolition of the maximum wage in the early 1960s. Chapter 4 considers some theoretical explanations for the extremely high earnings of the top superstars in sports and in similar fields such as film, music and publishing. Scarcity of supply of the highest talent, together with the very large audience reach of the top performers, are important factors which help to explain highly skewed earnings distributions. Another important aspect of footballers' compensation is the fact that wage structures are often extremely hierarchical, and players who are perhaps only a small fraction better than others frequently earn several times as much. By regarding the massive salaries of the top players as equivalent to a generous first prize in a tournament, encouraging all players to contribute maximum effort to the team's cause in an attempt to become the next prize winner, the rank-order tournament model provides one plausible explanation for observed wage differentials. Finally, chapter 4 concludes with an empirical investigation of the English football transfer market. The trading of players for cash is a feature of professional football worldwide, though one that is currently subject to the intense scrutiny of European legislators. The empirical model presented in chapter 4 shows how transfer fees are influenced by the characteristics of the players concerned, and of the buying and selling clubs.

Rottenberg considered briefly the nature of the production process in team sports, suggesting that the output of the club could be measured in terms of its attendance. Other researchers have taken up his idea of a team production function, but have typically employed team performance measures (such as win ratio), rather than attendance, as a measure of output. There have been numerous team production function studies based on North American sports such as baseball and basketball, in which many dimensions of playing skill are quantifiable, making it easy to measure individual productivity. But in American football and (association) football, there is greater interaction among the player inputs, so the measurement of productivity is more problematic. Chapter 5 includes a review of the empirical literature on team production functions, and describes the task of modelling team production in football.

An interesting application of the team production function approach is in quantifying the contribution of the manager to the team's performance. Typically, the managerial input is measured as part of a residual that is obtained after controlling for the players' contribution to performance. Having controlled for team quality, the variation in performance that remains unexplained is attributed either to the manager or to luck and other random factors. Chapter 5 concludes by describing some recent research which estimates team production functions using English football data, and uses them to obtain efficiency scores for football managers.

The measurement of managerial efficiency forms only one part of the research agenda on the role of managers in team sports. Sociologists and economists have also examined the link between team performance and the security of the manager's job tenure, and the effect of a change of manager on the subsequent performance of the team. This literature, which is reviewed in chapter 6, contributes to a broader research programme that is concerned with the two-way link between organisational performance and the managerial contribution.

Chapter 6 goes on to present some new empirical results for English football managers. Chronic job insecurity is undoubtedly one of the defining characteristics of the football manager's position. An important aim of the empirical analysis in chapter 6 is to quantify the factors that are most likely to trigger a change of manager, including match results over the short term, longer-term team performance measures and various personal and human capital attributes of the manager himself. Of course, changing the manager is a rational decision for club owners to take if it is likely to lead to an improvement in fortune under a new incumbent. Opinion as to the average effect on team performance of a change of manager seems to be quite mixed. The empirical results for English football presented in chapter 6 suggest that while a change of manager often has a disruptive effect that makes matters worse in the short term, in the longer term teams that change managers seem to recover faster from a run of poor results than teams that retain their manager following a poor run.

Until quite recently, the economic analysis of football was concerned almost exclusively with the determinants of demand, or with the statistical modelling of match and season attendances. Even in the present-day world of highly lucrative television contracts, merchandising and sponsorship, gate revenues still constitute a significant proportion of the total revenues of most football clubs. Furthermore, spectators who attend matches in person are not just passive consumers. Their presence contributes in a fundamental way to the quality of the product, by generating atmosphere and a sense of occasion. Most spectators also seek to influence match outcomes though the effects of vocal encouragement and criticism of players, managers and match officials. For these reasons, as well as the 'enthusiasm effect' suggested by Neale, supply and demand are really interdependent.

Identifying the causes of variations in attendances, from season to season and from match to match, is therefore the main objective of chapter 7. The chapter reviews the empirical literature on the demand for football attendance, highlighting some of the main problems of model specification, estimation and interpretation encountered by researchers in this area. Sociological case studies from Spain and Scotland are also used to illustrate the impact of broader social or cultural influences on patterns of demand for football attendance. Chapter 7 concludes by presenting an empirical analysis of English club-level attendances during the post-Second World War period. The analysis shows the effects on attendances of factors such as short-term loyalty, team performance and admission prices. It also investigates the relationship between various socio-economic, demographic and football-related characteristics of each club and its home town, and average attendances over the long term.

Neoclassical economics predicts that unco-ordinated interactions between large numbers of self-interested buyers and sellers operating in free, unregulated markets can normally be relied upon to deliver an efficient allocation of scarce resources. A key assumption is that all relevant information about the prices and characteristics of goods and services is transmitted rapidly and accurately among all participants in the relevant market. Chapter 8 presents two case studies, which focus on the efficiency with which relevant information about the performance of football teams on the field of play is impounded into the prices at which trade takes place in particular markets.

The first case study concerns the secondary market for trade in the shares of football clubs quoted on the London Stock Exchange (LSE). Following a description of the historical evolution of present-day structures of ownership and control in English club football, the empirical investigation seeks to quantify the extent to which major events that take place on the field of play, such as European qualification and elimination, or domestic promotion and relegation, carry implications for the share prices of football clubs that are floated on the LSE. If new information about team performance is transmitted and absorbed by the markets rapidly, a direct link between fluctuations in fortunes on the field of play and variations in share prices should be discernible empirically. The second case study in chapter 8 concerns the market for fixed-odds betting on the results of football matches. The main objective here is to establish whether a high-street bookmaker's published odds reflect all information that is relevant to predicting the match outcome.

This volume concludes in chapter 9 with a discussion of some of the major policy issues concerning football's future development as a sport and as a business that are currently facing the sport's governing bodies, club owners, broadcasters, sponsors and legislators. Among the policy issues considered, with the aid of the economic analysis presented in previous chapters of this volume, are the proposals for the formation of a European Super League; rocketing inflation in players' wages; plans to reform or even abolish the players' transfer market; the prospects for the survival of the smaller clubs; and the future of football's relationship with the broadcasting media. In one way or another, decisions concerning all such matters impinge upon what is surely the most fundamental issue in the economics of team sports: the need to maintain competitive balance. Forty-five years on, this is one issue that is still as relevant today as it was at the time Rottenberg's original ground-breaking article was published.

1.3 The use of econometrics in this volume

As indicated above, chapters 2–8 of this volume report the results of new empirical investigations of a number of the key topics that are covered in each chapter. Regression analysis, in various guises, is the main empirical technique used in these investigations. For readers who are familiar with econometrics, in the empirical sections of this volume we have attempted to strike a reasonable balance between the objectives of technical rigour and accessibility. With accessibility in mind, we have chosen not to burden the text with lengthy technical discussions about model specification or estimation issues. We have also chosen not to extend the tables of empirical results (many of which are already large) by including extensive listings of diagnostic test statistics. Readers who are interested or concerned about such matters should consult the relevant journal articles cited in the text, where the various technical issues are given proper emphasis and attention.

For the benefit of readers who are unfamiliar with econometrics, the presentation of the empirical results in this volume has been confined to specific sections within each chapter. These sections can be skipped without prejudicing understanding of the material contained elsewhere. Readers who skip the empirical sections will find a concise and completely non-technical summary of the main empirical findings in the concluding sections of each chapter. For readers without a background in statistics or econometrics who do wish to read the empirical sections, the rest of this sub-section provides a brief, non-technical description of the basics of regression analysis, and introduces some of the main terminology and jargon. Readers with an econometrics background are invited to skip the rest of section 1.3 and proceed directly to chapter 2.

Most econometric studies seek either to *explain* observed facts about the real world, or to construct a model that can *predict* the outcome of events that have not yet occurred. This volume includes examples of both types of econometric investigation. Typically, a regression model takes the following form:

$$y_i = \beta_1 + \beta_2 x_{2i} + \beta_3 x_{3i} + \ldots + \beta_k x_{ki} + u_i \qquad (1.2)$$

The definitions of variables and symbols used in (1.2) are as follows:

y_i	is the dependent variable
$x_{2i}, x_{3i}, \ldots, x_{ki}$	are the independent or explanatory variables
u_i	is the error term
$\beta_1, \beta_2, \beta_3, \ldots, \beta_k$	are the regression coefficients.

The dependent variable y_i is the variable whose behaviour the model seeks either to explain or to predict. The independent variables $x_{2i}, x_{3i}, \ldots, x_{ki}$ are other variables thought to influence or determine y_i. The coefficients $\beta_2, \beta_3, \ldots, \beta_k$ identify the impact on y_i of small changes in the values of each of $x_{2i}, x_{3i}, \ldots, x_{ki}$ respectively. For example, if x_{2i} increases by one unit while all other variables in (1.2) are held constant, the numerical adjustment to the value of y_i is given by the coefficient β_2. The one remaining coefficient, β_1, allows for the scaling of the dependent and independent variables; in most (but not all) regression models β_1 does not have any important interpretation.[4] Finally the error term u_i allows for any variation in the dependent variable that is not accounted for by corresponding variation in the independent variables. In most regression models, the value taken by the error term is assumed to be purely random. For purposes of statistical inference (see below) it is often useful

---

[4] Occasionally, other notational conventions are used in an expression such as (1.2). Different symbols may be used for both variables and coefficients. It is sometimes convenient to write an expression such as (1.2) more concisely using matrix notation, i.e. $y_i = \beta' x_i + u_i$, where $\beta' = (\beta_1 \ \beta_2 \ldots \beta_k)$ and $x_i' = (1 \ x_{2i} \ldots x_{ki})$. Alternatively it is sometimes convenient to use variable names rather than *y*s and *x*s, i.e. *DEPVAR* = $\beta_1 + \beta_2$ *INDVAR2* $+ \ldots + \beta_k$*INDVARk* + *ERROR*, where the names actually used describe the variables.

to assume that the error term follows some specific probability distribution, such as the *normal distribution*.

The 'i'-subscripts on the variables $y_i, x_{2i}, x_{3i}, \ldots, x_{ki}$ and u_i in (1.2) indicate that the relationship between the independent variables and the dependent variable holds over a number of *observations* contained within a sample of data. The observations are indexed over $i = 1 \ldots N$, where N is the total number of observations.[5] The sample therefore comprises N complete sets of observed numerical values of $x_{2i}, x_{3i}, \ldots, x_{ki}$ and y_i. The numerical values of the coefficients $\beta_1, \beta_2, \beta_3, \ldots, \beta_k$ are all unknown, and the purpose of the regression analysis is to process the data in order to obtain the best possible numerical estimates of these coefficients. The choice of estimation method depends on the specification of the model. Estimation methods used in this volume (and referred to in the text) include Ordinary Least Squares (OLS), Generalised Least Squares (GLS), Weighted Least Squares (WLS), Fixed Effects and Random Effects (FE and RE), Maximum Likelihood (ML) and Seemingly Unrelated Regressions estimation (SUR). Estimated regression coefficients are usually denoted $\hat{\beta}_1, \hat{\beta}_2, \hat{\beta}_3, \ldots, \hat{\beta}_k$, to distinguish them from the corresponding true (but unknown) coefficients $\beta_1, \beta_2, \beta_3, \ldots, \beta_k$.

Once a regression model has been estimated, the signs and numerical magnitudes of the estimated coefficients convey information about the direction and strength of the relationship between each independent variable and the dependent variable. Because the estimated coefficients are based on a limited sample of data, there is always a suspicion of imprecision or unreliability attached to them. For this reason, estimation methods for regression coefficients provide a *standard error* with each coefficient estimate. The standard error reflects the reliability of the estimate: the smaller the standard error, the greater the reliability. It can also be used to construct a *confidence interval* for the true value of the coefficient. A confidence interval is simply a range of likely values for the true coefficient located on either side of the estimated coefficient. We can claim that the true coefficient should lie somewhere within this range, subject only to a small (and specified) probability of being wrong.

The ratio of an estimated coefficient to its standard error, usually known as a *z-statistic* or *t-statistic* (depending on which type of regression model is being used), provides a convenient method for assessing whether the estimation has succeeded in identifying a relationship that is reliable

---

[5] In cases where data are observed over a number of different time periods, 't'-subscripts are used instead of 'i'-subscripts in order to denote time. For data with both a cross-sectional and a time series dimension, variables may be indexed using both 'i'- and 't'-subscripts.

in a statistical sense. This is one of the main tasks of *statistical inference*. The z-statistic (or t-statistic) for the coefficient estimate $\hat{\beta}_2$ is calculated as $z = \hat{\beta}_2/\text{se}(\hat{\beta}_2)$ where $\text{se}(\hat{\beta}_2)$ is $\hat{\beta}_2$'s standard error. If the absolute value of the z-statistic exceeds a certain critical value, we say that $\hat{\beta}_2$ is *statistically significant* or *significantly different from zero*. This means that we have sufficient statistical evidence to reject the *null hypothesis* that the true value of the coefficient β_2 is zero, in favour of the *alternative hypothesis* that β_2 is non-zero. In this case the null and alternative hypotheses would be written $H_0:\beta_2 = 0$ and $H_1:\beta_2 \neq 0$. This is an example of a *two-tail* hypothesis test. Another possibility is a *one-tail* test, in which the null and alternative hypotheses might take the form $H_0:\beta_2 \leq 0$ and $H_1:\beta_2 > 0$, respectively. Whenever a *hypothesis test* is carried out, it is usual to quote an accompanying *significance level*, such as 1, 5 or 10 per cent. This expresses the probability that the test may cause us to draw a wrong inference by rejecting a null hypothesis that is actually true. With a significance level of 5 per cent, if β_2 really were zero the test would run a 5 per cent risk of incorrectly concluding that β_2 is non-zero. The smaller the significance level the greater the confidence we can have in any inference that an estimated coefficient is statistically significant, and that the true coefficient is therefore different from zero.

If the purpose of a regression analysis is explanation, then by following the procedures outlined above, we may be able to infer (with only a small risk of making a mistake) that β_2 is non-zero. If so, then according to (1.2) we have shown that the independent variable x_{2i} does have an effect on the dependent variable y_i. In other words, some of the variation in y_i has been explained by corresponding variation in x_{2i}. The estimated coefficients, standard errors and z- or t-statistics are therefore of considerable interest: they show which independent variables are important in explaining the behaviour of the dependent variable. Consequently, much of the discussion of the empirical results in this volume concentrates on this aspect of the estimated regression models.

If the purpose of the regression analysis is prediction, the estimated coefficients, standard errors and z- or t-statistics are important, because they enable us to determine which independent variables should be included in the model that is to be used to generate the best possible prediction. In order to obtain a prediction, we need a set of values for all of the independent variables for an out-of-sample observation. These are substituted into the estimated model (already estimated using the in-sample data), so as to produce a prediction for the out-of-sample value of the dependent variable.

The *linear regression model*, also known as the *multiple regression model*, is probably the best known and most widely used type of regression model.

It is used in most situations where the dependent variable is continuous, and can take any numerical value. The linear regression model is employed a number of times in this volume: in chapter 2, to estimate models of convergence in football club gate revenues; in chapter 4, to estimate a model that explains transfer fees in terms of player and club characteristics; in chapter 6, to estimate the effect of a change of manager on team performance during the season after the change takes place; in chapter 7, to estimate models that explain variations in match attendances; and in chapter 8, to estimate models that explain movements in football club share prices.

Not all data, however, are amenable to analysis using the linear regression model. A model capable of predicting match results, for example, has a discrete or qualitative dependent variable, which can take only one of three non-numerical values: 'win', 'draw' or 'lose'. The *ordered probit model*, one of a broader class of *discrete choice models*, is the appropriate regression model to use in this case. This type of model is estimated for the first time in chapter 3, and is employed again in chapters 6 and 8. A second example arises when the relationship between measurable team inputs (playing talent or financial resources) and team performance is considered. In estimating this relationship, it is useful to be able to decompose the error term (the variation in team performance that cannot be explained by variations in the measurable inputs) into two parts: one reflecting the manager's contribution to performance, and the other reflecting random influences or luck. In chapters 5 and 6 *stochastic frontier analysis* is used to specify a regression model that has a special error term with the required structure. A final example arises when we seek to identify the factors most important in triggering the decision to terminate a manager's appointment. In this case the dependent variable in the regression model is an indicator variable, which takes the form $y_i = 0$ if the manager was retained and $y_i = 1$ if the manager was removed after match i was played. In chapter 6 yet another type of regression model is needed to estimate what are known as job-departure *hazard functions* for football managers.

In the space available in section 1.3, it has been possible to provide only a brief and highly selective outline of some of the basics of regression analysis. Readers who wish to discover more are strongly encouraged to explore one or more of the excellent econometrics texts that are currently available. In teaching econometrics to undergraduates and postgraduates for a number of years, the authors have found the texts by Gujarati (1995), Kennedy (1998), Pindyck and Rubinfeld (1998) and Greene (1999) to be especially helpful. Gujarati and Pindyck and Rubinfeld both provide a detailed and comprehensive beginner's guide to econometrics, while Kennedy explains the terminology of econometrics in a clear, succinct and non-technical manner. Greene, meanwhile, offers a more advanced treatment, including full technical details of a large number of more highly specialised econometric models and estimation techniques.

2 Professional football: historical development and economic structure

Professional football's characteristics as a sport have always been linked inextricably with its attributes as a business, but never more so than at present. Complaints are aired regularly in the media and elsewhere that players are over-paid; that the transfer market is out of control; that shareholders' priorities are over-riding the interests of supporters; that exorbitant ticket prices are driving long-standing spectators away from football; and that the priorities of television are dictating both the strategic and the operational decisions of football clubs and the sport's organising bodies. Horton (1997) voices a typical supporter's concerns over a wide range of matters of this kind, all of which are essentially issues of economics, commerce or finance.

This chapter presents an overview of the historical development of English club football as a business, and provides some international comparisons. The contents will serve as background to the more detailed analyses of various aspects of the economics of professional football, which are the subject of subsequent chapters. Section 2.1 begins by presenting some broad comparisons between the present-day commercial structures of the five leading European football leagues, in England, France, Germany, Italy and Spain. This material helps place the analysis of the history and present-day commercial structure of English league football that follows in subsequent sections of chapter 2 into its proper international context.

The more detailed analysis of English club football begins in section 2.2, with a description of the competitive structure of the major English league and cup tournaments. Some historical trends and patterns in the performance of groups of clubs distinguished by characteristics such as geographical location, city size and date of entry into the league are also identified. Section 2.3 describes trends in attendances, and the explanations for changing patterns of attendance which have been proposed by historians, sociologists and economists. Attendances and clubs' policies on admission prices determine gate revenues which, together with other sources including television fees, sponsorship, merchandising and transfer fees received, provide the main contributions to the revenue side of the football club's profit and loss account. Historical trends in the size and composition of English football's revenue base are described in sections 2.4 and 2.5.

The main component of a football club's costs is expenditure on players, through both wages and transfer fee expenditure. Sections 2.6 and 2.7 provide a brief account of the historical development of English football's labour and transfer markets. Historically, restrictions on the mobility of players, together with a net flow of transfer expenditure from the stronger to the weaker clubs, were perceived to have played an important role in maintaining a certain degree of equality between the richer and the poorer clubs, in both sporting and financial terms. But, more recently, the capacity of these mechanisms to function as they have in the past has come under considerable strain. Particularly challenging to the traditional organisation of the transfer market has been the landmark Jean-Marc Bosman ruling in the European Court of Justice (ECJ) in 1995 (see below).

Together, sections 2.2–2.7 provide a comprehensive account of the historical development and present-day condition of English football's commercial structure. Section 2.8 widens the perspective again, by providing a brief description of the historical evolution of football into its present-day form in two other countries: France and Japan. The histories of professional football in these two countries provide some fascinating contrasts, both with each other and with the English story that has been told in previous sections of chapter 2.

The distribution of financial resources between clubs is the main theme of the final, empirical part of chapter 2, in section 2.9. A number of economic measures of convergence and divergence are applied to an English league revenues data set covering all seasons between the mid-1920s and the late 1990s. The objective is to gauge the extent to which disparities between the revenue bases of clubs operating at different levels within the league have widened over time. Unsurprisingly, the convergence analysis shows that inequalities within English football were considerably greater by the end of the 1990s than they were in the mid-1920s. More surprising, perhaps, is the finding that almost all of the increase in inequality can be attributed to two much shorter periods within the last 75 years. The first big rise in inequality happened over a period of less than 20 years' duration, between the late 1950s and the mid-1970s. The second period of rising inequality began at the start of the 1990s, and is still underway at the time of writing. These findings tend to reinforce the interpretation of English football's economic history advanced in the earlier sections of chapter 2. The 1960s and the 1990s in particular appear to be transitional decades, when football's economic structure was subject to quite radical and fundamental change. In other decades, football's economic structure exhibited signs of much greater stability.

2.1 The commercial structure of Europe's 'big five' football leagues

This section presents some 'snapshot' comparisons of features of the present-day commercial structures of the big five European leagues of England, France, Germany, Italy and Spain. Data on average attendances, club revenues and budgets, players' wages and transfers and the international mobility of players are used to draw comparisons between the first divisions in each of the five leagues. The material in section 2.1 provides background and context to the more detailed analysis of the history and present-day commercial structure of English league football that follows in the next six sections of chapter 2.

Average league attendances increased in all five countries during the 1990s. Figure 2.1 shows the average home league attendances of each top-division club in each country for the 2000 season. Three clubs achieved average home attendances above 60,000: Internazionale (65,930), Barcelona (65,526) and Borussia Dortmund (64,535). Four more fell just short of the 60,000 mark: Real Madrid (59,316), Roma (58,915), AC Milan (58,376) and Manchester United (58,017). Average attendances across all first-division clubs were very similar in Germany (31,882), England (30,707) and Italy (29,887), but were somewhat lower in Spain (26,984) and France (21,861). Figure 2.1 highlights some significant differences between countries in the distributions of attendances among first-division clubs. Moving from left to right along the charts in figure 2.1 the gradient is much steeper for Italy than for England; the distribution of attendances is therefore less equal in Italy than in England. The variance of the natural logarithms of attendance provides a convenient summary measure of this kind of dispersion. The values of this statistic for the 2000 season were, in ascending order, 0.13 (England), 0.25 (Germany), 0.31 (Spain), 0.32 (France) and 0.33 (Italy). The average attendances for second-division clubs also suggest that support is more evenly distributed between clubs in England than elsewhere. The 2000 season second-division averages were 14,149 (England), 12,165 (Germany), 8,688 (Italy), 6,577 (Spain) and 5,692 (France).

According to data published by *World Soccer* (June 2000), the estimated total revenue of clubs in the English Premier League for the 2000 season was around £530 million. On this criterion, the Premier League was

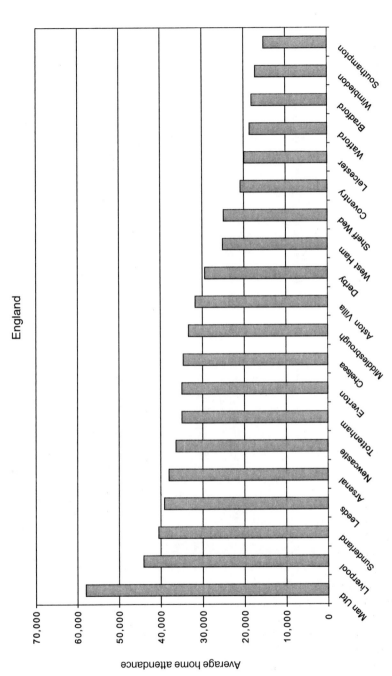

England

Average home attendance

Man Utd, Liverpool, Sunderland, Leeds, Arsenal, Newcastle, Tottenham, Everton, Chelsea, Middlesbrough, Aston Villa, Derby, West Ham, Sheff Wed, Coventry, Leicester, Watford, Bradford, Wimbledon, Southampton

Figure 2.1 Average home attendances, first-division clubs, five European leagues, 2000 season
Source: <http://www.football.sportsites.co.uk/>.

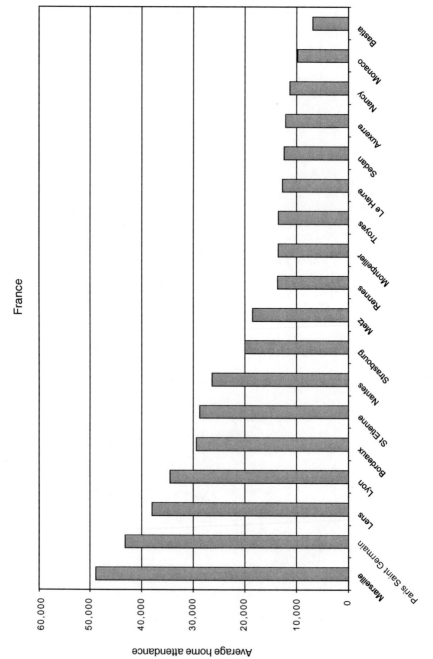

Figure 2.1 (*cont.*)

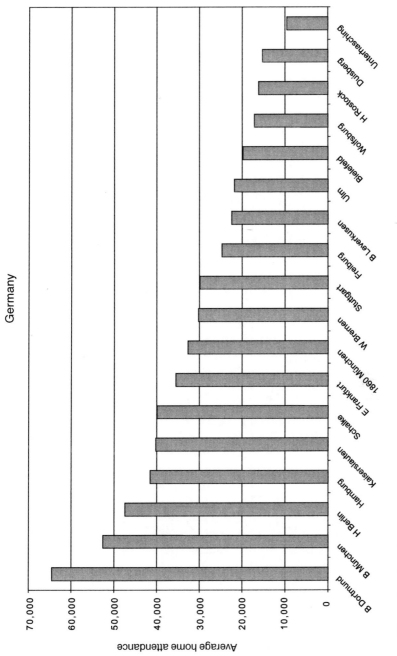

Germany

Average home attendance

Figure 2.1 (cont.)

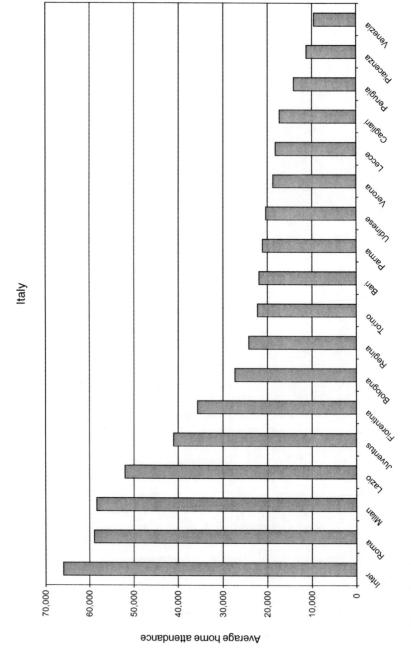

Italy

Figure 2.1 (*cont.*)

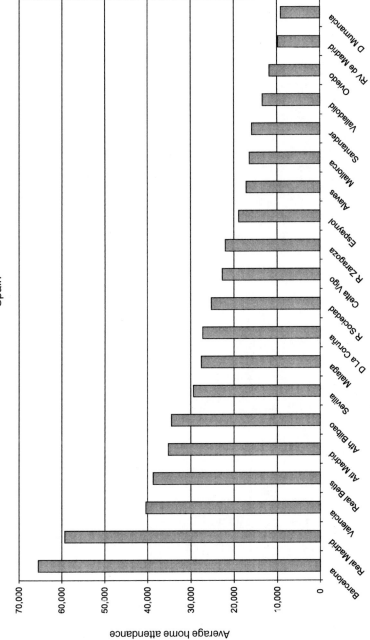

Spain

Figure 2.1 (*cont.*)

comfortably the wealthiest of the big five leagues. Approximate data for total revenues or total club budgets elsewhere were £430 million (Italy), £380 million (Spain), £360 million (Germany) and £230 million (France). English clubs tend to charge high ticket prices, producing relatively large gate receipts. They are also some way ahead of most of their continental rivals in terms of their ability to generate merchandising revenues. In the past, the leading continental clubs have been able to generate higher sponsorship income than their English counterparts; but recent deals secured by Manchester United and Liverpool will go some way towards reducing this gap. Estimates of total television income for the 2000 season were £200 million (England), £210 million (France), £105 million (Germany), £260 million (Italy) and £190 million (Spain). For the foreseeable future, however, the income of the top English clubs from the Premier League's collective television contracts is unlikely to match the earnings of their Italian and Spanish counterparts, as the latter reap the rewards of individually negotiated deals. Depending on the number of appearances, the Premier League's contract with BSkyB covering seasons 1998–2001 is worth around £15 million per annum to the Premier League winners. This figure should increase to between £25 million and £30 million from the 2002 season onwards. But in the 2000 season Juventus and AC Milan each received more than £30 million from individual contracts for their domestic television rights. Highly lucrative individual deals have also been signed by Real Madrid and Barcelona, to take effect in the 2004 season.

In all five countries, the World Soccer data show that distribution of revenues between clubs is considerably more skewed than the distribution of attendances. In England the revenues of Manchester United and Chelsea accounted for between 25 and 30 per cent of all Premier League club revenues for the 1999 season. In Germany the share of the top two, Bayern München and Borussia Dortmund, was between 30 and 35 per cent. In Spain three clubs, Barcelona, Real Madrid and Atlético Madrid, accounted for just under 50 per cent of all First Division club budgets for the 2000 season. But in Italy and France the pattern was rather different. Six Italian clubs, Juventus, Milan, Lazio, Internazionale, Parma and Roma, all had roughly comparable 2000 season budgets, of between £35 million and £55 million each. Together these six clubs accounted for over 60 per cent of all Serie A club budgets. In France Marseille and Paris Saint Germain (PSG) had the highest 1999 season budgets, of around £30 million each. But three more clubs, Lens, Lyon and Monaco, each spent between £20 million and £25 million. Together these five clubs accounted for over 50 per cent of all First Division club budgets. Applying the 'variance of the natural logarithms' measure to the dispersion of club revenues or budgets, the French league turns out to be the most egalitarian. The values of this statistic were 0.34 (France), 0.39 (Germany), 0.49 (Italy), 0.52 (England) and 0.79 (Spain).

By allowing out-of-contract players complete freedom of movement within EU boundaries, the 1995 ECJ ruling in the Jean-Marc Bosman case has had major implications for both mobility and levels of compensation within the footballers' labour market. The case arose when Bosman was offered new terms inferior to those of his previous contract by his Belgian club, RFC Liège. Having declined the new contract, Bosman was refused permission by Liège to join the French club Dunkerque. Bosman sued Liège citing restraint of trade, took his case to the ECJ, and won. At the same time the Court outlawed all restrictions on the eligibility of European Union (EU) nationals to play elsewhere within the EU; previously the three-foreigner rule had prevented clubs from fielding more than three foreign nationals in the same team at the same time. This change has enabled clubs to recruit players from beyond national boundaries to a far greater extent than ever before. Table 2.1 shows data on the nationalities of all squad players with first-division clubs in the big five European leagues at the end of the 1999 season. The same data are shown in summary form in figure 2.2.

For France, Germany, Italy and Spain, figure 2.2 groups players into five broad categories by nationality: players who were home nationals of each country; and players from the rest of Europe; Sub-Saharan Africa; Central or South America; and the rest of the world. Because English recruitment patterns are significantly different, a different set of categories is used in this case. Of the four continental leagues, Germany's was the most cosmopolitan, with German nationals accounting for only 58 per cent of all German club squad players. The corresponding percentages for Spain, Italy and France were 61 per cent, 68 per cent and 74 per cent, respectively. Only 57 per cent of English squad players were from England and Wales; but if players from Scotland and Northern Ireland are also counted, the proportion of British Premier League squad players rises to 64 per cent.

German and English clubs employed higher proportions of foreign Europeans than clubs in the other three countries. Poland (16 players) and Croatia (15) were the most heavily represented European countries in Division 1 of the Bundesliga, but in general German clubs seem willing to employ non-German Europeans from a very wide range of countries. In contrast, employment of non-British Europeans by English clubs was more highly concentrated by nationality: apart from the Irish Republic (with 29 players), Norway (23), France (22), Italy (17) and Holland (15) were all strongly represented. The Italian and Spanish proportions of

Table 2.1. *Nationalities of squad players at first-division clubs, five European leagues, summer 1999*

ENGLAND		FRANCE		GERMANY		ITALY		SPAIN	
England	346	France	327	Germany	311	Italy	289	Spain	323
Rest of UK	44	Belgium	18	Poland	7	France	16	Argentina	47
Ireland	29	Yugoslavia	11	Croatia	5	Croatia	15	Brazil	21
France	22	Rest of Europe	8	Holland	24	Yugoslavia	12	Uruguay	15
Italy	17	Sub-Saharan Africa	52	Hungary	43	Scandinavia	10	Rest of Central/South America	13
Holland	15	Central/South America	14	Former USSR	19	Rest of Europe	10	France	13
Scandinavia	41	North Africa	27	Rest of Europe	9	Central/South America	81	Yugoslavia	12
Rest of Europe	44	Rest of World	19	Sub-Saharan Africa	1	Sub-Saharan Africa	23	Portugal	10
Sub-Saharan Africa	12			Central/South America	15	Rest of World	23	Rest of Europe	58
Central/South America	12			Rest of World	23			Sub-Saharan Africa	12
Rest of World	22							Rest of World	3
TOTAL	**604**	**TOTAL**	**481**	**TOTAL**	**419**	**TOTAL**	**494**	**TOTAL**	**527**

Source: Macias (2000).

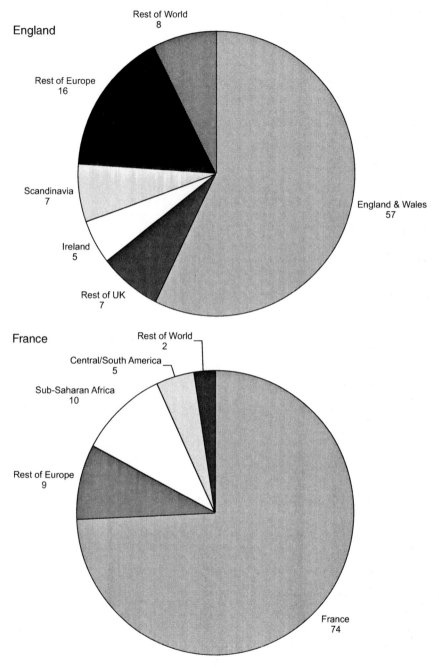

Figure 2.2 Nationalities of all squad players of all first-division clubs, five European leagues, end of 1999 season, per cent
Source: Macías (2000).

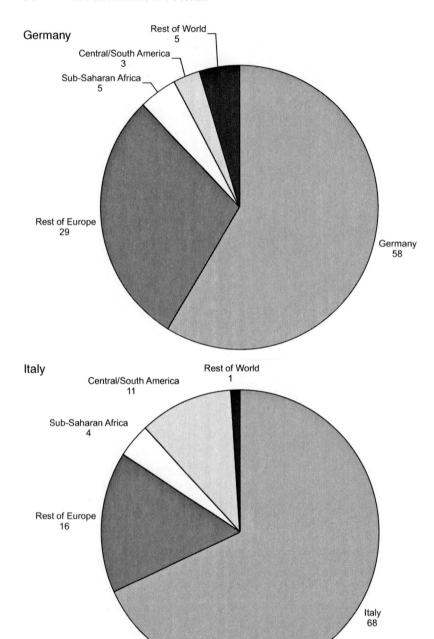

Figure 2.2 (*cont.*)

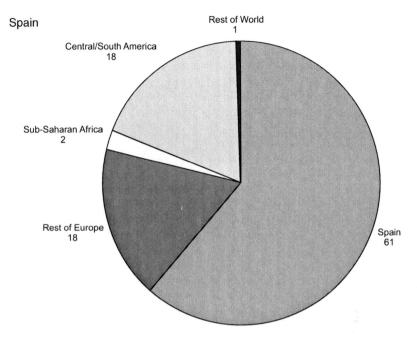

Figure 2.2 (*cont.*)

foreign Europeans were similar, at 18 and 16 per cent, respectively; but the French First Division, with a corresponding proportion of only 9 per cent, was a relatively unusual destination for non-French Europeans. Spain, Italy and France were the heaviest employers of non-Europeans. 18 per cent of Spanish players were from Central or South America, with Argentina in particular strongly represented. Spanish employment of players from Africa and the rest of the world was relatively low. Italian clubs also employed a relatively high proportion of Central or South Americans, while France had the highest concentration of players from Sub-Saharan Africa.

While the English Premier League has the highest total revenue of any first division in the world, England's wealthiest clubs tend to lag behind their counterparts in Italy and Spain in terms of spending on players' wages and on the acquisition of players through the transfer market. Table 2.2 shows the highest weekly wage earners in each of the big five leagues (*World Soccer*, November 1999). At the time, the highest-paid players in Italy (Alessandro del Piero of Juventus) and Spain (ironically an Englishman, Steve McManaman of Real Madrid) were earning more than twice as much as the highest-paid player in England (Alan Shearer of

Table 2.2. *Highest-paid players, five European leagues, 1999*

		£			£
ENGLAND			**ITALY**		
Alan Shearer	Newcastle United	28,000	Alessandro del Piero	Juventus	69,230
Michael Owen	Liverpool	24,000	Christian Vieri	Internazionale	55,769
Duncan Ferguson	Newcastle United	21,000	Ronaldo	Internazionale	50,000
			Juan Veron	Lazio	48,076
Chris Sutton	Chelsea	21,000	Filippo Inzaghi	Juventus	41,208
Marcel Desailly	Chelsea	20,000	Alessandro Nesta	Lazio	40,384
Kanu	Arsenal	20,000	Gabriel Batistuta	Fiorentina	34,615
Patrick Viera	Arsenal	20,000	Roberto Baggio	Internazionale	34,340
Emmanuel Petit	Arsenal	20,000	George Weah	AC Milan	34,340
			Pavel Nedved	Lazio	32,692
FRANCE			Oliver Bierhoff	AC Milan	26,923
Fabien Barthez	Monaco	42,307	Francesco Totti	Roma	26,923
Sonny Anderson	Lyon	26,923	Edgar Davids	Juventus	26,923
Robert Pires	Marseille	26,923			
Marco Simone	Monaco	23,076	**SPAIN**		
Fabrizio Ravinelli	Marseille	23,076	Steve McManaman	Real Madrid	65,384
Ali Bernarbia	Paris St Germain	23,076			
			Patrick Kluivert	Barcelona	57,692
			Nicolas Anelka	Real Madrid	55,769
GERMANY			Jimmy Floyd Hasselbaink	Atlético Madrid	44,230
Stefan Effenberg	Bayern München	48,076	Roberto Carlos	Real Madrid	40,000
Krassimir Balakov	Stuttgart	48,076	Raul	Real Madrid	40,000
Giovane Elber	Bayern München	32,692	Jari Litmanen	Barcelona	38,461
Andreas Moller	Dortmund	30,769	Ronald De Boer	Barcelona	25,000
Ze Roberto	Leverkusen	28,846	Frank De Boer	Barcelona	25,000
Fredi Bobic	Dortmund	25,000	Rivaldo	Barcelona	25,000
Ciriaco Sforza	Kaiserslauten	25,000	Luis Figo	Barcelona	25,000

Note:
Data are weekly earnings after tax converted into sterling. All figures are approximate owing to fluctuating exchange rates. They do not include match bonuses, signing-on fees or endorsements.
Source: World Soccer (November 1999).

Newcastle United). Table 2.3 charts the upward progress of the world record transfer fee since the first £1 million transfer of Guiseppe Savoldi from Bologna to Napoli in 1975. Table 2.3 also lists the 10 highest transfer fees paid worldwide, as of summer 2000. Only once since 1975 has an English club broken the Italian–Spanish monopoly of the world record

Table 2.3. *World record transfers and 12 highest transfers, summer 2000*

Player	Selling club	Buying club	Fee (£million)	Year
World record transfers				
Giuseppe Savoldi	Bologna	Napoli	1.2	1975
Paolo Rossi	Juventus	Vicenza	1.75	1978
Diego Maradona	Boca Juniors	Barcelona	3	1982
Diego Maradona	Barcelona	Napoli	5	1984
Ruud Gullit	PSV Eindhoven	Milan	6	1987
Roberto Baggio	Fiorentina	Juventus	8	1990
Jean-Pierre Papin	Marseille	Milan	10	1992
Gianluca Vialli	Sampdoria	Juventus	12	1992
Gianluigi Lentini	Torino	Milan	13	1996
Alan Shearer	Blackburn Rovers	Newcastle United	15	1996
Ronaldo	Barcelona	Internazionale	19	1998
Denilson	São Paulo	Real Betis	22	1999
Christian Vieri	Lazio	Internazionale	31	1999
Hernan Crespo	Parma	Lazio	36	2000
Luis Figo	Barcelona	Real Madrid	37	2000
Highest transfers as at summer 2000				
Luis Figo	Barcelona	Real Madrid	37	2000
Hernan Crespo	Parma	Lazio	36	2000
Christian Vieri	Lazio	Internazionale	31	1999
Marc Overmars	Arsenal	Barcelona	25	2000
Nicolas Anelka	Arsenal	Real Madrid	23.5	1999
Nicolas Anelka	Real Madrid	Paris St Germain	22	2000
Gabriel Batistuta	Fiorentina	Roma	22	2000
Denilson	São Paulo	Real Betis	22	1998
Marcio Amoroso	Udinese	Parma	21	1999
Juan Veron	Parma	Lazio	20	1999
Ronaldo	Barcelona	Internazionale	19	1997
Christian Vieri	Juventus	Atlético Madrid	19	1998

Source: World Soccer (August, September 2000).

(when Alan Shearer moved from Blackburn Rovers to Newcastle United for £15 million in 1996). Four years later, however, this transfer does not even figure among the world's top ten. Shearer's English club record stood for over four years, before eventually being overtaken by Rio Ferdinand's £18 million transfer from West Ham United to Leeds United in November 2000.

There are several explanations for English clubs' relatively modest showing in tables 2.2 and 2.3. The willingness of a number of Italian and Spanish club owners to subsidise spending on players is certainly a prime factor, contrasting starkly with the responsibilities of a number of floated English clubs to earn profits for the benefit of their shareholders. Another important factor is the greater level of public subsidy generally available for stadium construction and maintenance on the continent than in England. Also significant is the fact that English clubs tend to earn more revenue than their continental counterparts from sources such as merchandising and catering, which impose significant costs and deliver relatively low profit margins. Areas in which continental clubs excel, such as sponsorship and the sale of broadcasting rights, are virtually cost-free and therefore deliver much higher margins (*World Soccer*, June 2000). For the foreseeable future, the gap between the spending power of the leading continental clubs and their English rivals (such as Manchester United and one or two others) is likely to continue to impose strains on the relationship between the latter and the rest of England's Premier League and Football League clubs. The internal structure of English club football is examined in detail in the next six sections of this chapter.

2.2 The English football league: competitive structure and team performance

Origins and competitive structure

In England, the origins of the game of football can be traced back to the late Middle Ages. Originally football was a rough and violent game, involving unspecified numbers of younger men pursuing a ball through urban or rural locations, often resulting in serious damage to property, personal injury and even death. Despite repeated attempts by both church and state to ban the sport, street or village football remained popular until the arrival of industrialisation, when new patterns of urban residence and employment imposed constraints and disciplines that changed forever previously popular forms of recreation. In the first half of the nineteenth century football survived mainly within the upper-class public schools and universities, where the codes that define the modern sports of association football and rugby football were first developed. By imposing rules and conventions on school sports that previously were perhaps no less disorderly than their street and village antecedents, reform-minded schoolmasters such as Sir Thomas Arnold of Rugby sought to inculcate qualities of discipline, courage and leadership among pupils. Slowly, as successive generations of pupils graduated from education into adult life, the popularity of sports such as football and rugby spread beyond the schools and universities, and clubs started to form. At a landmark meeting of representatives of a number of London and suburban clubs in October 1863, English football's present-day governing body, the Football Association (FA), was established (Walvin, 1994).

English football's two most durable and important club competitions both emerged soon afterwards) Fifteen clubs first contested the FA Cup during the winter of 1871–2. The Wanderers, a team comprising players who had attended the leading public schools and Oxford or Cambridge Universities, defeated the Royal Engineers in the first final, watched by 2,000 spectators. During the 1880s, football's geographical centre of power shifted away from the predominantly southern ex-public school and ex-university clubs, towards teams based in manufacturing towns and cities in the midlands and the north west. Enlightened factory owners and employers, many of whom were themselves graduates of the public school system, began to see the benefits for workplace morale and productivity of regular Saturday afternoon holidays, which created the opportunity for the development of organised forms of working-class leisure activity. New football clubs began to form throughout England, often at the instigation of local church leaders, during the late 1870s and 1880s. A northern team, Blackburn Olympic, won the FA Cup for the first time in 1883, followed by Blackburn Rovers, three times winners between 1884 and 1886.

The principle of professionalism was accepted by the Football Association in July 1885. Its recognition was a key development in the processes leading to the eventual formation of the Football League in 1888. Twelve teams were members of the league during its first three seasons, with Preston North End the inaugural champions in the 1889 and 1890 seasons, followed by Everton in 1891. During the next three decades, membership of the Football League expanded progressively. In the 1893 season, a second division of 12 teams was created, while membership of the top division was expanded to 16. Several of the leading names of the modern era made their debut appearances in the 1890s, including Manchester United (then Newton Heath) in the 1893 season and Liverpool in the 1894 season. Woolwich Arsenal was the first southern club admitted, also in the 1894 season. Total membership of the two divisions was expanded to 32 teams in the 1895 season, then 36 in the 1899 season and 40 in the 1906 season.

The league finally achieved a membership of magnitude comparable to the combined strength of the present Premier League and Football League (92 teams) shortly after the First World War) In the 1921 season, 22 teams from the Southern League were added to the existing two-division membership (which had by then grown to 44 teams) to form the new Division 3 (South). In the 1922 season a new Division 3 (North) was created, initially comprising 20 teams, but with membership increased to 22 two seasons later.

The most important structural changes to the league's format since the 1920s were as follows:

- A further increase in league membership from 88 to 92 teams in the 1951 season
- The reorganisation of the lower two divisions into Divisions 3 and 4 from the 1959 season, with membership determined on merit (by promotion and relegation) rather than by geographical location
- An increase in mobility within the league with three (rather than two) teams promoted and relegated between Divisions 1 and 2 and Divisions 2 and 3 each season from the 1974 season onwards, and a play-off system introduced in the 1987 season to determine one of the promotion places for each division
- Several adjustments to the size of the divisions during the late 1980s and early 1990s, with automatic promotion and relegation between Division 4 and the top league outside the Football League also implemented in a number of seasons during this period
- The withdrawal from the Football League of Division 1 teams to form a breakaway Premier League, starting in the 1993 season. This development has not affected professional football's basic competitive structure, but it has had profound organisational and financial implications.

Since the Second World War, the number of tournaments has proliferated. Although the FA Cup has continued in a sudden-death format essentially unchanged since its inception in the 1870s, many more clubs (both amateur and professional) now enter, with the major clubs competing only in the final stages. By the 1999 season, the total entry had expanded to 567 teams, with the qualifying stages starting in August and the showpiece final played at the end of the domestic season the following May. The most important domestic competition of post-war vintage is the League Cup. Entry to this sudden-death knockout tournament is open to league clubs only. The League Cup made an uncertain start with a number of leading clubs either refusing to enter, or to take the competition seriously, for several years following its introduction in the 1961 season. Aston Villa of Division 1 defeated Rotherham United of Division 3 over two legs in the first final, and several other lower-division teams reached the final during the 1960s. By the start of the 1970s, however, the League Cup had become established as a prestigious competition which all clubs considered worth taking seriously. In recent seasons its reputation seems to have declined again, with some of the leading clubs choosing to field reserve teams for fixtures in the early rounds, in order to keep their best players fresh for the more important league and European fixtures.[1]

Regular competitive football at European level was first introduced in 1955. Birmingham City and a combined London team both competed in the first Fairs Cup tournament (the predecessor of the UEFA Cup) staged between 1955 and 1958. Meanwhile, Manchester United was the first English team to enter the European Cup in the 1957 season. By the 1961 season, both the Fairs Cup and a new European Cup Winners' Cup were also operating on an annual basis. From then until 1985, when English clubs were excluded from European tournaments following the hooligan-related Heysel stadium disaster at the European Cup Final in Brussels, the three European competitions attracted a combined quota of up to eight leading English clubs per season. England's ban was rescinded in the 1991 season. Since then, European competition has acquired an increasingly prominent position in the fixture lists of the leading clubs. The importance of regular European participation has been enhanced by rapid growth in the financial rewards available from increasingly lucrative television contracts. During the 1990s, a league format was introduced for the early stages of the European Cup, which was renamed the Champions League. This removed the threat of early elimination and guaranteed all entrants a certain minimum number of fixtures. In the 1999 season, 32 teams, including two or three from each of the leading European domestic leagues (rather than just the domestic champions) gained entry to the Champions League. Some teams (the champions and runners-up from the major football powers) enter the league direct, while others (third-placed teams from the major powers, and champions from lesser powers) participate in a qualifying tournament, which provides a means of eliminating some of the weaker aspirants before the main competition gets underway. The 1999 season also saw the consolidation of the UEFA and Cup Winners' Cups into a single UEFA Cup tournament.

Team performance

Although the main focus of this chapter is on the financial rather than the sporting performance of football clubs, it is obvious that there are direct linkages between the two. At the micro level, a club's capacity to generate revenue depends on its team's success on the field of play. On the other

---

[1] Manchester United's withdrawal from the 2000 season's FA Cup, in order to take part in the inaugural FIFA World Club Championship in January 2000, is a clear sign that the older and traditionally more prestigious FA Cup competition is subject to similar pressures.

hand, a club's capacity to strengthen its team by purchasing better players in the transfer market and by offering remuneration at a level that will attract and retain the best players depends on the strength of its finances.[2] At the macro level, a number of economists have argued that the attractiveness to spectators, and therefore the revenue-generating potential of any sports league, depends on the maintenance of a reasonable level of competitive balance. This is necessary to produce genuine uncertainty of outcome at three related levels: first, concerning individual match results; second, concerning championship or divisional outcomes within each season; and third, concerning championship outcomes from season to season (Jennett, 1984; Peel and Thomas, 1988). Competitive balance and uncertainty of outcome for individual match results are the main topics of chapter 3. Before considering the various economic and financial aspects of English football's historical development as a business, it is useful to identify a few key historical facts concerning team performance and championship dominance.

Table 2.4 summarises data about the best-performing teams in the league championship and the cup (domestic and European) competitions. The first panel shows the number of championship victories per team in each decade since the end of the First World War. As an alternative and slightly broader measure of championship dominance, the second panel shows the best-performing teams at the top of Division 1 or the Premier League in each decade, measured by awarding three, two and one points, respectively, to the teams finishing first, second and third in each season. The third and fourth panels show, for each decade, all teams that won the FA Cup and League Cup. The fifth panel shows the number of wins in European competition in each decade.

On both sets of measures of championship dominance, Arsenal in the 1930s, Liverpool in the late 1970s and 1980s and Manchester United in the 1990s all managed to establish a degree of dominance that has not been matched by any other team in the other decades. Many commentators attribute Arsenal's success in the 1930s to superior training methods and mastery of tactics, initially under the management of Herbert Chapman until his death in 1934. Continuity of an effective managerial style, maintained through a series of successful internal appointments (Bill Shankly, Bob Paisley, Joe Fagan, Kenny Dalglish) is regarded as a key factor in Liverpool's success during the 1970s and 1980s. While Alex Ferguson's managerial contribution during the 1990s is also widely acknowledged,

---

[2] Davies, Downward and Jackson (1995) and Dobson and Goddard (1998a) report statistical analyses of the two-way link between team performance and financial performance, for rugby league and for football, respectively.

detractors tend to see a degree of inevitability in Manchester United's recent success, in view of the club's overwhelming financial strength. It remains to be seen whether or not United's current dominance will eventually be challenged and overcome, as has that of other clubs that have dominated previous eras to the same extent as United today.

Table 2.4 indicates that the 1920s and 1960s were the decades in which championship outcomes from season to season were most open. Huddersfield Town was by some way the most successful team of the 1920s, but this decade was unusual in respect of the number of teams (16) that achieved a top three position on at least one occasion. Two clubs shared top honours almost evenly during the 1950s: Wolverhampton Wanderers and Manchester United. The 1960s and the first half of the 1970s can be seen as a continuum, with 10 different clubs winning the championship during 16 seasons, and no team winning in consecutive seasons. Then, by taking three of the last four championships in the 1970s, another six during the 1980s, and the first of the 1990s, Liverpool established an unprecedented 15-year stranglehold. Manchester United's present spell of dominance, however, is now close to equalling or surpassing that of Liverpool.

Another notable feature of table 2.4 is a shift in demographic base of the most successful clubs. In all decades since the 1930s, clubs from the six largest English cities (London, Birmingham, Liverpool, Manchester, Sheffield and Leeds) have claimed the majority (at least six out of every 10) of championship wins. As late as the 1960s, however, Burnley and Ipswich Town repeated the successes of teams like Huddersfield Town and Portsmouth in earlier decades, by winning championships despite having a relatively small population base. In the 1970s, Derby County and Nottingham Forest also interrupted temporarily the dominance of the clubs from the largest cities. During the 1980s and 1990s, however, only Blackburn Rovers has achieved the same feat, in the 1995 season. In any event, as arguably the wealthiest club in the league at the time thanks to the extraordinary *largesse* of their benefactor Jack Walker, Blackburn have some claim to be regarded as a special case.

To what extent has the dominance of the league championship by a handful of powerful clubs (such as Liverpool and Manchester United in the English case) been a typical experience in other European countries? Table 2.5 provides some international comparisons, by reproducing the equivalent of the first two panels of table 2.4 (showing the number of championship wins, and the best-performing teams on the criterion of points for top three finishes) for the post-1945 period, for five other European leagues: France, Germany, Italy, Scotland and Spain. For the six leagues (including England) table 2.6 shows the most successful

Table 2.4. *Most successful English league teams in league and cup competition, 1920–1999*

Championships

1920–9	1930–9	1947–59	1960–9	1970–9	1980–9	1990–9
Huddersfield 3	Arsenal 5	Man Utd 3	Liverpool 2	Liverpool 4	Liverpool 6	Man Utd 5
Liverpool 2	Everton 2	Wolves 3	Man Utd 2	Derby 2	Everton 2	Arsenal 2
Burnley 1	Man City 1	Arsenal 2	Burnley 1	Arsenal 1	Arsenal 1	Blackburn 1
Everton 1	Sheff Wed 1	Portsmouth 2	Everton 1	Everton 1	Aston Villa 1	Leeds 1
Newcastle 1	Sunderland 1	Chelsea 1	Ipswich 1	Leeds 1		Liverpool 1
Sheff Wed 1		Liverpool 1	Leeds 1	Nottm Forest 1		
WBA 1		Tottenham 1	Man City 1			
			Tottenham 1			

Championship – points for a top three finish

1920–9	1930–9	1947–59	1960–9	1970–9	1980–9	1990–9
Huddersfield 14	Arsenal 18	Man Utd 19	Man Utd 10	Liverpool 19	Liverpool 24	Man Utd 21
Burnley 6	Sheff Wed 7	Wolves 16	Liverpool 9	Leeds 10	Everton 8	Arsenal 9
Liverpool 6	Everton 6	Arsenal 8	Tottenham 8	Derby 7	Man Utd 6	Liverpool 7
Sunderland 5	Sunderland 5	Tottenham 8	Burnley 7	Arsenal 5	Ipswich 5	Blackburn 5
WBA 5	Aston Villa 4	Portsmouth 7	Leeds 7	Nottm Forest 5	Arsenal 4	Newcastle 5
Everton 3	Derby 4	Preston 5	Everton 5	Everton 4	Aston Villa 3	Aston Villa 4
Leicester 3	Man City 4	Blackpool 3	Ipswich 3	Ipswich 2	Nottm Forest 3	Leeds 3
Newcastle 3	Wolves 4	Chelsea 3	Man City 3	Man City 2	Southampton 2	Chelsea 1
Sheff Wed 3	Charlton 3	Liverpool 3	Wolves 3	QPR 2	Tottenham 2	Crystal Pal 1
Arsenal 2	Huddersfield 3	WBA 2	Nottm Forest 2	Chelsea 1	Watford 2	Norwich 1
Bolton 2	Preston 1	Burnley 1	Sheff Wed 2	Man Utd 1	West Ham 1	Nottm Forest 1
Cardiff 2	Tottenham 1	Derby 1	Chelsea 1	Tottenham 1		Sheff Wed 1
Man City 2		Huddersfield 1		WBA 1		Tottenham 1
Tottenham 2		Sunderland 1				
Aston Villa 1						
Chelsea 1						

FA Cup Wins

Bolton 3	Arsenal 2	Newcastle 3	Tottenham 3	Arsenal 2	Man Utd 2	Man Utd 4
Aston Villa 1	Everton 1	Arsenal 1	Everton 1	Chelsea 1	Liverpool 2	Arsenal 2
Blackburn 1	Man City 1	Aston Villa 1	Liverpool 1	Ipswich 1	Tottenham 2	Chelsea 1
Cardiff 1	Newcastle 1	Bolton 1	West Ham 1	Leeds 1	Coventry 1	Everton 1
Huddersfield 1	Portsmouth 1	Blackpool 1	Man City 1	Liverpool 1	Everton 1	Liverpool 1
Newcastle 1	Preston 1	Charlton 1	Man Utd 1	Man Utd 1	West Ham 1	Tottenham 1
Sheff Utd 1	Sheff Wed 1	Derby 1	WBA 1	Southampton 1	Wimbledon 1	
Tottenham 1	Sunderland 1	Man City 1	Wolves 1	Sunderland 1		
	WBA 1	Man Utd 1		West Ham 1		
		Nottm Forest 1				
		WBA 1				
		Wolves 1				

League Cup wins (from 1961)

		Aston Villa 1		Aston Villa 2	Liverpool 4	Aston Villa 2
		Birmingham 1		Man City 2	Arsenal 1	Arsenal 1
		Chelsea 1		Nottm Forest 2	Luton 1	Chelsea 1
		Leeds 1		Tottenham 2	Norwich 1	Leicester 1
		Leicester 1		Stoke 1	Nottm Forest 1	Liverpool 1
		Norwich 1		Wolves 1	Oxford 1	Man Utd 1
		QPR 1			Wolves 1	Nottm Forest 1
		Swindon 1				Sheff Wed 1
		WBA 1				Tottenham 1

European Competition wins (from 1956)

		Leeds 1		Liverpool 4	Liverpool 2	Man Utd 2
		Man Utd 1		Chelsea 1	Aston Villa 1	Arsenal 1
		Newcastle 1		Leeds 1	Everton 1	Chelsea 1
		Tottenham 1		Man City 1	Ipswich 1	
		West Ham 1		Nottm Forest 1	Nottm Forest 1	
				Tottenham 1	Tottenham 1	

Sources: Butler (1987); Smailes (1992), Rothmans.

Table 2.5. *Most successful teams in league competition, European comparisons, 1946–1999*

FRANCE

1946–59	1960–9	1970–9	1980–9	1990–9
Championships				
Nice 4	St Etienne 4	St Etienne 4	Bordeaux 3	Marseille 4
Stade Reims 4	Monaco 2	Marseille 2	Monaco 2	Auxerre 1
Lille 2	Nantes 2	Nantes 2	Nantes 2	Bordeaux 1
Bordeaux 1	Stade Reims 2	Monaco 1	Marseille 1	Lens 1
Marseille 1		Strasbourg 1	Paris SG 1	Monaco 1
Roubaix 1			St Etienne 1	Nantes 1
St Etienne 1				Paris SG 1
Championship – points for a top three finish				
Stade Reims 19	St Etienne 12	St Etienne 15	Bordeaux 13	Marseille 16
Lille 15	Stade Reims 9	Nantes 13	Nantes 12	Monaco 11
Nice 12	Monaco 8	Marseille 11	Monaco 10	Paris SG 11
Bordeaux 7	Nantes 8	Nice 4	Paris SG 6	Auxerre 5
Lens 5	Bordeaux 6	Strasbourg 4	St Etienne 6	Bordeaux 5
St Etienne 5	RC Paris 5	Monaco 3	Marseille 5	Lens 3
Marseille 4	Nîmes 3	Lens 2	Sochaux 3	Lyon 3
Nîmes 4	Nice 2	Lyon 2	Roubaix 2	Metz 2
Roubaix 4	Valenciennes 2	Nîmes 2	Auxerre 1	Nantes 4
Sochaux 2	Angers 1	Sochaux 2	Montpellier 1	
Toulouse 2	Lens 1	Bastia 1	Toulouse 1	
Angers 1	Metz 1	Sedan 1		
Le Havre 1	Sedan 1			
Monaco 1	Sochaux 1			
RC Paris 1				
Strasbourg 1				

Note: Olympique Marseille's 1993 championship was subsequently rescinded, but is included here.

Table 2.5. (cont.)

GERMANY

1964–9	1970–9	1980–9	1990–9
Championships			
B München 1	B Möncheng'bach 5	B München 6	B München 4
1860 München1	B München 3	Hamburg 2	B Dortmund 2
Eintr. Braunschweig 1	Hamburg 1	Stuttgart 1	Kaiserslauten 2
Köln 1	Köln 1	Werder Bremen 1	Stuttgart 1
Nürnberg 1			Werder Bremen 1
Werder Bremen 1			
Championship – points for a top three finish			
1860 München 5	B Möncheng'bach 20	B München 21	B München 20
Köln 5	B München 14	Hamburg 14	B Dortmund 9
Werder Bremen 5	Hamburg 5	Werder Bremen 10	Kaiserslauten 8
B München 4	Hertha Berlin 5	Köln 6	B Leverkusen 6
B Dortmund 4	Köln 5	Stuttgart 6	Werder Bremen 6
Eintr. Braunschweig 3	Schalke 04 4	B Möncheng'bach 2	Eintr. Frankfurt 3
Nürnberg 3	Fortuna Düsseldorf 2	Bayer Üdingen 1	Köln 2
Alemannia Aachen 2	Stuttgart 2		Stuttgart 2
B Möncheng'bach 2	Eintr. Braunschweig 1		Freiburg 1
Duisberg 2	Eintr. Frankfurt 1		Hertha Berlin 1
Eintr. Frankfurt 1	Kaiserslauten 1		Schalke 04 1

Note: Data from 1964 to 1991 are for West Germany.

ITALY

1947–59	1960–9	1970–9	1980–9	1990–9
Championships				
AC Milan 4	Internazionale 3	Juventus 5	Juventus 4	AC Milan 4
Juventus 3	Juventus 3	AC Milan 1	AC Milan 2	Juventus 3
Torino 3	AC Milan 2	Cagliari 1	Internazionale 2	Napoli 1
Internazionale 2	Bologna 1	Internazionale 1	Napoli 1	Sampdoria 1
Fiorentina 1	Fiorentina 1	Lazio 1	Roma 1	
		Torino 1	Verona 1	
Championship – points for a top three finish				
AC Milan 23	Internazionale 16	Juventus 21	Juventus 18	AC Milan 19
Juventus 17	AC Milan 14	AC Milan 10	Roma 11	Juventus 15
Internazionale 14	Juventus 12	Torino 7	Internazionale 9	Internazionale 7
Fiorentina 9	Fiorentina 6	Internazionale 5	Napoli 9	Lazio 5
Torino 9	Bologna 5	Lazio 4	AC Milan 5	Parma 4
Udinese 2	Napoli 3	Napoli 4	Fiorentina 3	Sampdoria 4
Lazio 1	Cagliari 2	Cagliari 3	Verona 3	Napoli 3
Modena 1	Torino 1	Perugia 2	Torino 2	Fiorentina 1
Padova 1		Vicenza 2		Torino 1
Roma 1		Fiorentina 1		Udinese 1
		Roma 1		

Table 2.5. (*cont.*)

SCOTLAND

1947–59	1960–9	1970–9	1980–9	1990–9
Championships				
Rangers 7	Celtic 4	Celtic 7	Celtic 4	Rangers 9
Hibernian 3	Rangers 3	Rangers 3	Aberdeen 3	Celtic 1
Aberdeen 1	Dundee 1		Rangers 2	
Celtic 1	Hearts 1		Dundee Utd 1	
Hearts 1	Kilmarnock 1			
Championship – points for a top three finish				
Rangers 30	Rangers 20	Celtic 24	Celtic 23	Rangers 29
Hibernian 16	Celtic 14	Rangers 19	Aberdeen 16	Celtic 12
Hearts 11	Kilmarnock 12	Aberdeen 7	Rangers 9	Aberdeen 9
Aberdeen 6	Hearts 5	Hibernian 7	Dundee Utd 7	Hearts 4
Celtic 6	Dundee 3	Dundee Utd 2	Hearts 4	Motherwell 3
Dundee 3	Dunfermline 2	St Johnstone 1	St Mirren 1	Dundee Utd 1
East Fife 2	Clyde 1			Hibernian 1
Partick 2	Hibernian 1			St Johnstone 1
Kilmarnock 1	Partick 1			
Motherwell 1	Third Lanark 1			

SPAIN

1946–59	1960–9	1970–9	1980–9	1990–9
Championships				
Barcelona 5	Real Madrid 8	Real Madrid 5	Real Madrid 5	Barcelona 6
Real Madrid 4	Atlético	Atlético	Athletic	Real Madrid 3
Atlétic	Madrid 1	Madrid 3	Bilbao 2	Atlético
Madrid 2	Barcelona 1	Barcelona 1	Real Sociedad 2	Madrid 1
Athletic		Valencia 1	Barcelona 1	
Bilbao 1				
Sevilla 1				
Valencia 1				
Championship – points for a top three finish				
Barcelona 25	Real Madrid 28	Real Madrid 15	Real Madrid 22	Barcelona 22
Real Madrid 18	Barcelona 13	Barcelona 15	Barcelona 12	Real Madrid 16
Valencia 12	Atlético	Atlético	Real Sociedad 10	Atlético
Atlético	Madrid 10	Madrid 14	Athletic	Madrid 6
Madrid 11	Las Palmas 3	Valencia 5	Bilbao 8	D La Coruña 6
Athletic	Real Zaragoza 2	Athletic	Atlético	Valencia 4
Bilbao 9	Athletico	Bilbao 4	Madrid 5	Athletic
Sevilla 7	Bilbao 1	Real Zaragoza 3	Español 1	Bilbao 2
D La Coruña 2	Español 1	Sporting Gijon 2	Sporting Gijon 1	Real Betis 1
	Real Betis 1	Español 1	Valencia 1	Real Mallorca 1
	Real Oviedo 1	Sevilla 1		Real Sociedad 1
				Real Zaragoza 1

teams overall for the entire post-1945 period, obtained by aggregating the points awarded for top three finishes. Because there were variations between countries in the date of resumption of the national league competition after 1945, the points scores in table 2.6 have been converted to percentages, to permit meaningful comparisons of championship dominance between countries.

By the criterion of the number of teams that have achieved a top three finish during the post-1945 period, the English league turns out to be the most democratic of the six that are analysed in tables 2.4–2.6. In total, 29 different English teams have achieved top three finishes. Several of these appeared in the top three for the first time during the 1980s (Southampton, Watford, West Ham) or 1990s (Crystal Palace and Norwich). France with 25 different top three finishers, and Germany with 20 are the next highest on this criterion. The German total is based on a significantly smaller number of seasons, however, the West German Bundesliga having only resumed on a national basis in the 1964 season. Italy, Scotland and Spain, with 18, 17 and 15 teams, respectively, had the smallest numbers of top three finishers.

In terms of the success achieved by the most successful teams during the post-1945 period, the English league has clearly been dominated to a greater extent by Liverpool and Manchester United than has France by its most successful teams. France, indeed, seems to be something of a special case, with no team apparently capable of maintaining a dominant position for more than a few years at a time. Stade Reims, the most successful team of the 1950s and early 1960s and twice European Cup runners up to Real Madrid, were eventually relegated in 1967 and have not returned to the First Division. The dominance of St Etienne, champions 10 times between 1957 and 1981 and a major force in European competition during the 1970s, had also run its course by the start of the 1980s, although the club did manage to preserve First Division status until 1996. Spells of success for Bordeaux and Marseille in the 1980s and 1990s ended abruptly in scandal and enforced relegation in both cases. Paris Saint Germain (PSG), currently the wealthiest French club, was formed only in the early 1970s and therefore has no historical tradition of championship success.

Elsewhere, the most successful teams in Germany, Italy, Scotland and Spain have enjoyed greater championship dominance than have Liverpool and Manchester United in England. The clear lead over all rivals achieved by Germany's Bayern München in table 2.6 is untypical; in the other five countries the scores of the first and second most successful teams are much closer together (although in Scotland a significant gap between Rangers and Celtic has developed in recent seasons). Bayern

Table 2.6. *League championship dominance, European comparisons, 1940–1999*

ENGLAND	FRANCE	GERMANY	ITALY	SCOTLAND	SPAIN
Liverpool 19.5	St Etienne 11.7	B München 27.3	Juventus 26.2	Rangers 33.6	Real Madrid 30.6
Man Utd 17.9	Nantes 11.4	B Mönchengl'bach 11.1	AC Milan 22.4	Celtic 24.8	Barcelona 26.9
Arsenal 8.2	Marseille 11.1	W Bremen 9.7	Inter 16.1	Aberdeen 11.9	Atlético Madrid 14.2
Leeds 6.3	Monaco 10.2	Hamburg 8.8	Fiorentina 6.3	Hibernian 7.9	Athletic Bilbao 7.4
Tottenham 6.3	Bordeaux 9.6	Köln 8.3	Torino 6.3	Hearts 7.5	Valencia 6.8
Wolverhampton 6.0	Stade Reims 8.6	B Dortmund 6.0	Napoli 6.0	Kilmarnock 4.1	R Sociedad 3.4
Everton 5.3	Nice 5.6	Stuttgart 5.1	Roma 4.1	Dundee Utd 3.1	D La Coruña 2.5
Nottm Forest 3.5	Paris SG 5.2	Kaiserslautern 4.2	Lazio 3.2	Dundee 1.9	Sevilla 2.5
Ipswich 3.1	Lille 4.6	B Leverkusen 2.8	Bologna 1.6	Motherwell 1.2	Real Zaragoza 1.9
Burnley 2.5	Lens 3.4	Hertha Berlin 2.8	Cagliari 1.6	Partick 0.9	Español 0.9
Derby 2.5	Nimes 2.8	1860 München 2.3	Parma 1.3	Dunfermline 0.6	Las Palmas 0.9
Aston Villa 2.2	Sochaux 2.5	Entracht Frankfurt 2.3	Sampdoria 1.3	East Fife 0.6	Sport Gijon 0.9
Portsmouth 2.2	Auxerre 1.9	Schalke 04 2.3	Udinese 0.9	St Johnstone 0.6	Real Betis 0.6
Chelsea 1.9	RC Paris 1.9	E Braunschweig 1.9	Verona 0.9	Clyde 0.3	Real Mallorca 0.3
Blackburn 1.6	Roubaix 1.9	Nürnberg 1.4	Perugia 0.6	St Mirren 0.3	Real Oviedo 0.3
Man City 1.6	Lyon 1.5	Alemannia 0.9	Vicenza 0.6	Third Lanark 0.3	
Newcastle 1.6	Strasbourg 1.5	Duisberg 0.9	Modena 0.3		
Preston 1.6	Metz 0.9	Düsseldorf 0.9	Padova 0.3		
Blackpool 0.9	Toulouse 0.9	B Üdingen 0.5			
Sheff Weds 0.9	Angers 0.6	Freiburg 0.5			
West Brom 0.9	Sedan 0.6				
QPR 0.6	Valenciennes 0.6				
Southampton 0.6	Bastia 0.3				
Watford 0.6	Le Havre 0.3				
Crystal Palace 0.3	Montpellier 0.3				
Huddersfield 0.3					
Norwich 0.3					
Sunderland 0.3					
West Ham 0.3					

Notes:
Scores are calculated by awarding three points for a championship win, two for second place and one for third place. Totals are converted to percentages.
See also notes to Table 2.2.

München have maintained a presence at the top of the Bundesliga since it resumed in the 1964 season, while the successes of other championship winning teams have been shorter in duration. The trajectory of Borussia Mönchengladbach was comparable to that of St Etienne in France: champions five times between 1970 and 1977, European Cup runners-up in 1977, UEFA Cup winners in 1975 and 1979, but relegated in 1999. Since the late 1970s Hamburg, Stuttgart, Kaiserslauten and most recently Borussia Dortmund (domestic champions in 1995 and 1996, and European champions in 1998) have all launched challenges to Bayern München's dominance which have been sustained over only relatively short periods.

The triumvirate of Juventus, AC Milan and Internazionale have maintained a stranglehold on Italy's Serie A throughout most of the post-1945 period. Teams such as Torino, Fiorentina, Roma, Napoli and Sampdoria have all won occasional championships but have not maintained a constant presence at the very highest level. At present Rome's Lazio, champions in the 2000 season and currently among the heaviest spenders in the European transfer market, appear to be capable of achieving a lasting shift in the balance of power in Serie A.

The championships of Scotland and Spain, in contrast, have been dominated to an even greater extent by just two teams in each case: Rangers and Celtic, and Real Madrid and Barcelona, respectively. Only when one of the leading two teams has experienced a particularly fallow period have opportunities arisen for a third team. Aberdeen's three championships, for example, were won during the early 1980s when Rangers were enduring a lengthy period of poor form and loss of direction. In Scotland, the gulf in terms of resources between Rangers and Celtic and the rest has now widened to the extent that it is difficult to imagine that any other team is even capable of winning the championship in the foreseeable future. The lack of competition has fuelled speculation that these two clubs (and perhaps a handful of others) will eventually withdraw from the Scottish League and join forces with their counterparts from Belgium, Holland, Portugal and Scandinavia to form a new Atlantic League (see chapter 9). By contrast in Spain, Deportivo La Coruña's championship win in 2000 and Valencia's European Cup final appearance in the same season (beaten, ironically, by Real Madrid) shows that domestic competition capable of challenging the big two does still exist, despite their formidable financial advantages.

Returning to England, it is useful to identify some broader patterns in the performance of clubs throughout the entire league, as well as at the very top end as shown in tables 2.4 and 2.6. For this purpose, table 2.7 identifies five groups of clubs with broadly similar characteristics (Group

Table 2.7. *Group definitions*

Group 1 Major London clubs and clubs from other towns with populations larger than 500,000, which entered the league before its expansion in the early 1920s:

Arsenal, Aston Villa, Birmingham City, Chelsea, Everton, Leeds United, Liverpool, Manchester City, Manchester United, Sheffield United, Sheffield Wednesday, Tottenham Hotspur, West Bromwich Albion, West Ham United (14 clubs)

Group 2 Clubs from towns with populations in the range 250,000–500,000 in the midlands and north (i.e. all English regions from the East and West Midlands northwards), all of these clubs entered the league before 1920:

Bradford City, Bradford Park Avenue, Coventry City, Derby County, Hull City, Leicester City, Newcastle United, Notts County, Nottingham Forest, Port Vale, Stoke City, Sunderland, Wolverhampton Wanderers (13 clubs)

Group 3 Other clubs from towns in the south (i.e. the South East, South West and East Anglia regions, plus south Wales) with populations below 500,000, as well as the smaller London clubs not included in Group 1; most of these clubs (except Bristol City, Luton Town, Fulham and Leyton Orient) entered the League during or after its early 1920s' expansion:

Aberdare, Aldershot, Barnet, Bournemouth, Brentford, Brighton and Hove Albion, Bristol City, Bristol Rovers, Cambridge United, Cardiff City, Charlton Athletic, Colchester United, Crystal Palace, Exeter City, Fulham, Gillingham, Ipswich Town, Leyton Orient, Luton Town, Maidstone United, Merthyr Town, Millwall, Newport County, Norwich City, Oxford United, Peterborough United, Portsmouth, Plymouth Argyle, Queens Park Rangers, Reading, Southampton, Southend United, Swansea City, Swindon Town, Thames, Torquay United, Watford, Wimbledon (38 clubs)

Group 4 All clubs from smaller towns in the midlands/north which entered the League before 1920:

Barnsley, Blackburn Rovers, Blackpool, Bolton Wanderers, Burnley, Bury, Chesterfield, Crewe Alexandra, Doncaster Rovers, Gateshead, Grimsby Town, Huddersfield Town, Lincoln City, Middlesbrough, Oldham Athletic, Preston North End, Rotherham United, Stockport County, Walsall (19 clubs)

Group 5 Clubs from the midlands/north which entered the League during or after its early 1920s expansion:

Accrington Stanley, Ashington, Barrow, Carlisle United, Chester City, Darlington, Durham City, Halifax Town, Hartlepool United, Hereford United, Mansfield Town, Macclesfield Town, Nelson, New Brighton, Northampton Town, Rochdale, Scarborough, Scunthorpe United, Shrewsbury Town, Southport, Stalybridge Celtic, Tranmere Rovers, Wigan Athletic, Workington Town, Wrexham, York City (26 clubs)

1 to Group 5), using three simple criteria to define the clubs that make up each group:

- the club's *home-town population* recorded in the 1961 Census of Population
- the date of the club's *initial entry into the league*
- the club's *geographical location* (for which there are two broad categories: south and midlands/north).

Figure 2.3 shows the percentage share of the clubs in each of the five groups in an aggregate performance score, calculated by awarding 92 points to the club which finished first in Division 1 (or the Premier League), 91 points to the club which finished second, and so on, in each season. Minor adjustments to the points system are made for seasons when the number of teams in the league was greater or less than 92. Teams finishing in equal positions in the old Division 3 (South) and Division 3 (North) are awarded equal points: first position in either division gains 48 points, second gains 46 points, and so on.

The relative constancy of Group 1's performance score emphasises the fact that the dominance of the clubs from the largest cities has been a consistent feature throughout the league's history, and is by no means a uniquely recent phenomenon. In contrast, the Group 2 clubs from the next city size-band, which include three championship winners from the 1920s, 1930s and 1950s (Newcastle United, Sunderland and Wolverhampton Wanderers), experienced a significant decline in their performance as a group between the late 1930s and late 1950s. Since then, the average performance of the Group 2 clubs has also been quite stable.

Group 3 clubs enjoyed a steady and sustained improvement in their average performance between the 1920s and the end of the 1980s. Their progressive advance represents the most important long-term shift in the geographical balance of football power. Since the Second World War, the majority of clubs gaining admission to the league have been located in the south: Colchester United (admitted in the 1951 season), Peterborough United (1961), Oxford United (1963), Cambridge United (1971), Hereford United (1973), Wimbledon (1978), Maidstone United (1990), Barnet (1992) and Wycombe Wanderers (1994).[3] More important, however, has been a progressive rise in the status of many of the southern clubs which entered the league during its early 1920s' expansion or later, and which have been engaged in a catching-up process during much of

---

[3] Post-war entrants to the league from the north and midlands were Scunthorpe United and Shrewsbury Town (both in the 1951 season), Wigan Athletic (1979), Scarborough (1988) and Macclesfield Town (1998). These lists do not include several clubs that temporarily exited and re-entered.

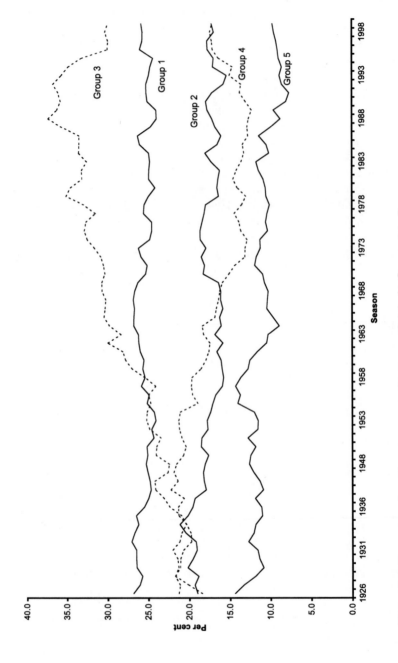

Figure 2.3 Percentage shares in aggregate performance of clubs in Groups 1 to 5
Sources: Butler (1987); Smailes (1992); Rothmans (various years).

the period since. Charlton Athletic, Crystal Palace, Ipswich Town, Norwich City, Portsmouth, Queens Park Rangers, Southampton and Swindon Town all rose from modest starting positions in Division 3 (South) eventually to figure prominently in the top two divisions. Collectively, however, Group 3 clubs have not been the main beneficiaries of English football's popular revival during the 1990s, in terms of either performance or revenues (see below). According to figure 2.3, the 1988 season was their most successful ever on the field of play. Since then their fortunes have declined significantly. By the end of the 1990s, Crystal Palace, Norwich and Queens Park Rangers were among several clubs in the previous list finding it difficult to sustain the levels of success they had enjoyed at times over the previous 25 years.

Group 4 consists mainly of northern clubs from smaller towns, all of which were already established in the top two divisions at the time of the league's early 1920s' expansion. These clubs appear to have been the main victims of the southern clubs' upward progression between the 1920s and 1980s. Many of these clubs, located in traditional industrial or manufacturing towns especially hard-hit by three major recessions during the 1970s, 1980s and 1990s, have not been able to keep pace with their more upwardly mobile southern counterparts. Nevertheless, a number of Group 4 members, including Blackburn Rovers, Bolton Wanderers and Middlesbrough, seem to have responded adroitly to the new opportunities created by the recent recovery in football's popular appeal. Accordingly, Group 4's performance score has improved significantly during the 1990s.

The long-term performance of the Group 5 clubs, many of which were the founder members of Division 3 (North) in the early 1920s, has been in marked contrast to that of their southern counterparts in Group 3. From the start, there was an imbalance between the respective strengths of the southern and northern Division 3 clubs. In the 1920 season, the last before the formation of Division 3 (South), the league comprised 37 clubs from the north and midlands, and only seven from the south. The pool of aspiring southern clubs still outside the league was therefore very strong, while most of the larger northern and midland towns were already represented. This meant that Division 3 (North) was formed from a weaker pool of clubs than Division 3 (South). Between the 1920s and 1990s, several of the Group 5 clubs lost their league status, and few of those that have survived have enjoyed anything more than the briefest spells in the top two divisions.

2.3 Match attendances

Trends in attendances

This section describes broad trends in English league match attendances at an aggregate level. A statistical analysis of the long-term determinants of attendance for individual clubs during the post-Second World War period is included in chapter 7. Data on aggregate English league attendances between the 1922 and 1999 seasons inclusive are shown in table 2.8. During the inter-war period, trends in attendances mirrored the fortunes of the national economy closely, with a short post-war boom after 1918 followed by a period of decline from the 1922 season onwards, and then a gradual recovery starting in the 1932 season. Following the Second World War, attendances surged, achieving an all-time high of 41 million in the 1949 season. Again, the post-war boom was relatively short-lived, and was followed by sustained decline in attendances that continued, almost uninterrupted, until the 1986 season. The downward trend was punctuated only by a few brief interludes, most notably following England's World Cup victory in 1966. The decline in aggregate attendance accelerated briefly in the early 1980s, and then levelled out in the middle of the decade. The 1987 season witnessed an unexpected improvement, which has continued ever since. By the turn of the century, however, despite 13 seasons of sustained growth, aggregate attendances had recovered only to levels last seen in the mid-1970s. The rather sluggish rate of growth is partly due to capacity constraints at refurbished all-seated stadia, with many leading clubs currently experiencing demand for tickets far in excess of ground capacities.

Table 2.8 also shows attendances by division and the percentage share of each division in the aggregate attendance over the same period. The divisional shares in aggregate attendance remained roughly constant through the 1920s and most of the 1930s. During the last three seasons before the Second World War, however, the attendances of the Division 1 clubs were 5.5 per cent higher than during the previous three seasons; those of the clubs outside Division 1 were 24.1 per cent higher. Consequently, Division 1's attendance share fell by around 5 per cent just before the Second World War. The story was similar during the post-war boom, but as aggregate attendances started to decline, the lower-division clubs shed spectators at a faster rate than their Division 1 counterparts. Between the 1949 season when the aggregate attendance peaked, and the 1986 season when the nadir was finally reached, Division 1's aggregate attendance fell by 49.7 per cent, while the combined attendance of the three lower divisions fell by 67.5 per cent. Consequently, Division 1's

Table 2.8. *English league attendances, aggregate and by division,*
1922–1999

Season	Total	Aggregates (million)				Percentage shares			
		D1/ Prem	D2/ One	D3/ Two	D4/ Three	D1/ Prem	D2/ One	D3/ Two	D4/ Three
1922	25.6	12.5	6.1	4.4	2.5	48.8	23.9	17.4	9.9
1923	23.6	10.8	6.2	4.2	2.4	45.6	26.4	17.8	10.1
1924	23.3	10.8	5.9	4.1	2.5	46.1	25.5	17.7	10.6
1925	23.1	10.4	6.2	4.1	2.3	45.2	27.0	17.7	10.1
1926	23.1	10.4	6.1	3.9	2.6	45.3	26.6	16.8	11.4
1927	23.4	10.6	6.5	3.8	2.5	45.2	27.9	16.1	10.8
1928	23.5	10.6	6.9	3.6	2.5	44.9	29.3	15.2	10.6
1929	23.9	10.5	6.7	4.0	2.7	43.9	28.0	16.6	11.5
1930	22.9	10.5	6.3	3.9	2.3	45.6	27.5	17.1	9.8
1931	21.0	9.5	6.1	3.2	2.3	45.0	28.9	15.3	10.8
1932	21.8	9.9	5.6	3.9	2.2	45.7	25.9	18.0	10.3
1933	21.4	9.5	6.1	3.5	2.3	44.6	28.4	16.3	10.7
1934	22.5	10.4	5.8	3.8	2.5	46.5	25.8	16.8	11.0
1935	23.1	10.8	6.1	3.8	2.4	46.8	26.4	16.4	10.5
1936	24.7	11.4	6.9	4.0	2.4	46.1	28.0	16.1	9.8
1937	26.4	11.4	8.0	4.4	2.6	43.0	30.3	16.8	9.9
1938	27.9	11.6	8.6	4.6	3.1	41.7	30.9	16.5	11.0
1939	27.0	11.5	8.6	4.0	2.9	42.4	31.9	14.8	10.8
1947	35.4	14.9	11.0	5.6	3.9	42.1	31.1	15.9	10.9
1948	40.2	16.7	12.3	6.7	4.6	41.5	30.5	16.5	11.4
1949	41.0	17.9	11.1	7.0	5.0	43.7	27.1	17.0	12.2
1950	40.6	17.4	11.7	7.1	4.4	42.8	28.8	17.5	10.9
1951	39.5	16.7	10.8	7.3	4.8	42.2	27.3	18.5	12.0
1952	39.0	16.1	11.1	6.9	4.9	41.3	28.4	17.8	12.5
1953	37.1	16.1	9.7	6.7	4.7	43.2	26.0	18.0	12.7
1954	36.4	16.1	9.7	6.3	4.2	44.4	26.7	17.4	11.5
1955	34.1	15.1	9.0	6.0	4.0	44.2	26.4	17.6	11.9
1956	33.2	14.2	9.1	5.7	4.3	42.7	27.3	17.1	12.9
1957	32.7	13.8	8.7	5.6	4.6	42.2	26.6	17.1	14.0
1958	33.5	14.4	8.6	6.1	4.3	43.1	25.8	18.2	12.9
1959	33.7	14.7	8.6	6.1	4.2	43.6	25.6	18.2	12.6
1960	32.5	14.4	8.4	5.7	4.0	44.4	25.8	17.6	12.3
1961	28.6	12.9	7.0	4.8	3.9	45.3	24.5	16.7	13.5
1962	28.0	12.1	7.5	5.2	3.3	43.1	26.6	18.6	11.7
1963	28.8	12.4	7.4	5.7	3.2	43.3	25.8	19.7	11.3
1964	28.5	12.5	7.6	5.4	3.0	43.8	26.6	19.0	10.6
1965	27.6	12.7	7.0	4.4	3.5	46.0	25.3	16.0	12.7
1966	27.2	12.5	6.9	4.8	3.0	45.8	25.4	17.6	11.1
1967	28.9	14.2	7.3	4.4	3.0	49.2	25.1	15.3	10.3
1968	30.1	15.3	7.4	4.0	3.4	50.8	24.7	13.4	11.1
1969	29.2	14.5	7.4	4.3	3.0	49.8	25.2	14.8	10.2
1970	29.5	14.8	7.6	4.2	2.9	50.2	25.7	14.2	9.9

Table 2.8. (*cont.*)

Season	Total	Aggregates (million)				Percentage shares			
		D1/ Prem	D2/ One	D3/ Two	D4/ Three	D1/ Prem	D2/ One	D3/ Two	D4/ Three
1971	28.2	14.0	7.1	4.4	2.8	49.6	25.1	15.5	9.8
1972	28.7	14.5	6.8	4.7	2.7	50.5	23.6	16.4	9.5
1973	25.4	14.0	5.6	3.7	2.1	55.0	22.1	14.7	8.3
1974	25.0	13.1	6.3	3.4	2.2	52.3	25.3	13.7	8.7
1975	25.6	12.0	7.5	4.1	1.9	47.0	29.5	16.0	7.5
1976	24.9	13.1	5.8	3.9	2.1	52.6	23.3	15.8	8.3
1977	26.0	13.6	6.2	4.1	2.1	52.2	23.9	15.8	8.1
1978	25.4	13.3	6.5	3.3	2.3	52.2	25.5	13.1	9.2
1979	24.5	12.7	6.1	3.4	2.3	51.7	25.1	13.8	9.4
1980	24.6	12.2	6.1	4.0	2.4	49.4	24.8	16.2	9.5
1981	21.9	11.4	5.2	3.6	1.7	52.0	23.6	16.6	7.7
1982	20.0	10.4	4.8	2.8	2.0	52.1	23.8	14.1	10.0
1983	18.8	9.3	5.0	2.9	1.6	49.6	26.5	15.7	8.3
1984	18.3	8.7	5.4	2.7	1.6	47.4	29.2	14.9	8.5
1985	17.8	9.7	4.0	2.7	1.4	54.7	22.6	15.0	7.7
1986	16.5	9.0	3.6	2.5	1.4	54.8	21.5	15.1	8.5
1987	17.4	9.1	4.2	2.4	1.7	52.6	24.0	13.5	9.9
1988	18.0	8.1	5.3	2.8	1.8	45.1	29.7	15.3	9.9
1989	18.5	7.8	5.8	3.0	1.8	42.3	31.6	16.4	9.7
1990	19.5	7.9	6.9	2.8	1.9	40.5	35.4	14.4	9.7
1991	19.5	8.6	6.3	2.8	1.8	44.2	32.2	14.6	9.0
1992	20.4	10.0	5.8	3.0	1.6	49.0	28.5	14.7	7.8
1993	20.6	9.7	5.9	3.5	1.5	47.2	28.5	16.9	7.5
1994	21.7	10.7	6.5	3.0	1.6	49.1	29.9	13.7	7.3
1995	21.9	10.7	6.6	3.2	1.4	48.7	30.2	14.8	6.2
1996	21.9	10.5	6.6	2.9	2.0	47.7	30.0	13.3	9.0
1997	22.8	10.8	6.9	3.2	1.9	47.4	30.5	14.0	8.1
1998	24.8	11.1	8.3	3.5	1.8	45.0	33.7	14.2	7.1
1999	25.4	11.6	7.5	4.1	2.1	45.8	29.6	16.3	8.3

Note:
Up to and including the 1958 season, D3 is Division 3 (South) and D4 is Division 3 (North).
Sources: Tabner (1992); Rothmans (various years).

attendance share increased by about 10 per cent in total. As table 2.8 shows, however, most of the improvement in Division 1's relative position took place over a rather shorter period than this. Specifically, between the late 1950s and the mid-1970s, Division 1's attendance share increased by between 8 and 9 per cent, predominantly (but not exclusively) at the expense of the clubs in the newly formed Divisions 3 and 4.

Between the mid-1970s and the mid-1980s, as aggregate attendances continued to fall, there was little further change in the divisional attendance shares, with Division 1's share hovering just above 50 per cent through most of this period. Since the mid-1980s, Division 2 clubs (now Division One) have enjoyed the fastest growth in attendances, while growth has been more sluggish in Division 1 (now the Premier League). In fact, Division 1 attendances did not start to increase until the 1990 season, fully three seasons after the aggregate figure first started to rise. As Szymanski and Kuypers (1999) point out, this may be partly due to the temporary presence in Division 2 of several of the best-supported clubs (Aston Villa, Leeds United, Chelsea, Newcastle United and Manchester City) in the late 1980s. More significantly over the longer term, as already noted, ground-capacity constraints have been partly responsible for keeping the Division 1/Premier League attendance share below 50 per cent in all seasons since 1988.

The percentage shares in aggregate attendance of the clubs in each of the five groups defined previously (see table 2.7) are shown in figure 2.4. The graphs confirm the narrowing of differentials between clubs in terms of attendance share immediately before and after the Second World War, and the widening that has taken place since, especially between the late 1950s and the mid-1970s. It is also notable that the trends in the fortunes of Group 1 and Group 3 clubs, measured in terms of performance on the one hand and attendance on the other, differ strikingly between figures 2.3 and 2.4. While the average performance of the Group 1 clubs hardly changed between the 1920s and 1990s, their attendance share has fluctuated markedly, between about 27 per cent (in the early 1950s) and 39 per cent (in the mid-1980s). Group 3 clubs in contrast have enjoyed significant improvements in performance until recently, but have found it difficult to achieve a corresponding increase in attendance share. The attendance share of the 27 Group 3 clubs in the league in the 1922 season (one of which was in Division 1, and four in Division 2) was 22.1 per cent. By the 1988 season, the number of Group 3 clubs had increased to 33 (nine of which were in Division 1 and six in Division 2). Despite the increase in numbers and the improvement in performance, Group 3's attendance share had increased only modestly, to 29.1 per cent. By the 1999 season, the attendance share of the 32 Group 3 clubs (three of which were in the Premier League and nine in Division One) had fallen back to 25 per cent.

Figure 2.5 presents some international comparisons of trends in average attendances since the 1970s, for selected clubs in England, Scotland, France and Germany. The sustained decline in English attendances during the 1970s and early 1980s is clearly reflected in the data for

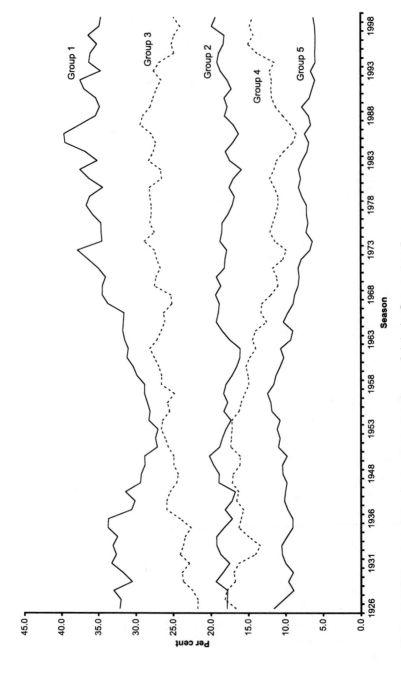

Figure 2.4 Percentage shares in aggregate attendance of clubs in Groups 1 to 5
Sources: Tabner (1992); Rothmans (various years).

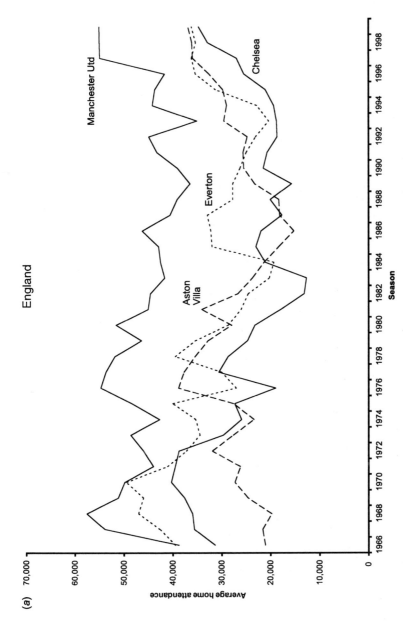

Figure 2.5 Trends in average home-league attendances, selected clubs, four European leagues
Sources: <http://rernes.free.fr/>; Rothmans.

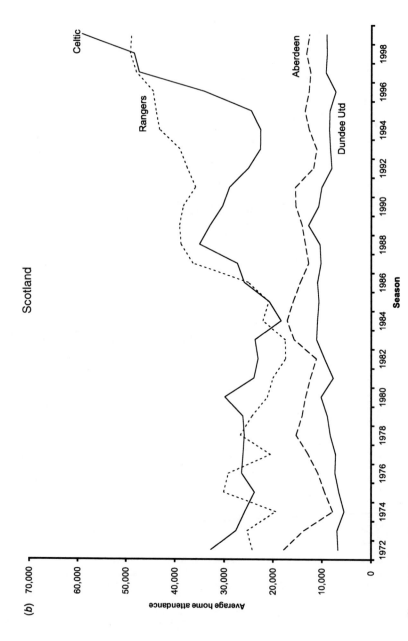

(b)

Scotland

Average home attendance

70,000
60,000
50,000
40,000
30,000
20,000
10,000
0

1972 1974 1976 1978 1980 1982 1984 1986 1988 1990 1992 1994 1996 1998

Season

Celtic

Rangers

Aberdeen

Dundee Utd

Figure 2.5 (*cont.*)

France

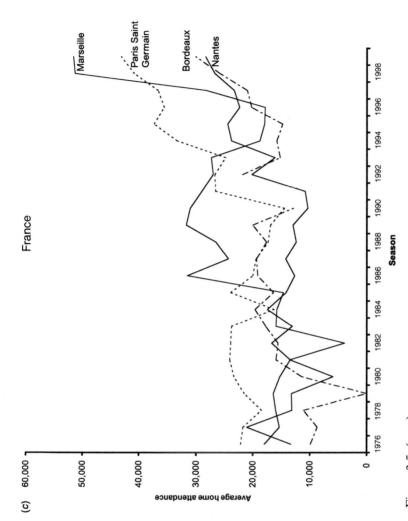

Figure 2.5 (*cont.*)

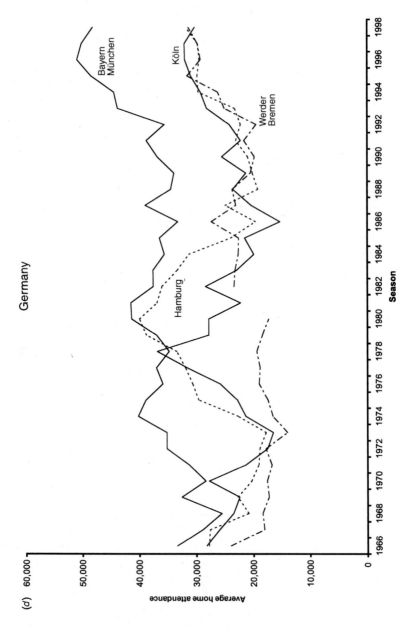

Germany

Bayern München

Köln

Werder Bremen

Hamburg

(d)

Average home attendance

60,000

50,000

40,000

30,000

20,000

10,000

0

1966 1968 1970 1972 1974 1976 1978 1980 1982 1984 1986 1988 1990 1992 1994 1996 1998

Season

Figure 2.5 (*cont.*)

Aston Villa, Chelsea, Everton and Manchester United shown in panel (a). So too is the 1990s upturn; although as indicated above, in many cases the numbers of spectators lost in earlier decades have been only partially recovered. In recent years, ground capacity restraints have restricted the magnitude of the improvement, especially for Chelsea and Manchester United.

For Celtic and Rangers, the 1970s and early 1980s' Scottish data shown in panel (b) tell a similar story of sustained decline in attendances. During this period, Celtic and Rangers were more typical of Scottish clubs in general than Aberdeen and Dundee United, which did not suffer from the same problem, thanks mainly to improvements in performance on the field of play. Since the mid-1980s, however, the divergence in fortunes between the two pairs of clubs could hardly be more pronounced. In the 1970s Celtic and Rangers filled their stadia for matches against each other, but regularly played home matches against lesser opposition in grounds two-thirds or three-quarters empty. Nowadays both clubs normally fill their grounds effortlessly for league matches, regardless of the opposition. Meanwhile, as the fortunes of Aberdeen and Dundee United on the pitch receded (relative to the highs attained in the mid-1980s), attendances at both clubs fell somewhat during the 1990s.

A similar story of spectacular recent attendance gains for the big-market teams, accompanied by more modest performance by others, is also apparent in the French data shown in panel (c). The tabulations begin only after the worst effects of French football's declining popularity in the 1960s and early 1970s had been experienced. Average attendances remained quite steady during the 1980s and early 1990s, prior to the recent uplift. Clearly the 1998 World Cup did much to improve the popularity of domestic club football in France during the 1999 and 2000 seasons. But in common with trends apparent in other countries, the two big-market teams included in panel (c), Marseille and Paris Saint Germain (PSG), have benefited far more than the other two, Bordeaux and Nantes.

For Germany, the long-term pattern differs somewhat from the other three countries. Perhaps because attendances started from a relatively low base when a national league competition resumed in the 1964 season, West German attendances remained reasonably buoyant throughout the 1970s. Victories for the national team in the 1972 European Championships and 1974 World Cup were also helpful. As elsewhere, attendances did fall during the early 1980s, while the 1990s were a period of sustained improvement. As panel (d) shows, in recent seasons the attendances of Bayern München, Germany's most successful and economically powerful club, have pulled away from those of others including Hamburg, Köln and Werder Bremen.

Explanations for changes in attendances

Economists, sociologists and social historians have all made strenuous efforts to explain the trends in attendances that have been summarised in the previous sub-section. Social and demographic change, increasing material affluence, the growth of televised football, football hooliganism, the state of football's physical infrastructure and the quality of the entertainment on the field of play are among the many factors considered to have contributed to the long post-war decline in attendances. More recently, a number of the same factors have begun to operate in directions that are more favourable from football's perspective. This sub-section provides a brief survey of the debate in respect of English club football attendances, starting in the inter-war period.

It is undoubtedly the case that the geographical bond between English football clubs and their spectators was much stronger in the first half of the twentieth century than it became later. Specific evidence on the geographical composition of football crowds is rather sparse, but it seems certain that the proportion of home supporters drawn from each club's immediate vicinity was higher in the past than at present. For example, 21 of the 33 spectators who died in the 1947 Bolton Wanderers stadium disaster lived within 10 miles of the stadium (Fishwick, 1989). Although both financial and time constraints militated against regular travel to away matches in the 1930s and 1940s, Dunning, Murphy and Williams (1988) show that occasional big games (especially FA Cup ties) were capable of attracting several thousand travelling spectators. Fishwick (1989) also cites anecdotal evidence that some Wiltshire spectators preferred to travel regularly to watch Reading, West Bromwich Albion or Aston Villa rather than see the local team Swindon Town struggling in the lower reaches of Division 3 (South) during the early 1930s.

In a historical survey which focuses primarily on the hooliganism phenomenon, Dunning, Murphy and Williams (1988) characterise the typical football crowd of the inter-war period as slightly more respectable than its pre-First World War counterpart. While inter-war crowds remained predominantly working-class and male, there were significant and probably increasing middle-class and female minorities. Russell (1999) suggests that local rivalries were sometimes less intense than wider regional hostilities: while spectators often took pleasure in the successes of any team from their own region, football provided a convenient outlet for resentments arising from the contrasting economic fortunes of northern and southern England. Although football hooliganism was never eliminated completely, it seems to have been less pervasive during the inter-war period than before the First World War. Subsequently it seems to have declined further during the 1940s and early 1950s, before returning with a vengeance in the mid-1950s.

Demobilisation and the relaxation of restrictions after the Second World War released a widespread and unprecedented pent-up demand for recreation and entertainment, which manifested itself not only in booming football attendances, but also in record-breaking cinema audience figures and packed beaches at British seaside holiday resorts during the summers. In explaining the subsequent sustained decline in football's popularity as a spectator sport, social historians have emphasised the impact of broader socio-economic changes. The growth of the affluent society saw the emergence of more home-oriented and privatised patterns of leisure activity, with the range of options extended in particular by television and the car. Many women became less willing to acquiesce in a home-based or child-minding function while men's leisure was centred on the pub, club or football terrace. The spread of home ownership led to an increase in the popularity of alternative weekend activities such as DIY and gardening (Dunning, Murphy and Williams, 1988; Walvin, 1994).

The increase in incidents of crowd misconduct both inside and outside football stadia, of which the train-wrecking exploits of Everton and Liverpool supporters in the late 1950s were an early manifestation, can also be attributed at least in part to broader social changes. Dunning, Murphy and Williams (1988) see football hooliganism as one unfortunate consequence of a general upsurge in working class assertiveness and decline in social deference, stimulated by a new self-confidence boosted by high and stable levels of employment and increasing affluence in the late 1950s and 1960s. This also manifested itself more positively through the novels, films, plays and popular music of the period. Whatever the causes, there is no doubt that over time, hooliganism and the counter-measures taken by clubs and the police prompted many spectators to switch from the terraces to the living room and TV set. Football grounds became increasingly the preserve of the more fanatical supporters, as the less committed came to the conclusion that the entertainment on offer was simply inadequate to compensate for the inconvenience, discomforts and occasional physical dangers caused by the hooligan phenomenon.

From the late 1950s onwards, rising affluence combined with improvements in both public and private transport, including the spread of car ownership and the construction of the motorway network, led to important changes in the geographical composition of demand. With long-distance travel now practical both financially and logistically, the top clubs began to drain support from their smaller counterparts. In the late 1960s there emerged a distinctive and vociferous London contingent among the hooligan fringe of Manchester United's support. This was symptomatic not only of the growing hooligan problem, but also of the increasing tendency of the leading clubs to draw support at a national rather than purely local or regional level. Greater personal mobility increased the propensity for some fans to travel regularly to away fixtures. Demographic changes also tended to erode the bonds between communities and their local clubs. Suburbanisation led to movements of large numbers of people away from city-centre districts where most grounds were located, to be replaced by incomers who did not necessarily have any affinity or interest in the local club, or in football in general. But paradoxically, spectators who remained loyal to their local sides appeared to become increasingly hostile towards the supporters of neighbouring teams, adding further fuel to the flames of hooliganism.

By the mid-1970s, there was a growing atmosphere of financial desperation enveloping many football clubs. Neither the clubs nor the police seemed able to curb the hooligan-related incidents, which had become a regular Saturday afternoon occurrence, both inside football stadia and outside in town centres and railway stations. There were also widespread perceptions of declining standards of conduct on the field of play. Much of this seemed to reflect unerringly a malaise afflicting English society on a broader scale, as politicians grappled with problems such as inflation, unemployment, industrial unrest and social breakdown. While the economy entered its deepest recession since the war at the start of the 1980s, football's public reputation had never been lower. It is hardly surprising that there was further acceleration in the downward trend in attendances. Fears of impending financial meltdown were heightened, with several major clubs (including Wolverhampton Wanderers, Middlesbrough and Bristol City) approaching, but also returning from, the very brink of insolvency and closure during the early 1980s. Meanwhile, Margaret Thatcher's Conservative government came increasingly to favour direct political intervention to confront football's problems head-on, including punitive legislation to tackle the hooliganism problem, and proposals (never implemented) for compulsory identity cards for all spectators.

English football hooliganism finally reached its apotheosis with the deaths of 38 mainly Italian supporters at the Heysel Stadium in Brussels at the Liverpool–Juventus European Cup Final in May 1985. Heysel's poor physical condition, which was similar to that of many major stadia in Britain, was a contributory factor in this tragedy, as was misbehaviour among the Liverpool section of the crowd. The declining state of domestic football's physical infrastructure had already been demonstrated catastrophically a few days earlier: 55 spectators died when a wooden stand caught fire during the Division 3 Bradford City–Lincoln City fixture on the final day of the 1985 league season. But it was only after 96 Liverpool supporters were crushed to death against a collapsed section of perimeter fencing at the start of the Liverpool–Nottingham Forest FA Cup semi-final played at Hillsborough (the home of Sheffield Wednesday) in April 1989 that the momentum for fundamental change finally became irresistible. One of the main recommendations of the ensuing report by the late Lord Justice Taylor (1990), that the stadia of all clubs in the top two divisions should be converted to all-seated accommodation in time for the start of the 1995 season, was accepted and implemented with scarcely a murmur of dissent from the football industry.

During the 1990s, the demand for conversion to all-seated accommodation provided both the opportunity and the impetus for more general refurbishment, and in some cases the wholesale reconstruction of England's major football stadia. According to data compiled by Deloitte and Touche (2000), £844 million was spent on stadia and facilities by Premier League and Football League clubs between the 1992 and 1999 seasons inclusive. Although terracing had been removed from most major stadia by the mid-1990s, the rate of expenditure has recently shown no sign of decreasing: the 1998 and 1999 season totals (£159 million and £152 million, respectively) were the two highest for the entire decade. A number of clubs have vacated stadia situated in congested inner-city or residential locations, where in many cases they had been located since the late nineteenth century, and moved to new sites offering better access to road links and space for car-parking. Improved facilities and surveillance technologies, together with a new public mood of revulsion following the worst excesses of the 1980s, have clearly contributed much to the marginalisation of the hooliganism phenomenon. Russell (1997) is surely correct to draw the obvious connection between the improvement in standards of crowd behaviour (at club level at least) and the reversal in the downward trend in attendances.

Football's rehabilitation as the most popular and fashionable national sport has also been aided by skilful exploitation by the industry of selective aspects of its own 'heritage'. This has helped to rekindle the interest of many people who had become disaffected during the 1970s and 1980s, and to attract new generations of football followers. On the one hand, it is true that whether viewing in person or on television, spectator and (especially) media interest is now focused perhaps to a greater extent than ever before on a handful of big-market clubs. On the other hand, it is still the case that the large majority of spectators who attend English professional football in person do *not* watch Manchester United, Liverpool, Arsenal and Chelsea. As table 2.8 shows, over 54 per cent of the total Premier

League attendance in the 1999 season went to matches in the Football League.

There is a widespread perception that by the end of the 1990s English football had largely succeeded in 'rebranding' itself as a middle-class spectator sport. Williams (1997) puts forward two alternative stylised views of the cultural transformation that seems to have taken place. Viewed in a positive light the 1990s saw the re-emergence of 'the Victorian tradition of the modern English football stadium as an important source of civic pride, in terms of its up-to-date amenities and facilities . . . [and] the popular "rediscovery" of the much cherished and at least part-mythical traditions of the English sports crowd for its mutual tolerance and sociability'. Viewed negatively the same period witnessed 'the effective end of the local and "organic", the self-administering and creative, English football crowd . . . [and] the emergence of the regulated, individuated, surveilled and high spending seated bourgeoisie football audience' (Williams, 1997, pp. 243, 244). The two views take opposing positions concerning the desirability of these developments, but neither questions the proposition that fundamental changes have occurred.

It is therefore a little surprising that hard empirical evidence on the social composition of football crowds is in rather short supply. On the basis of a review of 11 different surveys conducted at various times over a 14-year period between 1983 and 1997 in England and Scotland, Malcolm, Jones and Waddington (2000) question the common perception that the demographic composition of a typical 1990s' football crowd was markedly different to that of its predecessors in earlier decades.[4] Eight of the 11 surveys included in the British review were club-specific, while the other three were general. In several cases the generality of the results is limited by low response rates and small numbers. Nevertheless, there is no convincing evidence that the age composition of the typical crowd has changed very much overall. The proportion of female spectators also seems to have remained fairly constant throughout the 14-year period, at between 10 and 13 per cent in most of the surveys. There is some evidence, however, that female spectators tend to be younger on average than males, and less likely to be married or living with a partner.

Attempts to trace changes in the social composition of crowds are hampered by definitional problems and inconsistencies. But again there is little sign of a change over time in the proportions of unemployed or retired spectators. The proportion of students does appear to have declined over time, perhaps as a result of the deteriorating state of student

---

[4] Waddington and Malcolm (1998) also provide some comparative data, based on a number of surveys carried out in Britain, France, Spain, Austria and Belgium.

Table 2.9. *Aggregate revenues and costs, Premier League and Football League clubs, 1999 season*

Item	Premier League (£ million)	Football League (£ million)	All clubs (£ million)
Revenue			
Matchday	247	136	383
Television	196	35	231
Other	226	110	336
Costs			
Wages and salaries	392	229	621
Net transfer fees	127	13	140
Other costs	194	106	300
Trading surplus or deficit	−44	−67	−111

Source: Deloitte and Touche (2000).

finances. In general Malcolm, Jones and Waddington suggest that the composition of the typical British football crowd may have changed less than many commentators seem to assume. Group and individual loyalties to their team's identities are strong and persistent, and probably relatively impervious to changes either in the physical environment as a result of stadium reconstruction, or in the marketing and packaging of the experience of attending a match. Stability over time in patterns of demand has probably contributed much to the sheer endurance of the English league's 92-club membership, most of it steeped in proud historical tradition which remains one of the sport's most fascinating and appealing characteristics.

2.4 Admission prices and gate revenues

Sections 2.4–2.7 describe historical and recent trends in the main revenue and expenditure items that appear in a football club's company accounts, including gate and television revenues, other sources of revenue such as sponsorship and merchandising, expenditure on players' wages and salaries and transfer expenditure. Based on figures compiled by Deloitte and Touche (2000), table 2.9 summarises the relative magnitudes of these items for Premier League and Football League clubs collectively for the 1999 season. Table 2.10 shows key financial data for the six Premier League clubs with the largest total revenue in the same season, and for an 'average' club in each of the league's four divisions.

Table 2.10. *Financial and employment data, top six Premier League clubs and divisional averages, 1999 season*

Club	Total revenue (excluding transfers)	Wages and salaries	Operating profit (before transfers)	Pre-tax profit	Number of employees
Top six clubs (based on total revenue)					
Man Utd	110,920	36,965	30,533	22,411	498
Chelsea	59,092	30,180	8,929	23	415
Arsenal	48,623	26,478	7,307	2,068	180
Liverpool	45,265	36,273	−2,585	−8,061	251
Newcastle	44,718	24,491	3,930	1,373	225
Tottenham	42,585	21,699	8,917	1,293	185
Average Premier League club					
	33,482	19,545	3,441	684	216
Average Division One club					
	6,720	5,343	−1,317	−1,547	127
Average Division Two club					
	3,602	2,866	−913	−1,217	88
Average Division Three club					
	1,387	1,317	−626	−410	83

Note: All monetary amounts are in £000.
Source: Deloitte and Touche (2000).

Overall, Tables 2.9 and 2.10 show that most of the leading Premier League clubs, as well as the average Premier League club, made a profit in 1999, while the average Football League club made a loss.

Until recently, gate revenues from league matches represented by far the largest source of revenue for most football clubs. It was not until the start of the 1990s that clubs' revenue sources became sufficiently diversified that the share of league gate revenues in aggregate revenue fell below 50 per cent for the league as a whole. Of course, television, sponsorship, merchandising and other forms of commercial activity all make much bigger contributions now than ever before. Over the longer term, however, gate revenues data provides an accurate representation of trends in football's overall revenue-raising capability and performance. This section draws on a data set comprising annual gate revenues from league matches for all Premier League and Football League clubs, obtained from Football League archives and (for recent seasons) from Football Trust (various issues). The 1926 season is the first for which comprehensive records are available. An attraction of the gate revenues' data set for researchers is that it can be combined with the attendance data described in section 2.3, in order to calculate an average admission price for each club in each season. Average admission price is obtained simply by dividing total gate revenue by total attendance.

Table 2.11 shows the average admission price per spectator in nominal and real terms and average nominal admission prices by division, for each season between 1926 and 1999. For the period up to the mid-1970s, admission prices for spectators paying at the gate were subject to a statutory minimum determined by the Football League, which is also shown in table 2.11. At certain times, however, concessions were available to groups such as juniors, pensioners and the unemployed. Clubs were also permitted to charge more than the minimum. Many did so for seated accommodation (especially) and, increasingly as time went by, for standing accommodation as well. The original objective of the League's minimum admission price was to prevent clubs from attempting to attract spectators at the expense of other clubs in the same geographical catchment area by cutting prices. Table 2.12 shows aggregate gate revenue data in nominal and real terms, together with divisional gate revenue shares. Figure 2.6 shows the percentage shares of the Group 1 to Group 5 clubs (see table 2.7) in aggregate gate revenue.

Table 2.11 suggests that there was little difference between clubs in admission prices during the inter-war period, with most clubs charging the league minimum of 1 shilling (£0.05) to all but a relatively small minority of more affluent, seated spectators. The gentle increase in the real admission price series up to the mid-1930s and its subsequent reversal reflects the constancy of admission prices in nominal terms, against a background of retail prices that were falling in the late 1920s and early 1930s, and rising thereafter. When football resumed after the Second World War, the increase in admission prices was just sufficient to compensate for price inflation during the war. The post-war attendance boom therefore generated revenues more than 50 per cent higher than before the war in real terms for several seasons until the early 1950s.

The relative homogeneity of football's pricing structure was preserved throughout the 1950s. In the 1960 season, Division 1 clubs were charging only 25 per cent more on average than their Division 4 counterparts, a ratio not much greater than that which had prevailed during the inter-war period. From the 1960s onwards, however, the story is one of steadily increasing divergence between the prices of clubs at different levels within the league. By the 1970 season, Division 1 clubs were charging 48 per cent more per spectator on average than Division 4 clubs. This gap increased to 64 per cent in 1980, 70 per cent in 1990 and 155 per cent in

Table 2.11. *English league admission prices, 1926–1999*

Season	Average admission price Nominal (£)	Average admission price Real (1926=100)	Average nominal admission price (£) D1/Prem	D2/One	D3/Two	D4/Three	Minimum admission price (£)
1926	0.06	100	0.06	0.06	0.06	0.05	0.05
1927	0.06	103	0.06	0.06	0.06	0.05	0.05
1928	0.06	106	0.06	0.06	0.06	0.05	0.05
1929	0.06	107	0.06	0.06	0.06	0.05	0.05
1930	0.06	112	0.06	0.06	0.06	0.05	0.05
1931	0.06	118	0.06	0.06	0.06	0.05	0.05
1932	0.06	119	0.06	0.06	0.06	0.05	0.05
1933	0.06	124	0.06	0.06	0.06	0.05	0.05
1934	0.06	123	0.06	0.06	0.06	0.05	0.05
1935	0.06	122	0.06	0.06	0.06	0.05	0.05
1936	0.06	118	0.06	0.06	0.06	0.05	0.05
1937	0.06	114	0.06	0.06	0.06	0.05	0.05
1938	0.06	113	0.06	0.06	0.06	0.05	0.05
1939	0.06	110	0.06	0.06	0.06	0.05	0.05
1947	0.08	120	0.09	0.08	0.08	0.07	0.0625
1948	0.09	118	0.09	0.09	0.08	0.08	0.0625
1949	0.09	120	0.10	0.10	0.09	0.08	0.0625
1950	0.09	120	0.10	0.10	0.09	0.08	0.0625
1951	0.10	112	0.10	0.10	0.09	0.08	0.0625
1952	0.11	112	0.11	0.11	0.10	0.09	0.075
1953	0.12	126	0.13	0.12	0.11	0.10	0.075
1954	0.12	124	0.13	0.12	0.12	0.10	0.075
1955	0.12	120	0.13	0.12	0.12	0.10	0.075
1956	0.13	122	0.14	0.13	0.12	0.11	0.10
1957	0.13	118	0.14	0.13	0.12	0.11	0.10
1958	0.13	115	0.14	0.13	0.12	0.11	0.10
1959	0.14	117	0.15	0.14	0.12	0.11	0.10
1960	0.14	120	0.15	0.14	0.13	0.12	0.10
1961	0.16	135	0.18	0.17	0.14	0.13	0.125
1962	0.18	141	0.20	0.18	0.16	0.13	0.125
1963	0.18	141	0.20	0.19	0.16	0.14	0.125
1964	0.19	141	0.21	0.19	0.16	0.15	0.125
1965	0.21	151	0.24	0.21	0.18	0.16	0.125
1966	0.23	160	0.26	0.22	0.20	0.18	0.20
1967	0.24	162	0.27	0.23	0.21	0.18	0.20
1968	0.26	164	0.29	0.24	0.22	0.20	0.20
1969	0.29	176	0.33	0.26	0.24	0.22	0.25
1970	0.30	172	0.34	0.28	0.24	0.23	0.25
1971	0.35	186	0.41	0.32	0.29	0.27	0.30
1972	0.38	185	0.43	0.35	0.31	0.28	0.30
1973	0.46	209	0.52	0.43	0.38	0.36	0.40

Table 2.11. (*cont.*)

Season	Average admission price Nominal (£)	Real (1926=100)	Average nominal admission price (£) D1/Prem	D2/One	D3/Two	D4/Three	Minimum admission price (£)
1974	0.53	204	0.59	0.49	0.43	0.39	0.40
1975	0.59	185	0.66	0.60	0.46	0.41	0.40
1976	0.76	202	0.83	0.75	0.61	0.59	0.65
1977	0.85	197	0.96	0.83	0.68	0.58	n/a
1978	1.05	224	1.19	0.99	0.82	0.75	n/a
1979	1.18	222	1.29	1.16	0.99	0.91	n/a
1980	1.50	239	1.67	1.53	1.21	1.02	n/a
1981	1.84	261	2.05	1.85	1.43	1.20	n/a
1982	2.03	265	2.32	1.93	1.59	1.35	n/a
1983	2.24	281	2.55	2.17	1.83	1.45	n/a
1984	2.44	291	2.76	2.42	1.91	1.63	n/a
1985	2.77	312	3.21	2.46	2.11	1.79	n/a
1986	2.97	323	3.42	2.63	2.33	2.05	n/a
1987	3.21	336	3.70	2.92	2.48	2.35	n/a
1988	3.56	354	4.26	3.22	2.83	2.51	n/a
1989	3.95	365	4.73	3.71	3.13	2.69	n/a
1990	4.48	378	5.39	4.21	3.42	3.17	n/a
1991	5.32	424	6.46	4.82	3.94	3.70	n/a
1992	6.25	481	7.55	5.47	4.45	4.28	n/a
1993	7.09	537	8.77	6.21	5.11	4.31	n/a
1994	7.55	557	9.17	6.64	5.32	4.49	n/a
1995	8.75	625	11.58	6.46	5.46	5.60	n/a
1996	9.64	672	12.74	7.62	5.97	5.37	n/a
1997	10.74	722	14.59	7.96	6.66	5.72	n/a
1998	11.37	749	14.99	9.30	7.51	5.85	n/a
1999	12.30	799	16.27	9.81	8.64	6.45	n/a

Notes:
Up to and including the 1958 season, D3 is Division 3 (South) and D4 is Division 3 (North). 1999 season data are based on estimates for some clubs.
Sources: Football League; Football Trust; Bird (1982).
n/a = not available.

Table 2.12. *English league gate revenues, 1926–1999*

| Season | Aggregate league gate revenues | | Divisional percentage share in aggregate league gate revenues | | | |
	Nominal (£ million)	Real (1926=100)	D1/Prem	D2/One	D3/Two	D4/Three
1926	1.352	100	46.9	26.8	16.3	10.0
1927	1.373	105	47.0	28.2	15.5	9.3
1928	1.410	109	47.2	28.9	14.7	9.2
1929	1.419	111	45.7	28.3	16.1	9.9
1930	1.372	111	47.8	27.5	16.5	8.2
1931	1.246	108	47.4	28.5	15.0	9.1
1932	1.263	112	48.1	25.8	17.6	8.5
1933	1.261	115	46.9	28.8	15.4	9.0
1934	1.321	120	48.9	26.2	16.0	8.9
1935	1.373	123	49.9	26.3	15.3	8.5
1936	1.456	127	48.5	28.2	15.3	7.9
1937	1.575	131	45.2	30.3	16.1	8.4
1938	1.661	136	44.5	30.5	15.6	9.4
1939	1.594	129	45.8	31.1	13.9	9.2
1947	2.933	185	45.0	30.9	14.7	9.4
1948	3.578	205	43.8	30.4	15.7	10.2
1949	3.780	214	45.5	28.2	15.9	10.5
1950	3.801	211	44.3	29.9	16.5	9.3
1951	3.786	192	44.2	28.4	17.3	10.1
1952	4.135	189	44.1	28.5	16.7	10.7
1953	4.541	202	46.4	26.2	16.8	10.6
1954	4.431	196	46.9	27.2	16.4	9.5
1955	4.215	177	47.4	26.5	16.5	9.6
1956	4.355	176	45.4	27.6	16.0	11.0
1957	4.311	167	45.3	26.8	16.1	11.9
1958	4.448	167	46.9	25.6	16.8	10.6
1959	4.557	171	47.2	25.7	16.4	10.7
1960	4.549	168	48.1	26.0	15.8	10.1
1961	4.677	168	49.6	24.8	14.7	10.9
1962	4.981	171	47.6	27.2	16.5	8.8
1963	5.242	176	47.2	26.3	17.7	8.9
1964	5.341	174	48.0	27.1	16.5	8.4
1965	5.829	181	52.4	24.7	13.5	9.5
1966	6.308	189	52.0	24.0	15.2	8.7
1967	6.931	203	55.0	23.8	13.3	7.9
1968	7.682	214	56.7	23.1	11.6	8.5
1969	8.388	222	57.1	22.9	12.2	7.8
1970	8.828	220	56.9	23.9	11.5	7.7
1971	9.960	227	56.9	22.7	12.8	7.6
1972	10.814	229	57.8	21.7	13.4	7.1
1973	11.823	230	61.4	20.4	11.9	6.3

Table 2.12. (*cont.*)

| Season | Aggregate league gate revenues | | Divisional percentage share in aggregate league gate revenues | | | |
	Nominal (£ million)	Real (1926=100)	D1/Prem	D2/One	D3/Two	D4/Three
1974	13.174	221	58.8	23.7	11.0	6.4
1975	15.180	205	52.6	29.8	12.4	5.2
1976	18.822	218	57.7	23.0	12.8	6.4
1977	22.220	222	58.6	23.3	12.6	5.5
1978	26.651	246	59.3	23.9	10.3	6.5
1979	28.960	236	56.6	24.6	11.6	7.3
1980	36.911	255	55.0	25.4	13.1	6.5
1981	40.239	248	58.2	23.8	12.9	5.0
1982	40.523	230	59.6	22.6	11.1	6.6
1983	42.096	229	56.3	25.6	12.8	5.3
1984	44.760	232	53.7	29.0	11.6	5.7
1985	49.276	240	63.5	20.1	11.4	5.0
1986	48.901	231	63.2	19.1	11.9	5.9
1987	55.844	253	60.6	21.8	10.4	7.2
1988	63.906	276	54.0	26.9	12.2	7.0
1989	72.885	292	50.7	29.7	13.0	6.6
1990	87.219	319	48.8	33.3	11.0	6.9
1991	103.691	359	53.7	29.2	10.8	6.3
1992	127.329	425	59.2	25.0	10.5	5.3
1993	146.238	480	58.3	24.9	12.2	4.5
1994	163.655	524	59.7	26.3	9.7	4.3
1995	191.610	593	64.4	22.3	9.3	4.0
1996	211.500	639	63.0	23.7	8.3	5.0
1997	244.838	714	64.4	22.6	8.7	4.3
1998	283.313	804	59.4	27.5	9.4	3.7
1999	312.056	879	60.6	23.6	11.5	4.3

Notes:
Up to and including the 1958 season, D3 is Division 3 (South) and D4 is
Division 3 (North). 1999 season data are based on estimates for some clubs.
Sources: Football League; Football Trust.

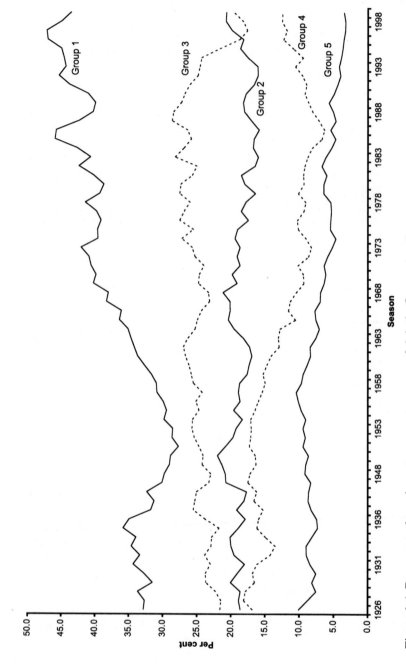

Figure 2.6 Percentage shares in aggregate gate revenue of clubs in Groups 1 to 5
Sources: Football League; Football Trust.

1997. Together with the eight or nine percentage-point increase in Division 1's attendance share which took place between the late 1950s and mid-1970s (see table 2.8), these relative price increases explain the increase of about 18 per cent in Division 1's gate revenue share over the same period shown in table 2.12. Similarly, the growth of the revenue share of Group 1 clubs between the late 1950s and mid-1970s (figure 2.6) was even faster rate than the growth in their attendance share (figure 2.4).

The increases in nominal admission prices in all divisions kept pace with inflation during the 1950s, but started to outstrip inflation in the 1960s, especially in the higher divisions. Cost pressures emanating from the removal of the maximum wage and changes affecting the terms of players' contracts (see section 2.7 below) were partly responsible for the imposition of real increases in admission prices during the 1960s. When retail price inflation began to soar and attendances continued to fall, for a few years clubs became more circumspect about raising prices by more than the rate of inflation. Consequently, admission prices remained almost unchanged in real terms between the 1971 and 1977 seasons. As inflation started to fall in the late 1970s and early 1980s and attendances continued to plummet, the clubs attempted to protect their dwindling real revenue base by imposing further price increases. But with attendances falling even faster than admission prices were rising (in real terms), football's capacity to insulate itself from the effects of its declining spectator base appears to have reached or even exceeded its limit by the start of the 1980s.

As the recovery in football's popularity gathered pace during the late 1980s and 1990s, there were further large real increases in admission prices, as anyone who has paid to attend a football match during the last 10 years knows all too well. The clubs can argue that higher prices are justified by improvements in the quality of the product: talented but expensive foreign players on the field of play (in the Premier League at least) are now viewed from comfortable seats in glistening new stands, built over the ruins of the crumbling rain-soaked terraces of yesteryear. Furthermore, stadium capacities have generally fallen while attendances have risen. Simple economics predicts that prices should rise sharply once capacity constraints are reached, and this is precisely what has happened. Pricing behaviour of this kind explains why the Group 1 clubs' revenue share has risen sharply during the 1990s (figure 2.6), while their attendance share has hardly changed (figure 2.4).

For the leading clubs in particular, paying spectators arriving through the turnstiles on match days now represent only one part of the target audience, of course. Pay-television audiences form an increasingly important component of present-day football's customer base. Section 2.5

describes the changing nature of football's long-standing and intricate relationship with the broadcasting media.

2.5 English football and the broadcasting media

The history of televised football

The British Broadcasting Company was first established in 1922. According to its first manager John Reith, its mission was to bring into every home 'all that was best in every department of human knowledge, endeavour and achievement' (Taylor, 1965). The company was replaced by the state-owned British Broadcasting Corporation (BBC) in 1926, funded by means of a flat-rate licence fee payable by all owners of wireless sets. The BBC's first television transmissions took place in the late 1930s, though it was not until the 1950s that sufficient households owned sets for television to begin to play a significant part in national life. The Independent Television (ITV) network of regional broadcasting companies was created in 1955. Funding was by means of advertising revenues. A second BBC channel was launched in 1964, to be followed by the introduction of colour transmissions in the late 1960s. Further free-to-air terrestrial channels were added in 1982 (Channel 4) and 1996 (Channel 5), both of which are advertising-funded. The two competing satellite broadcasters British Satellite Broadcasting (BSB) and Sky introduced Britain's first pay-television services in the late 1980s. These two companies merged in 1991 to form British Sky Broadcasting (BSkyB). Competition for BSkyB in the pay-television market is provided by cable television, and since 1999 by the terrestrial digital broadcaster ONdigital. BSkyB also launched its own digital services in 1999.

The BBC transmitted English football's first radio commentary of a match between Arsenal and Sheffield United in January 1927. Concern on the part of the Football League, however, about the potentially damaging effects on match attendances, led to a broadcasting ban being imposed in 1931. Regular radio coverage of league fixtures did not resume until after the Second World War, although cup matches and internationals were transmitted regularly during the 1930s. Televised transmission of football began on 9 April 1938 with the broadcast of an England–Scotland international match. Three weeks later the FA Cup final between Sunderland and Preston North End was also televised. Highlights of league matches were transmitted sporadically from 1955 onwards, but regular coverage did not start until the launch of the BBC's recorded highlights programme *Match of the Day* in 1964. This was followed by the launch of regional highlights programmes on the ITV network in 1968. From then until the late 1970s, as buyers of broadcasting rights the BBC and ITV appear to have operated an informal cartel, the main effect of which was to limit the fees paid to football by the television companies. The proceeds were distributed evenly among all league members, with each club receiving a meagre £1,300 from the fee of £120,000 paid during the 1968 season. The total payment had increased modestly to £5,800 per club, or just under £534,000 in total, by the 1979 season (Goldberg and Wragg, 1991).

The first attempted breach in the BBC–ITV stranglehold occurred in 1978 when London Weekend Television (LWT) broke ranks with the other ITV companies, and attempted to negotiate exclusive rights to cover and distribute televised football to the rest of the ITV network. An Office of Fair Trading (OFT) ruling prevented the deal from going ahead, but in the subsequently renegotiated contract, the amount received by each club rose to £23,900 from an aggregate annual fee of £2.2 million from the 1980 season onwards. Regular live coverage of league fixtures, shared between BBC and ITV, took place for the first time in the 1984 season, in a two-year deal which provided for coverage of 10 matches per season at a cost of £2.6 million per season. Live coverage was suspended temporarily during the 1986 season, following the breakdown of negotiations for a new contract. Football's parlous financial condition at the time, combined with increasing tensions between the larger and smaller clubs over the distribution of the proceeds, probably allowed the TV companies to retain the upper hand in the negotiations. A contract was eventually settled at the start of 1986, reinstating live coverage during the remainder of the 1986 season and for the following two seasons. The annual price was £3.1 million for 14 matches, which implied the price per match had fallen relative to the previous contract. The 1986 contract was also the first to breach the principle of equal distribution of revenues between all 92 league member clubs; instead, Division 1 clubs received 50 per cent of the proceeds, Division 2 clubs 25 per cent and Divisions 3 and 4 clubs 12.5 per cent each.

The arrival of the two satellite broadcasters BSB and Sky in the late 1980s signalled a significant shift in the relative bargaining power of the football industry as the seller of broadcasting rights and the television companies as buyers. The BBC–ITV duopsony was gone for good, and the television companies were competing against one another to acquire broadcasting rights far more intensely than ever before. The implications of the shift were already apparent in the earliest days of satellite broadcasting. In the 1988 round of negotiations, ITV secured exclusive rights to show 18 matches per season over the next four seasons, from 1989 to 1992 inclusive. The annual fee was £11 million. The balance of bargaining power within football was also changing rapidly. Threats from the leading clubs to withdraw from the Football League and enter into separate negotiations with the television companies secured a settlement in which roughly three-quarters of the ITV fee went to the Division 1 clubs. Of this, more than 40 per cent was shared between the so-called 'big five', which were to become the subject of the majority of ITV's coverage: Arsenal, Everton, Liverpool, Manchester United and Tottenham Hotspur. By way of consolation for losing altogether the right to cover league football, BBC formed a partnership with BSB to purchase broadcasting rights for FA Cup and international matches. Collaborative arrangements of this kind between the satellite and terrestrial broadcasters, intended to allay public concerns about the progressive disappearance of sports coverage from free-to-air television channels, were a key component of the satellite companies' strategies to expand their portfolio of live sports coverage during the 1990s.

As the ITV contract's 1992 expiry date started to approach, it was clear that the next round of negotiations would be shaped both by the ambitions of the newly merged satellite operator BSkyB to secure a significantly greater share of the coverage, and by the manoeuvrings of the leading clubs anxious to maximise their own share of the proceeds. Strategically, BSkyB identified the acquisition of regular live coverage of league football as the key step that would generate sufficient take-up of satellite services to enable the company to extend subscription charges beyond films, to sports and other channels. Meanwhile in early 1991, the Football Association's Blueprint for the Future of Football (Football Association, 1991) announced that at the end of the 1992 season, the 22 Division 1 clubs would withdraw completely from the Football League to form the new Premier League, with its own governing body under the auspices of the Football Association. Naturally, the Premier League would negotiate its own television contract, which would be separate from any arrangements made by the Football League on behalf of its 70 remaining members.

In negotiations documented extensively by Fynn and Guest (1994), BSkyB succeeded (narrowly) in outbidding ITV for the contract providing exclusive live broadcasting rights during the Premier League's first five seasons, from 1993 to 1997 inclusive. Subsequently the BSkyB contract was extended for a further four seasons from 1998 to 2001. The partnership with BBC inherited by BSkyB following the BSB–Sky merger was to continue, with BBC screening regular Saturday evening highlights of league matches played earlier the same day, from the 1993 season onwards. The headline cost of the combined BSkyB–BBC Premier League coverage was £304 million for the initial five-year contract, and then £743 million for the subsequent four-year extension. The total amounts received by the Premier League clubs are smaller than these headline figures, however, as some of the revenue flows to the Football Association. In each of the 1993 to 1996 seasons, the Premier League clubs received around £40 million from the BSkyB–BBC contract. In 1997 the aggregate receipts increased to £83 million. In 1998, as the new contract got underway, the Premier League clubs received £125 million. These proceeds are shared according to a formula that depends upon each team's finishing position in the league, and on the number of television appearances. The distribution of the television coverage is more equitable than under the old ITV contract, a feature influential in encouraging the majority of Premier League clubs to favour BSkyB over ITV, when the first BSkyB contract was concluded in 1992.[5] In the 1998 season, Arsenal, Manchester United, Liverpool, Chelsea and Leeds United were the top five earners from the contract, accounting for around 35 per cent of the Premier League clubs' total proceeds.

The arrangement whereby BBC and BSkyB shared live coverage of FA Cup and international matches also continued until the end of the 1998 season, when ITV replaced BBC in this role. ITV's initial consolation for failing to secure Premier League coverage for the 1993 season was a contract to show selected Football League matches live on a regional basis on Sunday afternoons, for varying fees that amounted to more in total than had been paid to the former Division 2, 3 and 4 clubs under the old ITV contract. But from the 1997 season onwards the rights for live Football League coverage were also acquired by BSkyB. The television earnings of Football League clubs have increased dramatically as a result, from around £16 million in 1996, to more than £30 million per season between 1997 and 2000. In 1997 Division One clubs received around 57 per cent of Football League television revenues, Division Two around 26 per cent and Division Three around 17 per cent (Football Trust; Deloitte and Touche, 1999).

The outcome of the third sale of televised broadcasting rights since the formation of the Premier League was announced in June 2000. BSkyB's bid to secure the continuation of its Premier League coverage from the 2002 season onwards was successful. Initially, a second live Premier

---

[5] Four of the 'big five' are reported to have opposed the BSkyB contract. As the main beneficiaries of the old ITV contract, Arsenal, Everton, Liverpool and Manchester United naturally favoured its continuation. It is reported that Aston Villa and Leeds United also voted in favour of ITV. The decision of the fifth 'big-five' member, Tottenham Hotspur, to vote in favour of BSkyB, was crucial in ensuring the two-thirds majority needed for the deal to go through. Tottenham chairman Alan Sugar's interest in the consumer electronics (and satellite dish) manufacturer Amstrad, was declared at the meeting (Conn, 1997, pp. 19–20).

League package was sold to the cable operator NTL, to permit matches to be screened on a pay-per-view basis; though a few weeks later NTL announced their withdrawal. ITV replaced BBC as provider of the Saturday evening Premier League highlights package, while ONdigital won the rights to live Football League coverage from BSkyB. All of the contracts awarded in June 2000 were secured by bids far in excess of the prices paid in the previous round. As yet, football's gravy train does not appear to have run out of steam, though the momentum may be slowing. Chapter 9 considers the prospects for the future of football's relationship with the broadcasting media.

The BSkyB takeover bid for Manchester United, and the collective sale of broadcasting rights

The issue of vertical integration between football clubs and television companies first attracted headline attention in England with the announcement on 7 September 1998 that BSkyB were bidding £575 million to achieve a 100 per cent takeover of Manchester United. Two days later, the United board recommended acceptance of an improved offer valuing the company at £623 million. Trade Secretary Peter Mandelson subsequently referred the BSkyB bid to the Monopolies and Mergers Commission (MMC). On 12 March 1999 the MMC delivered its findings: the merger would damage competition between broadcasters, and would be detrimental to the wider interests of British football (Monopolies and Mergers Commission, 1999). On 9 April 1999, the Trade Secretary Stephen Byers announced his acceptance of the MMC's recommendations, and blocked the BSkyB takeover.

The arguments put forward for and against the BSkyB–Manchester United bid are worth rehearsing briefly. From BSkyB's perspective, the attractions were obvious: first, to obtain control of the world's most profitable and most widely supported football club at a price which many analysts considered conservative; second, to obtain influence in possible future negotiations over the creation of a European Super League, if such negotiations ever take place; and third, to obtain similar influence in negotiations over the next domestic television contract, due to begin in 2001.

Significantly, it was the impact of the merger in the domestic (rather than the European) arena that provided the main grounds for the MMC's rejection of the bid. To have the same company involved simultaneously on both sides of the negotiations for broadcasting rights, it was argued, would damage competition between broadcasters. Assurances that the company's broadcasting arm would refrain from influencing the football arm in such negotiations were considered unenforceable. In any event, BSkyB would have a natural advantage over competitors in the bidding contest, since a proportion of its bid would return automatically to the company through the football club. A successful takeover would probably encourage a series of retaliatory mergers involving other media groups and major clubs. This would be likely to widen the financial gap between the latter and the less marketable members of the Premier League and the Football League. The MMC was also concerned that BSkyB's influence over the organisation of English football (for example, in the scheduling of fixtures) might be exploited unfairly, either to the benefit of Manchester United or to the detriment of its main rivals (Lee, 1999; Michie and Oughton, 1999).

The MMC report has been criticised in some quarters for taking an unduly anglocentric view of Manchester United as a club and as a business. In both respects, United operates not only in the domestic arena, but also at the European and global levels where the anti-competitive impact of vertical integration should be considerably smaller (Deloitte and Touche, 1999). The MMC decision was nevertheless widely welcomed domestically, not least by the majority of Manchester United supporters, concerned that the club had been about to fall under the control of a profit-oriented business group with no understanding of its historical traditions and sporting ambitions. Politicians were evidently nervous about being seen to sanction the notion that football clubs are merely tradeable commodities, to be bought and sold according to the dictates of the free market. Official recognition that the wholesale application to sport of norms applicable elsewhere in business and finance might be detrimental to the broader public interest, is also a highly welcome (if perhaps overdue) development.

BSkyB also played a central role in a landmark case brought to the Restrictive Practices Court (RPC) by the OFT in 1999. The OFT sought to show that the Premier League had acted unlawfully as a cartel in negotiating the sale of broadcasting rights on behalf of its member clubs. It was argued that the Premier League's decision to award exclusive live broadcasting rights to BSkyB unfairly restricted the number of live matches screened on television and inflated the price paid by subscribers. But in a judgement published in July 1999 rejecting the OFT case, the RPC took the view that on balance these arrangements did not operate against the public interest. The RPC was required to judge the merits of collective selling against an alternative and perhaps chaotic scenario involving completely decentralised selling of broadcasting rights; possible compromises involving the collective and individual sale of different bundles of matches could not be considered. Szymanski (2000a) suggests that this technicality may have been influential in persuading the Court to endorse the status quo.

The OFT's case also hinged upon the question as to whether access to exclusive live Premier League coverage conferred monopoly power upon BSkyB as sole suppliers to a distinct market of a specific programme type, or whether it merely enabled BSkyB to compete more effectively with other broadcasters for audiences, within a much wider market for television programmes in general (Cave, 2000). If Premier League coverage constituted a market in its own right, the existing arrangements, by restricting access and driving up price, could well be anti-competitive and against the public interest. But if Premier League coverage was simply one of many programme types competing for audience share, the existing arrangements could be beneficial in helping to promote competition through improved programme quality. Overall, the RPC was sympathetic to this latter argument (Cave, 2000). From football's point of view the collective sale of broadcasting rights enabled the Premier League to market its championship as a single entity. It also ensured greater equality between the television revenues earned by richer and poorer clubs than would be the case if clubs sold their broadcasting rights individually. The existing arrangements therefore helped to promote not only competition between broadcasters, but also competitive balance between clubs within football; a consideration recognised by the Court as beneficial to the public interest.

In the long term, the 1999 rulings in the BSkyB–Manchester United takeover bid and the OFT–Premier League case at the RPC are unlikely to represent the final word on the matters which the two cases have raised. On the issue of vertical integration, it is perhaps significant that a number of media groups already hold controlling interests in leading clubs on the continent.[6] Since the BSkyB–Manchester United bid was turned down, there has been a spate of acquisitions of minority shareholdings in English clubs by media groups determined to press their influence on football as far as Football Association regulations on cross-ownership will allow. At the time of writing, BSkyB holds shares in Manchester United, Leeds United, Chelsea, Sunderland and Manchester City; NTL has stakes in Newcastle United, Middlesbrough, Aston Villa and Leicester City; and Granada Media has stakes in Arsenal and Liverpool. Technological developments such as the introduction of multi-channel digital television and internet broadcasting, ensure that technology will soon permit virtually

---

[6] For example, Finivest controls AC Milan; Canal Plus controls Paris Saint Germain and Servette Geneva; and Pathé holds a large minority interest in Olympique Lyonnais (Deloitte and Touche, 1999).

unlimited screenings of live matches, on either a subscription or a pay-per-view basis, assuming that the market will bear such a level of exposure (Cameron, 1997). On the issue of broadcasting rights, it seems likely that the leading English clubs may eventually decide to take matters into their own hands, and follow their Italian and Spanish counterparts in negotiating their own individual deals.

2.6 Other sources of revenue and cross-subsidy

Section 2.4 has identified a number of historical trends in a comprehensive data set covering gate revenues from league fixtures. Data on the total revenues the clubs have generated from all sources is much more difficult to obtain, because historically many clubs have not produced company accounts on a regular or consistent basis. Szymanski and Kuypers (1999) have compiled annual data on turnover, wages and salaries, net transfer expenditure and profit for a number of clubs that have filed accounts at Companies House. Their wages and salaries data include all employees; at present, Deloitte and Touche (1999) estimate that players' salaries account for around two-thirds of total wages and salaries at larger clubs, and up to four-fifths at smaller clubs.

The Szymanski and Kuypers data set shows that for most of the post-war period, smaller clubs were more dependent than larger clubs on income from sources other than league gate revenues. Recently, however, the position has reversed. During the 1990s gate revenues from league matches were a smaller proportion of total revenues for Premier League and Division One clubs than for clubs in Divisions Two and Three. For all clubs reliance on gate revenues from league matches has fallen considerably. In the 1950s, revenues from league matches constituted over 80 per cent of total revenues. By the 1990s, the corresponding figure was below 40 per cent. Growth in revenues from television, as described in section 2.5, accounts for much of the shift. According to table 2.9 television money accounted for 29.3 per cent of Premier League and 12.5 per cent of Football League revenues in the 1999 season. The growth of sponsorship and other types of commercial activity, especially merchandising, has also been very important. According to table 2.9 these sources accounted for 33.8 per cent of Premier League revenues and 39.1 per cent of Football League revenues in the 1999 season. Comprehensive data on the revenue contribution made by different types of commercial activity is not available, but table 2.13 shows the estimated annual values of the shirt sponsorship deals of all Premier League clubs current during the 2000 season. At the start of the 2001 season, Vodafone's £30 million four-year shirt sponsorship deal with Manchester United set a new English record.

Table 2.13. *Shirt sponsorship contracts, Premier League clubs, 2000 season*

Club	Sponsor	Fee p.a. (million)	Start season	Club	Sponsor	Fee p.a. (million)	Start season
Arsenal	Sega	£3.3	2000	Man Utd	Sharp	£1.3	1997
Aston Villa	LDV	£0.8	1999	Middlesbrough	BT Cellnet	£0.3	1996
Bradford	JCT600	£0.3	1999	Newcastle	Newcastle Breweries	£1.0	2000
Chelsea	Autoglass	£1.1	1998	Sheff Weds	Sanderson	£0.5	1995
Coventry	Subaru–Isuzu	£0.7	1998	Southampton	Friends Provident	£0.5	2000
Derby	ED5	£0.7	2000	Sunderland	Reg Vardy	£0.5	2000
Everton	One-2-One	£0.7	1998	Tottenham	Holsten	£1.3	2000
Leeds	Packard Bell	£2.0	1997	Watford	Phones 4 U	£0.5	2000
Leicester	Walkers Crisps	£0.5	2000	West Ham	Dr Martens	£1.0	1999
Liverpool	Carlsberg	£1.0	1999	Wimbledon	Tiny	£0.3	2000

Source: Daily Mirror (12 February 2000).

Both cause and consequence of the widening financial gulf separating the leading clubs from the rest has been the gradual erosion of arrangements for revenue sharing within the league. Until the early 1980s, 20 per cent of the notional receipts from every league match were paid to the visiting club. Notional receipts were based on minimum admission charges, with certain deductions permitted (e.g. for costs of policing and stewarding). Since the 1984 season, however, clubs have retained all of the proceeds from their home fixtures. Under another revenue sharing arrangement, 4 per cent of all notional receipts were paid into a pool, the proceeds from which were distributed evenly among all 92 league member clubs. The 4 per cent levy was reduced to 3 per cent from the 1987 season onwards, prior to the complete withdrawal from this scheme of the Premier League clubs at the start of the 1993 season. The 3 per cent levy and arrangements for equal distribution of the proceeds are still effective within the Football League.

The reduction in the reliance of clubs at all levels on revenues from league matches is also attributable partly to an increase in the number of cup and other tournaments. For the top clubs, the revenue contribution of participation in European competition has grown significantly over time, and especially in recent seasons. For the rest, the introduction in the 1987 season of the end-of-season play-offs to determine one promotion place from each division of the Football League, culminating (from the 1990 season onwards) in a series of three divisional Wembley finals, has added a dramatic and lucrative postscript to the domestic season. Up to and including the 1999 season as many as 69 different clubs had participated at least once in the play-offs, while four clubs (Bolton Wanderers, Crewe Alexandra, Scunthorpe United and Tranmere Rovers) had registered no fewer than five play-off appearances each.

A separate cup competition for teams from the lower two divisions has operated successfully (under the names of successive sponsors) since the 1985 season. But an attempt to establish a third cup tournament open to all league clubs eventually foundered in the early 1990s, suggesting that saturation point had finally been reached. Cup competitions provide an implicit cross-subsidy from the richer clubs to the poorer in several ways:

- a lower-division club may be able to attract an abnormally large attendance by being drawn to play a top club
- the rules for pooling gate receipts allow for a greater element of redistribution than is the case for league fixtures
- all clubs share in the proceeds of sponsorship agreements.

As with the explicit arrangements for sharing league gate revenues, however, the willingness of the leading clubs to provide these implicit cross-subsidies by participating wholeheartedly in the two main cup tournaments, the FA Cup and the League Cup, has come under strain in recent seasons. The extension of the European calendar in particular has brought genuine problems of fixture congestion, which have been tackled in a number of ways: by delaying the entry of teams involved in Europe to the League Cup; by substituting penalty shoot-outs for replays as a means of settling drawn cup ties; by the clubs themselves choosing to field teams comprising reserve team players for cup matches; and by the complete withdrawal of Manchester United from the 2000 season's FA Cup. Manchester United's decision sparked an unprecedented level of debate and complaint in the media and even in Parliament. In the eyes of many traditionalists, all of the developments mentioned above have tended to devalue the two domestic cup competitions, to the detriment of the league's smaller member clubs in particular and, in the case of the FA Cup, non-league clubs as well.

2.7 Football's labour market: players' wages and the transfer system

The retain-and-transfer system and the maximum wage were both key features of English football's labour market from the very earliest days of professionalism. Both were designed to prevent the clubs with the most resources from acquiring all of the most talented players simply by out-bidding other clubs for their services – the outcome which, it was argued, might occur if the football players' labour market operated without any restrictions. Both survived in their original form until the maximum wage was abolished in 1961, and the retain-and-transfer system was substantially overhauled in 1963.

The retain-and-transfer system originated in an FA regulation introduced in 1885, requiring clubs to register their players annually with the Football Association. Player registrations immediately became tradeable commodities between clubs, since unregistered players were not permitted to appear (Morrow, 1999). All player contracts were renewable annually at the club's discretion, and clubs were entitled to retain a player's registration even if his contract was not being renewed. In theory and sometimes in practice, this enabled a club to prevent an out-of-contract player from earning a living. A player could move only if his present club was prepared to sell or release his registration. Under this system all clubs had the discretion to retain individual players for as long as they wished, as well as the guarantee of financial compensation when players were eventually permitted to depart.

The incentive for players to seek to move was also restricted by the existence of the maximum wage, originally fixed at £4 per week when it was introduced in 1901. But according to Russell (1997), Football Association rules introduced at the same time to outlaw bonus payments were regularly flouted during the next decade, resulting in many players receiving more than the maximum and a number of clubs being punished by the football authorities. By 1922 the official maximum had risen to £8 per week (£6 during the summer); meanwhile, the average weekly earnings of male employees in engineering in 1924 were £2.65. By the time the maximum had risen to £20 per week (£17 during the summer) in 1958 the differential had narrowed further: average weekly earnings for male manual employees in 1958 were £12.83 (Department of Labour and Productivity, 1971).

By restraining both the growth in players' salaries overall, and divergences between the remuneration of players operating at the top and bottom ends of the league, the maximum wage seems to have helped impose considerable uniformity on the financial structure of professional football at all levels. Between the early 1920s and the late 1950s the proportionate increases in the minimum and average admission price, and the maximum wage were all very similar. Clubs seem to have responded to fluctuations in attendances and revenues primarily by adjusting the number of players employed on professional terms. For example, the total number of professional players in England and Wales increased from 5,000 in 1939 to 7,000 by the end of the 1940s, at the height of the postwar attendance boom (Fishwick, 1989). Roughly 4,000 of these were registered with league clubs. By 1961 the number of professionals registered with league clubs had fallen to just over 3,000 (Sloane, 1969). Circumstantial evidence also suggests that a uniform financial structure helped foster competitive balance on the field of play. As already seen, the number of different clubs that either won or were in serious contention for the league championship at some point during the 1920s, 1930s and 1950s was far greater than the equivalent number in subsequent decades.

Towards the end of its lifetime, the main economic beneficiaries of the maximum wage were the paying spectators. As late as the 1960 season, the average admission price was only 23 per cent higher in real terms than in 1926, despite the very much larger rise in real disposable incomes that had taken place in the meantime. It is no coincidence that the pressure for abolition mounted progressively as the post-war economic recovery gathered pace, and as the magnitude of the spectators' implicit consumer surplus also increased. As soon as the maximum wage was lifted and players' salaries started to escalate, especially at the top end of the league, admission prices also started to rise. Much of the surplus then began to shift away from the spectators towards the players (Dobson and Goddard, 1998b).

With both proven and suspected cases of illegal payments to players on the increase, and with the football authorities coming under intense pressure from a campaign organised by the Professional Footballers Association (PFA, the players' trade union), the maximum wage was eventually abolished in 1961. Soon afterwards, the 1963 High Court ruling in the case of the player George Eastham against his employer Newcastle United adjudged the retain-and-transfer system as it had previously operated to be an unreasonable restraint on trade. From then on the club holding the player's registration had to offer a new contract at least as rewarding and of the same duration as the expired contract (which could be for one or two years) in order to retain his registration. If such a contract was not forthcoming, the player became a free agent. Transfers, however, were still at the discretion of the selling club, which retained the ultimate power to frustrate a player's desire for a move, so long as it was prepared to continue to pay at the same level as under the old contract.

As anticipated, the most direct consequence of these changes was wage inflation. Famously, the weekly wage of Fulham and England captain Johnny Haynes increased almost immediately to £100: a rise of more than 400 per cent relative to the old maximum. For the large majority of professionals, the immediate effect on wages was less dramatic. According to Russell (1997) several leading clubs, including Liverpool and Manchester United, attempted to maintain their own unofficial maximum during the 1960s.[7] Many clubs also responded to the increase in costs by cutting back the number of professionals employed; the total was down to 2,400 by the 1967 season (Sloane, 1969).

Nevertheless, over a period of years the cumulative effect on football's finances of the decision to lift the lid on players' wages was profound. According to the Szymanski and Kuypers (1999) data set, the inflation-adjusted increase in wages and salaries during the 1950s for clubs with complete records was less than 10 per cent. Between the 1961 and 1974 the corresponding inflation-adjusted increase for the same clubs was around 90 per cent. Revenues had fallen by about 5 per cent in real terms during the 1950s. Between 1961 and 1974 the real increase was over 30 per cent. Between 1961 and 1974 growth in wages appears to have outstripped growth in revenues among both the larger and the smaller clubs, but growth in both revenues and wages was very much faster for the larger clubs than for the smaller. Clearly, football's internal financial structure was already starting to diverge. The adjustment of football's financial

---

[7] Even in the 1990s several leading English clubs have been unwilling to break internal pay structures in order to match the salaries paid to superstar players in Italy and Spain.

structure to the removal of the maximum wage appears to have been virtually complete by the mid-1970s. Between 1974 and the late 1980s, the
rates of increase in revenues and wages were very similar. Having crept
from below 40 per cent in the 1950s to above 50 per cent by the mid-
1970s, the average ratio of total wages and salaries to total revenues
remained stable thereafter. Naturally, however, the average data tend to
mask considerable intra-club and year-on-year variation.

A further important change to the transfer system was introduced in
1978, when players were awarded the right to decide themselves whether
to move on the expiry of their contracts. Though the new system was
termed freedom-of-contract, in practice the out-of-contract player was
still constrained to some extent. If his existing club was offering a new
contract at least as rewarding as the expired contract, it could still
demand a compensation fee, either to be agreed between the two clubs, or
(in cases where agreement could not be reached) to be decided by a FA
tribunal. The tribunal decision was binding on both parties. This meant
that in order to move, an out-of-contract player had to find a new club
that would either agree a fee with his existing club, or be willing to take
the risk of going to arbitration at the Football Association.

Comprehensive data on transfer expenditure prior to the 1970s is not
available. Even so, it seems certain that the labour market reforms of the
early 1960s tended to encourage increased levels of expenditure in the
transfer market, by creating the opportunity for the richer clubs to attract
players by offering more generous packages of remuneration. On the
other hand, freedom-of-contract, by limiting the value to his present club
of the player whose contract was drawing towards its conclusion, might be
expected to have had the opposite effect from 1978 onwards.

Relative to gate revenues, however, there has been no clear trend in
aggregate expenditure on transfers between league clubs since the 1970s,
as table 2.14 shows. There is certainly considerable year-on-year variabil-
ity: in part this reflects the relatively small number of transactions which
make up each annual total. The data, however, do not seem to justify the
frequent complaint that the transfer market is 'out of control'. In fact,
perhaps the most surprising feature of table 2.14 is the long-term stability
of the ratio of total transfer expenditure to gate revenue. The one apparently unsustainable burst of transfer activity, in which some of the characteristics of a boom–bust cycle are apparent, followed English football's
first £1 million transfer (Trevor Francis from Birmingham City to
Nottingham Forest) in February 1979 and peaked during the following
season. A spate of transfers for fees of £1 million or more, involving
players such as Steve Daley, Gary Birtles (twice), Andy Gray and Peter
Ward, culminated in Bryan Robson's £1.5 million move from West

Table 2.14. Gross expenditure on transfers between English league member clubs, 1973–1999

Season	Gross expenditure on transfers of players from other league member clubs (current prices; £ million)					Gross expenditure on transfers of players from other league member clubs (real: 1973=100)					Total as per cent of league gate revenues
	D1/Prem	D2/One	D3/Two	D4/Three	All	D1/Prem	D2/One	D3/Two	D4/Three	All	
1973	3.2	1.8	0.7	0.2	5.9	100	100	100	100	100	49.1
1974	3.7	2.0	0.9	0.3	6.9	106	104	117	136	108	52.4
1975	4.2	1.8	0.8	0.2	7.0	102	102	77	92	93	46.1
1976	2.2	0.5	0.5	0.2	3.4	43	18	50	63	37	18.6
1977	4.7	1.5	0.6	0.2	7.0	78	46	45	56	64	31.1
1978	7.6	2.6	1.1	0.4	11.7	112	68	82	90	95	43.5
1979	9.1	4.8	2.5	0.8	17.2	124	117	168	185	129	59.4
1980	18.3	9.3	3.7	1.5	32.8	214	196	206	290	210	88.9
1981	11.9	6.3	2.7	0.3	21.2	121	115	130	53	118	52.7
1982	18.0	2.6	1.3	0.5	22.4	163	42	56	76	111	55.0
1983	6.3	2.3	1.5	0.1	10.2	53	36	62	17	48	24.2
1984	8.4	2.7	1.5	0.4	13.0	68	40	57	50	58	28.8
1985	9.5	3.3	1.1	0.3	14.2	73	46	41	44	60	28.8
1986	10.9	2.8	1.4	0.4	15.5	80	37	49	50	63	31.9
1987	16.4	3.9	1.8	0.7	22.8	117	50	61	85	89	40.8
1988	23.0	9.5	3.2	1.0	36.7	157	117	105	113	138	57.6
1989	25.3	15.9	3.4	1.6	46.2	162	183	106	164	162	63.4
1990	26.6	19.4	5.8	3.3	55.1	159	208	167	318	180	63.2
1991	26.4	13.5	4.9	1.2	46.0	143	131	129	102	137	44.4
1992	46.4	24.4	2.7	1.4	74.9	241	228	67	115	213	58.7
1993	50.8	19.1	2.8	0.5	73.2	256	173	67	42	202	50.1
1994	66.9	20.4	3.2	1.3	91.8	332	182	77	102	250	56.1
1995	84.0	19.0	5.8	1.1	109.9	403	164	135	83	289	57.4
1996	94.2	36.4	6.1	2.8	139.5	441	306	139	207	358	66.0
1997	94.8	36.8	7.1	2.0	140.7	428	299	156	143	349	57.5
1998	95.3	46.5	16.7	1.5	160.0	422	370	359	105	389	50.0
1999	136.2	24.3	12.2	2.0	174.7	594	190	258	139	418	45.1

Sources: Football Trust, Deloitte and Touche (1999, 2000), Football League, Premier League.

Bromwich Albion to Manchester United in October 1981. Subsequently, the British transfer record was not broken again until Peter Beardsley moved from Newcastle United to Liverpool for £1.9 million in July 1987.

The 1978 'freedom-of-contract' system survived intact in England and Wales until the landmark 1995 ECJ ruling in the Jean-Marc Bosman case, which prompted further major steps towards acceptance of the principle of complete freedom of movement for out-of-contract players. The requirement for the payment of compensation to the former club of an out-of-contract player who was signing for a new club was found to be incompatible with provisions in Article 48 of the Treaty of Rome for the freedom of movement of labour. The existing 'three-foreigner' rule, which had the effect of limiting the number of individuals from countries outside the jurisdiction of each national football federation allowed onto the field of play at any one time, also contravened Article 48, by restricting the opportunity for EU nationals to play for clubs located in other EU countries.

The Bosman ruling concerning out-of-contract players applied originally only to player transfers that crossed EU national boundaries. But many European governing bodies quickly brought regulations governing transfers between clubs within their national jurisdiction in line with the principles established by Bosman. Since the end of the 1998 season, all transfers of out-of-contract players over age 24 between English clubs have been uncompensated. The retention of the fee element for out-of-contract players below age 24 recognises that in a completely free player labour market, clubs that invest in player development may be unable to realise the proceeds of their investment owing to poaching. The post-1998 English arrangements attempt to preserve some element of compensation for clubs that discover or develop talented young players. But the ECJ was unconvinced that the entire pre-Bosman transfer system had been justified by the 'compensation' argument; instead, it took the view that transfer fees often bore little or no relation to the efforts or costs incurred in developing players (Simmons, 1997; Morrow, 1999).

A detailed statistical analysis of the determinants of domestic transfer fees pre-Bosman, and of changes in the characteristics of the playing staffs of Premier and Football League clubs which have occurred since, is included in chapter 4. At this stage, however, some general conclusions can be drawn concerning the domestic impact of the Bosman ruling. Several years after the event, it is certainly clear that the players' labour market has changed fundamentally, and in ways that were mostly predictable at the time.

First, the removal of all restrictions on the eligibility of players from EU countries, as well as non-EU players of international standing, has led to a huge influx of foreign players now being employed by English clubs, especially in the Premier League (see also section 2.1 and chapter 4). Many have been attracted by remuneration perhaps well above what they would be likely to attain elsewhere. According to data reported by Deloitte and Touche (1999), the net transfer expenditure outflow of the English league football clubs as a whole has increased dramatically, from around £11 million in the 1993 season to £15 million (1994), £36 million (1995), reaching a peak of £93 million in the 1996 season. After falling to around £70 million in each of the 1997 and 1998 seasons, it increased sharply to £140 million in the 1999 season. While the post-Bosman increase was spectacular, the trend was already underway before 1995. The spectacular success achieved by Eric Cantona, first at Leeds United and then at Manchester United, following his transfer from Nîmes in 1991, seems to have been particularly influential in raising awareness within the traditionally insular British game of the kind of contribution gifted overseas players might be capable of bringing.

Second, since the price of acquiring an out-of-contract player is now paid entirely to the player (rather than shared between the player and his former club) wage inflation is a predictable consequence of Bosman. Players seeking a new club are in a much stronger position to bargain for high remuneration if their acquisition is not encumbered with the obligation to pay a transfer fee. As table 2.15 shows, wage inflation in English football has certainly been exceptional during the post-Bosman period, but so too has growth in revenue. Bosman has clearly assisted some individuals, especially star players, to capture more of the large surpluses that are being generated from sources such as television and merchandising. It seems likely, however, that high wage inflation would have occurred in any case (as it did before 1995) as a consequence of the popular revival football has enjoyed during the 1990s.

Third, many clubs have attempted to protect themselves against the possibility of losing their best players without compensation by offering longer-term contracts, especially to their younger stars. Morrow (1999) suggests that this development may also have contributed to wage inflation in the short term, if a higher initial level of remuneration is needed to persuade a player to commit for a longer period. Longer contracts may also be attractive to players, however, since they insure future earnings against the consequences of serious injury or loss of form. They may also help restrain wage inflation over the longer term, if they are enforced over their full duration. There are nevertheless incentives for clubs to offer enhanced terms to their top stars far in advance of the expiry of their present contracts, to avoid involvement in an eventual bidding contest for the players' signatures. The 'insurance' argument provides

Table 2.15. *Revenue, wages and salaries and net transfer expenditure,*
1994–1999

Year	Premier League	Div One	Div Two	Div Three	All
Average revenue (£000)					
1994	11,441	3,768	1,451	1,046	4,348
1995	14,675	3,569	1,740	1,103	5,158
1996	17,311	4,331	1,681	1,380	5,692
1997	23,698	5,599	2,482	1,159	7,562
1998	29,088	7,597	2,771	1,312	9,370
1999	33,482	6,666	3,700	1,417	10,353
Average wages and salaries (£000)					
1994	5,312	2,541	1,096	743	2,397
1995	6,568	2,485	1,256	788	2,735
1996	8,494	3,263	1,324	941	3,289
1997	10,905	3,768	1,734	1,051	4,080
1998	15,222	5,605	2,179	1,201	5,653
1999	19,545	5,343	2,861	1,302	6,729
Average net transfer expenditure (£000)					
1994	−1,109	98	243	114	−149
1995	−1,744	100	−98	54	−404
1996	−5,278	276	141	159	−997
1997	−4,106	27	320	76	−782
1998	−5,241	−719	−175	267	−1,303
1999	−6,562	324	−468	239	−1,402
Total wages and salaries as percentage of total revenue					
1994	46.4	67.4	75.5	71.1	65.4
1995	44.8	69.6	72.2	71.4	64.8
1996	49.1	75.4	78.7	68.2	68.7
1997	46.0	67.3	69.9	90.6	69.4
1998	52.3	73.8	78.6	91.5	75.0
1999	58.4	80.1	77.3	91.8	77.7
Total net transfer expenditure as percentage of total revenue					
1994	−9.7	2.6	16.7	10.9	5.3
1995	−11.9	2.8	−5.7	4.9	−2.4
1996	−30.5	6.4	8.4	11.5	0.2
1997	−17.3	0.5	12.9	6.6	1.5
1998	−18.0	−9.5	−6.4	16.0	−3.9
1999	−19.6	4.9	−11.3	15.2	−2.0
Number of clubs in sample					
1994	22	24	19	16	81
1995	22	24	21	14	81
1996	20	24	21	16	81
1997	20	23	22	16	81
1998	19	21	18	14	72
1999	20	20	18	14	72

Source: Deloitte and Touche (1999, 2000).

incentives for risk-averse players to accept improved terms: a contracted player who declines an improved offer received within the lifetime of his existing contract cannot be certain that his value to potential bidders will still be as high when the contract eventually expires. With reference to Major League Baseball, Lehn (1990a, 1990b) argues that long-term contracts also create possibilities for opportunistic behaviour on the part of players, whose prospensity to miss games through injury appeared to increase once under secure contract.

A final predicted consequence of Bosman, which was widely debated at the time, was its potential to cut off what has in the past been a major source of revenue for lower-division clubs: proceeds from the sale of their most talented players to clubs in the higher divisions. At best, the erosion of the implicit cross-subsidy generated by the domestic transfer market might damage competitive balance by widening the financial gap between rich and poor; at worst, the loss of transfer fee earnings might threaten the survival of some of the league's smaller member clubs. While the ECJ accepted that it was legitimate for the football industry to use various means of financial cross-subsidy to promote competitive balance, the Court felt that the transfer system as it had operated pre-Bosman was neither a necessary nor an effective means of achieving this objective (Morrow, 1999).

Europe's legislators served further notice of their intention to pursue to its logical conclusion the application of European employment law to football's labour market in the summer of 2000. The European Commission announced that the existing transfer system for in-contract players breached the principle that employees of any organisation should be free to change employers whenever they wished, subject only to serving a short period of notice (typically three months). FIFA, football's world governing body, was invited to put forward proposals for alternative arrangements. At the time of writing, it appears that intense lobbying has resulted in some softening of the EC's original position, as well as qualified recognition of the principle that professional sports can, in some circumstances, be treated as a special case in respect of European employment and competition. The full details of the new system were unclear at the time of writing, but some of the possible implications are discussed in chapter 9.

The initial reaction of many owners and managers of big- and small-market clubs alike, as well as officials of football's governing bodies, to the possible demise of the transfer system, was one of dismay. Predictions that the loss of transfer income would lead to the closure of many small-market clubs were widespread, even though similar predictions made at the time of the Bosman ruling have as yet failed to materialise. In fact, the evidence concerning the impact on the domestic transfer market of the Bosman ruling is rather mixed. Table 2.14 shows that while the rate of increase in aggregate transfer expenditure between English league clubs slowed significantly during the late 1990s, the total has nevertheless continued to rise. Aggregate expenditure by Premier League clubs, however, was virtually constant in nominal terms in the 1996, 1997 and 1998 seasons, before rising sharply in 1999. Between 1996 and 1998 there was particularly heavy spending in Division One, a number of clubs having taken the view that heavy investment on players in the short term would be more than compensated by the revenues that would flow if Premier League status could be secured and maintained. Fulham's decision to become the first lower-division club to adopt a similar strategy on a significant scale accounts for a large proportion of the total Division Two expenditure in the 1998 and 1999 seasons.

The extent of cross-subsidy emanating from the transfer market is more clearly visible in table 2.16, which shows net expenditure on transfers within the league, by division, since 1973. In all but two seasons since 1973, Division 1/Premier League clubs have been net spenders. In most seasons, there has been a net inflow favouring clubs in the lower two divisions. Relative to the gate revenues of the lower-division clubs, the cross-subsidy has increased in importance over time (Dobson and Goddard, 1998b). This pattern has continued since 1995; in fact, a by-product of the short-term post-Bosman turbulence in the domestic transfer market during the 1996 and 1997 seasons seems to have been a sharp *increase* in the implicit cross-subsidy. The 1998 season appears to have been a quirk, as were 1981 and 1990 when the net flows were actually in favour of Division 1 clubs. As noted above, the 1998 data are distorted by the unusual transfer activity of Fulham in Division Two. In any case, net expenditure, equal to the balance between two very much larger gross flows, is highly volatile from year to year. In the 1999 season net expenditure by the Premier League clubs increased to a record level of £27.5 million. But even this sum represents only around 5 per cent of the income that the Premier League will generate annually under the new television contracts that come into force in the 2002 season. It is perhaps understandable if the European Commission feels that the transfer system is only one of a number of mechanisms (and perhaps one that is rather arbitrary and inefficient) for a cross-subsidy of this magnitude to be achieved.

All commentators agree that changes such as the formation of the Premier League, the exponential growth of television and other revenues, freedom-of-contract and the internationalisation of the player labour market have widened both the financial and the competitive gulf between

Table 2.16. *Net transfer expenditure within the league, 1973–1999*

Season	D1/Prem	D2/One	D3/Two	D4/Three
	Net expenditure on transfers of players from other league member clubs (current prices; £ million)			
1973	0.4	−0.1	−0.3	−0.1
1974	0.2	0.3	−0.2	−0.3
1975	0.6	−0.2	−0.3	−0.1
1976	0.7	−0.7	0.0	0.0
1977	0.5	0.0	−0.3	−0.2
1978	1.8	−1.1	−0.5	−0.2
1979	0.2	−0.6	0.3	0.2
1980	0.6	0.6	−0.7	−0.5
1981	−0.9	0.5	0.6	−0.2
1982	2.4	−1.9	−0.3	−0.3
1983	0.4	−0.4	0.5	−0.5
1984	2.2	−1.3	−0.5	−0.4
1985	2.2	−1.2	−0.9	−0.1
1986	1.2	−0.7	−0.3	−0.2
1987	4.1	−2.4	−1.4	−0.4
1988	5.5	−2.6	−1.5	−1.3
1989	0.8	1.2	−1.3	−0.7
1990	−3.5	0.8	1.5	1.1
1991	7.4	−5.1	−0.3	−2.0
1992	3.6	3.7	−5.3	−2.0
1993	6.0	−2.0	−3.2	−0.8
1994	13.0	−6.0	−5.9	−1.1
1995	9.6	−8.9	0.3	−1.0
1996	25.2	−18.3	−4.0	−2.9
1997	14.5	−3.1	−9.3	−2.1
1998	1.5	0.6	1.8	−3.9
1999	27.5	−25.3	0.7	−2.9

Sources: Football Trust, Deloitte and Touche (1999, 2000).

the leading clubs and the rest. For several Division One clubs that have achieved promotion to the Premier League in recent seasons, the chasm has turned out to be unbridgeable. Deloitte and Touche (1999) have likened the jump from Division One to the Premier League to that which would be faced by a convenience store attempting to become a supermarket in the space of just 10 weeks. But the temptation for Football League to gamble on elevation to Premier League status by increasing wage and transfer expenditure is ever-present, even though at the aggregate level such effort cancels itself out completely if all teams increase spending simultaneously (see also chapter 9). One of the more alarming trends of recent seasons has been the sharp rise in wages and salaries as a percentage of revenue in the Football League (see table 2.15). Nevertheless, predictions of the imminent financial demise of the lower division clubs were just as prevalent during the early 1980s as they are today, and were perhaps even more credible given that the finances of the football industry as a whole were in seemingly terminal decline at the time.

Clearly, football's finances are now passing through a period of structural change at least as far-reaching as that which followed the reforms of the early 1960s. Even if the transfer system is eventually reformed or even abolished as a result of the European Commission's interventions, the present authors are more optimistic than many that the resilience that has seen many clubs overcome the most outrageous financial duress in the past, will continue to favour the future survival of English professional club football at all its levels, in a form not too dissimilar to that which has proven so durable over the past 80 years.

2.8 The historical development of professional football: international comparisons

Sections 2.2 to 2.7 have provided an account of the historical development of professional football in England and Wales, as both a sport and a business. The fact that the codified game of football now played throughout the world originated on the playing fields of the public schools of Victorian Britain naturally makes the story that unfolded in the previous sections of chapter 2 a hugely important part of the history of the sport's international development. When one investigates the history of football worldwide, however, one finds that for every country there is a unique story to be told, which explains the evolution of the sport into its present-day form. Section 2.8 aims to provide just a flavour of this international diversity, by outlining the historical development of professional football in two cases which contrast starkly, both with each other and with England.

In France as in England, the historical development of football has been mainly 'organic' rather than consciously planned, but the sport has always struggled to achieve the heights of popularity attained in a number of other European countries. Despite spectacular recent French success at European and world level, club football appears to be at a crossroads: on the one hand commercial pressures are threatening to undermine a distinctive national model of sports organisation, while on the other the leading French clubs seem to be struggling to keep up with their Italian, Spanish, German and British counterparts.

In Japan in contrast, professional football is an exclusively recent phenomenon. As in France the origins of Japanese amateur football can be traced as far back as the 1870s, but the sport has always struggled for recognition under the shadow of baseball. The formation of the J.League in 1993 represents a conscious 'top-down' attempt to launch a new sports 'brand' in the consumer marketplace, requiring radical innovation capable of shifting entrenched cultural values, and deploying the full battalions of modern marketing and advertising techniques toward this end. Although initial public enthusiasm for the new brand has waned recently to some extent, professional football does appear to have established a foothold sufficiently secure to permit it to develop further in the future.

France

As in many countries, football was first introduced into France by travelling British businessmen during the late nineteenth century. The first club was founded in the port city of Le Havre in 1872 by members of shipping and transit companies who wished to play both football and rugby. A number of other multi-sports clubs were formed in the 1870s and 1880s, before clubs devoted exclusively to football began to appear during the 1890s. The first national cup tournament was won by Standard AC in 1894, and an embryonic league competition was won by Club Français in 1896. By the turn of the century, football was played extensively throughout northern France including Paris (Pickup, 1999).

At the start of the twentieth century, football spread rapidly to the east and south of France. France's first international fixture was played against Belgium in 1904, but the administration of the sport during the pre-war period was chaotic, owing to rivalries between a number of alternative governing bodies. This situation was resolved in 1919 by unification of the competing bodies under the Federation Française de Football (FFF). A French official, Jules Rimet, was the first president of the newly created international football federation FIFA when it was formed in 1920, and became the prime mover behind the creation of the first international World Cup tournament, played in Uruguay in 1930.

In domestic football, a major advance came with the acceptance of professionalism in 1932, followed by the introduction of a national league competition won by Sête in its inaugural 1934 season. The 1935 winners were Sochaux, a club which had been formed in 1929 on a professional basis with the backing of the Peugeot car manufacturer. This development had been instrumental in prompting the authorities to adopt professionalism. Racing Club (RC) Paris, formed by a Parisian estate agent in 1932, became the next champions in 1936.

The legal framework for the organisation of professional football clubs was provided by the 1901 freedom of association law, permitting the formation of associations of citizens on a non-profit basis for any purpose. Clubs such as Sochaux and RC Paris, dominated by local business personalities seeking influence and prestige (rather than financial reward) through their involvement in football, became the norm from the 1930s onwards. From the outset, there was also a strong tradition of local authority involvement in the financing and administration of football (including municipal ownership of most major football stadia), deriving from a statutory duty for municipalities to promote and develop sport. Prior to the introduction of fixed-term contracts in 1968, professional players were tied contractually to a single club up to the age of 35. The relatively draconian pre-1968 contractual position may explain football's relatively unattractive status as a working-class occupation following the introduction of professionalism: most players were middle-class and semi-professional. A relatively high proportion of players were imported: according to Lanfranchi (1994) 329 foreigners played in the French First Division before 1939, and a similar pattern was maintained after the war. Indigenous working-class representation did increase gradually, however, from the 1950s onwards (Eastham, 1999; Pickup, 1999; Mignon, 2000).

French officials were highly influential in the development of the first European club tournaments during the 1950s, as they had been in the creation of the World Cup 30 years before. Stade Reims, domestic champions five times between 1953 and 1962, were runners up to Real Madrid in the first European (Champions) Cup tournament in 1956, and again in 1959. In domestic football, however, the 1960s and 1970s were a period of retrenchment. The successes of St Etienne, domestic champions nine times between 1964 and 1981 and participants in the latter stages of the European Cup three times in succession in the mid-1970s, took place against a background of declining spectator interest and financial crisis on the domestic scene. Population decline in many smaller industrial towns led to reductions in municipal funding, and several clubs reverted to amateur status (Pickup, 1999; Mignon, 2000).

The French tradition of state involvement in the organisation of sport has received some of the credit for steps taken during the 1970s that have subsequently contributed to a renaissance in the fortunes of French football, both at club and (especially) at international level. In 1974 the National Football Institute was established to provide training to 40 of the most promising young players. At the same time, all professional clubs were required to set up their own training centres with links to local schools and other community organisations (Eastham, 1999). At international level many of the products of this system went on to achieve

Table 2.17. *Average league attendances, French First Division, 1981–2000*

Season	Average (000)	Season	Average (000)	Season	Average (000)	Season	Average (000)
1981	11.4	1986	10.9	1991	12.2	1996	16.0
1982	10.8	1987	12.6	1992	12.4	1997	16.4
1983	11.5	1988	13.5	1993	15.1	1998	17.9
1984	11.2	1989	11.8	1994	13.1	1999	19.3
1985	10.9	1990	14.3	1995	14.6	2000	22.3

Source: <http://rernes.free.fr./>

unprecedented success. France were World Cup semi-finalists in 1982 and 1986, World Cup winners in 1998 and European Champions in 1984 and 2000. Domestically the benefits were more ambiguous, with many of the leading players choosing to enhance their earnings by playing for Italian, Spanish, German or British clubs, rather than remaining with their (relatively impoverished) French counterparts. Naturally, the Bosman ruling has made this ambition easier to achieve. Meanwhile Arsenal's acquisition of the 18-year-old Nicolas Anelka on completion of his apprenticeship with Paris St Germain in 1997 without paying compensation highlighted a worrying anomaly in the contractual basis of the French training system. Nevertheless, the 1990s have witnessed a strong revival in the fortunes of French football at club level. Table 2.17 shows that average First Division attendances have increased steadily from just over 10,000 at the start of the decade, to over 20,000 by the end.

Despite its unique organisational and ownership structure, French club football has not proven impervious to the kinds of pressures for commercialisation which have had such a profound impact in England (and elsewhere) during the last two decades. Weaknesses in the administrative and financial control of French club football were apparent following the implication of officials of St Etienne, Paris St Germain and Bordeaux in a series of financial scandals during the 1970s and 1980s. An important modernising development was a change to the legal constitution of the larger professional clubs made in 1984, allowing for greater involvement of private investors while still preventing profits from being paid to chairmen and directors. Nevertheless, several early experiences of the involvement of the 1980s breed of entrepreneur were far from happy ones. Most notorious was Bernard Tapie's flamboyant reign as Chairman of Marseille (OM), which included five successive domestic championships between 1989 and 1993 (the last of which was subsequently rescinded) and the first French European Cup triumph in 1993. This period ended in enforced relegation for the club in 1994, and in Tapie (and several other club officials) being jailed in 1995 for a variety of bribery and corruption offences including match fixing during the 1993 season.[8]

Perhaps more sustainable models for the commercial management of French football at the highest level are provided by Olympic Marseille's gradual rehabilitation under the presidency of Robert-Louis Dreyfus, head of the Adidas sportswear manufacturer; and by the recent progress of Paris Saint Germain, under the effective control of the subscription television company Canal Plus (Eastham, 1999). Formed in 1984, Canal Plus' success in marketing subscriptions to view live football on terrestrial television provided an early exemplar for BSkyB's subsequent success in Britain. In another move that proved to be prescient Canal Plus acquired a 40 per cent share in the ailing Paris Saint Germain in 1991. Although one of the television company's aims was to influence the future development of relations between football and television, their financial and organisational support led to a revival in Paris Saint Germain's competitive and commercial fortunes: the club were French champions in 1994, and European Cup Winners Cup winners in 1996. By the end of the decade Paris Saint Germain had by far the largest turnover of any French club, and in summer 2000 were (ironically) able to pay £22 million in order to re-sign Anelka from Real Madrid.

The conflict between the traditional national model and what Bourdieu (1999) has described as the neoliberal commercial model for the control of French football is still underway. Current symptoms include the continuing exodus of leading players to foreign clubs; the debate and legal actions concerning the proposed termination of municipal funding for football clubs on the grounds that it is anti-competitive; and the expressed desire of a handful of major clubs, including Olympic Marseille and Paris Saint Germain, to float on the stock exchange. Clearly these clubs believe that the commercial freedom that flotation would secure is essential if they are to keep pace with other leading European clubs in the future. But France is not the only country in which the high ambitions of the richest clubs have raised fears about the competitive and commercial implications for the rest.

Japan

The first football match to be played in Japan is reported to have taken place just one year after the sport first appeared in France. In 1873

---

[8] Eastham (1999) describes the Marseille case in detail. Eastham also describes the entrepreneur Jean-Luc Lagardère's attempt to revive the fortunes of Racing Club Paris in the late 1980s. This venture also ended in sporting and commercial failure, but there was no illegal or criminal activity.

Lieutenant Commander Archibald Douglas of the British navy organised a game at the Naval Academy in Tokyo Bay. Trade links with Britain ensured that Japan received continued exposure to football during the rest of the nineteenth century, and by the turn of the century football featured on the curricula of a number of teacher training schools. A schools championship was introduced in 1918, and the Japanese Football Association (JFA) was formed in 1921 to administer the first national football tournament. The JFA joined FIFA in 1929 (Horne, 1996, 2000; Sugden and Tomlinson, 1998).

Despite these early developments, the growth in football's popularity was severely constrained by the pre-eminence of baseball as Japan's leading national sport. The initial introduction and subsequent development of baseball was certainly due to the American influence, which extended throughout the Pacific rim and was paramount in Japan between the late nineteenth century and the 1930s, and again after 1945. Academics following Whiting (1977), however, have attempted to explain baseball's popularity in terms of its compatability with certain attributes of the Japanese national character, most clearly identified (in the west at least) with the *samurai* warrior class. According to this interpretation, the distinctive Japanese variant of baseball shares many characteristics with the martial arts, including a rigorous training and disciplinary regime, an emphasis on the repetition of set moves, a focus on the psychological duel between pitcher and hitter, and the suppression of individuality for the benefit of the team (Horne, 1996, 2000).

Whether such insights are helpful, or whether they merely reflect the stereotypical cultural prejudices of outsiders, has become a matter of debate among sociologists. Either way, there is no doubt that baseball remained Japan's most popular national sport throughout the twentieth century. Professional baseball was introduced in 1936, and the present-day competitive structure comprising the Central League and the Pacific League was introduced, along US lines, in 1950. Baseball rather than football is played at the elite universities, which are the main recruiting grounds for the top positions in industry and commerce, the media and the professions. Ownership of the leading professional baseball teams rests with large corporations. Japan's most popular team, Tokyo's Giants (of the Central League) regularly attract crowds of 50,000, and in general the level of television exposure is high.

Despite its tendency to celebrate rather than suppress individuality, football maintained its subsidiary position within the schools curricula throughout the twentieth century. The Japan Soccer League (JSL), a national-league competition comprising non-professional company teams (whose players typically worked in the mornings and trained in the afternoons) was first launched in 1965. Foreign players were admitted from 1967, but had to become employees of the sponsoring company. The principle of professionalism was not accepted by the JSL until 1985 (Nogawa and Maeda, 1999). At international level Japan entered the World Cup qualifying tournament for the first time in 1954, but prior to the 1990s success for the national team was confined mainly to the Olympics. As host nation Japan were quarter-finalists in 1964 and then semi-finalists in Mexico four years later. Japan hosted the FIFA World Youth Championships in 1979, and staged a challenge match between the top European and South American club sides a number of times during the 1980s. Eventually, however, repeated failure by the national team to achieve World Cup qualification convinced officials of the need to introduce professionalism. In 1986 a committee was set up to investigate the issue, and in 1990 plans for the launch of the professional J.League in May 1993 were announced (Sugden and Tomlinson, 1998; Horne, 2000).

It would be hard to argue, as in the case of England in the 1880s or France in the 1930s, that the introduction of professionalism in Japanese football in the 1990s was a natural and inevitable stage in the sport's organic development. Instead Birchall (2000) has described the creation of the J.League as 'perhaps one of the greatest mass-marketing events even Japan, and probably the world, has ever seen'. All aspects of the launch were subject to detailed and carefully co-ordinated planning. While the commercialisation of football has evolved gradually elsewhere, in Japan commercial concerns were paramount from the outset. For example, Japan's second largest advertising company, Hakuhodo, were given responsibility for marketing and publicity, while Sony Creative Products took charge of all aspects of product design, including the design of team shirts and other items of merchandise (Birchall, 2000). Initial three-year J.League sponsorship deals were arranged with drinks manufacturer Suntory and consumer credit firm Nippon Shinpan (Nicos) for Y400 million (over £2 million) each, while the sale of television rights raised more than Y1000 million (over £5 million) in 1993, and twice this amount in 1994 (Horne, 1996, 2000).

Another component of the launch strategy was for the J.League to assume a role in urban redevelopment, so no team was allowed to locate in central Tokyo. A stadium capacity of at least 15,000 and a youth policy linked to local schools were among the criteria for league membership. All teams had to employ qualified coaches. Broadcasting rights and sponsorships were to be sold collectively by the J.League. The initial membership of 10 teams increased progressively to 18 teams by 1998. In 1999 a second division was created, with 16 teams remaining in the J1 Division, and 10 teams in the J2 Division.[9] An important part of football's 'rebranding' was the creation of team identities associated with places of residence rather than employment, and with parts of team names borrowed from Europe and North America; for example, Furukawa Electric from the JSL became JEF United Ichihara, Mitsubuishi Motors became Urawa Red Diamonds, Sumitomo Metals became Kashima Antlers and Yomiuro FC became Verdy Kawasaki (the first J.League champions). Several foreign coaches, including Arsène Wenger and Osvaldo Ardiles, have been employed, and a number of high-profile foreign players were recruited, including England's Gary Lineker, Germany's Pierre Litbarski, and Brazil's Zico and Dunga. Links with Brazil are especially strong owing to Brazil's large ethnic Japanese community (Nogawa and Maeda, 1999; Birchall, 2000; Horne, 2000).

In 1993 and 1994, the J.League's popularity exceeded the expectations of its creators, with many stadia experiencing regular sell-out attendances, televised broadcasts attracting unprecedented audience ratings and revenues from sponsorship and merchandising outstripping their original projections. Since 1995, however, there has been a marked decline in the J.League's commercial fortunes as some of the initial gloss and excitement has worn off. Average match attendances which peaked at 19,500 in 1994 fell to 10,100 by 1997, before recovering to just under 12,000 in 1998 (although the decline partly reflects the introduction of new teams). Over the same period, average attendances for professional baseball games were between 25,000 and 30,000. Television and sponsorship revenues have remained static since 1995, while sales of merchandise have slumped dramatically (Horne, 2000). In 1998 financial problems forced the Yokohama Flugels to merge with local rivals the Marinos, while Yomiuro withdrew their sponsorship of Verdy Kawasaki. A number of clubs have been forced to economise by releasing expensive foreign players. Nevertheless, Japanese progress at international level, including participation in the final stages of the 1998 World Cup and automatic qualification as co-hosts with South Korea in 2002, can only raise the profile and enhance the credibility of domestic football. The foundations of the J.League now appear to be sufficiently secure to allow professional football to survive and prosper.

[9] American or baseball influences are apparent in several aspects of the J.League's competitive structure. In all seasons but one, the championship has been played in two stages separated by a mid-season break, with the winners of each stage meeting in a play-off to determine the overall champions. An experiment with a European-style single-stage format was abandoned after one season in 1996. At first, penalty shoot-outs were used to settle draws. Now, matches level after 90 minutes go into 30 minutes' extra time under the 'golden goal' rule. Three league points are awarded for a win in 90 minutes, two for a win in extra time and one for a draw at the end of extra time.

2.9 Convergence and divergence in the league gate revenues of English football clubs

The previous sections of chapter 2 have described a number of fundamental changes in the competitive and business structure of professional football that took place during the twentieth century, and especially in recent times. In England as elsewhere, their cumulative effect has been to widen the economic and financial chasm that now separates clubs operating at different levels within the league. Inevitably, the magnitude of the gulf which currently exists raises concerns about the future viability of English football's traditional competitive structure of 92 clubs organised into four divisions, all employing a squad of full-time professional players. These concerns have been prominent during football's recent renaissance, but it is worth recalling that they are by no means solely a recent phenomenon. Discussion of the merits and demerits of proposals such as break-away competitions for the top clubs at national or European levels, semi-professional status for lower-division players, or a return to regionalisation of the lower divisions was just as extensive during the early 1980s when football's revenue base was in decline, as it has been recently.

This section does not attempt to provide answers or solutions to all of these issues. Instead, it pursues a less ambitious objective: to quantify the rise in inequality that has taken place over the long term. To this end, a number of standard economic measures of convergence, divergence and inequality are applied to the league gate revenues data set that was described in section 2.4. A direct comparison of the economic structure of professional football between the 1920s and the 1990s will of course show that economic inequality between clubs has risen considerably during the period. But the analysis will also reinforce the impression, conveyed less formally in the earlier sections of this chapter, that much of the increase in inequality within the 75-year period which the gate revenues data set describes has taken place in relatively short bursts. Specifically, the period between the late 1950s and the mid-1970s, which includes the abolition of the maximum wage and the reform of the retain-and-transfer system, was one of fundamental change in the economic structure of English football. So too was the period (still underway) since the start of the 1990s, which takes in the formation of the Premier League, the development of pay-television, and the Bosman ruling.

Measuring convergence, divergence and inequality

Describing the pattern and modelling the process by which a group of economic units increases or decreases in size (on some appropriate measure) over time, both in absolute terms and relative to one another, is a key endeavour in a number of fields of empirical economic enquiry, as the following examples illustrate:

- International economists may wish to know whether the *average prosperity* of a group of countries, measured by their *per capita* Gross Domestic Product (GDP), can be expected to converge or diverge over time. Do wealthier countries enjoy faster or slower growth in *per capita* GDP than their poorer counterparts? If the rich are becoming richer at a faster rate than the poor are becoming richer (or if the poor are actually becoming poorer) there may be a need for interventionist policies by development agencies and the governments of the richer countries to offset rising inequality. Alternatively, if the poor are becoming richer at a faster rate than the rich, then inequalities between nations may tend to diminish naturally over time without the need for any such intervention (Solow, 1956; Baumol, 1986; Barro, 1991; Temple, 1999).

- On a slightly smaller scale, industrial economists may wish to identify and predict *trends in industry concentration measures*, which indicate the extent to which an industry is dominated by a small number of large firms. To model the evolution of an industry's structure, it is useful to study the empirical relationship between the relative sizes of the member firms, and their growth performance. Do the larger firms tend to grow faster than the smaller ones? If so, we should expect to see market concentration increase over time. Alternatively, is there no statistical relationship between firm size and growth? Is the probability of growing at a certain rate over any given period the same for a large firm and a small firm? If so (perhaps less obviously) market concentration can also be expected to increase over time. Or, finally, do the smaller firms tend to grow faster on average than their larger counterparts? In this case, market concentration might either increase or decrease in the short term. But in the long term, concentration will converge towards an equilibrium, beyond which there is no further tendency for it either to increase or decrease (Gibrat, 1931; Hart and Prais, 1956; Sutton, 1997).

Returning to football, the type of empirical model that has been used to investigate the evolution of *per capita* GDP in international economics, and the evolution of industry structure and concentration in industrial economics, can be adapted to model the distribution of aggregate gate revenues among the member clubs of the English football league. To do so, some mathematical notation is needed, and some standard economists' definitions of convergence and divergence must be introduced. The notation is as follows:

$\log_e(r_{i,t})$ = natural logarithm of club i's total gate revenue from league matches in season t

$\Delta^T\text{-}\log_e(r_{i,t+T}) = \log_e(r_{i,t+T}) - \log_e(r_{i,t})$ = logarithmic growth of the league gate revenue of club i between seasons t and $t+T$

$\log_e(p_i)$ = natural logarithm of the population recorded in the 1961 Census of Population for the local authority district in which club i's ground is situated

$\log_e(a_i)$ = natural logarithm of the number of years between club i's first season as a league member and the 1997 season

n_i = the number of other clubs situated within a 30-mile radius of club i's ground which competed in the league at any time between the 1926 and 1997 seasons.

The level and growth of gate revenues are expressed in logarithmic form in order to focus on the distribution of revenues between clubs. The logarithmic transformation eliminates distortions arising from inflation and other influences on gate revenues that are common to all clubs.

The first measure of convergence or divergence is based on movements over time in the standard deviation across clubs of logarithmic gate revenues, $\log_e(r_{i,t})$. There is *sigma convergence* if the standard deviation, denoted $s(\log_e(r_{i,t}))$, is decreasing over time, and no sigma convergence or *sigma divergence* if this standard deviation is constant or increasing.

It is also possible to measure convergence using regression analysis of the relationship between $\log_e(r_{i,t})$ and $\Delta^T \log_e(r_{i,t+T})$. Consider the following regression model:

$$\Delta^T \log_e(r_{i,t+T}) = \alpha + \beta \log_e(r_{i,t}) + u_{i,t+T} \tag{2.1}$$

where $u_{i,t+T}$ is a random error term with a mean of zero and a standard deviation of σ_u, and α and β are coefficients to be estimated. The numerical value of the coefficient β in (2.1) determines the relationship between revenue at time t, and growth in revenue over the period t to $t+T$:

- If $\beta > 0$, growth in revenue over any period tends to be related positively to initial revenue at the start of the period, so on average *the larger clubs grow faster than the smaller clubs*. As suggested above, the dispersion of revenues between clubs will tend to widen over time, and there is no sigma convergence.
- If $\beta = 0$, there is no relationship between growth in revenue and initial revenue. In this case as well, *the distribution of revenues between clubs tends to widen over time*, and there is no sigma convergence. If growth is

unrelated to size, each club's growth rate in each period is effectively drawn randomly from the theoretical distribution of all possible growth rates, which is the same for all clubs. Over time, however, the cumulative effects of 'good luck' (clubs that by chance get slightly more than their fair share of high growth) and 'bad luck' (clubs that get slightly more than their fair share of low growth) are such that the dispersion of revenues between clubs tends to widen.

- If $\beta < 0$, growth in revenue over each period tends to be related negatively to initial revenue at the start of the period, so on average *the smaller clubs grow faster than the larger clubs*. In the long term, the revenues of all clubs tend to be mean-reverting towards some average value, and there is no tendency for the dispersion of revenues to widen over time.[10]

Figure 2.7 illustrates the three cases described above: (i) $\beta > 0$, (ii) $\beta = 0$ and (iii) $\beta < 0$. In each panel, the diagram on the left shows the scatter-plot of the cross-sectional relationship between growth in revenue and initial revenue (in logarithmic form), represented by (2.1). The diagram on the right shows the implications of this relationship for the time-path of revenues for two representative clubs. In panel (i), the gulf between the clubs that were initially richer and poorer tends to widen over time. So too does the dispersion of revenues. In panel (ii), the revenues of the two clubs tend to 'wander' randomly. It is possible by chance for the club that was initially poor to overtake its richer counterpart, but the dispersion of revenues again tends to widen over time. Finally, in panel (iii), the revenues of the two clubs always tend to revert towards the same long-term average value (denoted by the dotted line). The club that was initially richer does not maintain any long-term advantage over its poorer counterpart, and the dispersion of revenues remains the same in the long term.

It is clear that the numerical value of the parameter β in (2.1) plays a critical role in determining whether there is convergence or divergence in revenues. An alternative measure of convergence or divergence, based on the numerical value of β, is *unconditional beta convergence*. If $\beta < 0$ there is unconditional beta convergence, and if $\beta \geq 0$ there is no unconditional beta convergence. From the previous discussion, it is evident that unconditional beta convergence is a necessary, but not a sufficient, condition for sigma convergence.

---

[10] In terms of the parameters of (2.1), the expression for the long-term average revenue is $-\alpha/\beta$. The expression for the standard deviation of the distribution of revenues at any given time around this average is $\sigma_u/\surd(2\beta + \beta^2)$. In the short term, if the current standard deviation of revenues is smaller than $\sigma_u/\surd(2\beta + \beta^2)$, the distribution of revenues will tend to widen, so there is no sigma convergence. If the current standard deviation is larger than $\sigma_u/\surd(2\beta + \beta^2)$, the distribution will tend to narrow, and there is sigma convergence.

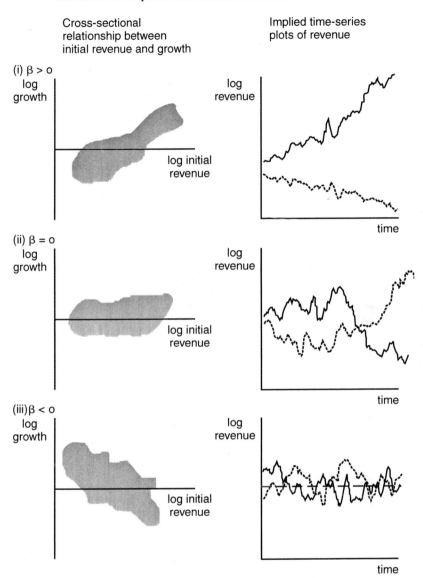

Figure 2.7 Cross-sectional relationships between revenue and growth, and implications for the time-path of revenue

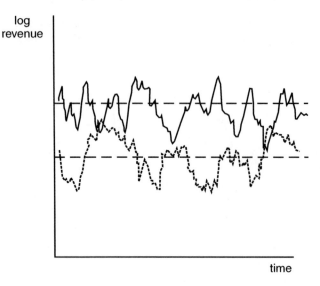

Figure 2.8 Time-path of revenue under conditional beta convergence

Sigma convergence and unconditional beta convergence offer adequate convergence measures, as long as (2.1) provides an accurate representation of the processes that are generating the rates of growth of revenues for all clubs in each period.[11] It is possible, however, that this is not the case. There may be factors other than the size of the club's revenue at the start of each period, which influence the growth in revenue over the same period. In the case where $\beta < 0$, this is equivalent to saying that, in the long term, each club's revenue may be mean-reverting towards an average value which is specific to that club, and which depends on observable characteristics of the club. This is illustrated in figure 2.8, in which the two clubs' revenues tend to be mean-reverting towards different long-term average values.

The three additional variables defined above, $\log_e(p_i)$, $\log_e(a_i)$ and n_i, will be used in the empirical analysis to test whether club-specific characteristics are in fact relevant in determining the long-term average values of revenues. In the long term, it might be expected that each club's attendance would be positively related to its local population base, negatively related to its age (if early entry into the league allowed the clubs concerned to benefit from first-mover advantages in establishing a high initial base

---

[11] Equation (2.1) provides an accurate description if the *only* systematic (non-random) influence on growth in revenue over each period is the value of revenue at the start of the period.

level of support), and negatively related to the number of other clubs in its near geographical vicinity. If so, then (2.1) should be reformulated as follows:

$$\Delta^T \log_e(r_{i,t+T}) = \alpha + \beta \log_e(r_{i,t}) + \gamma_1 \log_e(p_i) + \gamma_2 \log_e(a_i)$$
$$+ \gamma_3 n_i + u_{i,t+T} \tag{2.2}$$

where γ_1, γ_2 and γ_3 are additional parameters to be estimated. The same logic as before applies to the implications of the numerical value of the coefficient β for convergence. Specifically, if $\beta < 0$ in (2.2) there is *conditional beta convergence*, and if $\beta \geq 0$ there is no conditional beta convergence.[12] Beta convergence can therefore be unconditional or conditional, depending whether additional conditioning variables are included in the growth model (as in (2.2)), or not (as in (2.1)).

Finally, another popular measure of cross-sectional equality and inequality among a group of economic units is the *Gini coefficient*. In the present context, this is calculated by arranging the revenues of all n clubs with league membership in season t in ascending numerical order, and defining $r_{i,t}$ to be the revenue of the ith club (so $r_{1,t}$ is the smallest revenue value, and $r_{n,t}$ is the largest). It is then possible to define the cumulative revenue function,

$$F_{m,t} = \sum_{i=1}^{m} r_{i,t}$$

for $m = 1 \ldots n$. $F_{m,t}$ is the sum of the m smallest revenues in the data set, for any value of m.

The Gini coefficient compares the shape of $F_{m,t}$ as m increases from 1 to n, with the shape $F_{m,t}$ would take if there was perfect equality between the revenues of the n clubs. This is illustrated in figure 2.9. The straight line linking O and B is the shape of $F_{m,t}$ if total league revenue was shared equally between the n member teams. The curve OAB lying beneath the straight line is the actual shape of $F_{m,t}$. The greater the degree of inequality, the lower down in figure 2.9 will be the mid-point A, and the greater will be the curvature of OAB. The Gini coefficient is the ratio of the shaded area between the straight line OB and the curve OAB, to the triangle OBC. The greater the degree of inequality, the closer is the Gini coefficient to one.[13]

---

[12] In the case $\beta < 0$, the average value to which the revenues of club i are mean-reverting in the long term is $-(\alpha + \gamma_1 \log_e(p_i) + \gamma_2 \log_e(a_i) + \gamma_3 n_i)/\beta$.

[13] The formula for the Gini coefficient is

$$G_t = \frac{nF_{n,t} - 2\sum_{m=1}^{n} F_{m,t}}{nF_{n,t}}$$

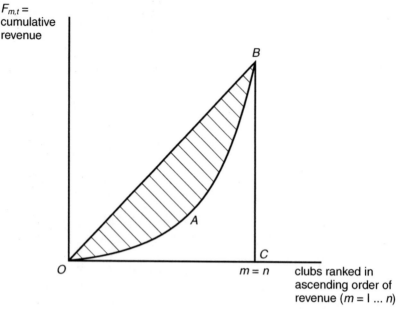

Figure 2.9 Calculation of Gini coefficient using football revenue data

To summarise, in a period for which revenues show evidence of beta convergence, or during which the standard deviation of revenues or the Gini coefficient shows no tendency to change systematically, the professional football industry's economic structure exhibits characteristics of equilibrium, in the sense that there is no tendency for the dispersion of revenues across clubs at all levels within the league to widen over time. Conversely, a period during which beta convergence breaks down, or the standard deviation of revenues or Gini coefficient tends to increase over time, can be characterised as one of transition between an old and a new structural order.

Convergence tests: empirical results

The results of the convergence tests are summarised in table 2.18. Column (1) shows the standard deviation of log revenue for all clubs that were league members in each season, $s(\log_e(r_{i,t}))$. The trend in $s(\log_e(r_{i,t}))$ indicates whether or not there is sigma convergence. $s(\log_e(r_{i,t}))$ was slightly higher in the 1920s and 1930s than in the late 1940s and 1950s but, overall, the dispersion of revenues between clubs remained quite stable until the late 1950s.

Thereafter, $s(\log_e(r_{i,t}))$ increased steadily from its 1950s average of just

Table 2.18. *Convergence in gate revenues from English league matches, 1926–1997*

Season	Sigma convergence $s(\log_e(r_{i,t}))$ (1)	Gini coefficient G_t (2)	Unconditional beta convergence $\hat{\beta}$ (3)	Conditional beta convergence $\hat{\beta}$ (4)	$\hat{\gamma}_1$ (5)	$\hat{\gamma}_2$ (6)	$\hat{\gamma}_3$ (7)
1926	0.690	0.349	−0.067	−0.178[b]	0.128[a]	−0.013	0.218
1927	0.756	0.365	−0.136[c]	−0.237[a]	0.128[a]	−0.014	0.227
1928	0.777	0.378	−0.161[b]	−0.241[a]	0.104[a]	−0.012	0.098
1929	0.740	0.352	−0.129[b]	−0.216[a]	0.101[a]	−0.010	0.161
1930	0.754	0.368	−0.111[c]	−0.143[b]	0.045	−0.014[c]	0.245
1931	0.744	0.376	−0.203[a]	−0.246[a]	0.032	−0.005	0.297[b]
1932	0.726	0.366	−0.186[a]	−0.232[a]	0.035	−0.006	0.266
1933	0.731	0.379	−0.151[a]	−0.179[a]	0.022	−0.007	0.194
1934	0.731	0.373	−0.153[a]	−0.172[a]	0.014	−0.008	0.215[c]
1935	0.778	0.397	−0.204[a]	−0.215[a]	0.018	−0.011[c]	0.146
1936	0.781	0.396	−0.230[a]	−0.215[a]	−0.011	−0.009	0.146
1937	0.752	0.369	−0.180[a]	−0.197[a]	0.013	−0.004	0.124
1938	0.728	0.360	−0.188[a]	−0.212[a]	0.012	−0.005	0.243
1939	0.734	0.369	−0.215[a]	−0.210[a]	0.000	−0.014[c]	0.254
1947	0.757	0.368	−0.213[a]	−0.231[a]	0.010	0.000	0.101
1948	0.686	0.344	−0.088[c]	−0.112[c]	0.038	−0.006	−0.034
1949	0.694	0.346	−0.057	−0.077	0.025	−0.005	0.016
1950	0.695	0.343	−0.028	−0.076	0.056	−0.008	0.024
1951	0.681	0.341	−0.073	−0.116	0.053	−0.005	−0.033
1952	0.680	0.341	−0.057	−0.095	0.077[c]	−0.008	−0.169
1953	0.690	0.349	−0.020	−0.078	0.099[b]	−0.007	−0.151
1954	0.708	0.362	−0.010	−0.023	0.059	−0.008	−0.224
1955	0.701	0.361	−0.021	−0.072	0.124[b]	−0.017	−0.255

Table 2.18. (*cont.*)

Season	Sigma convergence $s(\log_e(r_{i,t}))$ (1)	Gini coefficient G_t (2)	Unconditional beta convergence $\hat{\beta}$ (3)	Conditional beta convergence $\hat{\beta}$ (4)	$\hat{\gamma}_1$ (5)	$\hat{\gamma}_2$ (6)	$\hat{\gamma}_3$ (7)
1956	0.692	0.354	-0.045	-0.088	0.100[b]	-0.003	-0.280
1957	0.659	0.347	0.060	0.006	0.094[c]	-0.001	-0.251
1958	0.682	0.355	0.095	0.035	0.069	0.000	-0.053
1959	0.736	0.370	0.016	-0.051	0.105[b]	0.003	-0.218
1960	0.767	0.382	0.065	-0.001	0.086[c]	0.003	-0.118
1961	0.744	0.387	0.045	-0.052	0.123[b]	-0.004	-0.047
1962	0.755	0.388	0.083	-0.037	0.150[a]	-0.017	0.103
1963	0.795	0.403	0.074	-0.018	0.127[b]	-0.017	0.090
1964	0.801	0.415	0.107	0.018	0.121[b]	-0.016	0.129
1965	0.837	0.435	0.078	0.016	0.071	-0.007	0.186
1966	0.798	0.422	0.072	-0.009	0.100[c]	-0.013	0.174
1967	0.851	0.446	0.081	0.009	0.105[b]	-0.021[c]	0.199
1968	0.878	0.451	0.059	-0.027	0.119[b]	-0.012	0.064
1969	0.880	0.463	-0.026	-0.080	0.068	-0.008	0.114
1970	0.928	0.468	0.006	-0.012	0.021	-0.005	0.118
1971	0.928	0.471	-0.030	-0.074	0.062	-0.014	0.164
1972	0.963	0.477	-0.089	-0.098	0.001	0.007	0.039
1973	0.985	0.494	-0.143[b]	-0.204[a]	0.076	-0.001	0.108
1974	1.013	0.489	-0.137[b]	-0.220[a]	0.119[b]	-0.004	0.076
1975	1.052	0.498	-0.156[b]	-0.215[a]	0.124[b]	0.000	-0.022
1976	1.009	0.488	-0.174[a]	-0.215[a]	0.086	0.004	-0.064
1977	1.043	0.495	-0.174[a]	-0.196[a]	0.042	0.006	-0.165
1978	1.030	0.500	-0.221[a]	-0.262[a]	0.087	0.001	-0.183

Year							
1979	0.979	0.478	-0.213^a	-0.301^a	0.146^a	-0.010	0.014
1980	1.002	0.483	-0.218^a	-0.306^a	0.162^a	-0.012	-0.034
1981	1.029	0.504	-0.224^a	-0.301^a	0.154^a	-0.005	-0.102
1982	0.994	0.502	-0.143^b	-0.211^a	0.126^b	-0.003	-0.099
1983	1.015	0.497	-0.184^a	-0.261^a	0.129^b	0.000	-0.035
1984	1.003	0.505	-0.102^c	-0.159^b	0.071	0.001	0.074
1985	1.050	0.539	-0.101	-0.160^b	0.057	0.006	0.230
1986	0.998	0.525	-0.052	-0.115	0.047	0.011	0.280
1987	0.963	0.511	0.016	-0.040	0.035	0.015	0.415^a
1988	0.963	0.486					
1989	0.929	0.476					
1990	0.934	0.478					
1991	0.979	0.500					
1992	1.038	0.518					
1993	1.033	0.513					
1994	1.074	0.522					
1995	1.124	0.552					
1996	1.124	0.565					
1997	1.146	0.576					

Notes:

^{a} = significantly different from zero, two-tail test, 1 per cent level;

^{b} = 5 per cent level; ^{c} = 10 per cent level.

under 0.70. Between the mid-1970s and the end of the 1980s, a new plateau was established, with an average value just over 1.00. After falling slightly at the start of the 1990s, $s(\log_e(r_{i,t}))$ has since increased further, achieving its highest-ever value in the 1997 season. For the period covered by table 2.18 as a whole, there is clearly no evidence of sigma convergence in the gate revenues data. Instead the dispersion of aggregate gate revenue between clubs has widened considerably. As suggested above, however, much of the increase in the standard deviation has taken place over relatively short sub-periods within the last 75 years, specifically between the late 1950s and mid-1970s, and again more recently during the 1990s. The trend in the Gini coefficient, shown in column (2) of table 2.18, tells a very similar story to the sigma convergence measure. Overall, G_t increased from around 0.34 in the late 1940s to just under 0.58 by the late 1990s.

For the 75 clubs that were league members in both the 1926 and 1997 seasons, tests for unconditional and conditional beta convergence of revenue over the entire observation period involved estimation of (2.1) and (2.2), using 1926 as the base season and the change in log revenue during the 55 seasons completed between 1926 and 1997, denoted $\Delta^{55} \log_e(r_{i,97})$, as the dependent variable. The estimation results are as follows:

$$\Delta^{55}\log_e(r_{i,97}) = 1.263 + 0.368^b \log_e(r_{i,26}) + \hat{u}_{i,97}$$
$$(1.321)\ (0.138)$$

$$n = 75 \qquad \hat{\sigma}_u = 0.731 \qquad R^2 = 0.089 \tag{2.3}$$

$$\Delta^{55}\log_e(r_{i,97}) = 0.814 + 0.301^c \log_e(r_{i,26}) + 0.096 \log_e(p_i)$$
$$(1.945)\ (0.155) \qquad\qquad (0.075)$$

$$-0.011 \log_e(a_i) - 0.011\ n_i + \hat{u}_{i,97}$$
$$(0.325) \qquad\quad (0.017)$$

$$n = 75 \qquad \hat{\sigma}_u = 0.762 \qquad R^2 = 0.111 \tag{2.4}$$

Note: [b] = significantly different from zero, two-tail test, 5 per cent significance level; [c] = 10 per cent level.
Standard errors of estimated coefficients are shown in parentheses.

In both estimated equations, the estimated coefficients on $\log_e(r_{i,26})$ are positive. The estimated coefficient is significantly different from zero at the 5 per cent level in the unconditional convergence model (2.3), but significant at only the 10 per cent level in the conditional convergence model (2.4). In both cases, however, there clearly is no evidence of beta convergence. The results are to be expected in view of the increase in $s(\log_e(r_{i,t}))$ reported in table 2.18.

While there is evidence of neither beta convergence nor sigma convergence in the results reported so far, there is still the possibility of observing convergence in revenues over shorter sub-periods within the observation period. Indeed, this might well be expected in view of the pattern exhibited by $s(\log_e(r_{i,t}))$, which as column (1) of table 2.18 shows, is quite stable over relatively long sub-periods. Columns (3)–(7) of table 2.18 report the results of a series of estimations of (2.1) and (2.2), using each season from 1926 to 1987 in turn as the base season, and the change in log revenue over the next $T = 10$ seasons as the dependent variable. Therefore the first row reports regressions of log growth between the 1926 and 1936 seasons on log revenues in the 1926 season. The gap created by the Second World War is ignored in defining the 10 season intervals, so (for example) the fifth row reports regressions of log growth between 1930 and 1947 on log revenue in 1930.

Column (3) of table 2.18 reports the estimated values of β in (2.1) (denoted $\hat{\beta}$). In the unconditional convergence model, negative estimates of β are obtained in all estimations up to and including base season 1956. At the 5 per cent level, the estimated coefficients are significantly smaller than zero for all base seasons between 1931 and 1947. Therefore there was unconditional beta convergence in revenues during this period. During the early and mid-1950s, the negative estimated values of β become smaller in absolute terms, before eventually turning positive for all but one base season between 1957 and 1970. During this period, unconditional beta convergence broke down. From base season 1971 onwards, negative estimates of β are obtained for all base seasons up to and including 1986. These are significantly different from zero for all base seasons between 1973 and 1983. From base season 1981 onwards, however, the negative estimates of β start to become smaller in absolute terms. In the final estimation for base season 1987, a small positive estimated value of β is obtained.

Columns (4)–(7) report the estimated values of β, γ_1, γ_2 and γ_3 in the conditional convergence model (2.2). In general, the conditional beta convergence results are similar to their unconditional counterparts. The estimated values of β are significantly different from zero for all base seasons up to and including 1947, and from 1973 to 1985 inclusive. During the 1920s and 1930s, the negative conditional convergence estimates are generally larger in absolute terms than the corresponding unconditional estimates. Similarly, between the late 1950s and early 1970s, the conditional estimator shows less tendency than the unconditional to return positive estimates. For the 14 base seasons between 1957 and 1970, the unconditional estimator returns 13 positive estimates, while the conditional estimator does so on only five occasions.

The estimates of γ_1, the coefficient on log population, are positive in all 55 estimations of (2.2), and significantly different from zero at the 5 per cent level in 21 cases. This represents reasonably strong and consistent evidence that when there is beta convergence, the equilibria to which individual clubs' revenues are mean-reverting are dependent on the local population base. Despite a progressive increase over time in the geographical mobility of spectators (as described in section 2.3) there is no indication that the relationship between population and revenue was any weaker at the end of the observation period than at the start. Several of the largest estimates of γ_1 are obtained for base seasons in the early 1980s. Presently the most fashionable clubs are mainly located in the largest cities, but because they attract support from all parts of the country these clubs no longer depend on their local population base for their popularity.

The signs of the estimates of γ_2, the coefficient on the number of other local clubs, are also mostly as expected, with 41 negative and only 14 positive estimates obtained. The negative sign of the majority of these coefficients suggests that other things being equal, a larger amount of local competition tends to depress a club's equilibrium gate revenue. However, none of the 41 negative estimates is significantly different from zero at the 5 per cent level, so the influence does appear to be relatively weak. In this case, there is some indication of a change over time: most of the negative estimates of γ_2 (and most of those which come closest to being statistically significant) are found near the beginning of the observation period. In the 1920s, a large local population base was presumably necessary to generate a large level of (local) support, because spectators would go to watch the nearest team. The presence of other teams in the same locality would tend to diminish a club's revenue base. In the 1990s a large local population base was still necessary to generate a large level of (national) support, because the big-city teams are the most fashionable. The presence of other teams in the same locality, however, would make little or no difference to these clubs' revenue base.

Finally, the duration of the club's league membership appears to exert only a very weak influence (if any) on equilibrium revenue, with sequences of both positive and negative estimates of γ_3 obtained for different sub-periods. The positive estimate obtained in the very final estimation for base season 1987 is the only one in column (7) that is significantly different from zero, at the 1 per cent level. This result could perhaps be meaningful, however, in view of the findings in section 2.2 concerning the revival in the fortunes of several of the league's oldest member clubs during the 1990s.

2.10 Conclusion

Chapter 2 has presented an analysis of both the historical development and the current state of English club football's commercial structure, and has provided some international comparisons. The empirical results reported section 2.9, together with the description of the historical development of English professional football as a business in sections 2.2–2.8, suggest that between the early 1920s and the end of the century, the economic structure of English football has passed through two distinct equilibrium phases, interrupted by two transitional periods.

The first and highly durable equilibrium phase lasted from the early 1920s until the late 1950s. Considerable uniformity in the financial structure of clubs operating at all levels within the league was preserved through regulation of both admission prices (which determined the main component of revenue) and players' wages (the principal item of cost). By the end of the 1950s, however, as the post-war recovery gathered momentum and general living standards rose dramatically, the pressure for relaxation of these regulations became irresistible. The abolition of the maximum wage in 1961, and the reform of the retain-and-transfer system in 1963, heralded a period of rising financial inequality between clubs operating at different levels within the league hierarchy, as football made the transition towards a new (and considerably less durable) equilibrium economic structure.

The period from the mid-1970s to the end of the 1980s is identified as the second equilibrium phase. During this period football's economic fortunes were in decline on a number of fronts. Pressures emanating from social and demographic changes, the hooligan phenomenon, and the failure of football clubs themselves to maintain their own physical infrastructure, had taken their toll on attendances over many years, to the extent that the future survival of large numbers of clubs (both large and small) seemed to be in jeopardy. As the crisis deepened, the earlier trend towards rising inequality between clubs appears to have been checked; the financial positions of all clubs were deteriorating at roughly the same rate. Tragically, however, it was only after the disasters of Heysel, Bradford and Hillsborough that the momentum for fundamental reform became overwhelming.

Football's rehabilitation during the 1990s as the most popular and fashionable national sport in England and elsewhere has coincided with a further sharp rise in financial and competitive inequality between clubs. This increase has taken place against a background of rising rather than falling demand at all levels, which has done much to offset the most adverse financial consequences for the league's smaller members. Of course there are many positive aspects to the changes of recent years. Mainly as a consequence of technological change in broadcasting, football's dual status as both spectator sport and television spectacle has become more realistically reflected in the balance between the revenues it derives from both sources. The wholesale reconstruction and conversion of all major stadia to all-seated status, together with the marginalisation of the hooliganism phenomenon, have been hugely influential in strengthening football's appeal as a spectator sport. An influx of talented overseas players is widely perceived to have led to marked improvements in playing standards in the Premier League. Liberalisation of the rules governing football's labour market has widened disparities between the earnings capability of the top players and the rest: a trend that seems certain to continue in the future if further reform, required to comply with European employment law, results in the eventual abolition of the transfer system.

3   Competitive balance and uncertainty of outcome

Over the past 45 years, a consensus has evolved among most sports economists that in a professional sports league, the free operation of market forces should maintain a reasonable degree of competitive balance among member teams. The interdependencies between teams inherent in the competitive structure of any sports league create disincentives for a wealthy team to attempt to accumulate talent to the extent that the league as a whole loses competitive viability. Contrary to widely held belief, measures such as a salary cap or maximum wage, a reserve clause restricting player mobility between clubs, or gate revenue sharing, are not expected to create closer competitive balance than would tend to emerge naturally as a result of the free play of market forces. Such measures may have implications, however, for the distribution of revenues between strong clubs and weak clubs and between clubs (in general) and players.

In this chapter, section 3.1 describes the North American model for the organisation and regulation of professional team sports, and draws some comparisons with the British and European models. This is followed by a review of the theoretical literature on competitive balance within sports leagues, most of which has been developed with North American team sports in mind. After the main findings of this literature have been examined, its applicability to European football is considered. Two important premises of the US literature seem questionable in respect of European football: first, the assumption of profit maximising behaviour on the part of clubs; and, second, the assumption that the available stock of playing talent is fixed. The implications of relaxing or altering these assumptions are explored. Section 3.1 also reviews the empirical evidence on the effects of the introduction of free agency in a number of North American professional team sports on competitive balance within the leagues concerned.

Competitive balance matters, of course, because it ensures uncertainty of outcome, both for individual matches and for the league championship as a whole. Uncertainty of outcome is the lifeblood of any sporting event: take away the element of uncertainty and competitive sport degenerates into sterile exhibition. Unpredictability is a key characteristic of the product that professional sports teams sell to their spectators, and an analysis of the nature of unpredictability forms an essential element of any survey of the economics of sport. Examining the extent to which individual match results in football are predictable or unpredictable is the main objective of sections 3.2 and 3.3. For consistency with the emphasis on competitive balance in sports leagues in the theoretical literature, the empirical analysis focuses on the predictability and unpredictability of league (rather than cup or European) match results.

In section 3.2 the patterns and trends contained in a comprehensive English league match results data set, covering the seasons 1973 to 1999 inclusive, are identified and compared with equivalent data from a number of other European leagues. The main long-term feature of this data is a progressive improvement in the performance of away teams and a corresponding decline in the magnitude of home advantage. Using goal scoring records, it is possible to identify the contributions to this trend made by changes in the relative strengths of the attacking and defensive capabilities of home and away teams. Another topic of enduring fascination to many sports fans is the nature of 'persistence' effects in sequences of consecutive match results. Does a recent run of good results tend to build confidence, and so increase the probability that the next match will also be won? Or does it tend to create complacency, and so increase the risk that the next match will be lost? Appropriate statistical techniques are applied to the match results data set in an effort to resolve this issue empirically. The findings appear to support the second hypothesis of negative persistence.

Section 3.3 tackles the problem of developing a statistical model which takes advantage of the systematic or predictable component in sequences of past results, to assess the probabilities and provide forecasts for future matches. In the present context, the model identifies the extent to which match results are predictable from historical data and the extent to which results are random. Later in this volume, the same model is used to assess the effect on the match result of a recent change of manager by either team (chapter 6), and to assess the efficiency of the prices quoted by a leading high-street bookmaker for fixed-odds betting on the outcome of football matches (chapter 8).

3.1 Economic theory of competitive balance in sports leagues

The North American professional team sports model

The theoretical literature on the determinants of the degree of competitive balance within sports leagues has been developed mainly by US sports economists, with North American team sports primarily in mind. Naturally the development of this literature reflects the characteristics of the North American model for the organisation and regulation of team sports. This differs from the British or European model in a number of important aspects. Before reviewing the US literature, it is therefore important to be aware of some of the key similarities and differences between the two models. This sub-section outlines the organisational structure of three North American professional team sports: baseball, basketball and football.[1]

Perhaps the most fundamental difference between the North American and European models concerns the highly restricted nature of supply in North America. In all three sports league membership is controlled through the award of franchises by the leagues' organising bodies. A franchise grants a territorial monopoly to the team's owner: no other team can operate within the owner's territory, and no owner can relocate to another town without the approval of 75 per cent of all team owners. In Major League Baseball (MLB), at the time of writing 16 teams compete in the National League (NL), and 14 in the American League (AL). In American football there are 31 teams in the National Football League (NFL). In basketball there are 29 teams in the National Basketball Association (NBA). In each case, league competition takes place within a number of regionalised sections, and end-of-season play-offs determine championship outcomes.

To appreciate the highly restrictive nature of the franchise system, it is worth noting that the 1997 US population was 267 million. The top divisions of the big five European football leagues each support 18 or 20 teams, with national populations of 52 million (England and Wales), 59 million (France), 82 million (Germany), 58 million (Italy) and 39 million (Spain). Even more important, league membership in North America is determined exclusively through the franchise system; there is no hierarchical divisional structure and no promotion and relegation. In theory and in practice, membership of the top European football divisions is open to a much larger number of teams competing in the lower divisions of the respective leagues. Promotion and relegation between divisions depends solely on competitive prowess.

Profit maximisation is the prime objective of North American leagues and team owners, so profitability is the main factor influencing decisions concerning the award of franchises and relocation. There is also intense competition between municipalities to attract and retain franchise

---

[1] Quirk and Fort (1992, 1999) and Scully (1995) provide fascinating descriptions of the historical development of the institutional structures of the main North American professional team sports. This sub-section draws on these accounts.

holders. Inducements take the form of offers to construct lavish new stadiums at public expense: a significant source of public subsidy for leagues and teams that are already rich in cash. To demonstrate that threats on the part of team owners to relocate are far from idle, Quirk and Fort (1999) document 11 team moves that took place in MLB between 1950 and 1997; nine in the NFL; and 18 in the NBA. The leagues have been able to maintain their monopoly positions largely because the US courts, acknowledging the peculiarities of the economics of team sports (see chapter 1), have tended to accept the legitimacy of restrictions on the production of sporting events that would be inadmissible elsewhere. In a landmark ruling in 1922, the Supreme Court granted MLB exemption from the Sherman antitrust laws. In 1961 the Sports Broadcasting Act was passed by Congress, entitling the leagues to sell broadcasting rights collectively on behalf of their member teams (Quirk and Fort, 1992; Scully, 1995).

The main role of the leagues within this framework is to implement rules aimed at furthering the collective interest of the teams in achieving joint profit maximisation. The leagues therefore impose restrictions on the behaviour of the teams in both the product and labour markets, which seek to prevent any individual team from achieving a level of competitive dominance that would be damaging to the interest that all teams share in maintaining a reasonable degree of competitive balance. In the early history of all three sports, the most important restriction of this kind was the reserve clause, described in chapter 1. Having signed a contract as a professional, the player's team retained the option to renew his contract, effectively binding the player to his present employer. The reserve clause was justified on the grounds that it was necessary to prevent the richest teams from outbidding the rest for the services of the top players; but its tendency to depress players' compensation was a highly convenient side-effect from the team owners' perspective.

Baseball's reserve clause, effective since 1880, was challenged successfully in the Supreme Court in 1976, on the grounds that it should be interpreted as only a one-year option clause. The Court ruled that by playing for a year without signing a new contract, a player could satisfy his obligations under the reserve clause, and subsequently become a free agent. Under the 1976 settlement, all MLB players became free agents after completing a minimum number of years of major league service (currently six years). In basketball, the one-year interpretation had always applied, but teams that signed a free agent had to pay compensation to his former employer. This system was also abandoned in 1976, when moves towards the full implementation of free agency were initiated. Players became free agents after four years' NBA service or upon expiry of their second contract if this happened sooner. In American football, free agency did not come until 1993, when a similar one-year option was abandoned. The delay is attributed by Quirk and Fort (1999) to the relatively weak bargaining position of the players' union, explained in turn by the short average duration of playing careers and the dominant role played in the sport by coaches (who tend to be even more influential than star players). From 1993 NFL players became free agents after a five-year qualifying period.

In all three sports trades involving in-contract players normally take the form of player-exchange deals, or swaps of players for draft picks (see below). Trading players for cash is unusual, though not completely unknown, and there is no North American equivalent of European football's multi-million-pound transfer system.

Other restrictions on the free play of market forces in North American sports include the draft system, salary caps and revenue sharing. The reverse-order-of-finish draft system allows the weakest teams from the previous season the first pick of rookie players moving from college (or school in the case of baseball) to professional level for the first time. The NFL introduced the draft in 1936; the NBA followed suit soon after its formation in 1949; and MLB adopted the draft in 1965 (though the draft does not apply to new players arriving from overseas). In 1983 the NBA became the first organising body to adopt a salary cap, in an attempt to offset the potentially harmful effects of free agency for competitive balance. Each team is subject to a salary cap limiting its total wage expenditure to 53 per cent of gross league revenues divided by the number of teams in the league. There is also a salary floor set at 47 per cent of gross revenues divided by the number of teams. An exemption applies if a team wishes to exceed the cap so as to match an offer made by another team to one of its first-team players. As part of its 1993 free-agency settlement, the NFL adopted a similar arrangement, with wages limited to 67 per cent of designated revenues. An attempt to impose a salary cap in MLB resulted in a strike by players in 1994 and 1995, before it was abandoned.

In theory, by equalising expenditure on players' compensation throughout the league, the salary cap should enable the small-market teams to compete for championship success on equal terms with the big-market teams. In practice, however, the NBA salary cap has not succeeded in equalising expenditures, mainly because the exemption clause is invoked routinely by the big-market teams. Consequently total wages regularly exceed 60 per cent of revenues, and the high-spending teams' wage bills are typically more than twice those of the low-spending teams. Critics point out that if anything, championship success in the NBA has become more rather than less concentrated since the cap was introduced (Quirk and Fort, 1999).

In all three sports revenue sharing plays an important part in offsetting the basic inequalities in drawing power between teams. Practices concerning the distribution of gate revenues vary between sports. NFL home and away teams share gate revenues on a 60:40 split. In baseball, the split is 95:5 in the NL and 80:20 in the AL. In the NBA there is no sharing of gate revenues. Broadly speaking, national television revenues are shared equally between all league member teams, while the home team keeps local television revenues. Broadcasting rights in all three sports are sold in separate packages to national and local broadcasters. In contrast to their European counterparts, North American sports have not pursued the pay-television option at national level. National television contracts are with the free-to-air networks ABC, CBS, NBC and Fox, which seek to recoup their fees through advertising revenues. As in Europe television revenues increased exponentially during the 1990s. Quirk and Fort (1999) quote 1996 estimates for total television and radio income of $706 million for MLB, $615 million for the NBA and $1.29 billion for the NFL. The latter figure has since been eclipsed by a new set of contracts yielding $2.2 billion per year between 1998 and 2005.

With the leagues maintaining a stranglehold over the supply of professional team sports, it is unsurprising that the histories of the three sports are littered with attempts on the part of outsiders to set up rival competitions. Following the creation of the NL in 1876, there were several attempts to establish rival leagues, including the AL which was set up in 1901. The current NL–AL monopoly, achieved by agreement between the two leagues in 1903, has survived subsequent challenges from the Federal League (1914), the Mexican League (in the 1940s) and a threatened Pacific Coast League (which was averted in 1958, partly as a result of the moves of the Brooklyn Dodgers and New York Giants to Los Angeles and San Francisco, respectively). In basketball the NBA was created in 1949 from the remains of two rival leagues. Its most powerful challenger since has been the American Basketball Association (ABA), set up in 1967. Mounting financial difficulties eventually led to the demise of the ABA, with four of its surviving teams being incorporated into the NBA in 1976. Since the creation of the American Professional Football Association (the forerunner to the NFL) in 1920, there have been several attempts to establish rival leagues in American football; the most successful being the fourth American Football League (AFL), set up after the NFL had refused to award a number of expansion franchises in the late 1950s. The AFL operated alongside the NFL between 1960 and 1969, before a merger incorporating the AFL teams into the NFL realised the original aims expressed by the AFL's founders' 10 years earlier.

Although there is a prolific and colourful history of attempts to create rival leagues, only the AL has endured for more than a few years, and then only by operating together with the NL as a *de facto* joint monopoly supplier. In some instances, however, rival league proposals (whether implemented or only threatened) have been successful in forcing the established leagues to make policy changes. Clearly, there is a strong imperative in any sport to operate a competitive structure which delivers a single champion. But while the established leagues remain effectively closed to new entrants, excluding a number of cities capable of supporting potentially valuable franchises, the incentives that have previously brought so many rival league proposals to (temporary) fruition will undoubtedly remain in place.

Of course, it is important not to exaggerate the differences between the markets for professional team sports in North America and Europe. As shown, there are a number of significant institutional differences. But as Fort (2000) argues, spectators wherever they live exhibit an overwhelming preference for seeing their own team win, while in both regions 'sports organizations put the highest level of sports quality before the fans that can afford to support it. And the joint ventures undertaken by teams through their organizations make them financially better off than they would be acting alone' (Fort, 2000, p. 451). Organisational and institutional structures have implications for the division of the spoils (both pecuniary and non-pecuniary) among the main protagonists: owners, players, broadcasters, spectators and governing bodies. But the similarities between North America and Europe in the underlying incentives motivating these parties perhaps far outweigh the differences.

Theoretical models of sports leagues: some preliminaries

As seen in chapter 1, Rottenberg (1956) first articulated the idea that market mechanisms can be relied upon to maintain a reasonable degree of competitive balance among the member teams of a sports league, without the need for extensive regulation of player compensation or mobility by the sport's governing body. In discussing the economic structure and characteristics of the North American baseball players' labour market, Rottenberg considers the case of two teams located in different towns, one of which has a larger population (or potential market) than the other. Other things being equal the marginal revenue product of a player of a given level of ability is greater with the big-market team than with the small-market one. But because the marginal revenue function declines as the quantity of playing talent already held increases, it does not pay the big-market team to accumulate the most talented players to the point where complete competitive dominance is achieved.

In essence, this argument does not depend upon contractual arrangements or the structure of player compensation. It is valid under free agency, in which case the player may be in a strong position to secure most or all of his marginal revenue product in wage negotiations, since his reservation wage is the wage he could command by signing for another team. It is also valid under a reserve clause, in which case teams may have the opportunity to drive player compensation down, towards the highest wage the player could command in employment outside the sport.[2]

El-Hodiri and Quirk (1971) develop a mathematical model of an n-team professional sports league that captures these and other insights. Specifically, they demonstrate that perfect competitive balance, with all teams having equal playing strengths, is consistent with an assumption of profit maximising behaviour only if there is no buying and selling of players' contracts, or if the revenue functions of all teams are the same. In the type of model presented below, the latter would require that all teams are located in towns of equal (or similar) population size, so that each team's potential market is the same. Since neither of these requirements is likely to be met in practice, '[i]t is not surprising, then, that casual empiricism indicates that in no professional team sport under current rules of operation is there a tendency toward equal playing strengths' (El-Hodiri and Quirk, 1971, p. 1313).

Subsequently, Quirk and El-Hodiri (1974), Quirk and Fort (1992), Fort and Quirk (1995), Vrooman (1995, 1996, 1997), Hausman and Leonard (1997), Rascher (1997) and Késenne (2000a, 2000b) have used variants of the same model to investigate various policy issues. The main findings of this body of work are reviewed below, using a modified version of the model described by Vrooman (1995). Several of these authors present simplified and stylised versions of the original n-team model, in which the league consists of just two teams. Without sacrificing any of the important insights available from the n-team version, the two-team model can be derived using less algebra, and is also suitable for a diagrammatic form of presentation.

It is assumed that team i (for $i = 1, 2$) has the following functions for total revenue, R_i and total cost, C_i:

---

[2] Prior to its gradual elimination from most US sports between the 1970s and 1990s, the reserve clause operated in a manner similar to the original retain-and-transfer system in English football, by tying a player for his entire career to the holder of his registration.

$$R_i = rP_i^\alpha W_i^\beta \qquad C_i = cP_i^\gamma W_i^\delta \qquad (3.1)$$

where P_i = team i's population or market size; it is assumed $P_1 > P_2$
   T_i = team i's stock of playing talent
   W_i = team i's win ratio = $T_i / (T_1 + T_2)$
   α is the elasticity of revenue with respect to market size
   β is the elasticity of revenue with respect to win ratio
   γ is the elasticity of cost with respect to market size
   δ is the elasticity of cost with respect to win ratio
   r and c are constants.

The US studies develop a closed model, in which the total stock of playing talent is fixed, so any reallocation of talent between the two teams is a zero-sum activity. This assumption is reasonable for North American sports which draw principally on home-grown talent and which do not trade players with teams in other countries to any great extent. It is less appropriate for football, especially following the liberalisation of the rules governing the European football players' labour market in the mid-1990s, since when the leading clubs in particular have recruited large numbers of players from overseas. After the closed version of the model has been reviewed, an open model, in which the total stock of playing talent is allowed to vary, is developed below.

Fort and Quirk (1995) simplify the cost function in (3.1), by assuming that $\gamma = 0$ and $\delta = 1$ (the marginal cost of winning, equivalent to the marginal cost of talent, does not depend on city size, and does not vary with the quantity of talent). For the most part, the assumptions $\{\gamma = 0, \delta = 1\}$ are also adopted below, though they are relaxed at one point. Most US studies assume profit maximising behaviour on the part of teams individually. The effect of altering this assumption for the case of football is considered below in the context of the open model.

The closed model

For convenience, it is assumed that playing talent is measured on a scale such that $T_1 + T_2 = 1$ in the closed model. The marginal revenue and marginal cost of team i (for $i = 1, 2$), obtained by differentiating (3.1) assuming $\gamma = 0$ and $\delta = 1$, are as follows:

$$MR_i = \frac{\partial R_i}{\partial T_i} = \beta P_i^\alpha W_i^{\beta-1} \qquad MC_i = c \qquad (3.2)$$

Under the profit maximising assumption, each team seeks to employ playing talent up to the point at which the marginal revenue generated by an extra unit of talent, MR_i, is just equal to the marginal cost of employing the extra unit, MC_i. As shown below, however, depending on the assumptions made about the rules governing player compensation, $MR_i = MC_i$ may or may not be an attainable condition in the closed model, owing to the limited availability of playing talent. If the stock of talent is fixed and the cost of hiring talent is low, all teams may be forced to operate with marginal revenue above marginal cost.

If both teams face the same marginal cost of talent ($\gamma = 0$ and $\delta = 1$ in (3.1)), the marginal revenues of both teams should be the same in equilibrium ($MR_1 = MR_2$). If $MR_1 > MR_2$, a transfer fee can be found at which it is attractive to both teams for some talent to be transferred from team 2 to team 1. If the transfer fee is pitched somewhere between the discounted values of the future revenue gains to team 1 and losses to team 2, both teams are made better off by the transfer. It is profitable for both teams to continue to trade in this way, until the condition $MR_1 = MR_2$ is attained.

This equilibrium condition $MR_1 = MR_2$ can be used to obtain an expression for the equilibrium 'ratio of win ratios', a simple measure of competitive balance, as follows:

$$W_1/W_2 = (P_1/P_2)^{\alpha/(1-\beta)} \tag{3.3}$$

Equation (3.3) indicates that any departure from competitive equality ($W_1 = W_2$) is caused by the effect on the respective revenue functions of the difference between the home-town populations of the two teams ($P_1 > P_2$). The degree of competitive imbalance is positively related to both α (the elasticity of revenue with respect to population) and β (the elasticity of revenue with respect to win ratio).

The equilibrium is depicted in figure 3.1. The downward-sloping $MR_1(P_1)$ shows team 1's marginal revenue based on its actual home-town population of P_1, as a function of T_1 represented on the horizontal axis. $MR_2(P_2)$ shows team 2's marginal revenue. Since by assumption $T_1 = 1 - T_2$, $MR_2(P_2)$ plotted against T_1 is the inverse of the same function plotted against T_2, and is therefore upward-sloping. Finally, the dotted $MR_1(P_2)$ shows team 1's hypothetical marginal revenue, if team 1's home-town population were P_2 (the same as team 2). For any value of T_1, $MR_1(P_1) > MR_1(P_2)$ because $P_1 > P_2$. If team 1's home-town population were P_2, each team would hire the same quantity of talent, $T_1 = T_2 = 0.5$ at point A, and each would achieve an identical win ratio of 0.5. Since team 1's home-town population is P_1, however, the equilibrium occurs at the intersection of $MR_1(P_1)$ and $MR_2(P_2)$ at B. Team 1 hires T_1^* units of talent, and team 2 hires $T_2^* = 1 - T_1^*$, where $T_1^* > 0.5$ and $T_2^* < 0.5$. The ratio of the equilibrium win ratios is as shown in (3.3). The shaded area ABD in figure 3.1 represents the gain in total league revenue that is realised by moving

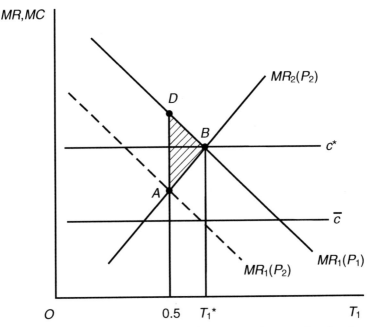

Figure 3.1 Competitive balance under reserve clause and under free agency

from perfect competitive balance at A to the efficient distribution of playing talent at B.

An important property of this model is that the equilibrium is the same under different institutional arrangements in the player labour market. Initially, suppose the labour market is highly regulated, with either a reserve clause or a maximum wage in force. Under a reserve clause, each player is tied contractually to the team that currently holds his registration. Depending on their bargaining power, maximising team owners can drive the wage down, perhaps as far as the next highest wage the player could command in alternative employment outside the sport, represented by the horizontal marginal cost function $\bar{c}$ in figure 3.1. With a maximum wage, the model's formal properties are the same, with $\bar{c}$ representing the maximum that can be paid to any player. At the equilibrium, the marginal revenues of all teams at B exceed the exogenously determined marginal cost of $\bar{c}$. All teams would like to hire more talent, but are unable to do so because the total supply is fixed.

Now consider the situation under free agency, with players at liberty to choose which team they will play for. In this case, each player's reservation wage is the wage he could command by signing for another team.

Economic competition between the teams to attract players causes the wage to be bid up, until the point is reached at which both teams are hiring as much talent as they wish at the equilibrium wage.[3] The latter is therefore determined endogenously, within the model. The location of the free-agency equilibrium, however, is still the same as before, at B. In this case, competition to hire players drives the free-agency equilibrium wage up to c^*, so marginal revenue and marginal cost are equal for both teams.

This important, and to some extent counter-intuitive finding is known as the *invariance result*. It asserts that changing from a reserve clause (or a maximum wage) to free agency should have no effect on competitive balance. The invariance result conforms to Ronald Coase's well-known Theorem, that the economically optimal distribution of a resource (in this case, playing talent) is independent of the legal ownership of the property right to that resource (Coase, 1960). Although the introduction of free agency shifts rent from the teams to the players, it does not change the optimal allocation of resources (the efficient distribution of playing talent) between teams, and therefore does not affect competitive balance in equilibrium.

According to the invariance result, the rookie draft, which in several North American professional team sports offers first pick of the new professionals graduating from college to the teams finishing lowest in their leagues at the end of the previous season, is also expected not to affect competitive balance, at least in the long term. The draft does not alter the position of the marginal revenue functions, and therefore does not affect the position of B in figure 3.1, where $MR_1 = MR_2$. Although the draft does determine the first destinations of rookie players, it does not affect the incentives for teams subsequently to trade players until their marginal revenues are brought into equality.

There are some qualifications to the invariance result, however, which arise if more complex labour market structures are considered, or if the simplifying assumptions concerning cost structure are removed. Fort and Quirk (1995) and Vrooman (1995) both discuss the salary cap mechanism adopted by the NBA in 1983 (see above), under which each team's total expenditure on wages must fall within specified minimum and maximum limits. In the theoretical model, if all teams are required to spend exactly the same on wages, and if a reverse-order-of-finish draft allocates the best new players to the lowest-finishing teams, the long-term

---

[3] Although it would be perhaps easy for club owners to collude to hold down the wage in a two-team league, the two-team model is only a stylised version of the more realistic n-team case, in which effective collusion would be harder, though perhaps not impossible to achieve.

equilibrium is perfect competitive balance. In this case, $MR_1 > MR_2$ in equilibrium: team 1 would like to spend more and team 2 would like to spend less, but both are prevented from doing so by the rules of the salary cap. The equilibrium achieved is also inefficient in the sense that total league revenues are not maximised.

One reason why sports' governing bodies may wish to interfere with the allocation of resources or playing talent which market forces would otherwise produce is that in the free-market equilibrium there is no guarantee that small-market teams will earn sufficient revenue to cover their costs. If small-market teams go out of business, the viability of the league as a whole might be undermined. The desire to prevent this outcome could justify the salary cap. Hausman and Leonard (1997) argue, however, that a combination of a flat-rate tax on all teams, and lump-sum payments to the less profitable or loss making teams, could be used to ensure the viability of the small-market teams, without distorting competitive balance and the efficient allocation of resources.

This type of analysis assumes that the purpose of the cap is to achieve greater competitive balance and/or to maintain the economic viability of the small-market teams. Using a model with different structural assumptions, Vrooman (1995) considers an alternative scenario, in which the real purpose of the cap is to maximise league revenues. Reverting to the two-team model Vrooman begins by assuming $\gamma > 0$ and $\delta > 1$ in (3.1). The marginal cost functions of both teams are increasing as the quantity of talent already employed increases, and $MC_1 > MC_2$ for any given level of talent because with $\gamma > 0$, the big-market team has to pay more than the small-market team to attract and retain its players. The equilibrium condition for the allocation of talent between the two teams becomes $MR_1 - MC_1 = MR_2 - MC_2$. Under free agency, equilibrium is at D_1 and D_2 in figure 3.2 ($MR_1 = MC_1$ and $MR_2 = MC_2$), with team 1 hiring T_1^{**} units of talent. Competition is more balanced than at B where $MR_1 = MR_2$: team 1's big-market revenue advantage is partially offset by its cost disadvantage, so it does not dominate competition to the same extent. The effect of the salary cap under a league revenue maximising assumption, however, would be to restore the less balanced equilibrium at B. Under the rules of the cap, total player costs are shared equally between the two teams, so the marginal cost of talent does not affect either team's optimising decision. Individual team and total league revenues are maximised when $MR_1 = MR_2$, as before.

Another influential finding of the US literature is that the existence or nature of arrangements for revenue sharing among league members should have no effect on competitive balance. In section 2.5 it was shown

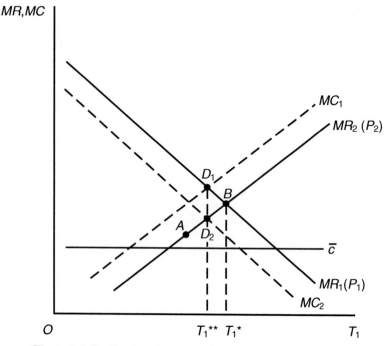

Figure 3.2 Implications for competitive balance of a salary cap

that, over time, there has been a trend towards the erosion of both explicit and implicit mechanisms for revenue sharing in English league football. Intuition might suggest that by causing the gap between rich and poor to widen, this is likely to create greater competitive imbalance. But as before, intuition turns out to be misleading. Suppose each team keeps only a proportion, λ, of its own gate revenues, while the remaining $(1-\lambda)$ are awarded to the other team (with $0.5 < \lambda \le 1$). The net revenues of teams 1 and team 2, after sharing, are as follows:

$$NR_1 = \lambda R_1 + (1-\lambda)R_2 \qquad NR_2 = (1-\lambda)R_1 + \lambda R_2 \tag{3.4}$$

The revised marginal revenue functions are:

$$MNR_1 = \frac{\partial NR_1}{\partial T_1} = \lambda \beta P_1^\alpha W_1^{\beta-1} - (1-\lambda)\beta P_2^\alpha W_2^{\beta-1}$$

$$MNR_2 = \frac{\partial NR_2}{\partial T_2} = -(1-\lambda)\beta P_1^\alpha W_1^{\beta-1} + \lambda \beta P_2^\alpha W_2^{\beta-1} \tag{3.5}$$

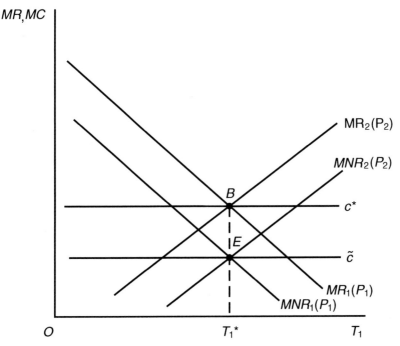

Figure 3.3 Implications for competitive balance of revenue sharing

Using (3.5) and returning to the assumption of equal marginal costs ($\gamma = 0$ and $\delta = 1$ in (3.1)), it is easy to demonstrate that the condition for $MNR_1 = MNR_2$ is the same as (3.3), and is therefore unaffected by λ. As shown in figure 3.3, the competitive balance equilibrium is at E, with team 1 hiring T_1^* units of talent as at B. Under free agency, however, the equilibrium wage rate is reduced to $\tilde{c} < c^*$. As before, there is a transfer of rent, this time from the players to the teams. The small-market team benefits most from the revenue sharing arrangement.

Intuitively, the marginal benefit to each team of hiring an extra unit of talent is λ times the marginal effect on its own gate revenue resulting from the increase in its win ratio, plus $(1 - \lambda)$ times the (negative) marginal effect on the other team's gate revenue resulting from the reduction in its win ratio. Both teams' marginal revenues are reduced when revenue sharing is introduced. Because both teams are affected equally, the location of the equilibrium distribution of playing talent does not change. But there is a reduction in the equilibrium free-agency wage rate: teams do not compete as fiercely to attract talent if part of the additional revenue which that talent generates is pooled. Revenue sharing therefore tends to depress player compensation, but does not affect competitive balance.[4] Conversely, wage inflation would be an expected consequence of the erosion or abolition of revenue sharing arrangements.

The conclusion that the equilibrium distribution of talent and competitive balance are unaffected by revenue sharing has been qualified by Atkinson, Stanley and Tschirhart (1988), Kesenne (1996, 2000) and Rascher (1997). If teams pursue utility or revenue rather than profit maximising objectives, with each team's utility or revenue depending on its win ratio, then revenue sharing does affect the equilibrium distribution of talent. If revenue depends not only on the relative values of T_1 and T_2 (which determine the win ratio) but also on their absolute values, on the grounds that spectator demand is sensitive to the overall quality of talent on view, it can be shown that revenue sharing affects the equilibrium distribution of talent under both profit maximising and utility maximising assumptions.

Vrooman (2000) makes a number of policy recommendations on the basis of the North American professional team sports literature. In MLB, the continued application of the reserve clause to players with below six years' service simultaneously leads to over-payment of free-agent talent (owing to its limited supply) and the exploitation of reserved players. Reducing the free-agency service requirement from six to four years would address both distortions, without reinforcing the competitive dominance of the big-market teams (according to the invariance result). The suggested introduction in MLB of a salary cap, in contrast, would be a retrograde step, likely to simultaneously increase player exploitation and reduce competitive balance.

The open model

This sub-section describes an adaptation of the closed model, to the case where player labour market conditions are open. In the open model, there is no constraint on the availability of talent, which can be traded freely with teams from outside the domestic league. Each team can therefore increase its stock of playing talent, without simultaneously depleting the stock held by the other team. Each player's reservation wage is the wage he could command by signing for another team either within or outside

---

[4] Fort and Quirk (1995) show that this conclusion is qualified if, as is actually the case in North America, revenue comprises two components: gate revenue which is shared, and local TV revenue which is captured wholly by the home team. In this case, variation in the proportion of gate revenue which is shared does affect the distribution of talent between the two teams.

the domestic league. For simplicity, it can be assumed that the wage per unit of talent, c, is determined in the international players' labour market, and is therefore exogenous to the model.

This formulation seems more useful than the closed model for the analysis of European football, especially since the liberalisation of various institutional features of the players' labour market in the mid-1990s. In fact, it is of some interest to compare directly the equilibrium properties of the closed and open models. Although the analogy is rather stylised, the pre-1995 regulations in European football, under which teams could field no more than three overseas players, might be interpreted as comparable to a (partially) closed model, in which teams had to rely primarily on the domestic transfer market to improve their playing squads. Since 1995, however, the labour market has become very much more open, with many of the top teams now more likely to acquire new players from continental Europe or further afield,[5] than from other clubs in their domestic leagues (see also chapter 4).

In the open model, the marginal revenues of teams 1 and 2, obtained by differentiating (3.1) under the assumption that the total stock of playing talent $T_1 + T_2$ is variable, are as follows:

$$MR_1 = \frac{\partial R_1}{\partial T_1} = \beta P_1^\alpha W_1^{\beta-1} T_2/(T_1+T_2)^2$$

$$MR_2 = \frac{\partial R_2}{\partial T_2} = \beta P_2^\alpha W_2^{\beta-1} T_1/(T_1+T_2)^2 \qquad (3.6)$$

Retaining the assumption of equal marginal costs ($\gamma = 0$ and $\delta = 1$ in (3.1)), using the equilibrium condition $MR_1 = MR_2$, and exploiting the fact that $T_1/T_2 = W_1/W_2$, (3.6) can be manipulated to obtain a revised expression (corresponding to (3.3)) for the equilibrium 'ratio of win ratios':

$$W_1/W_2 = (P_1/P_2)^{\alpha/(2-\beta)} \qquad (3.7)$$

For any given set of values for P_1, P_2, α and β, (3.7) produces a smaller equilibrium value of W_1/W_2 in the open model than does (3.3) in the closed model. In the open model, the acquisition of an extra unit of talent by one team does not deplete the talent held by the other. Its impact on the acquiring team's win ratio and revenue is therefore smaller than in the

---

[5] In a Premier League match against Southampton played in December 1999, Chelsea made a small piece of history by becoming the first English team to name 11 non-British players in their starting line-up for a league fixture.

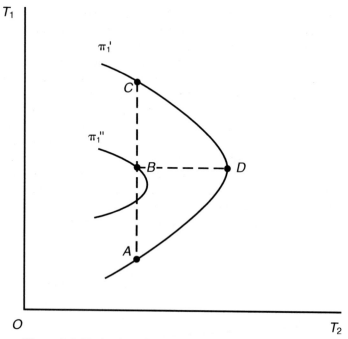

Figure 3.4 Derivation of teams' iso-profit curves, open model

closed model. It becomes harder for the big-market team to achieve dominance; by buying players it strengthens its own squad, but it does not weaken the other team's squad. The big-market team does not find it profitable to dominate the league to the same extent as in the closed model, so competition becomes more balanced.

At this point, the algebra for the open model becomes more complex and will not be pursued. A diagrammatic treatment of this model, however, is still possible. Because T_1 and T_2 can vary independently, a new diagram showing *iso-profit curves* for the two teams is required. An iso-profit curve for team 1 shows all combinations of values for T_1 and T_2 that produce identical profits for team 1. For each value of profit that team 1 could earn, there is a separate iso-profit curve. Similarly there is another complete set of iso-profit curves for team 2.

Figure 3.4 illustrates the construction of iso-profit curves for team 1. Starting at A, where T_1 is small relative to T_2, team 1 earns a certain profit, say π_1', but could improve by employing more talent (especially as team 1 has the higher home-town population). As T_1 is increased while T_2 is held constant, B is approached. Team 1's win ratio increases, and so too does its revenue, by an amount that exceeds its increase in costs. Team 1's profit therefore increases to π_1'' at B. Will profit continue to increase if team 1 carries on increasing T_1 indefinitely? The answer must be 'no'. Eventually, diminishing returns set in: T_1 becomes so large relative to T_2 that team 1's win ratio approaches one. Further increases in talent make little difference to the win ratio or to revenue, but they do add to costs. Team 1's profit starts to fall, eventually returning to π_1' at C.

Suppose team 1 had remained at B, but team 2 had responded to the initial increase in T_1 by hiring some additional talent itself. An increase in T_2 while T_1 is held constant must reduce team 1's win ratio and revenue, while leaving its costs unaltered. Therefore team 1's profit falls, eventually returning to π_1' at D. There is now enough information to locate team 1's iso-profit curve for a profit of π_1', which connects points A, D and C. Similarly, there must be another iso-profit curve for the higher profit of π_1'', passing through (and following a similar path on either side of) point B.

Figure 3.5 shows the complete sets of iso-profit curves for both team 1 and team 2 on the same diagram. Those for team 2 have a curvature similar to those for team 1, but relative to the vertical (rather than the horizontal) axis. Also shown on figure 3.5 are the *reaction functions* for the two teams. Team 1's reaction function DE shows, for each value of T_2, the value of T_1 that would produce the maximum profit attainable by team 1. It is located by joining the 'peaks' (relative to the vertical axis) of the team 1 iso-profit curves. Similarly, team 2's reaction function FG shows, for each value of T_1, the value of T_2 that would produce the maximum profit attainable by team 2. It is located by joining the peaks (relative to the horizontal axis) of the team 2 iso-profit curves. The dotted 45-degree ray from the origin OA shows all points at which $T_1 = T_2$, and at which there is perfect competitive balance. The ray OB shows all points which satisfy (3.7), at which $MR_1 = MR_2$ in the open model. For purposes of comparison, the ray OC shows all points which satisfy (3.3), at which $MR_1 = MR_2$ in the closed model.

Under profit maximising assumptions, the Cournot–Nash equilibrium is at the intersection of the two reaction functions, at point L. Here, both teams are maximising their own profit, on the assumption that the quantity of talent employed by the other team is fixed at its current level. L is located on OB, so the condition $MR_1 = MR_2$ is satisfied. L is not necessarily the only equilibrium consistent with profit maximising assumptions, however. Starting from L, suppose team 1 is aware of team 2's reactions. Team 1 can anticipate that if it reduces its quantity of talent from T_1' to T_1'', team 2 will react by adjusting from T_2' to T_2'', thereby returning to team 2's reaction function at M. Despite having departed from its own reaction function, team 1 is rewarded for its ability to anticipate team 2's

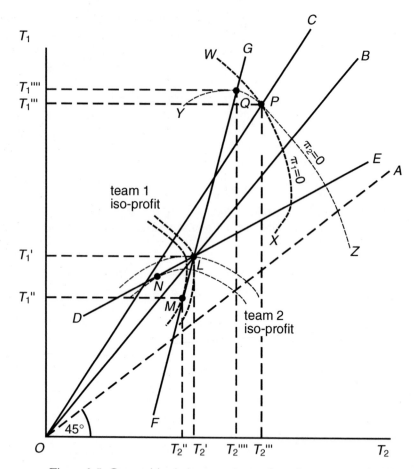

Figure 3.5 Competitive balance under profit and revenue maximising assumptions, open model

reaction by earning a higher profit at point M than at L. In the terminology of classical duopoly theory, M is a Stackelberg equilibrium.

It is worth noting that $MR_1 > MR_2$ at M. Team 1 refrains from buying players (either from team 2 or from outside the league), however, because it anticipates that if it did so, team 2 would respond in kind, and the equilibrium would quickly revert back towards L. If, as described above, the big-market team acts strategically (by using its ability to anticipate the other team's reaction to enhance its profit), competition becomes more balanced than at the Cournot–Nash equilibrium.

Conversely if the small-market team acts strategically, the Stackelberg equilibrium is at N, and competition becomes less balanced.[6]

As seen previously, the profit maximisation assumption is perhaps more controversial in European football than in North American professional team sports.[7] What happens to competitive balance in the open model if it is assumed instead that all teams seek to maximise their win ratio, subject only to a financial constraint that limits the talent they can afford to hire? In economic terms, this can be formalised using an assumption of revenue maximisation, subject to a minimum profit constraint. This is suitable because revenue is a direct function of win ratio. For simplicity a zero profit constraint can be assumed (each club must at least break even). It would make no difference to the formal properties of the model, however, if the profit constraint were negative, implying that club owners were prepared to tolerate a specified level of loss.

By setting revenue equal to cost for both teams in (3.1), it is easily demonstrated that the equilibrium condition under constrained revenue maximisation is the same as (3.3). This equilibrium is located at P in figure 3.5, at the intersection of the two teams' zero profit iso-profit curves WX and YZ, and on the ray OC showing the combinations of T_1 and T_2 that satisfy (3.3). Both teams spend more heavily on talent than under profit maximising assumptions (team 1 relatively more so than team 2), although in terms of its effect on win ratios, much of the extra spending tends to cancel itself out. Competition, however, tends to be less balanced under constrained revenue maximisation than under profit maximisation.

As before, by acting strategically and anticipating team 2's reactions, team 1 is capable of doing better than at P. Starting at P, if team 1 can afford to incur temporary losses by increasing its talent from T_1''' to T_1'''', it can force team 2 to reduce from T_2''' to T_2''''. Eventually Q is attained:

---

[6] An unrealistic feature of this formulation is that *both* teams could become more profitable than at point L by simultaneously reducing their stocks of talent in the same proportions, moving 'south-west' along the ray OB towards the origin. If revenue depends only on the relative values of T_1 and T_2 (which determine the win ratio) and not on their absolute values, both teams would have incentives to shed all of their talented players and field less expensive journeymen. To prevent this from happening in the model, revenues could (realistically) be made partly dependent on the quality of talent fielded by the home team or by both teams. This kind of adjustment adds to the algebra, but does not affect any of the main qualitative conclusions of this sub-section. Hausman and Leonard (1997) also make each team's revenue a function of the quality of other teams, in order to study the positive externality which arises if superstars help generate gate or television revenues for teams other than their own (see below).

[7] Ferguson *et al.* (1991) use a standard approach to test the assumption of profit maximising behaviour on the part of teams participating in the North American National Hockey League. The results tend to support the profit maximising hypothesis.

this is the only point at which team 2 can break even if team 1 hires T_1''''. At Q team 1 has a higher win ratio and higher revenue than at P, and also makes a positive profit. Competition, however, has become still more unbalanced. Since team 1 is not bound by the profit constraint at Q, would it be advisable for team 1 to invest even further in additional talent? The answer is probably not. Anywhere to the 'north' of Q, team 2 is unable to break even at any value of T_2, and is therefore insolvent. Because of the joint nature of production, this outcome is presumably in neither team's interest.

This sub-section concludes with a summary of the main findings. Other things being equal, a change from a closed to an open player labour market should make competition within the league more balanced. Under open conditions, it becomes harder for a rich team to use its spending power to achieve league dominance by monopolising the best of a limited supply of talent. In the open model, competition should be more balanced if teams pursue profit maximising objectives than if they pursue traditional sporting objectives of win ratio or revenue maximisation, subject to a financial constraint. Profit maximising teams tend not to over-spend on players, and this makes for a more balanced league competition. With constrained revenue maximisation, the strength of each club's financial muscle is the decisive factor in determining expenditure on talent, so competition tends to be less balanced. In either case, strategic behaviour by the big-market club is likely to strengthen these conclusions.

The two-team closed model does of course emphasise the degree of interdependence between the teams, which would be lower in an n-team league. On the other hand, the comments of Kevin Keegan, the buying manager in the £15 million transfer of Alan Shearer from Blackburn Rovers to Newcastle United in the summer of 1996, demonstrate that team managers at the top level are highly conscious of the interdependence of their actions. During the 1996 season, Newcastle had been Manchester United's closest rival for the Premier League title. '[W]hatever happened, we knew that if we had not beaten Manchester United to Shearer's signature, it would have finished the league as a contest . . . The combination of Shearer and United, the way they played and the pace they possessed, would have been devastating, and we could not let it take place' (Keegan, 1999, p. 327).

Empirical investigations and extensions

The most popular empirical test of the propositions of the closed model for North American sports is based on a simple measure of competitive balance in any one season:

(Actual standard deviation of win ratios across teams) ÷

(Expected standard deviation of win ratios if all teams were equal in strength)

If all teams competing in a league are of equal strength, the probability that any team wins or loses an individual match (ignoring draws and home advantage) is 0.5. It can be shown that the expected or ideal standard deviation in the denominator of the above expression is $0.5/\sqrt{n}$, where n is the number of matches played by each team. The higher the actual standard deviation of win ratios relative to this ideal standard deviation, the greater the degree of competitive imbalance. Fort and Quirk (1995) and Vrooman (1995) both demonstrate that this ratio did not change significantly following the introduction of free-agency in baseball in 1976, lending support to the invariance result. With limited data, Fort and Quirk find that the introduction of the rookie draft by the NFL in 1936 made no difference to competitive balance in football. Their findings for baseball are more ambiguous: there was no significant change in the NL, but some increase in competitive balance in the AL, following the introduction of the draft in 1965. Finally, Vrooman attributes a reduction in competitive balance in basketball in the late 1980s and early 1990s to the NBA's adoption of the salary cap in 1983, using the argument summarised in figure 3.2. Vrooman uses separate empirical estimates of the parameters of (3.1) for baseball, football and basketball to predict W_1/W_2 for a stylised two-team league in each case. These suggest that basketball should be the most unbalanced of the three sports: a prediction that is confirmed by the data.

Bennett and Fizel (1994) use similar methods to investigate the effect on college football of the Supreme Court's 1984 decision to end the collective negotiation of television contracts by the National Collegiate Athletic Association (NCAA), and award colleges the right to negotiate their own deals individually. The concern that this would reduce competitive balance by directing the majority of coverage and revenue towards the more powerful colleges is not substantiated by the empirical findings: there is no evidence of systematic changes in the standard deviations of win ratios after 1984. If anything competitive balance may have improved slightly. Regressions show that teams with high 'tradition' scores (compiled from historical television screenings' data), which would have been expected to benefit most from individual bargaining, actually performed slightly worse than expected in terms of win ratios post-1984.

Grier and Tollison (1994) use different methods to investigate the effect of the rookie draft in American football. By estimating regressions of win ratio on lagged win ratio and each team's average order in the draft over the previous three, four or five seasons, they find that teams that draft early tend to benefit subsequently by winning significantly more games. This suggests the draft does tend to enhance competitive balance, contrary to the invariance result.

Taking a longer-term perspective, Eckard (1998) examines the effect on competitive balance in college football of a range of restrictions on player recruitment, eligibility and compensation that were introduced by the NCAA in 1952. Pooled cross-sectional time series data is used to decompose the overall variance in win ratios into a time component for each team and a cumulative component across teams:

$$\sum_i \sum_t (W_{i,t} - 0.5)^2/NT$$

$$= \sum_i \sum_t (W_{i,t} - \overline{W}_i)^2/NT + \sum_i (\overline{W}_i - 0.5)^2/N \qquad (3.8)$$

where $W_{i,t}$ is team i's win ratio in season t; N is the number of teams; T is the number of years; and $\overline{W}_i = \sum_t W_{i,t}/T$. Post-1952, there was a reduction in the first term and an increase in the second term on the right-hand side of (3.8). This suggests that the regulations made competition less balanced: differences between strong and weak teams became more entrenched, resulting in a reduction in the variation of each team's performance over time and an increase in the variation in average performance between teams. This finding is confirmed using a variety of other competitive balance indicators, including several championship dominance measures.

Hausman and Leonard (1997) demonstrate empirically that between 1989 and 1992, the match attendances and television ratings achieved by clubs generally in the NBA were enhanced significantly in matches involving three basketball superstars: Larry Bird, Michael Jordan and Magic Johnson. As well as generating revenue for their own teams, superstars also have a positive effect on the revenues of opponents. This positive externality may have implications for competitive balance, and for the efficient distribution of talent between the league's member clubs. Under profit maximising assumptions, small-market teams tend to free ride and hire less talent than they would in the absence of the externality. The distribution of talent is therefore weighted more heavily in favour of big-market teams, and competition is less balanced. The equilibrium is also inefficient, in the sense that it fails to maximise league revenues.

Hausman and Leonard argue against the salary cap as a mechanism for correcting this imbalance. They suggest that the salary cap is likely to cause a substantial departure from the efficient equilibrium in the other direction, distributing talent too heavily in favour of small-market teams, and over-compensating for the effect of the superstar externality.

In a recent application of the closed model to European football, Hoehn and Szymanski (1999) investigate the implications for competitive balance in the domestic league of involvement of big-market teams in European competition. While team 2's revenue function depends only on its win ratio against team 1 in domestic competition, team 1's total revenues are obtained from both domestic and European competition. In the latter, team 1 competes against a European team with a similar (large) home-town population. Team 1 has an incentive to invest more heavily in talent than it otherwise would, in order to achieve a reasonable win ratio in Europe and maximise profits from both competitions. The effect is to make competition more unbalanced in the domestic league. The higher the proportion of team 1's total revenue derived from Europe, the greater is the degree of domestic imbalance. The decline in team 2's win ratio reduces team 2's revenue, perhaps to the point where profits become unattainable and losses inevitable. At this point the domestic league may cease to be financially viable, and may even close down. To avoid this outcome, Hoehn and Szymanski advocate the creation of a European league for the leading teams, which would entail their complete withdrawal from their domestic leagues. The present arrangements, requiring these teams to participate simultaneously in both domestic and European competition, are unlikely to be sustainable in the long term for the reasons outlined above.

Hoehn and Szymanski provide an analysis of a situation that manifestly does create serious tensions for the leading teams when balancing their domestic and European commitments. Not least among the concerns are the sheer physical demands on players of regular involvement in two matches per week. To some extent, however, these pressures may eventually help foster competitive balance in the domestic league: teams playing in Europe may choose to rest key players for domestic matches, or may lose matches they would normally expect to win as a result of tiredness or de-motivation. As yet, experience of regular league competition at European level may be insufficient for clubs or policy makers to be completely confident that gate and television revenues would hold up if 'Europe' were to become the norm for the leading clubs, rather than a glamorous distraction. The prospects for the eventual creation of a European Super League are discussed further in chapter 9.

3.2 Patterns in football league match results

Average home and away performance

The theoretical models of the economics of sports leagues reviewed in section 3.1 are concerned with the degree of competitive balance between league member teams, which in turn determines the extent of uncertainty of outcome for the destination of the league championship. In sections 3.2 and 3.3, the emphasis shifts towards an empirical analysis of uncertainty of outcome for individual match results in football. The discussion begins by identifying some simple facts about match results and goal scoring records.

Table 3.1 shows, for each season between 1973 and 1999 inclusive, the proportions of English league football matches that resulted in home wins, draws and away wins, and the average numbers of goals scored per match by the home and away teams and in total. Over this period as a whole, there has been a marked improvement in the average performance of away teams, and a corresponding deterioration in the performance of home teams. Between the early 1970s and the late 1990s, the proportion of matches resulting in away wins rose by about 7 per cent, from around 20 per cent to 27 per cent, while the proportion of home wins fell by the same amount, from around 52 per cent to 45 per cent. The proportion of draws hardly changed, remaining at around 28 per cent throughout the period. Perhaps the most striking feature of table 3.1 is the dramatic jump in the average number of goals scored by away teams, which coincided with the introduction of the award of three points (rather than two) for a win in the English league, from the 1982 season onwards.

Naturally, inspecting the data in table 3.1 makes one wonder whether the long-term erosion of the importance of home advantage is attributable solely to changes in incentives arising from the introduction of three rather than two league points for a win, or whether it reflects changes in the underlying processes or 'technologies' which generate match results. Such changes might include improvements in training methods enabling players to perform more consistently away from home, or improvements in the quality of transportation making away travel less onerous. Because England's adoption of 'three points for a win' pre-dated the implementation of the same change in a number of other leading football nations by more than a decade, some international comparisons of home and away win ratios and goal-scoring records should shed light on this matter.

Table 3.2 summarises the relevant data for teams in the top divisions of England, France, Germany, Scotland and Spain, for seasons 1973 to 1999 inclusive. For England the data are aggregated into three nine-

Table 3.1. *Percentages of home wins, draws and away wins and average number of goals scored by home and away teams per season, English league, 1973–1999*

Season	Home wins (per cent)	Draws (per cent)	Away wins (per cent)	Average goals per game: home team	Average goals per game: away team
1973	51.7	28.4	19.9	1.57	0.92
1974	48.9	30.2	21.0	1.51	0.92
1975	52.4	27.9	19.7	1.59	0.92
1976	50.2	27.7	22.1	1.59	0.99
1977	51.9	27.9	20.2	1.66	0.99
1978	50.1	30.9	19.0	1.62	0.98
1979	48.0	29.6	22.4	1.55	1.01
1980	49.9	27.9	22.2	1.58	0.98
1981	49.6	28.0	22.4	1.53	0.94
1982	47.1	27.4	25.5	1.53	1.07
1983	52.0	26.3	21.6	1.72	1.06
1984	50.8	26.0	23.2	1.69	1.06
1985	50.1	24.3	25.6	1.62	1.10
1986	50.1	24.6	25.3	1.69	1.11
1987	48.9	27.4	23.7	1.55	1.05
1988	46.1	27.3	26.6	1.55	1.08
1989	46.8	28.6	24.6	1.58	1.08
1990	46.8	27.3	25.9	1.54	1.09
1991	48.4	27.6	24.1	1.56	1.06
1992	47.3	27.1	25.6	1.51	1.07
1993	46.5	26.3	27.1	1.57	1.12
1994	45.6	27.4	27.0	1.53	1.14
1995	46.4	27.5	26.1	1.51	1.08
1996	45.0	29.6	25.3	1.48	1.06
1997	46.4	28.1	25.5	1.47	1.03
1998	47.9	27.8	24.3	1.51	1.05
1999	45.0	28.0	27.0	1.46	1.08

Source: Match results' data set.

season periods (seasons 1973 to 1981 inclusive; 1982 to 1990; and 1991 to 1999). Evidently the post-1982 improvement in the performance of away teams identified for the English league as a whole in table 3.1 also applies to the Division 1 teams shown in table 3.2. For the other four countries, the data are similarly aggregated, except for the final nine-year period which is split into two sub-periods at the point when 'three points for a win' was introduced: the 1995 season in France and Scotland, and the 1996 season in Germany and Spain.

The results for France, Germany and Spain indicate that long-term

Table 3.2. *Percentages of home wins, draws and away wins and average number of goals scored by home and away teams per season, international comparisons, 1973–1999*

Seasons	Home wins (per cent)	Draws (per cent)	Away wins (per cent)	Average goals per game: home team	Average goals per game: away team
England					
1973–81	49.6	28.7	21.7	1.58	1.00
1982–90[a]	48.4	26.3	25.3	1.58	1.07
1991–9[a]	45.7	28.5	25.8	1.52	1.09
France					
1973–81	57.0	25.1	18.0	1.92	1.01
1982–90	55.1	27.4	17.4	1.67	0.87
1991–4	51.7	31.7	16.6	1.45	0.76
1995–9[a]	49.2	31.0	19.8	1.47	0.87
Germany					
1973–81	54.3	25.5	20.1	2.29	1.32
1982–90	50.9	27.7	21.5	2.18	1.26
1991–5	45.4	31.2	23.4	1.76	1.19
1996–9[a]	44.9	29.3	25.8	1.73	1.22
Scotland					
1973–81	46.7	24.7	28.5	1.62	1.21
1982–90	45.4	25.3	29.3	1.53	1.14
1991–4	40.7	29.3	30.0	1.36	1.11
1995–9[a]	43.4	27.3	29.2	1.51	1.16
Spain					
1973–81	61.6	25.1	13.3	1.74	0.79
1982–90	53.6	26.9	19.5	1.57	0.88
1991–5	50.4	28.4	21.2	1.51	0.94
1996–9[a]	47.9	27.1	25.0	1.60	1.09

Note:
[a] Denotes three league points awarded for a win.
Source: Match results' data set.

erosion of the importance of home advantage is very much an international phenomenon, which has in fact been taking place at a faster rate in these three countries than in England. No doubt this partly reflects the fact that home advantage counted for more in these countries than it did in England in the 1970s. Since then a process of international convergence has been underway; the differences between countries were very much greater at the start of the period covered by table 3.2 than at the end. Nevertheless in France and Spain in particular, and in Germany to a lesser extent, the short-term impact of the introduction of 'three points for a win' in the mid-1990s was the same as in England at the start of the 1980s: an immediate increase in the average number of goals scored by the away team, and a corresponding increase in the proportion of matches finishing in away wins.

The pattern for Scotland is rather different. The proportion of away wins has always been significantly higher in Scotland than in any of the other four countries, but has changed very little over the 27-year period covered by table 3.2. There has been a slight reduction in the proportion of home wins, however, matched by a similar increase in the proportion of draws. The relatively strong performance of away teams presumably reflects a high level of competitive imbalance in the Scottish league: home advantage tends to have less effect on the results of matches between teams that are very unequal than between teams that are evenly balanced. It is likely that the Scottish data are also affected to a greater extent than those for other countries by a series of changes to the league and divisional structure during the 1970s, 1980s and 1990s, which had significant implications for competitive balance. This may also explain the absence of any clear 'three points for a win' effect in Scotland. The introduction of the latter in the 1995 season coincided with a reduction in the number of Premier Division teams from 12 to 10. Other things being equal this would be expected to improve competitive balance, and therefore increase the importance of home advantage. This latter effect appears to have dominated the 'three points for a win' effect in Scotland, since the proportion of home wins was higher and the proportion of away wins lower between 1996 and 1999 than between 1991 and 1995.

Returning to data for the English league in its entirety, tables 3.3–3.5 show the percentage distributions of the numbers of goals scored in each match by the home and away teams based on league match results between the 1973 and 1999 seasons (inclusive). The same tabulations are also compiled, from match results data for a smaller number of seasons, by Dixon and Coles (1997). Table 3.3 reports the results for the nine seasons from 1973 to 1981 inclusive, referred to in this section as $P1$ (period 1). Tables 3.4 and 3.5 report the same results for 1982 to 1990 ($P2$), and 1991 to 1999 ($P3$), respectively. The start of $P2$ corresponds to the change from two to three points being awarded for a win, from the 1982 season onwards.

By way of illustration, table 3.5 indicates that of all matches that took place in $P3$, 8.6 per cent finished as 0-0 draws, 11.2 per cent finished as 1-0 wins for the home team, and 7.5 per cent finished as 0-1 wins for the away team. A 1-1 draw was the most common outcome, in 12.9 per cent

Table 3.3. *Joint and marginal percentage distributions of goals scored by home and away teams, English league, 1973–1981*

		Goals scored by the away team							
		0	1	2	3	4	5	6+	Total
	0	9.3	6.7	3.2	1.1	0.3	0.0	0.0	20.7
Goals	1	12.0	13.2	5.1	2.0	0.5	0.1	0.0	32.9
scored	2	9.3	9.4	5.2	1.3	0.3	0.0	0.0	25.6
by	3	5.1	4.7	2.4	0.9	0.1	0.0	0.0	13.2
the	4	2.0	1.7	0.9	0.3	0.1	0.0	0.0	5.1
home	5	0.7	0.7	0.4	0.2	0.0	0.0	0.0	1.9
team	6+	0.2	0.2	0.2	0.0	0.0	0.0	0.0	0.6
	Total	38.6	36.6	17.3	5.9	1.3	0.3	0.1	100.0

Source: Match results' data set.

Table 3.4. *Joint and marginal percentage distributions of goals scored by home and away teams, English league, 1982–1990*

		Goals scored by the away team							
		0	1	2	3	4	5	6+	Total
	0	7.8	7.2	3.5	1.6	0.4	0.1	0.0	20.7
Goals	1	10.6	12.5	5.9	2.2	0.7	0.2	0.0	32.2
scored	2	8.2	9.5	5.2	1.7	0.4	0.1	0.0	25.2
by	3	4.4	4.8	2.7	1.0	0.2	0.1	0.0	13.3
the	4	2.2	2.0	1.0	0.5	0.1	0.0	0.0	5.8
home	5	0.7	0.7	0.4	0.1	0.1	0.0	0.0	2.0
team	6+	0.3	0.3	0.1	0.0	0.0	0.0	0.0	0.8
	Total	34.3	37.0	18.8	7.3	2.0	0.5	0.1	100.0

Source: Match results' data set.

of all matches. The results in table 3.4 for *P2* are very similar. A comparison of both of these sets of results with those for *P1* reported in table 3.3 lends further credence to the suggestion that the change from two to three points for a win had the desired effect and encouraged attacking play, particularly by away teams. In *P1*, the proportion of matches that finished 0-0 was 9.3 per cent, a higher percentage than in either of the two subsequent periods. Similarly among other low-scoring results, the proportions of 1-0 home wins (12.0 per cent) and 1-1 draws (13.2 per cent) were higher in *P1* than subsequently. There was, however, a smaller

Table 3.5. *Joint and marginal percentage distributions of goals scored by home and away teams, English league, 1991–1999*

| | | Goals scored by the away team | | | | | | | |
		0	1	2	3	4	5	6+	Total
	0	8.6	7.5	4.0	1.4	0.4	0.1	0.0	22.2
Goals	1	11.2	12.9	6.4	2.3	0.6	0.1	0.1	33.6
scored	2	8.1	9.4	4.9	1.7	0.5	0.2	0.0	24.9
by	3	4.3	4.5	2.5	1.1	0.3	0.0	0.0	12.7
the	4	1.4	1.6	0.9	0.4	0.1	0.0	0.0	4.5
home	5	0.6	0.6	0.3	0.1	0.0	0.0	0.0	1.6
team	6+	0.2	0.2	0.1	0.0	0.0	0.0	0.0	0.6
	Total	34.4	36.7	19.2	7.1	2.0	0.4	0.2	100.0

Source: Match results' data set.

proportion of 0-1 away wins before the introduction of three points for a win (6.7 per cent) than after.

The final columns and rows of tables 3.3–3.5 show the marginal probability distributions of goals per match scored by the home and away teams, respectively, calculated by summing horizontally across the other columns and vertically down the other rows of each table. For example, table 3.5 indicates that the home team failed to score in 22.2 per cent of matches played in $P3$, and the home team scored once in 33.6 per cent of these matches. Similarly, the away team failed to score in 34.4 per cent of these matches, and scored once in 36.7 per cent of these matches. For the away teams in particular, there has been a marked change in the shape of the marginal probability distribution of goals scored. The modal (most frequent) number of away goals scored changed from zero in $P1$, to one in $P2$ and $P3$. After increasing from 0.98 in $P1$ to 1.08 in $P2$, the average number of away team goals per game remained unchanged in $P3$. For the home teams, the marginal distribution of goals scored was similar in periods 1 and 2, but dropped significantly in $P3$. The average numbers of goals scored by the home team were 1.58, 1.61 and 1.51, respectively in the three periods. Overall, the improvement in the performance of away teams over the last two decades was attributable initially (in the 1980s) to an improvement in their offensive or goal scoring prowess, and has been sustained subsequently (in the 1990s) by an improvement in their defensive capacity to avoid conceding goals.

Tables 3.6 and 3.7 show the conditional distributions for the numbers of goals scored by the home and away team. To save space, only the results

Table 3.6. *Percentage distributions of goals scored by home team, conditional on the number of goals scored by away team, English league, 1991–1999*

| | | Goals scored by the away team | | | | | | |
		0	1	2	3	4	5	6+
	0	25.1	20.4	21.0	20.0	22.1	20.0	20.6
Goals	1	32.5	35.2	33.2	32.5	29.6	32.5	41.2
scored	2	23.6	25.7	25.7	24.2	24.6	36.3	17.6
by	3	12.4	12.1	13.1	15.5	15.6	5.0	5.9
the	4	4.2	4.4	4.7	6.1	5.9	5.0	14.7
home	5	1.6	1.6	1.6	1.1	1.7	1.3	0.0
team	6+	0.6	0.6	0.7	0.5	0.6	0.0	0.0
	Average	1.45	1.52	1.55	1.61	1.61	1.46	1.53

Source: Match results' data set.

for $P3$ covering the 1991 to 1999 seasons inclusive are included. The conditioning is on the number of goals scored by the opposing team. The conditional distributions can be used to identify whether there are interdependencies between the numbers of goals scored by the home and away teams in each match, or whether the numbers of goals scored by the two teams can be considered as approximately independent.

For example, the first column of table 3.6 shows, for matches in which the away team failed to score, the proportions of occasions on which the home team scored 0, 1, 2, 3, etc. goals. In 25.1 per cent of matches in which the away team failed to score, therefore, the home team also failed to score; in 32.5 per cent of matches in which the away team failed to score, the home team scored once, and so on. The second column shows the same for matches in which the away team scored once. In table 3.7, the conditioning is reversed. The first row shows, for matches in which the home team failed to score, the proportions of occasions on which the away team scored 0, 1, 2, 3 goals, and so on. The second row shows the same for matches in which the home team scored once.

If the number of goals scored by the home team and the away team are independent of each other, then the number of away goals should not affect the probabilities for the number of home goals. This means the probability distributions in each column of table 3.6 should look similar to one another (and similar to the marginal distributions for the number of home goals in table 3.5). Likewise, the number of home goals should not affect the probabilities for the number of away goals, so the probability distributions in each row of table 3.7 should also look similar to one

Table 3.7. *Percentage distributions of goals scored by away team, conditional on the number of goals scored by home team, English league, 1991–1999*

		Goals scored by the away team							
		0	1	2	3	4	5	6+	Average
	0	39.0	33.8	18.2	6.4	1.9	0.4	0.2	1.00
Goals	1	33.3	38.4	19.0	6.9	1.7	0.4	0.2	1.08
scored	2	32.7	37.9	19.8	6.9	1.9	0.6	0.1	1.10
by	3	33.7	35.1	19.8	8.7	2.4	0.2	0.1	1.12
the	4	31.7	35.3	19.7	9.6	2.5	0.5	0.6	1.20
home	5	35.2	37.2	20.0	5.2	2.1	0.3	0.0	1.03
team	6+	33.6	37.4	21.5	5.6	1.9	0.0	0.0	1.05

Source: Match results' data set.

another (and similar to the marginal distributions for the number of away goals in table 3.5). In fact, however, the probabilities do not appear to conform to this condition for independence. In table 3.7, for example, if the home team scores 0, then 0 is also the most likely score for the away team (with a probability of 0.390). The probability that the away team scores 1 is lower, at 0.338. If the home team scores 1, however, then the probability that the away team scores 0 is only 0.333, while the probability that the away team also scores 1 is higher, at 0.384. The conditional mean scores reported in the final column of table 3.7 indicate that the (conditional) average number of away goals was an increasing function of the number of home goals over the range 0 to 4 home goals. Similarly, according to the bottom row of table 3.6, the (conditional) average number of home goals was an increasing function of the number of away goals over the range 0 to 4 away goals.

In common with the results presented by Dixon and Coles (1997), these tabulations suggest that the greatest degree of interdependence occurs in low-scoring games, since the largest discrepancies between the probabilities in adjacent rows or columns are towards the top left-hand corners of tables 3.6 and 3.7. Nevertheless, it is apparent that the shapes of the conditional probability distributions do vary to some extent over the full range of values for the conditioning variable. The numbers of goals scored by the home and away teams are interdependent. This fact complicates the task of modelling match results through scores. As will be seen in section 3.3, many of the difficulties can be avoided by modelling match results directly (as home win, draw or away win) rather than indirectly (through the home and away team scores). Modelling results directly, however, does imply that potentially useful information in the scores data is discarded.

Good and poor sequences, and match result probabilities

The tabulations in the previous sub-section can be used to obtain probabilities that matches finish in home wins, draws or away wins based on historical analysis of match results. If such tabulations are used to assess these probabilities, however, no account is taken of the underlying strengths and the recent performances of the two teams contesting the match in question. In fact, it is obvious that different teams do have different strengths, which influence the probabilities for the outcome of any specific match. As well as the underlying strengths of the two teams, if either team has recently experienced a sequence of good results or poor results, this may also influence the outcome of the match in question. This influence could conceivably be in either direction:

- A recent run of good results may create confidence, increasing the probability of another good result. A recent run of poor results may sap confidence, reducing the probability of a good result. Below, this case is referred to as a positive persistence effect.

- A recent run of good results may create complacency, reducing the probability of another good result. A recent run of poor results may encourage a team to raise its efforts, or encourage the manager to make changes of personnel or tactics, increasing the probability of a good result. This case is referred to as a negative persistent effect.

Table 3.8 reports the longest sequences of consecutive results in the league match results data set between the 1973 and 1999 seasons inclusive, based on four criteria: (i) matches without a win, (ii) matches without a loss, (iii) consecutive wins, and (iv) consecutive losses. Each of these criteria can be applied to home matches, away matches and all matches.

Tables 3.9–3.12 show the probabilities of home wins, home losses, away wins and away losses, conditional on the duration of various sequences of recent results, calculated from the league match results data set. By way of illustration, the first row of table 3.9 shows that the unconditional probability of a home win is 0.485, reflecting the fact that 48.5 per cent of all matches in the data set were home wins. Subsequent rows show how the probability of a home win changes if it is calculated conditionally on the home team having experienced a sequence of results as described at the top of each column, of duration as identified at the start of each row, immediately prior to the match in question. In the first column, for example, if the home team had not lost its previous match,

Table 3.8. *Long runs of consecutive results, English league, 1973–1999*

Matches unbeaten			*Matches without a win*		
Nottm Forest	1979	42	Cambridge	1984	31
Bristol Rovers	1974	32	Oxford	1989	27
Liverpool	1988	31			
Consecutive wins			*Consecutive losses*		
Reading	1986	13	Walsall	1989	15
Newcastle	1993	13	Brighton	1973	12
Liverpool	1991	12	Stoke	1986	11
			West Bromwich	1996	11
Home matches unbeaten			*Home matches without a win*		
Liverpool	1981	63	Aldershot	1992	16
Nottm Forest	1980	51	Cambridge	1984	16
			Crystal Palace	1998	16
			Darlington	1989	16
			Nottm Forest	1999	16
Consecutive home wins			*Consecutive home losses*		
Southend	1981	18	Birmingham	1986	10
West Ham	1981	16	Doncaster	1998	8
Blackpool	1992	15	Walsall	1989	8
Fulham	1999	15			
Away matches unbeaten			*Away matches without a win*		
Nottm Forest	1979	20	Swansea	1985	46
Bristol Rovers	1974	17	Leyton Orient	1996	42
Liverpool	1988	16	Norwich	1979	41
Tottenham	1986	16			
Burnley	1973	15			
Consecutive away wins			*Consecutive away losses*		
Blackburn	1980	7	Birmingham	1979	18
Cardiff	1993	7	Bolton	1985	15
Chelsea	1989	7	Brentford	1973	15
Derby	1993	7	Brighton	1997	15
Man Utd	1994	7	Hereford	1978	15
Mansfield	1976 & 1992	7	Leicester	1987	15
Notts County	1998	7	Reading	1999	15
Reading	1986	7			

Note: Seasons quoted are the seasons in which each run ended.
Source: Match results' data set.

Table 3.9. *Probabilities of home win conditional on recent results*

					N =			
	Number of previous matches unbeaten	Number of previous matches without a win	Number of previous consecutive wins	Number of previous consecutive losses	Number of previous home matches unbeaten	Number of previous home matches without a win	Number of previous consecutive home wins	Number of previous consecutive home losses
Uncond.	0.485	0.485	0.485	0.485	0.485	0.485	0.485	0.485
N = 1	0.500	0.474	0.511	0.464	0.496	0.463	0.508	0.448
2	0.510	0.459	0.528	0.440	0.505	0.450	0.524	0.429
3	0.526	0.445	0.545	0.414	0.516	0.428	0.545	0.390
4	0.540	0.441	0.537	0.408	0.521	0.415	0.549	0.381
6	0.558	0.419	0.603	0.349	0.534	0.412	0.551	—
8	0.581	0.401	—	0.278	0.544	0.390	0.594	—
10	0.609	0.398	—	—	0.559	0.419	—	—
15	0.635	0.350	—	—	0.578	—	—	—
20	0.672	—	—	—	0.586	—	—	—

Source: Match results' data set.

Table 3.10. *Probabilities of home loss conditional on recent results*

				$N =$				
	Number of previous matches unbeaten	Number of previous matches without a win	Number of previous consecutive wins	Number of previous consecutive losses	Number of previous home matches unbeaten	Number of previous home matches without a win	Number of previous consecutive home wins	Number of previous consecutive home losses
Uncond.	0.238	0.238	0.238	0.238	0.238	0.238	0.238	0.238
$N = 1$	0.223	0.249	0.214	0.260	0.229	0.258	0.218	0.269
2	0.213	0.262	0.198	0.277	0.221	0.271	0.202	0.294
3	0.201	0.273	0.180	0.294	0.213	0.286	0.187	0.311
4	0.191	0.278	0.177	0.299	0.210	0.298	0.177	0.344
6	0.171	0.295	0.140	0.340	0.197	0.317	0.158	—
8	0.151	0.308	—	0.407	0.193	0.351	0.144	—
10	0.124	0.317	—	—	0.184	0.374	—	—
15	0.110	0.346	—	—	0.177	—	—	—
20	0.105	—	—	—	0.166	—	—	—

Source: Match results' data set.

Table 3.11. Probabilities of away win conditional on recent results

$N =$

	Number of previous matches unbeaten	Number of previous matches without a win	Number of previous consecutive wins	Number of previous consecutive losses	Number of previous away matches unbeaten	Number of previous away matches without a win	Number of previous consecutive away wins	Number of previous consecutive away losses
Uncond.	0.238	0.238	0.238	0.238	0.238	0.238	0.238	0.238
$N = 1$	0.246	0.229	0.251	0.220	0.252	0.231	0.260	0.224
2	0.257	0.223	0.270	0.211	0.269	0.224	0.288	0.215
3	0.264	0.212	0.290	0.209	0.283	0.220	0.334	0.209
4	0.279	0.209	0.308	0.220	0.298	0.215	0.347	0.201
6	0.304	0.195	0.374	0.142	0.332	0.205	—	0.188
8	0.314	0.191	—	—	0.349	0.196	—	0.185
10	0.349	0.187	—	—	0.338	0.183	—	0.168
15	0.385	0.191	—	—	—	0.170	—	—
20	0.385	—	—	—	—	0.159	—	—

Source: Match results' data set.

Table 3.12. *Probabilities of away loss conditional on recent results*

$N =$

	Number of previous matches unbeaten	Number of previous matches without a win	Number of previous consecutive wins	Number of previous consecutive losses	Number of previous away matches unbeaten	Number of previous away matches without a win	Number of previous consecutive away wins	Number of previous consecutive away losses
Uncond.	0.485	0.485	0.485	0.485	0.485	0.485	0.485	0.485
$N = 1$	0.473	0.500	0.465	0.514	0.464	0.495	0.455	0.508
2	0.458	0.509	0.437	0.532	0.446	0.503	0.421	0.521
3	0.446	0.525	0.420	0.550	0.430	0.509	0.361	0.534
4	0.431	0.529	0.407	0.565	0.413	0.517	0.359	0.543
6	0.405	0.553	0.330	0.653	0.382	0.525	—	0.562
8	0.396	0.561	—	—	0.361	0.531	—	0.584
10	0.357	0.593	—	—	0.390	0.543	—	0.575
15	0.320	0.590	—	—	—	0.543	—	—
20	0.333	—	—	—	—	0.561	—	—

Source: Match results' data set.

the (conditional) probability of a home win is 0.500, reflecting the fact that 50 per cent of all matches in which the home team had not lost its previous match finished in home wins. If the home team was unbeaten in its previous two matches, the (conditional) probability of a home win is 0.510, because 51 per cent of all matches in which the home team was unbeaten in its two previous matches finished in home wins. Subsequent columns of table 3.9 show the conditional home win probabilities for other sequences of results immediately prior to the match in question. Tables 3.10–3.12 repeat the exercise for unconditional and conditional home loss, away win and away loss probabilities. The conditional probabilities are not reported in cases where the data set provides fewer than 50 sequences of the required duration on which to base the calculation.

Tables 3.9–3.12 show that from each team's perspective, the match outcome probabilities can vary quite significantly if sequences of recent results are taken into account. For a team going into a home match on an unbeaten run of 10 matches, the unconditional probabilities of a home win, draw and away win of 0.485, 0.277 and 0.238, change to conditional probabilities of 0.609, 0.267 and 0.124, respectively.[8] For a team going into an away match on an unbeaten run of 10 matches, the same unconditional probabilities change to conditional probabilities of 0.357, 0.294 and 0.349, respectively. The conditional probabilities increase or decrease even more sharply with duration for sequences of consecutive wins or losses, than for unbeaten or win-less sequences. At the longer durations, however, the data set provides insufficient numbers of sequences of consecutive wins or losses to calculate the conditional probabilities reliably.

At first sight, tables 3.9–3.12 might appear to suggest that recent results do indeed have a major bearing on match outcomes. In general the conditional win probabilities tend to increase with the duration of a good spell (however defined), and decline with the duration of a poor spell. Can this pattern be attributed to a positive persistence effect? In fact, the answer is 'no', or at least 'not without further investigation'. The pattern in the conditional probabilities might well be explained by team heterogeneity (variation in the underlying strengths of the teams within each division) and not by short-term fluctuations in form or confidence. For example, the calculation of the probability of a win conditional on a long unbeaten spell is based mainly on the experience of the stronger teams in each division, since these naturally are the ones that tend to achieve long unbeaten spells. Such teams have an above-average probability of winning again because they are strong, but not necessarily because they

---

[8] In calculating these conditional probabilities, conditioning is on the recent results of the team in question only, and not on those of its opponent.

are recently unbeaten. In economists' terminology, sample selection effects might explain the pattern in the conditional probabilities.

A more technical approach is therefore required to disentangle the effect of team heterogeneity from that of short-term persistence effects on the conditional win, draw and loss probabilities. In the rest of this subsection, a simulation approach is used to address this issue. It does so by establishing how many unbeaten or win-less sequences, or how many sequences of consecutive wins or losses of each duration, should be observed over the course of 27 seasons, if the *only* systematic determinant of match results is team heterogeneity, and if recent results are irrelevant (except in the sense that they also reflect team heterogeneity). If the actual numbers of sequences at each duration are similar to the expected numbers obtained from the simulation exercise, this supports the hypothesis that only team heterogeneity matters. If the actual numbers of sequences of any given duration are significantly greater or smaller than the expected numbers, the same hypothesis is rejected. If the actual numbers of sequences at each duration are greater than the expected numbers, this suggests a positive persistence effect, which tends to prolong the durations of good or poor spells. Conversely, if the actual numbers are smaller than the expected numbers, this suggests a negative persistence effect, tending to curtail the durations of good or poor spells.

To generate the expected distribution of spells of various durations under the assumption that the confidence effect is zero, the modelling approach developed by Köning (2000) is adopted. It is assumed that the underlying strength of team i is represented by the parameter α_i. Importantly for the purposes of identifying persistence effects, and consistent with Köning's specification, the α_is are assumed to remain constant over the course of each season. The result of the match between home team i and away team j is simulated using the following statistical model:

$$
\begin{array}{lll}
\text{Home win} & \text{if} & \mu_2 < \alpha_i - \alpha_j + \varepsilon_{i,j} \\
\text{Draw} & \text{if} & \mu_1 < \alpha_i - \alpha_j + \varepsilon_{i,j} < \mu_2 \\
\text{Away win} & \text{if} & \alpha_i - \alpha_j + \varepsilon_{i,j} < \mu_1
\end{array}
\tag{3.9}
$$

In (3.9) μ_1 and μ_2 are parameters which control the overall proportions of home wins, draws and away wins the statistical model will generate over a large number of replications. In the simulations, values of $\varepsilon_{i,j}$ are drawn randomly from the standard normal distribution, to represent the unpredictable or random element in the match outcome.

To generate the simulated sequences of results under the assumption that only team heterogeneity matters, numerical estimates of the parameters reflecting team heterogeneity (the α_is) are first required. These are obtained using the actual data set to estimate the parameters of (3.9)

(α_i for $i = 1 \ldots n$ where n is the number of teams in the division, and μ_1 and μ_2) for each division in each of the 27 seasons. 108 estimations are required in total. Treating the 'dependent variable' as discrete and ordered (the three possible values being home win, draw and away win), the appropriate specification is the ordered probit model.[9]

The ordered probit parameter estimates for each division in each season are used to calibrate (3.9) for the purposes of generating the simulations. Having obtained these estimates, it is possible to 'replay history' and use the estimated model to create a full set of simulated match results, again under the assumption that the determinants of match results are team heterogeneity (the α_is) and luck (the $\varepsilon_{i,j}$s), but not short-term persistence effects. This is done by drawing a value of $\varepsilon_{i,j}$ randomly from the standard normal distribution for every match played in every season. The simulated match results are then generated from the team heterogeneity parameters (the estimated α_is), the estimated values of μ_1 and μ_2, and the randomly drawn $\varepsilon_{i,j}$s, according to (3.9). When the full set of simulated results for the 27-season period is complete, the numbers of 'simulated' good and poor spells (however defined) of various durations can be calculated and compared with the corresponding numbers of such spells observed in the actual data set. By examining a number of replications of the complete simulation process,[10] it is possible to establish whether the actual numbers of spells of any given duration are unusually high or low relative to the numbers generated on average by the simulations, allowing for a reasonable amount of random variation that will be found in the simulated numbers from one replication to the next.

Table 3.13 reports the actual and expected numbers of unbeaten and win-less spells, and spells of consecutive wins and losses, for various durations. The actual numbers are calculated from the league match results data set, and the expected numbers are obtained from the simulations. For purposes of illustration, the top left-hand panel of table 3.13 reports the results for unbeaten spells of durations 1 to 20 matches (as shown in column (1)). Column (2) indicates that there were 69,762 'unbeaten spells' of at least one match between the 1973 and 1999 seasons; 44,696 of these were extended to at least two matches unbeaten; 29,255 were extended to at least three matches unbeaten, and so on.

Columns (3)–(5) indicate the numbers of unbeaten spells of each duration that would be expected if the match results were generated as assumed in the statistical model, with no short-term persistence effects.

---

[9] See, for example, Greene (1999). The details of the ordered probit model are described in more detail in section 3.3, where a forecasting model for match results is developed.

[10] 200 simulations of the 27-season period are used to generate the results reported below.

Column (4) shows the mean number of unbeaten spells of each duration across the 200 replications. Columns (3) and (5) show the 5 per cent and 95 per cent percentiles for the number of unbeaten spells of each duration. The range of values between columns (3) and (5) can be interpreted as a 90 per cent confidence interval for the number of spells of each duration, based on the assumption that there are no short-term persistence effects. For example, 2,619 unbeaten spells of at least 10 matches should be observed if this assumption is correct. Making reasonable allowance for the random or unpredictable element in match results, any number of such spells between 2,435 and 2,824 would be consistent with the hypothesis that there are no short-term persistence effects. The actual number shown in column (2), however, falls outside this interval, at 2,366.

This example illustrates a consistent feature of the simulation results for all four types of spell considered in table 3.13: the actual numbers of spells of any duration are almost always smaller than the expected numbers, and often below the lower limit of the 90 per cent confidence interval. For unbeaten spells, the 'null hypothesis' of no short-term persistence effects is therefore rejected at the 10 per cent significance level at all durations between six and 13 matches. For win-less spells, the result is even stronger: the same null hypothesis is rejected at any duration of two or more matches. For spells of consecutive wins and consecutive losses, the results are similar. The actual numbers fall below the lower limit of the 90 per cent confidence interval at all durations of two or more matches for spells of consecutive wins, and for all durations between three and nine matches for spells of consecutive losses.

As discussed above, these findings suggest that there are *negative* short-term persistence effects, which tend to curtail the durations of both good and poor spells. A team currently enjoying a run of good results has a higher probability (relative to the probability conditioned only on the team's underlying strength) of a poor result in its next match, and a team on a run of poor results has a higher probability of a good result in its next match. Negative short-term persistence effects of this kind tend to curtail the durations of both good and poor spells, accounting for the patterns evident in the comparison between the actual and the simulated results shown in table 3.13.

3.3 Modelling and forecasting match results

Previous literature on modelling football results

In section 3.3 a regression model is developed to describe the patterns that can be identified in the 27-year English league match results data set

Table 3.13. *Actual and expected numbers of unbeaten and win-less spells, and spells of consecutive wins and losses, of various durations*

Duration (matches) (1)	Number of unbeaten spells				Number of win-less spells			
	Actual (2)	Expected			Actual (6)	Expected		
		Lower 5 per cent (3)	Mean (4)	Upper 5 per cent (5)		Lower 5 per cent (7)	Mean (8)	Upper 5 per cent (9)
1	69,762	69,507	69,751	69,980	69,775	69,531	69,776	70,016
2	44,696	44,435	44,747	45,055	44,463	44,512	44,815	45,143
3	29,255	29,084	29,438	29,807	28,875	29,141	29,494	29,850
4	19,527	19,465	19,806	20,182	19,140	19,473	19,816	20,161
5	13,265	13,253	13,583	13,952	12,733	13,214	13,537	13,850
6	9,158	9,212	9,487	9,814	8,589	9,121	9,391	9,666
8	4,565	4,624	4,854	5,121	4,047	4,478	4,707	4,923
10	2,366	2,435	2,619	2,824	1,982	2,303	2,473	2,649
15	580	563	668	772	361	484	583	709
20	163	141	204	268	64	112	168	240

| | Number of spells of consecutive wins | | | | | Number of spells of consecutive losses | | | |
| Duration (matches) (1) | Actual (2) | Expected | | | Actual (6) | Expected | | |
		Lower 5 per cent (3)	Mean (4)	Upper 5 per cent (5)		Lower 5 per cent (7)	Mean (8)	Upper 5 per cent (9)
1	39,592	39,322	39,575	39,813	39,582	39,346	39,574	39,785
2	14,284	14,381	14,621	14,846	14,511	14,365	14,578	14,789
3	5,422	5,657	5,847	6,028	5,605	5,613	5,759	5,917
4	2,174	2,394	2,514	2,635	2,259	2,316	2,425	2,529
5	888	1,059	1,142	1,218	931	990	1,071	1,154
6	382	487	547	612	411	439	497	557
8	88	110	142	184	92	93	123	153
10	21	24	41	64	21	20	36	54

Source: Match results' data set.

described above. Having been estimated from historical data, this model can be used to assess probabilities and generate forecasts for future match results.

In the academic literature, there are relatively few studies that seek to model match results data for football. Early contributions by Moroney (1956) and Reep, Polard and Benjamin (1971) use the poisson and negative binomial distributions to model the distributions of the numbers of goals scored per game. The aggregated approach adopted, however, precludes the generation of specific forecasts for individual matches based on information about the respective strengths of the two teams concerned. By comparing final league placings with experts' pre-season forecasts, Hill (1974) demonstrates that individual match results do nevertheless have a predictable element, and are not determined solely by chance.

Maher (1982) develops a model in which the home and away team scores follow independent poisson distributions, with means which are the product of parameters reflecting the attacking and defensive capabilities of the two teams. If H denotes the goals scored by home team i and A the goals scored by away team j, the respective probability functions are:

$$P(H=h) = \exp(-\alpha_i\beta_j) \, (\alpha_i\beta_j)^h \, / \, h!$$
and
$$P(A=a) = \exp(-\gamma_i\delta_j) \, (\gamma_i\delta_j)^a \, / \, a!$$

where α_i and β_j reflect the attacking capability of team i at home and the defensive capability of team j away, and γ_i and δ_j reflect the defensive capability of team i at home and the attacking capability of team j away. Tests show that γ_i and δ_j can be regarded as proportional to β_i and α_i respectively, so it is necessary to estimate only one set of attacking and one set of defensive parameters for each team. This can be done *ex post*, after the full set of match results has been observed, using maximum likelihood methods. The model does not predict scores or results *ex ante*. Although goodness-of-fit tests show that the model provides a reasonably accurate approximation to the data, separate examination of the observed and expected distributions of the difference between the scores of the two teams reveals a tendency to under-estimate the proportion of drawn matches. This is attributed to interdependence between the scores of the home and away teams, and is corrected by modelling scores using a bivariate poisson distribution. The marginal distributions are the same as before, but allowance is also made for positive correlation between the home and away team scores in each match.

Dixon and Coles (1997) employ Maher's (1982) modelling approach for different ends: they seek to develop a forecasting model capable of generating *ex ante* match outcome probabilities. Instead of using the bivariate poisson distribution, the marginal poisson probabilities for the scores of both teams in low-scoring games ($H \leq 1$ and $A \leq 1$) are adjusted directly to allow for interdependence, which, as already seen, appears to be greatest towards the top left-hand corners of tables 3.3–3.5. For forecasting purposes, estimation of the vectors of α_i and β_j must be based on historical data only. This is achieved using a 'pseudo-likelihood function', in which the attacking and defensive parameters are estimated from past scores, weighted by a factor that declines exponentially over time. Each team's parameters are updated from match to match, as the scores from the most recently completed matches enter the estimation.

Using a modelling framework similar to that of Dixon and Coles, Rue and Salvesen (2000) assume that the time-varying attacking and defensive parameters of all teams move up and down randomly over time. The prior estimates of these parameters are updated each time new match results information is received. An allowance is made for 'mean-reversion' in the team strength parameters (see chapter 6): this reflects the fact that neither winning runs nor losing runs tend to last forever. In the long term there is a tendency for the performance of all teams to revert towards the overall mean. Rue and Salvesen truncate all scores' data at five goals (so scores greater than five are treated as five), and incorporate a 'psychological effect' whereby team A is assumed to under-rate team B whenever A is stronger than B. The latter effect introduces an additional parameter, making the estimation more flexible.

Several researchers have investigated the impact of specific factors on match results. Barnett and Hilditch (1993), for example, investigate whether artificial playing surfaces, introduced and subsequently abandoned by several clubs during the 1980s and early 1990s, conferred (additional) home-team advantages. Ridder, Cramer and Hopstaken (1994) show that player dismissals have a negative effect on the match result from the viewpoint of the team completing the match with fewer than 11 players. Clarke and Norman (1995) use a range of non-parametric techniques to identify systematically the effect of home advantage on match results.

Dixon and Robinson (1998) investigate variations in the scoring rates of the home and away teams during the course of a match. It is well known that the scoring rate tends to increase with the duration of the match elapsed. Popular wisdom suggests this is because players tend to get tired as matches progress, increasing the likelihood of mistakes and therefore goals. There is, however, another possible explanation. When the scores of the two teams are unequal, the team that is behind has little to lose by committing more players to attack. This increases both the probability that it will score, and the probability that it will concede again.

Of course, the incentive for a trailing team to play recklessly in the hope of grabbing a goal increases as the end of the match draws near. So perhaps the observed tendency for the scoring rate to increase simply mirrors an increase (as time elapses) in the probability of the scores being unequal. In fact Dixon and Robinson find some evidence to support both hypotheses. The scoring rate does depend upon whether the scores are currently level; but even after controlling for the current score, the scoring rate still increases with the duration of the match elapsed.

Finally, Köning's (2000) approach to the modelling of match results (rather than individual team scores) using ordered probit estimation has been described in section 3.2. In common with Maher (1982), the aim is to obtain a set of parameters that describes a collection of match results *ex post*, rather than to generate forecasts or estimated probabilities *ex ante*. Köning advocates modelling results directly, rather than indirectly through scores, partly on grounds of simplicity: fewer parameters are required, the estimation procedures are more straightforward and the specified ordered probit model lends itself quite easily to the inclusion of dynamics or other explanatory variables. Furthermore, the thorny problem of interdependence between the home and away team scores is finessed completely using this approach.

Kuypers (2000) uses a variety of explanatory variables drawn from recent match results to estimate an *ex ante* forecasting model, also using ordered probit regression. These include: the average points per game and the cumulative points attained by the home and away teams in the current season; the league positions and goal differences of the two teams; and the points and goal differences obtained by the two teams from the last three games. The main focus of the paper, however, is on investigating whether the forecasts provide a basis for profitable fixed-odds betting on football match results. The full specification and estimations of the forecasting model are not presented. In the remainder of this section an explicit ordered probit regression model is developed to generate estimated *ex ante* probabilities for match outcomes, based on historical match results' data.

Specification of the model

For the purposes of describing the construction of the model, it is assumed initially that the underlying process causing matches to finish either as home wins, draws or away wins (or using statistical terminology, the underlying data generating process) was unchanged throughout the 27-year observation period (covering the seasons from 1973 to 1999 inclusive). As seen in section 3.2, this is an over-simplification. Having developed and estimated the model using data for the full 27-year period,

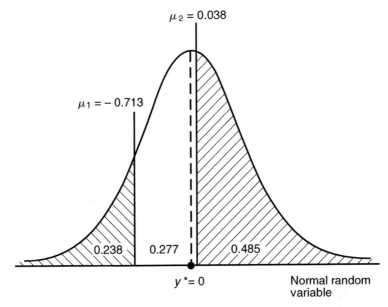

Figure 3.6 Standard normal probability density function

however, it will be possible to repeat the estimation using data for a shorter sub-period, within which the assumption of a constant data-generating process is more easily justified.

Of the 54,848 league matches played during the 27-year observation period, 26,614 (48.5 per cent) finished as home wins; 15,168 (27.7 per cent) were drawn; and 13,066 (23.8 per cent) were away wins. This implies that if any match is selected randomly from the data set, the probabilities that the match selected was a home win, a draw or an away win would be 0.485, 0.277 and 0.238, respectively (see also tables 3.9–3.12). The process of selecting a match from the data set at random and observing either a home win, a draw or an away win, can be replicated within a statistical model using the standard normal probability distribution (see figure 3.6). Because the shape of the standard normal distribution is known exactly by statisticians, the probability of drawing a value within any given numerical range can be specified precisely. For example, the probability of drawing a value less than $\mu_1 = -0.713$ is 0.238. The probability of drawing a value greater than $\mu_2 = +0.038$ is 0.485. Therefore the probability of drawing a value *within* the range $\mu_1 = -0.713$ to $\mu_2 = +0.038$ is $1 - 0.238 - 0.485 = 0.277$.

These examples are not selected arbitrarily. They are chosen to indicate the solution to the task of mimicking in a statistical model the process of selecting a match randomly and observing the result. Imagine drawing just one value at random from the standard normal distribution. Obtaining a value greater than $\mu_2 = 0.038$ is then 'equivalent' to (or has the same probability as) observing a home win. Similarly, obtaining a value between $\mu_1 = -0.713$ and $\mu_2 = +0.038$ is equivalent to observing a draw. Obtaining a value below $\mu_2 = -0.713$ is equivalent to observing an away win.

As developed so far, the statistical model treats all matches that could be chosen from the data set as having identical home-win, draw and away-win probabilities. This corresponds to the situation in which there is no information about the relative strengths of the two teams competing in the chosen match, before the match is played. Suppose, however, that when the match is chosen, information about the two teams taking part is also available, before the match outcome is observed. Such information might include data on the fundamental playing strengths of the two teams, data on their most recent results and information about the importance of the match to each team: does the match have significance for championship, promotion or relegation issues for either or both teams? Information of this kind might well change the assessment of the home-win, draw and away-win probabilities for the match in question.

In terms of the statistical model, reassessment of the probabilities can be captured by allowing variation in the mean of the normal distribution from which the random variable is drawn. Rather than drawing from the standard normal distribution with zero mean, a normal distribution with mean y^* (where y^* can be above or below zero), and a standard deviation of one can be used. Suppose for example y^* is adjusted from 0 to $+0.1$ as in figure 3.7(a). Then the probability of obtaining a value for the random variable greater than $\mu_2 = 0.038$ (still equivalent to the probability of observing a home win) becomes 0.525. The probability of obtaining a value between $\mu_1 = -0.713$ and $\mu_2 = 0.038$ (observing a draw) is 0.267, and the probability of obtaining a value below $\mu_1 = -0.713$ (observing an away win) is 0.208. Setting $y^* > 0$ therefore represents a match in which the probability of a home win is assessed to be greater than the average. Similarly, if $y^* = -0.1$ as in figure 3.7(b), the probability of a home win is below the probability when $y^* = 0$, and the probability of an away win is above the probability when $y^* = 0$.[11]

The one remaining question is, how can the data on the relative

[11] In fact, this account is an over-simplification. If y^* is allowed to vary from match to match, slight adjustments to the values of the cut-off points (in the example still assumed to be -0.713 and $+0.038$) are also needed, to ensure that the average estimated home-win, draw and away-win probabilities across all matches correspond to the actual proportions of home wins, draws and away wins in the data set.

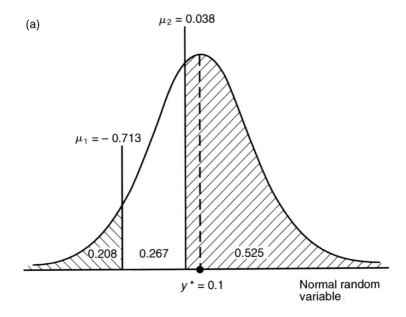

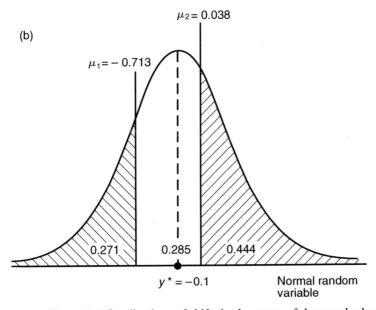

Figure 3.7 Implications of shifts in the mean of the standard normal probability density function

strengths and the recent form of the two teams be used to define the most appropriate value of y^* for the match in question? The answer comes by exploiting the wealth of statistical evidence in the 27-year data set, to construct a formula to convert suitably defined team strength, recent form and match significance variables into values of y^*. The formula is chosen so that the values of y^* which it delivers will generate match result probabilities that correspond as closely as possible to the patterns of home wins, draws and away wins that actually occurred in the data set.

The expression used to generate the value of y^* for the match between home team i and away team j, now denoted $y_{i,j}^*$, is as follows:

$$y_{i,j}^* = \alpha_{0,0}^0 P_{i,0,0}^0 + \sum_{d=-1}^{+1} \alpha_{0,1}^d P_{i,0,1}^d + \sum_{d=-1}^{+1} \alpha_{1,1}^d P_{i,1,1}^d + \sum_{d=-2}^{+2} \alpha_{1,2}^d P_{i,1,2}^d$$

$$+ \beta_{0,0}^0 P_{j,0,0}^0 + \sum_{d=-1}^{+1} \beta_{0,1}^d P_{j,0,1}^d + \sum_{d=-1}^{+1} \beta_{1,1}^d P_{j,1,1}^d + \sum_{d=-2}^{+2} \beta_{1,2}^d P_{j,1,2}^d$$

$$+ \sum_{m=1}^{M} \gamma_m^{HH} R_{i,m}^H + \sum_{n=1}^{N} \gamma_n^{HA} R_{i,n}^A + \sum_{n=1}^{N} \gamma_n^{AH} R_{j,n}^H + \sum_{m=1}^{M} \gamma_m^{AA} R_{j,m}^A$$

$$+ \delta_1 S_{i,j}^H + \delta_2 S_{i,j}^A \qquad\qquad (3.10)$$

where $P_{i,y,s}^d = p_{i,y,s}^d / n_{i,y}$, and

$p_{i,y,s}^d =$ Total 'points' (1 = win, 0.5 = draw, 0 = loss) gained by team i from matches played during 12 months prior to current match ($y = 0$), or between 12 and 24 months prior to current match ($y = 1$); in current season ($s = 0$), in previous season ($s = 1$), or two seasons previously ($s = 2$); in current division ($d = 0$), one division above or below current division ($d = +1$ or $d = -1$), or two divisions above or below current division ($d = +2$ or $d = -2$)

$n_{i,y} =$ Total matches played by team i during 12 months prior to current match ($y = 0$), or between 12 and 24 months prior to current match ($y = 1$)

$R_{i,m}^H =$ Result (1 = win, 0.5 = draw, 0 = loss) of mth most recent home match played by the home team ($m = 1 \ldots M$).

$R_{i,n}^A =$ Result (as defined above) of nth most recent away match played by the home team ($n = 1 \ldots N$)

$S_{i,j}^H =$ 1 if match has championship (D1/Prem), promotion (D2/One to D4/Three) or relegation (D1/Prem to D4/Three) significance for home team i, and does not have significance for away team j; 0 otherwise

$S_{i,j}^A =$ 1 if match has significance (as defined above) for away team j, and does not have significance for home team i; 0 otherwise.

The specification of the model is completed by specifying the link between $y_{i,j}^*$ and the result of each match, denoted $y_{i,j}$, as follows:

Home win $\Rightarrow y_{i,j} = 1$ if $\mu_2 < y_{i,j}^* + \varepsilon_{i,j}$

Draw $\Rightarrow y_{i,j} = 0.5$ if $\mu_1 < y_{i,j}^* + \varepsilon_{i,j} < \mu_2$

Away win $\Rightarrow y_{i,j} = 0$ if $y_{i,j}^* + \varepsilon_{i,j} < \mu_1$ (3.11)

where $\varepsilon_{i,j}$ is an error term which allows for the random element in the result of the match between teams i and j, and which is assumed to follow the standard normal distribution. Together, (3.10) and (3.11) constitute an ordered probit model. The estimated version of (3.11) can be rearranged to obtain probabilities for each outcome, as follows:

Home win probability $= p_{i,j}^H = p(\varepsilon_{i,j} > \hat{\mu}_2 - \hat{y}_{i,j}^*) = 1 - \Phi(\hat{\mu}_2 - \hat{y}_{i,j}^*)$

Draw probability $= p_{i,j}^D = p(\hat{\mu}_1 - \hat{y}_{i,j}^* < \varepsilon_{i,j} < \hat{\mu}_2 - \hat{y}_{i,j}^*)$

$$= \Phi(\hat{\mu}_2 - \hat{y}_{i,j}^*) - \Phi(\hat{\mu}_1 - \hat{y}_{i,j}^*)$$

Away win probability $= p_{i,j}^A = p(\varepsilon_{i,j} < \hat{\mu}_1 - \hat{y}_{i,j}^*) = \Phi(\hat{\mu}_1 - \hat{y}_{i,j}^*)$ (3.12)

where $\Phi(\ )$ is the standard normal distribution function. In (3.10), the variables $P_{i,y,s}^d$ (for team i, and their counterparts for team j) are the main team quality indicators. The higher the value of $y_{i,j}^*$, the higher the probability of a home win, so $\alpha_{y,s}^d > 0$ and $\beta_{y,s}^d < 0$ are expected. It is assumed that team i's underlying quality is captured by its win ratio over the 12 months prior to the match in question, represented by

$$P_{i,0,0}^0 + \sum_{d=-1}^{+1} P_{i,0,1}^d,$$ and by its win ratio between 12 and 24 months prior to

the match in question, represented by $\sum_{d=-1}^{+1} P_{i,1,1}^d + \sum_{d=-2}^{+2} P_{i,1,2}^d$. The model

allows the individual components of these sums to make different contributions to the team quality measure. For example, if present season results are a better indicator of current team quality than previous season results in the same division within the same 12-month period, $\alpha_{0,0}^0 > \alpha_{0,1}^0$ and $\beta_{0,0}^0 < \beta_{0,1}^0$ would be expected. If previous-season results from a higher division indicate higher quality than those from a lower division, $\alpha_{y,1}^{+1} > \alpha_{y,1}^0 > \alpha_{y,1}^{-1}$ and $\beta_{y,1}^{+1} < \beta_{y,1}^0 < \beta_{y,1}^{-1}$ for $y = 0,1$ would be expected. An important issue is the number of previous years over which team quality should be measured. Experimentation indicated that $\{P_{i,0,s}^d, P_{j,0,s}^d\}$ and

$\{P^d_{i,1,s}, P^d_{j,1,s}\}$ were both strongly significant sets of covariates in the ordered probit model, but $\{P^d_{i,2,s}, P^d_{j,2,s}\}$ (similarly defined for matches that took place between 24 and 36 months prior to the match in question) were insignificant. Therefore team quality is measured using win ratios measured over the periods 0–12 months and 12–24 months prior to the match in question, but the 24–36 month win ratios are not included.

The variables $R^H_{i,m}$ and $R^A_{i,n}$ (for team i, and their counterparts for team j) allow for individual inclusion of each team's few most recent home and away results in the calculation of $y^*_{i,j}$. Although these variables also contribute towards the values of $P^d_{i,y,s}$ (and are to some extent correlated with $P^d_{i,y,s}$) the evidence of short-term persistence in match results presented in section 3.2 suggests that $R^H_{i,m}$ and $R^A_{i,n}$ have particular relevance (over and above the information they convey about team quality) in helping to predict the result of the current match. An important issue is the number of lagged values of these variables to include. Experimentation indicated that the home team's most recent home results are more useful than its most recent away results as predictors, and similarly that the away team's most recent away results are more useful than its most recent home results. Statistically significant estimates of γ^H_m and γ^A_m were obtained for most values of m up to and including nine, while significant estimates of γ^A_n and γ^H_n were obtained for most values n up to and including four. $M = 9$ and $N = 4$ are therefore the lag lengths used in the estimations that follow.

The identification of matches with significance for championship, promotion and relegation issues has been an important and sometimes awkward issue in the literature on the estimation of the demand for attendance (see chapter 7). It is also relevant in the present context, however, since match outcomes (as well as attendances) are likely to be affected by incentives. Teams are more likely to contribute high effort when they need points to have a chance of winning the championship or promotion or avoiding relegation, than when the match has no bearing on such issues. In particular, if a match is significant for one of the competing teams and insignificant for the other, it is likely that the incentive difference has a bearing on the outcome. The algorithm used to assess whether or not a match is significant is crude but also has the merit of simplicity. A program calculates whether it would still be possible mathematically for the team in question to win the championship or be promoted or relegated, if all other teams currently in contention took one point on average from each of their remaining fixtures.[12] The match significance variable

---

[12] The model was also tested using a stricter definition, classifying a match as insignificant only when it was mathematically impossible for the team in question to win the championship, promotion or relegation under any assumptions concerning the performance

definitions are $S^H_{i,j} = 1$ if the match is significant for home team i but not for away team j, and $S^H_{i,j} = 0$ elsewhere. Similarly, $S^A_{i,j} = 1$ if the match is significant for away team j but not for home team i, and $S^A_{i,j} = 0$ elsewhere. Therefore $\delta_1 > 0$ and $\delta_2 < 0$ would be consistent with incentive effects of the kind described above.

Estimation of the model

Table 3.14 reports the results of two sets of estimations of the coefficients of (3.10) and (3.11). The set reported in columns (1)–(2) and (5)–(6) use all of the available data for the 1973 to 1999 seasons inclusive. Columns (1) and (5) show the coefficient estimates, and columns (2) and (6) show their standard errors. There are 53,820 useable match result observations.[13]

Although using all of the data maximises the information set available for the estimation, it relies on an assumption of parameter constancy which, as has already been seen from the trends in the proportions of home and away wins identified in section 3.2, is invalid. In columns (3)–(4) and (7)–(8) of table 3.14, therefore, the estimation is repeated using only the 19,746 useable match result observations for the 10 seasons 1989 to 1998 inclusive. Table 3.1 suggests that the proportions of home and away wins did not vary systematically within this period, so the assumption of parameter stability seems plausible. Slightly fewer coefficients are found to be significantly different from zero in the ten-season model. This is a natural consequence of the fact that the estimation is based on fewer observations. The estimation for this particular 10-season period is reported here, because this model is used in chapter 8 to make *ex ante* 'predictions' of match results for the 1999 season, in order to investigate hypotheses about the efficiency of prices in the fixed-odds betting market.

In general, the parameter estimates reported in table 3.14 are in accordance with prior expectations. For example, the estimated coefficients on $P^0_{i,0,0}$, $P^0_{i,0,1}$ and $P^0_{i,1,1}$ show that for the home team, the points ratio from matches played during the present season is a stronger indicator of current team quality than the points ratio from matches played in the

---

of other teams. The chosen algorithm, however, produced values of $S^H_{i,j}$ and $S^A_{i,j}$ which had greater explanatory power in the ordered probit model. Although the algorithm is rather crude, it does succeed in a simple manner in identifying those matches of significance to one or both teams during the last few weeks of the season, the results of which are most likely to be affected by incentive effects.

[13] The number of useable observations is slightly less than the 54,848 matches completed, because full sets of lagged results are unavailable for all teams at the start of the observation period, and for teams entering or re-entering the league during their first seasons of membership.

Table 3.14. *Ordered probit estimation of match results forecasting model, 1973–1999 and 1989–1998*

| | Estimation period | | | | | Estimation period | | | |
| | 1973–99 | | 1989–98 | | | 1973–99 | | 1989–98 | |
	(1) coeff.	(2) s.e.	(3) coeff.	(4) s.e.		(5) coeff.	(6) s.e.	(7) coeff.	(8) s.e.
$P^0_{i,0,0}$	1.555[a]	0.109	1.736[a]	0.183	$R^H_{i,1}$	0.066[a]	0.013	0.027	0.021
$P^{+1}_{i,0,1}$	1.523[a]	0.179	1.535[a]	0.292	$R^H_{i,2}$	0.032[b]	0.013	0.016	0.021
$P^0_{i,0,1}$	1.128[a]	0.100	0.979[a]	0.163	$R^H_{i,3}$	0.075[a]	0.013	0.074[a]	0.021
$P^{-1}_{i,0,1}$	0.830[a]	0.091	0.829[a]	0.151	$R^H_{i,4}$	0.010	0.013	−0.009	0.021
$P^{+1}_{i,0,1}$	0.592[a]	0.154	0.699[a]	0.257	$R^H_{i,5}$	0.020	0.013	0.010	0.021
$P^0_{i,1,1}$	0.541[a]	0.096	0.610[a]	0.157	$R^H_{i,6}$	−0.002	0.013	0.001	0.021
$P^{-1}_{i,1,1}$	0.460[a]	0.085	0.469[a]	0.143	$R^H_{i,7}$	0.015	0.013	0.013	0.021
$P^{+2}_{i,1,2}$	0.172	0.350	0.783	0.889	$R^H_{i,8}$	0.028[b]	0.013	−0.014	0.021
$P^{+1}_{i,1,2}$	0.716[a]	0.142	0.626[a]	0.230	$R^H_{i,9}$	0.042[a]	0.013	0.019	0.021
$P^0_{i,1,2}$	0.403[a]	0.094	0.364[b]	0.152	$R^A_{i,1}$	0.020	0.013	0.017	0.021
$P^{-1}_{i,1,2}$	0.313[a]	0.080	0.411[a]	0.130	$R^A_{i,2}$	0.037[a]	0.013	0.043[b]	0.021
$P^{-2}_{i,1,2}$	−0.111	0.158	−0.195	0.236	$R^A_{i,3}$	0.047[a]	0.013	0.033	0.021
$P^0_{j,0,0}$	−1.292[a]	0.109	−1.439[a]	0.180	$R^A_{i,4}$	0.007	0.013	−0.029	0.021
$P^{+1}_{j,0,1}$	−1.331[a]	0.177	−1.151[a]	0.287	$R^H_{j,1}$	−0.028[b]	0.013	−0.038[c]	0.021
$P^0_{j,0,1}$	−0.912[a]	0.099	−0.714[a]	0.160	$R^H_{j,2}$	−0.031[b]	0.013	−0.025	0.021
$P^{-1}_{j,0,1}$	−0.619[a]	0.091	−0.467[a]	0.152	$R^H_{j,3}$	−0.031[b]	0.013	−0.027	0.021
$P^{+1}_{j,1,1}$	−0.845[a]	0.154	−0.567[b]	0.257	$R^H_{j,4}$	−0.037[a]	0.013	−0.038[c]	0.021
$P^0_{j,1,1}$	−0.603[a]	0.095	−0.491[a]	0.156	$R^A_{j,1}$	−0.045[a]	0.013	−0.031	0.021
$P^{-1}_{j,1}$	−0.466[a]	0.086	−0.346[b]	0.145	$R^A_{j,2}$	−0.045[a]	0.013	−0.013	0.021
$P^{+2}_{j,1,2}$	−0.398	0.354	−0.867	0.893	$R^A_{j,3}$	−0.043[a]	0.013	−0.033	0.021
$P^{+1}_{j,1,2}$	−0.717[a]	0.141	−0.732[a]	0.228	$R^A_{j,4}$	−0.046[a]	0.013	−0.043[b]	0.021
$P^0_{j,1,2}$	−0.469[a]	0.093	−0.415[a]	0.150	$R^A_{j,5}$	−0.028[b]	0.013	−0.006	0.021

$P^{-1}_{j,1,2}$	−0.281[a]	0.080	−0.143	0.130	$R^A_{j,6}$	−0.037[a]	0.013	−0.027	0.021
$P^{-2}_{j,1,2}$	−0.413[a]	0.161	−0.536[b]	0.242	$R^A_{j,7}$	−0.031[b]	0.013	−0.022	0.021
$S^H_{i,j}$	0.148[a]	0.027	0.121[b]	0.048	$R^A_{j,8}$	−0.030[b]	0.013	−0.021	0.021
$S^A_{i,j}$	−0.114[a]	0.027	−0.118[b]	0.048	$R^A_{j,9}$	−0.021	0.013	−0.055[b]	0.021
μ_1	−0.629	0.055	−0.574	0.092					
μ_2	0.145	0.055	0.189	0.092	obs	53,820		19,746	

Notes:

[a] = significantly different from zero, two-tail test, 1% level; [b] = 5% level; [c] = 10% level.

Key:

$P^0_{i,0,0}$ = total points gained by home team: last 12 months, current season, current division; divided by matches played in last 12 months

$P^{+1}_{i,0,1}$ = as above: last 12 months, last season, one division above current division

$P^0_{i,0,1}$ = as above: last 12 months, last season, current division

$P^{-1}_{i,0,1}$ = as above: last 12 months, last season, one division below current division

$P^{+1}_{i,1,1}$ = as above: 12–24 months ago, last season, one division above current division; divided by matches played 12–24 months ago

$P^0_{i,1,1}$ = as above: 12–24 months ago, last season, in current division

$P^{-1}_{i,1,1}$ = as above: 12–24 months ago, last season, one division below current division

$P^{+2}_{i,1,2}$ = as above: 12–24 months ago, two seasons ago, two divisions above current division

$P^{+1}_{i,1,2}$ = as above: 12–24 months ago, two seasons ago, one division above current division

$P^0_{i,1,2}$ = as above: 12–24 months ago, two seasons ago, current division

$P^{-1}_{i,1,2}$ = as above: 12–24 months ago, two seasons ago, one division below current division

$P^{-2}_{i,1,2}$ = as above: 12–24 months ago, two seasons ago, two divisions below current division

$P^0_{j,0,0}, P^{+1}_{j,0,1} \cdots$, same as above for away team.

$S^H_{i,j}$ = 1 if match has significance for home team but not for away team

$S^A_{i,j}$ = 1 if match has significance for away team but not for home team

$R^H_{i,1}$ = result of most recent home match played by home team

$R^H_{i,2}$ = result of second most recent home match played by home team, and so on

$R^A_{i,1}$ = result of most recent away match played by home team

$R^A_{i,2}$ = result of second most recent away match played by home team, and so on

$R^H_{j,1}, R^A_{j,1} \cdots$, same as above for away team.

same division within the same 12-month period but during the previous season. In turn, the latter is a stronger indicator than the points ratio from matches played in the same division during the previous 12-month period and during the previous season. The estimated coefficients on $P^0_{j,0,0}$, $P^0_{j,0,1}$ and $P^0_{j,1,1}$ show the same for the away team. Only one of the four estimated coefficients on $P^{+2}_{i,1,2}$, $P^{-2}_{i,1,2}$, $P^{+2}_{j,1,2}$ and $P^{-2}_{j,1,2}$ is significantly different from zero, however. This is primarily owing to a shortage of data, since movement up or down by two divisions in consecutive seasons is a relatively rare occurrence.

The estimated coefficients on $R^H_{i,m}$, $R^A_{i,n}$, $R^H_{j,n}$ and $R^A_{j,m}$ are rather more erratic, both in terms of numerical magnitude and in terms of the significance of individual coefficients. Despite the finding of a negative persistence effect in section 3.2, the estimated coefficients on the home team's recent results are predominantly positive (and those for the away team predominantly negative). This is undoubtedly because recent results contribute information about the underlying strengths of the two teams. The estimated coefficients on these variables therefore combine information about team heterogeneity with information about persistence effects; and the former appears to dominate the latter. Finally, despite the crudity of the formula used to identify matches with significance for championship, promotion or relegation outcomes for either team, the coefficients on $S^H_{i,j}$ and $S^A_{i,j}$ are correctly signed and significantly different from zero in both estimations. This seems to confirm that the efforts contributed by football players (like most employees in other industries) are strongly influenced by incentives.[14]

Table 3.15 compares the 1989–1998 model's predictions for the 1999 season with the actual match results. The mechanics of the calculation of predictions are described in the next sub-section. On the basis of historical data, the model slightly over-estimates the proportions of home wins and draws, and under-estimates the proportion of away wins. 486 of the 877 home-win predictions (55.4 per cent) turned out to be correct; 173 out of the 545 draw predictions (31.7 per cent) were correct; and 178 out of the 522 away-win predictions (34.1 per cent) were correct. The number of matches that would be expected in each cell if the forecasting model had no predictive content are shown in parentheses. If the 877 home win predictions had been selected randomly, therefore, the expected number of correct predictions would be 409 (or 46.6 per cent). Likewise, 545 randomly predicted draws would be expected to yield 157

---

[14] In contrast, in a paper using data on end-of-season championship series in US baseball, basketball and hockey, Ferrall and Smith (1999) find negligible evidence of strategic or incentive effects. The match result does not seem to be influenced by the importance of the match for the outcome of the series.

Table 3.15. *Match results forecasting model's predicted results and actual results*

		Predicted			
		Home win	Draw	Away win	Total
Actual	Home win	486 *(409)*	227 *(252)*	194 *(244)*	907
	Draw	238 *(253)*	173 *(157)*	150 *(151)*	561
	Away win	153 *(215)*	145 *(133)*	178 *(128)*	476
	Total	877	545	522	1944

Note:
Cells show the actual number of matches in each category, and *(in italics)* the expected number in each category if the forecasting model had no predictive content.

correct predictions (28.8 per cent) and 522 randomly predicted away wins should yield 128 correct predictions (24.5 per cent). The forecasting model therefore outperforms random prediction significantly in the case of home wins and away wins, but only marginally in the case of draws, which appear to be near-random events.[15]

An illustration: Middlesbrough v. Arsenal, Premier League, 24 April 1999

This sub-section illustrates the calculation of win-draw-loss probabilities and a match result forecast, using the 1999 season's Middlesbrough v. Arsenal Premier League fixture as an example. This fixture was played on 24 April 1999.

The complete win-draw-loss records of the two teams over the 24 months prior to the fixture are shown in table 3.16. The total numbers of games played 0–12 months and 12–24 months before 24 April 1999 were $n_{i,0} = 36$ and $n_{i,1} = 48$ for Middlesbrough, and $n_{j,0} = 38$ and $n_{j,1} = 35$ for Arsenal. Using this data, the calculations of $P^d_{i,y,s}$ and $P^d_{j,y,s}$ for home team $i =$ Middlesbrough and away team $j =$ Arsenal are shown in column (1) of table 3.17. Column (2) shows the relevant coefficients from the estimated model, obtained from table 3.14. Column (3) shows the product of each variable and its coefficient. The sum of these products is carried forward to the final calculation of $\hat{y}^*_{i,j}$ below.

[15] A test of the hypothesis that the actual numbers of correct or incorrect predictions in each cell correspond to the numbers expected under random prediction rejects the null at all realistic significance levels. The test statistic is distributed chi-square with four degrees of freedom under the null, and the realised value is 52.4.

Table 3.16. *24-month playing records of Middlesbrough and Arsenal up to 24 April 1999*

Season	Matches played	Division	Played	Won	Drawn	Lost
Middlesbrough						
1997	on or after 24/4/97	Premier	4	1	3	0
1998	before 23/4/98	1	44	26	9	9
	on or after 24/4/98	1	2	1	1	0
1999	before 23/4/99	Premier	34	12	14	8
Arsenal						
1997	on or after 24/4/97	Premier	2	1	0	1
1998	before 23/4/98	Premier	33	20	9	4
	on or after 24/4/98	Premier	5	3	0	2
1999	before 23/4/99	Premier	33	18	12	3

Source: Match results' data set.

Table 3.17. *Part-calculation of $\hat{y}_{i,j}^{*}$ for Middlesbrough v. Arsenal (1)*

Variable	Calculation (1)	Coeff. (table 3.14) (2)	Product (3)
$P_{i,0,0}^{0}$	$\{(12 \times 1) + (14 \times 0.5)\}/36 = 0.528$	1.736	0.917
$P_{i,0,1}^{-1}$	$\{(1 \times 1) + (1 \times 0.5)\}/36 = 0.042$	0.829	0.035
$P_{i,1,1}^{-1}$	$\{(26 \times 1) + (9 \times 0.5)\}/48 = 0.635$	0.469	0.298
$P_{i,1,2}^{0}$	$\{(1 \times 1) + (3 \times 0.5)\}/48 = 0.052$	0.364	0.019
$P_{j,0,0}^{0}$	$\{(18 \times 1) + (12 \times 0.5)\}/38 = 0.632$	-1.439	-0.909
$P_{j,0,1}^{0}$	$\{(3 \times 1) + (0 \times 0.5)\}/38 = 0.079$	-0.714	-0.056
$P_{j,1,1}^{0}$	$\{(20 \times 1) + (9 \times 0.5)\}/35 = 0.700$	-0.491	-0.344
$P_{j,1,2}^{0}$	$\{(1 \times 1) + (0 \times 0.5)\}/35 = 0.029$	-0.415	-0.012
Total carried forward to $\hat{y}_{i,j}^{*}$			-0.052

Key:
See table 3.14.

Table 3.18. *Part-calculation of $\hat{y}^*_{i,j}$ for Middlesbrough v. Arsenal (2)*

Variable	Value (1)	Coeff. (table 3.14) (2)	Product (3)	Variable	Value (4)	Coeff. (table 3.14) (5)	Product (6)
$R^H_{i,1}$	0.5	0.027	0.014	$R^H_{j,1}$	1	−0.038	−0.038
$R^H_{i,2}$	1	0.016	0.016	$R^H_{j,2}$	1	−0.025	−0.025
$R^H_{i,3}$	1	0.074	0.074	$R^H_{j,3}$	1	−0.027	−0.027
$R^H_{i,4}$	1	−0.009	−0.009	$R^H_{j,4}$	1	−0.038	−0.038
$R^H_{i,5}$	0.5	0.010	0.005	$R^A_{j,1}$	0.5	−0.031	−0.016
$R^H_{i,6}$	0.5	0.001	0.001	$R^A_{j,2}$	1	−0.013	−0.013
$R^H_{i,7}$	0.5	0.013	0.007	$R^A_{j,3}$	0.5	−0.033	−0.017
$R^H_{i,8}$	0	−0.014	0	$R^A_{j,4}$	0.5	−0.043	−0.022
$R^H_{i,9}$	1	0.019	0.019	$R^A_{j,5}$	1	−0.006	−0.006
$R^A_{i,1}$	1	0.017	0.017	$R^A_{j,6}$	1	−0.027	−0.027
$R^A_{i,2}$	0.5	0.043	0.022	$R^A_{j,7}$	1	−0.022	−0.022
$R^A_{i,3}$	1	0.033	0.033	$R^A_{j,8}$	0	−0.021	0
$R^A_{i,4}$	0	−0.029	0	$R^A_{j,9}$	0.5	−0.055	−0.028
Total carried forward to $\hat{y}^*_{i,j}$			0.199	Total carried forward to $\hat{y}^*_{i,j}$			−0.279

Key:
See table 3.14.

The results achieved by the two teams in the matches immediately preceding 24 April 1999, in chronological order, were as follows:

Middlesbrough Last 9 home: WLDDDWWWD
Last 4 away: LWDW

Arsenal Last 4 home: WWWW
Last 9 away: DLWWWDDWD

Using these data, the values of $R^H_{i,m}$ and $R^A_{i,n}$ for $m = 1 \ldots 9$ and $n = 1 \ldots 4$ are shown in column (1), and the values of $R^H_{j,n}$ and $R^A_{j,m}$ are shown in column (4) of table 3.18. Columns (2) and (5) show the estimated coefficients obtained from table 3.14. Columns (3) and (6) show the product of each variable and its coefficient. As before, the sums of these products are carried forward to the final calculation of $\hat{y}^*_{i,j}$ below.

On the morning of 24 April 1999, the relevant parts of the Premier League table were as shown in table 3.19. Arsenal were still in contention

Table 3.19. *Premier League table on the morning of 24 April 1999*

Position	Team	Played	Won	Drawn	Lost	Points
1	Manchester United	32	19	10	3	67
2	Arsenal	33	18	12	3	66
7	Middlesbrough	34	12	14	8	50
18	Blackburn Rovers	33	7	11	15	32
19	Southampton	34	8	7	19	31
20	Nottingham Forest	34	4	9	21	21

Source: Match results' data set.

for the championship; but with only four matches remaining, Middlesbrough were neither in contention for the championship, nor in danger of relegation. The match therefore had significance (as defined as above) for Arsenal but not for Middlesbrough. This implies $S_{i,j}^{H}=0$ and $S_{i,j}^{A}=1$. Using the relevant coefficient from table 3.14, -0.118 is carried forward to the final calculation of $\hat{y}_{i,j}^{*}$.

The final calculation of $\hat{y}_{i,j}^{*}$ for the Middlesbrough v. Arsenal match is:

$$\hat{y}_{i,j}^{*}=-0.052+0.199-0.279-0.118=-0.250$$

Applying the estimated values $\hat{\mu}_{1}=-0.574$ and $\hat{\mu}_{2}=0.189$ from table 3.14, (3.12) can be used to obtain the estimated match result probabilities, as follows:

Home win probability, $p_{i,j}^{H}=p(\varepsilon_{i,j}>\hat{\mu}_{2}-\hat{y}_{i,j}^{*})$
$$=p(\varepsilon_{i,j}>0.439)$$
$$=1-\Phi(0.439)=0.330$$

Draw probability, $p_{i,j}^{D}=p(\hat{\mu}_{1}-\hat{y}_{i,j}^{*}<\varepsilon_{i,j}<\hat{\mu}_{2}-\hat{y}_{i,j}^{*})$
$$=p(-0.324<\varepsilon_{i,j}<0.439)$$
$$=\Phi(0.439)-\Phi(-0.324)=0.296$$

Away win probability, $P_{i,j}^{A}=p(\varepsilon_{i,j}<\hat{\mu}_{1}-\hat{y}_{i,j}^{*})$
$$=p(\varepsilon_{i,j}<-0.324)$$
$$=\Phi(-0.324)=0.374$$

where $\Phi(\ )$ is the standard normal distribution function (as in (3.12)). The average proportions of home wins, draws and away wins for seasons 1989 to 1998 inclusive (on which the estimated model is based) were 0.466, 0.278 and 0.256, respectively. In view of Arsenal's strong record during the previous 24 months, their excellent recent form and the fact that the match was significant for them but not for their opponents, the model adjusts these average probabilities to those obtained above: 0.330, 0.296 and 0.374, respectively. Arsenal are therefore significantly more strongly 'fancied' in this fixture than an average away team in an average fixture.

To obtain a specific match result prediction, the fitted values $\hat{y}^*_{i,j}$ for the 19,746 matches played between the 1989 and 1998 seasons and included in the estimation reported in table 3.14 are ranked in descending order. The two cut-off values of $\hat{y}^*_{i,j}$ separating the 46.6 per cent of matches with the highest values of $\hat{y}^*_{i,j}$ (the most likely home wins), the 27.8 per cent of matches with the next highest values (the most likely draws), and the remaining 25.6 per cent of matches with the lowest values (the most likely away wins) are 0.119 and −0.050. Therefore a suitable forecasting rule for matches played during the 1999 season is:

- forecast home win if $\hat{y}^*_{i,j} > 0.119$
- forecast draw if $-0.050 < \hat{y}^*_{i,j} < 0.119$
- forecast away win if $\hat{y}^*_{i,j} < -0.050$

On these criteria, the forecast for the Middlesbrough v. Arsenal fixture with $\hat{y}^*_{i,j} = -0.250$ is an away win. Readers who have worked right the way through this sub-section may recall or may be interested to learn that the match in question actually resulted in a 6–1 victory for the away team!

3.4 Conclusion

Competitive balance and uncertainty of match result outcomes have been the main themes linking the theoretical and empirical sections of chapter 3. The theoretical literature on competitive balance places considerable faith in the capacity of market forces to maintain a reasonable degree of competitive balance within professional team sports leagues. It tends to be suspicious of regulatory intervention intended to promote competitive balance, in the form of reserve clauses, salary caps, or revenue sharing arrangements. At best, the effect on competitive balance of such mechanisms may be neutral; at worst they could inadvertently make competition more unbalanced. North American assumptions of closed player labour markets and profit maximising behaviour do not necessarily transfer directly across the Atlantic. Nevertheless, the theoretical literature does suggest strongly that caution needs to be exercised before advocating simplistic remedies for perceived trends towards excessive championship dominance by a handful of big-market teams, both in England and elsewhere in Europe.

It has been argued that unpredictability is an essential characteristic of the product that professional sports teams sell to their spectators, so uncertainty of individual match result outcomes has been the main subject of the empirical sections of chapter 3. Analysis of trends contained in a comprehensive league match results data set reveals a progressive improvement in the performance of away teams in recent years, and a corresponding decline in the importance of home advantage. Analysis of the nature of persistence effects in sequences of consecutive match results lends support to the notion of a complacency or negative confidence effect, which aids the reversal of both good spells and bad spells sooner than would otherwise be expected, given the normal diversity of quality between the teams within each division in any season. Finally, a forecasting model has been developed, which assesses probabilities and generates forecasts of future match results from historical data, and identifies the extent to which match results are predictable and the extent to which they are random. The forecasting model also plays an important role in several of the empirical investigations that are reported in later chapters of this volume.

4   The labour and transfer markets

Since the early 1960s there has been a series of major institutional reforms to the organisation of the players' labour market in English football, starting with the abolition of the maximum wage in 1961, and culminating in the 1995 European Court of Justice (ECJ) ruling in the Jean-Marc Bosman case (see chapter 2). Some of the broader consequences of these changes are obvious and widely recognised. Spiralling wages, especially for superstar players, are a consequence of the progressive shift towards freedom-of-contract that has been underway throughout this period. Although naturally the chronology and detail of institutional reform varies between countries, the same long-term trend has been evident worldwide. The trend towards the globalisalisation of the players' labour market has accelerated significantly in recent years, especially among the major professional football playing nations located in the EU, as a consequence of the Bosman ruling.

This chapter begins in section 4.1 by presenting a descriptive profile of certain key personal and career characteristics of professional football players in the English league. The analysis focuses on those players who turned out most regularly, week-in-week-out, for league matches played in each of two seasons located 20 years apart: 1979 and 1999. Tabulations of the data are used to draw comparisons between the composition of the two samples. Among the players' characteristics investigated are age, place of birth and various aspects of each individual's career playing record. This analysis is followed in section 4.2 by a rather more general investigation of patterns of international migration on the part of professional footballers, which draws mainly on the results of previous sociological research.

Section 4.3 examines explanations for the very high wages earned by the leading stars in modern-day professional football. Above-inflation increases in players' wages, especially at the highest level, have been a permanent feature of English football since the abolition of the maximum wage in the early 1960s. In section 4.3 it is argued that scarcity in the supply of the highest talent is only part of the explanation. Before the

189

introduction of pay-television, football reached large television audiences but could not appropriate the full economic price for providing the service to individual audience members. Since the late 1980s, however, this situation has been transformed. The changing composition of the effective demand for football has undoubtedly played a central role in creating the explosion in both revenue and wages in football (and a number of other sports) in recent years.

Wage inflation at the aggregate level has been accompanied by rapidly increasing differentials between the earnings of individual football players, even within the same club. Section 4.3 also looks at a model of intra-team wage distributions. To an economist, it seems reasonable to assume that football players, like other economic agents, respond to incentives. If players' compensation is related to their performance, players will exert more effort and invest in developing their skills. The payment of extremely high wages to certain star players may be a rational strategy for clubs to adopt, if it provides an incentive structure which maximises effort and investment in skills development by all players, especially in the early stages of their careers.

According to the rank-order tournament model, the difference in performance between players determines their rank in a hierarchy of wages, but does not determine the margin of compensation. Players' wages at any point in time therefore do not necessarily reflect directly their individual contribution to the club's revenue-earning capability at the same time.

Empirical evidence on the determinants of football players' compensation is rather thin on the ground, mainly because of restrictions on disclosure. In a number of North American sports, however, there is sufficient individual disclosure to permit empirical investigation of these relationships at the micro level. Unequal pay for equal work is one form of racial discrimination, which has received particular attention in the literature on the determinants of sports stars' wages. Section 4.4 looks at some of the main North American evidence, as well as a recent empirical study of racial discrimination in English football.

Although the Bosman ruling has established the principle of free agency with no transfer fee payable when an out-of-contract player aged over 24 changes club, and despite the European Commission's recently declared intention to force the reform or abolition of the present ransfer system, at the time of writing big-money transfer deals for in-contract players are still commonplace throughout world football. Indeed, one obvious consequence of the introduction of free agency for out-of-contract players is to increase the incentive for a club to sell a talented player while he is still in-contract, so that the club can receive a fee. And as shown in section 2.6, within English football the transfer market still plays an important role in redistributing revenues from the richer to the poorer clubs. Using a pre-Bosman English transfers data set, section 4.5 concludes this chapter by presenting an empirical analysis of the determinants of transfer fees.

4.1 Player mobility, migration and career structure in the English league

Section 4.1 presents a new analysis of patterns of migration, mobility and career development among English football's regular workforce: the players who turn out most regularly, week-in-week-out, for league matches played at all levels within the Premier and Football Leagues. It draws on a data set which records a number of key personal and professional characteristics of the 12 players who made the most league appearances for each of the league's 92 member clubs, in each of two seasons located 20 years apart: 1979 and 1999. The data set therefore comprises two samples, each containing the 1,104 players who turned out most regularly for their clubs during the season concerned. The method of analysis is purely descriptive: tabulations of the data based on the players' characteristics are used to identify similarities and differences between the composition of the two samples.

The typical professional football player begins his career as an apprentice at the age of 16. If successful, he will sign for a club as a full-time professional around two years later. Most professional football players play one or two competitive matches per week throughout the season. On other days and during the close season, they either train or relax. Provided he stays free from injury and loss of form, an outfield player can expect to play until he reaches his early or mid-thirties. A successful goalkeeping career can be expected to last slightly longer. Some players are signed by a top club when young, and spend most of (or even all) their career in the top flight. Others begin in the lower divisions, to be transferred later to a club of higher status. Players who have appeared regularly at the top level may sometimes accept a move to the lower divisions when they get older, in order to prolong their playing careers. For many players, however, a career as a professional means playing only in the lower divisions, from when they first sign until they retire.

Ages and dates of birth

Table 4.1 shows the percentage distribution of all players by age on the 31 May immediately after the end of the two seasons. The data shows that the average age of the players included in the two samples increased by

Table 4.1. *Percentage distribution of all players, by age, 31 May 1979 or 1999*

Age	1979	1999	Age	1979	1999
16	0.2	0.0	31	5.1	6.3
17	0.5	0.2	32	4.0	4.4
18	1.6	0.9	33	2.2	3.2
19	4.3	2.5	34	1.4	3.3
20	6.0	3.9	35	0.7	2.0
21	7.1	4.3	36	0.3	0.9
22	9.8	6.2	37	0.3	0.5
23	8.2	6.6	38	0.1	0.2
24	7.3	7.5	39	0.0	0.0
25	9.3	8.6	40	0.0	0.3
26	8.4	7.5	41	0.0	0.1
27	6.9	9.0			
28	7.1	7.9			
29	4.9	6.1	Mean	25.3	26.8
30	4.4	7.6	St. dev.	4.2	4.4

Sources: Rothmans, Hugman (1998).

about 18 months, from 25.3 years in 1979 to 26.8 years in 1999. The age distribution appears to shift to the right in a fairly uniform manner across the full range of ages, so the shape of the distribution remains similar. 20–28 is the most frequent age range in the 1979 sample, and 22–31 is the most frequent range in the 1999 sample. There were fewer players 19 or under in 1999 (3.6 per cent) than in 1979 (6.6 per cent), and there were more players aged 32 or above in 1999 (14.9 per cent) than in 1979 (9.0 per cent).

A possible explanation for the shift in the age distribution is the recent influx of players born overseas, who were present in much greater numbers in 1999 than in 1979. If overseas players are older on average than their local-born counterparts (perhaps because they tend to move abroad at a relatively late stage in their career) this might account for the increase in the average age. Table 4.2 shows the average age of players on 31 May, disaggregated by birthplace and division. On the basis of the evidence in table 4.2, the hypothesis that overseas players were responsible for the increase in average age can be dismissed categorically; in 1999 the average age of the overseas players was almost identical to their local-born counterparts.[1] Table 4.2 also shows that there was relatively little variation

[1] There is rather more variation in the average age of the overseas-born players in the 1979 sample; this, however, is mainly a reflection of the small numbers involved.

Table 4.2. *Average age of players, by birthplace and division, 31 May 1979 or 1999*

| | Birthplace | | | | | |
| | Britain and Ireland | | Rest of world | | All players | |
	Average	No.	Average	No.	Average	No.
1979						
D1	25.8	254	26.9	10	25.9	264
D2	25.1	258	23.8	6	25.1	264
D3	25.4	283	21.6	5	25.3	288
D4	25.1	286	27.0	2	25.1	288
All	25.4	1081	25.0	23	25.3	1104
1999						
Prem	27.5	160	27.2	80	27.4	240
Div One	27.2	243	27.2	45	27.2	288
Div Two	26.5	267	26.4	21	26.5	288
Div Three	26.2	277	27.1	11	26.2	288
All	26.8	947	27.1	157	26.8	1104

Sources: Rothmans, Hugman (1998).

in the average age of players across the league's four divisions: in both seasons, the average age of Division 1/Premier League players was around six months higher than their counterparts in the other three divisions.

Further analysis of players' dates of birth reveals a feature of the data that is quite striking, and also consistent between the two samples. Table 4.3 shows the percentage distribution of all players by month of birth. This reveals that a significant majority of professional players (59.9 per cent in 1979 and 58.1 per cent in 1999) were born during months that fall in the first half of the school year, from September to February inclusive. The most likely explanation is that children whose birthdays fall in these months are physically bigger and stronger, and are therefore more likely to succeed in school sports, than children in the same school year with birthdays between March and August, who nevertheless play in the same school sports teams as their older counterparts. Although the physical disadvantage to the latter is most pronounced at the youngest ages, it seems certain that an aversion to sport acquired early on in life would effectively terminate an individual's prospects of ever becoming a professional sports person.

Birthplaces and first clubs

Table 4.4 shows the percentage distribution of players by birthplace, classified by standard region (old definitions) for British-born players and

Table 4.3. *Percentage distribution of all players, by month of birth, 1979 or 1999*

Month	1979	1999
Jan	8.9	8.0
Feb	10.1	7.3
Mar	8.2	8.5
Apr	5.9	6.7
May	7.2	6.8
June	6.6	6.3
July	6.0	6.1
Aug	6.3	7.5
Sept	10.2	10.7
Oct	11.3	12.0
Nov	10.1	10.4
Dec	9.3	9.7

Sources: Rothmans, Hugman (1998).

Table 4.4. *Percentage distribution of all players, by birthplace, 1979 or 1999*

Region	1979	1999		1979	1999
London/South East (L/SE)	18.7	20.7	France	—	1.3
South West (SW)	3.5	4.9	Germany/Austria/Switzerland	0.2	0.9
East Anglia (EA)	1.5	2.2	Benelux	0.2	1.5
East Midlands (EM)	7.9	6.2	Scandinavia	—	3.3
West Midlands (WM)	7.5	7.7	Spain/Portugal/Malta	—	0.3
Yorks and Humberside (YH)	10.9	10.0	Italy	—	0.5
North West (NW)	17.6	14.9	Greece/Turkey	0.3	0.3
North (N)	10.2	7.8	Eastern Europe/former USSR	0.1	0.6
Wales (Wal)	5.8	3.4	Asia	0.2	0.4
Scotland (Scot)	10.6	4.2	Africa	0.4	1.6
Northern Ireland (NI)	1.9	1.2	Australia/New Zealand	—	1.5
Rep. of Ireland (Ire)	1.7	2.4	North or South America	0.3	1.7
			West Indies	0.5	0.5
All Britain and Ireland	97.8	85.6	All outside Britain and Ireland	2.2	14.4

Sources: Rothmans, Hugman (1998).

Table 4.5. *Percentage distribution of players born in England and Wales, by birthplace, and population comparisons, 1979 or 1999*

| | 1979 season | | 1999 season | |
Region of birth	Footballers (per cent)	Population (1961, per cent)	Footballers (per cent)	Population (1981, per cent)
London/South East	22.4	34.8	26.6	34.3
South West	4.2	8.0	6.3	8.8
East Anglia	1.8	3.2	2.8	3.8
East Midlands	9.4	7.2	8.0	7.8
West Midlands	9.0	10.3	9.9	10.5
Yorks and Humberside	13.0	10.1	12.9	9.9
North West	21.1	13.9	19.2	13.0
North	12.2	6.7	10.0	6.3
Wales	6.9	5.7	4.4	5.7

Sources: Rothmans, Hugman (1998), CSO, *Regional Trends.*

by country or broader geographical area for overseas players. The proportion of players born outside Britain and Ireland increased from 2.2 per cent in 1979 to 14.4 per cent in 1999. France, Italy and the Scandinavian countries are among those that contributed significant numbers of players in 1999, but were not represented at all in 1979.

Although the overall proportion of British and Irish-born players fell from 97.8 per cent in 1979 to 85.6 per cent in 1979, the proportions of players from some English regions increased: specifically, London/South East, the South West, East Anglia and the West Midlands. But relative to population, all of these regions were under-represented in both seasons. This is shown in table 4.5, which compares the 1979 and 1999 percentage distributions of English- and Welsh-born players by region of birth with regional populations from the 1961 and 1981 Censuses, respectively. The North West, the North and Wales all produced significantly fewer players in 1999 than in 1979. Relative to population, table 4.5 shows that (with the exception of Wales in 1999) these regions were over-represented in both seasons. In table 4.4, the proportion of players born in Scotland declined sharply between 1979 and 1999, while the proportion born in the Irish Republic increased. The marked decline in the number of Scottish players is difficult to explain, but as table 4.4 shows, it is consistent with the similar experience of regions in the north of England.

The proportions of clubs located in each region of England and Wales changed very little over the period, because there were only minor adjustments to the league's 92-club membership. This suggests two possible

Table 4.6. *Percentage distribution of players'*
first clubs, 1979 or 1999 by region

Region	1979	1999
London/South East	23.3	24.9
South West	5.5	5.3
East Anglia	2.6	4.9
East Midlands	9.6	7.4
West Midlands	12.7	7.9
Yorks and Humberside	12.9	12.0
North West	19.8	17.7
North	6.0	6.0
Wales	3.3	2.5
Other	4.4	11.6

Sources: Rothmans, Hugman (1998).

explanations for the changing geographical profile of players within England and Wales:
• clubs located outside football's traditional heartland in the north of England may have become more successful at the recruitment and development of new talent; or
• clubs may have become more likely to recruit new talent nationally rather than locally, or from parts of the country other than football's traditional heartland.

Tables 4.6–4.9 provide some support for both of these hypotheses. Table 4.6 shows the percentage distribution of all players' first clubs by region. London/South East and East Anglia were the only regions in England and Wales whose clubs achieved increases in the numbers of players citing them as first club. The largest decreases were in the East and West Midlands and the North West. Table 4.7 shows the clubs that achieved the most citations as first club in both samples. Here, too, there is some evidence of improvement among southern clubs: Charlton Athletic, Ipswich Town, Luton Town, Millwall, Norwich City, Southampton and Watford all figure in the top 20 for 1999, but not for 1979. The geographical pattern, however, is not entirely consistent. In 1979, Manchester United were just one of a number of clubs with a good record in developing new players. By 1999, United had emerged as the clear leader in this respect. Chelsea's high position in 1979 was followed by a very modest showing (of only seven players) in 1999, presumably because the club's recent strategy has been to recruit its own first-team players heavily from overseas.

Table 4.7. *Most frequent first clubs: top 20, 1979 or 1999*

1979			1999		
Position	First club	No. of players	Position	First club	No. of players
1	Arsenal	27	1	Manchester United	29
2	Manchester City	26	2	Crystal Palace	24
3	Chelsea	24	3	Norwich City	21
	Leicester City	24	4	Luton Town	20
	Manchester United	24		Manchester City	20
6	Burnley	22		Southampton	20
	Crystal Palace	22	7	Leeds United	19
8	Leeds United	20	8	Millwall	18
	Wolverhampton Wdrs	20		Tottenham Hotspur	18
10	Middlesbrough	19	10	Arsenal	17
	Nottingham Forest	19		Huddersfield Town	17
12	Tottenham Hotspur	18	12	Aston Villa	16
	Huddersfield Town	18		Blackpool	16
	Blackpool	18		Crewe Alexandra	16
	Derby County	18		Ipswich Town	16
16	Birmingham City	17		Leicester City	16
	Coventry	17		Nottingham Forest	16
	Liverpool	17	18	Charlton Athletic	15
	West Bromwich Albion	17		Liverpool	15
20	Newcastle United	16		Middlesbrough	15
	Sunderland	16		Sheffield United	15
				Watford	15

Sources: Rothmans, Hugman (1998).

Among the players whose first club was in each region, columns (1) and (2) of table 4.8 show the proportions who were born in the same region. In both samples, clubs located in the North had the highest propensity to recruit new players locally, and clubs in East Anglia had the lowest. For all regions except the West Midlands, the proportion of new players recruited locally was smaller in the 1999 sample than in the 1979 sample. This suggests that in general, recruitment has become less concentrated geographically over time. Even for the biggest clubs, however, local recruitment is still high, as table 4.9 illustrates. In the 1999 sample, 12 of the 29 players whose careers began at Manchester United were born in the North West, and 10 of the 17 players whose first club was Arsenal were born in London/South East. Among the smaller clubs included in table 4.9, the proportions are even higher: 12 of the 16 players who began

Table 4.8. *Percentages of players whose first club and whose current club is in their region of birth, 1979 or 1999*

	Per cent of players whose first club is in stated region, who were born in the same region		Per cent of players whose current club is in stated region, who were born in the same region	
Region	(1) 1979	(2) 1999	(3) 1979	(4) 1999
London/South East	56.4	43.1	40.2	20.8
South West	45.9	44.8	21.4	19.0
East Anglia	41.4	27.8	8.3	20.8
East Midlands	53.8	43.9	28.7	13.0
West Midlands	42.9	58.6	28.3	22.2
Yorks and Humberside	64.8	58.3	39.6	27.1
North West	68.0	61.5	47.5	36.6
North	81.8	74.2	38.9	34.7
Wales	75.0	46.4	43.8	16.7

Sources: Rothmans, Hugman (1998).

at Blackpool were from the North West, and 21 of the 24 players who began at Crystal Palace were from London/South East.

Among the players whose current club (in 1979 or 1999) was in each region, columns (3) and (4) of table 4.8 show the proportions who were born in the same region. Again, in most cases these proportions declined significantly between 1979 and 1999. Clubs from the North West and the North had significantly higher concentrations of locally born players than clubs from all other regions in 1999.

Professional career histories

Table 4.10 shows the percentage distribution of players by duration of spell at present club, and table 4.11 shows the percentage distribution by number of clubs (past and present) in England and Wales. Loan spells are not included in table 4.11. Both tables indicate that there has been a marked increase in player mobility between 1979 and 1999. In 1979, for example, 22.3 per cent of all players had been with their present club for more than 5 years; in 1999, the corresponding figure was 12.8 per cent. In 1979, 39.2 per cent of all players were still with their first professional club in England and Wales; in 1999, the corresponding figure was 30.2 per cent. In both seasons, there was more mobility in the league's lower divisions than in the higher divisions, but the difference does appear to

Table 4.9. *Distribution of players, by birthplace, selected first clubs, 1979 or 1999*

Club		L/SE	SW	EA	EM	WM	YH	NW	N	Wal	Scot	NI	Ire	RoW	Total
Arsenal	1979	9	1	1	1	—	3	1	4	—	2	2	2	1	27
	1999	10	—	—	1	—	1	—	1	—	2	1	1	—	17
Blackpool	1979	1	—	—	—	—	—	12	1	—	2	—	—	2	18
	1999	2	—	—	—	1	—	12	1	—	—	—	—	—	16
Crystal Palace	1979	17	1	—	—	—	—	—	1	2	1	—	—	—	22
	1999	21	—	—	—	2	—	1	—	—	—	—	—	—	24
Leeds	1979	1	—	1	—	—	9	—	1	3	4	1	—	—	20
	1999	—	—	—	—	—	5	2	5	2	—	—	2	3	19
Manchester Utd	1979	—	—	1	—	—	2	8	2	2	2	2	5	—	24
	1999	1	1	—	1	1	1	12	1	3	1	3	2	2	29
Middlesbrough	1979	—	—	—	1	—	2	—	13	—	3	—	—	—	19
	1999	1	—	—	2	—	—	—	10	—	—	—	1	1	15

Sources: Rothmans, Hugman (1998).

Table 4.10. *Percentage distribution of players, by duration of present spell at present club, 1979 or 1999*

Duration at present club (years)	1979					1999				
	D1	D2	D3	D4	All	Prem	Div One	Div Two	Div Three	All
0–1	12.9	21.6	22.2	31.9	22.4	24.6	23.6	25.7	36.8	27.8
1–2	18.6	21.6	20.8	30.2	22.9	22.1	29.9	26.7	30.6	27.5
2–3	14.8	15.5	17.4	19.1	16.8	15.8	14.6	18.4	16.7	16.4
3–4	6.1	10.6	11.1	5.6	8.3	10.8	9.4	13.5	7.3	10.2
4–5	11.7	6.8	6.9	4.2	7.3	4.6	6.3	5.6	4.5	5.3
5–6	7.2	7.2	5.9	5.2	6.3	3.3	4.2	3.8	1.7	3.3
6–7	6.1	2.7	5.6	1.0	3.8	5.0	4.2	2.8	1.0	3.2
7–8	4.9	3.8	2.8	0.7	3.0	3.8	2.4	0.7	0.4	1.7
8–9	3.0	2.3	3.8	1.4	2.6	2.9	2.4	1.0	0.4	1.6
9–10	4.2	1.5	1.4	0.7	1.9	1.7	1.7	0.4	0.4	1.0
More than 10	10.5	6.4	2.1	0.0	4.7	5.4	1.3	1.4	0.2	2.0
Mean	5.2	4.0	3.7	2.6	3.8	3.8	3.3	2.9	2.4	3.1

Sources: Rothmans, Hugman (1998).

Table 4.11. *Percentage distribution of players, by number of clubs (past and present) in England and Wales, 1979 or 1999*

	No. of clubs in England and Wales (including current club)						
	1	2	3	4	5	6 or more	Mean
1979							
D1	50.4	29.9	14.0	4.2	1.5	0.0	1.8
D2	45.1	30.3	16.7	4.5	1.5	1.9	1.9
D3	35.4	33.3	19.1	9.7	2.1	0.3	2.1
D4	27.4	29.2	23.3	10.8	6.3	3.1	2.5
All	39.2	30.7	18.4	7.4	2.9	1.4	2.1
All – British/Irish born	38.6	31.0	18.5	7.6	3.0	1.4	2.1
1999							
Prem	45.4	22.5	17.5	7.1	5.8	1.7	2.1
Div One	33.0	24.3	19.8	12.8	4.2	5.9	2.5
Div Two	22.6	34.4	21.9	9.0	7.3	4.9	2.6
Div Three	22.2	27.1	20.8	12.2	7.3	10.4	2.9
All	30.2	27.3	20.1	10.4	6.2	5.9	2.6
All – British/Irish born	24.2	28.3	22.2	11.7	7.0	6.7	2.7

Sources: Rothmans, Hugman (1998).

have narrowed significantly. In Division 1/Premier League, the average duration of the present spell fell from 5.2 to 3.8 years, while in Division 4/Three, the corresponding figures were 2.6 and 2.4 years, respectively.

Because of the way in which the source data are presented, table 4.11 records only the number of clubs in England and Wales for which each player has played professionally during his career. A player signed by his first English club direct from Italy, for example, would be recorded as having played for only one club. Consequently, if the number of clubs is interpreted as a measure of player mobility, the aggregate data in table 4.11 may, if anything, tend to understate mobility. For this reason, the final row of each panel shows the percentage distribution of British and Irish born players only, by number of clubs. On these data, the reduction in the proportion of one-club players was even greater, from 38.6 per cent in 1979 to 24.2 per cent in 1999. The average number of clubs played for by British and Irish-born players increased from 2.1 in 1979 to 2.7 in 1999.

Table 4.12 summarises another aspect of player mobility, in respect of players who joined their present club by means of a transfer from another professional club in England and Wales. The total number within each sample of 1,104 who did so increased from 624 in 1979 to 710 in 1999.

Table 4.12. *Distribution of players who joined present club by transfer from another club in England and Wales, by division of current club (in May 1979 or 1999) and division of previous club at time of departure*

| | 1979 | | | | |
| | Previous division | | | | |
Current division	D1	D2	D3	D4	All
D1	67	39	14	9	129
D2	68	31	26	13	138
D3	50	49	47	23	169
D4	26	47	50	65	188
All	211	166	137	110	624

| | 1999 | | | | |
| | Previous division | | | | |
Current division	Prem/ D1	Div One/ D2	Div Two/ D3	Div Three/ D4	All
Prem	71	41	9	2	123
Div One	58	61	41	24	184
Div Two	36	64	69	32	201
Div Three	14	38	81	69	202
All	179	204	200	127	710

Sources: Rothmans, Hugman (1998).

Table 4.12 tabulates their current divisional status (in May 1979 or 1999) against the divisional status of their previous club at the time of departure. The results suggest that over time, large jumps between divisions have become rarer. In the 1979 season, there were nine individuals playing regularly in Division 1 who had transferred to their present club from Division 4; in 1999, the corresponding figure was only two. Similarly, in 1979, 26 individuals were playing regularly in Division 4 having transferred from Division 1; in 1999, the corresponding figure was 14. It seems reasonable to infer that reductions in the numbers of large jumps between divisions probably reflect a widening in the gap in playing standards between divisions during the intervening period.

The main findings of section 4.1 can be summarised as follows:
• The average age of regular professional players in England and Wales has increased by about 18 months over the past 20 years. The age

distribution is very similar in all divisions of the league, and is similar for British- and Irish-born players and players from overseas.

- Males born between September and February have around a 50 per cent higher chance of becoming professional footballers than those born between March and August.
- Players born outside Britain and Ireland accounted for over 14 per cent of those who appeared most regularly for their clubs in 1999.
- There were more regular players born in southern regions of England, the West Midlands and the Irish Republic in 1999 than in 1979, but many fewer from the northern regions of England and from Wales, Scotland and Northern Ireland. Even so, the north of England was still over-represented (relative to population) in 1999, and the south was under-represented. As a whole, southern clubs appear to have become more successful over time in recruiting and developing new players, while clubs generally appear to have become slightly less reliant on local recruitment.
- Player mobility between clubs increased significantly between 1979 and 1999. Mobility is higher at the bottom than at the top end of the league, but the difference has narrowed somewhat over time. It has, however, become less common for players to make large jumps in divisional status, between the top and bottom divisions, in a single transfer.

4.2 Patterns of international migration for professional footballers

The migration of professional sports labour at international level, both in football and in other sports, has been investigated in a series of articles by Maguire (1994), Maguire and Stead (1998) and Maguire and Pearton (2000). Section 4.2 reviews the main findings of this body of work. At the end of section 4.2 a snapshot of current patterns of (mainly) intra-European migration at the highest level is provided by analysis of cross-tabulations by country of origin and country of current employment of the 352 players named in the squads of the 16 nations that took part in the final stages of the European National Championships (Euro 2000) in the summer of 2000. Section 4.2 complements and extends the 'snapshot' picture of the distribution of squad players by nationality in the big five European leagues presented in section 2.1.

Maguire (1994) and Maguire and Stead (1998) suggest that observed patterns of migration of professional sports players across national boundaries reflect the interactions between a complex set of social, economic, historical, geographical and cultural influences. These include:

- the degree of geographical proximity between countries and the ease of travel

- the residual impact of historical, imperial or colonial ties
- countries' attitudes towards their own nationals seeking employment opportunities abroad
- countries' treatment of foreign nationals seeking employment opportunities within their own boundaries
- wage differentials, offering players the opportunity to increase their earnings by playing abroad, or (the other side of the same coin) clubs the opportunity to recruit talented players more easily or cheaply than is possible in the domestic transfer market
- the reputation, status and characteristics (including, for example, tactics, styles of play or the strength of physical competition) of the sport in different countries
- the extent to which media exposure raises interest and awareness in the sport across countries
- inter-personal links, which may influence groups of players from the same nation in deciding to play in the same foreign country or join the same club simultaneously.

In an analysis of the nationalities of all players participating in the first divisions of 32 European countries in the 1993 season, Maguire and Stead (1998) find that 1,295 players, or 11.4 per cent of the total workforce, were employed by clubs located in countries other than their country of nationality. Of these, the proportions from non-European countries, non-EU European countries and EU countries were 27 per cent, 54 per cent and 19 per cent, respectively. Flows of players into and out of Europe were concentrated most heavily on South American countries. In 1994, there were 297 transfers (at all levels) involving moves from non-European to European countries. Of these, 46 per cent were from South America, 22 per cent from North and Central America and the Caribbean, 20 per cent from Asia, 7 per cent from Africa and 5 per cent from Oceania. European countries located around the Mediterranean rim were the principal destinations for players imported from South America.

Intra-European trade in players was dominated by flows from Eastern Europe into the EU. According to Maguire and Stead (1998), 47.3 per cent of all non-EU players playing in the EU were from Eastern Europe. Such flows have naturally increased significantly since the collapse of communism at the end of the 1980s. Previously the majority of former communist countries permitted only a handful of players to move to the west, and in most cases not until the latter stages of their careers. During the 1990s, apart from the 'pull' factor of the higher earnings available in Western Europe, significant 'push' factors include the ethnic conflicts in the former Yugoslav territories, and considerable political and economic turmoil elsewhere, mirrored at the sporting level by the disappearance or wholesale reconstruction of various leagues and individual clubs. Players from Croatia and the rump Yugoslav Federation formed the two biggest groups among non-EU Europeans playing in the EU in 1993. Their principal destinations (in descending order) were Greece, Spain, Austria and Portugal.

One of the most striking aspects of Maguire and Stead's analysis of the intra-European player flows is the imbalance between the number of players moving from north to south and the number moving in the opposite direction. In the 1995 season, there were 29 northern Europeans playing in the south, but only five from southern Europe playing in the north. Speculating on the causes of this asymmetry, Maguire and Stead suggest that the (actual or perceived) professionalism, adaptability, language competence and high educational standards of Dutch and Scandanavian players, together with their physical attributes, tend to make them attractive targets for leading clubs in any country. In contrast, northern European perceptions of southern Europeans tend to focus on concerns about temperament or the ability to adapt to the physical demands of the northern style of play. Whether such attributes are imagined or real is to some extent beside the point, since it is the perception that counts in determining recruitment practices.

Naturally, the wealthy Italian league was and still is an especially popular destination for the most talented EU players. In the 1995 season 24 of Italy's 59 imports were from the EU, while 15 were from elsewhere in Europe and 20 from the rest of the world (Maguire and Stead, 1998). In the early 1990s a number of high-profile Dutch players, including Gullit, van Basten and Riijkard, were prominent in Serie A. Until the middle of the decade, however, the export of Italian players (at any level) to other EU leagues was rare. More recently this situation has changed to some extent, with Zola, di Matteo, Vialli, Ravinelli, Carbone and di Canio, for example, all joining English clubs during the late 1990s. Similarly very few players of Spanish nationality were found playing in other European countries in the 1995 season. Spain's First Division was even more cosmopolitan than Italy's Serie A, with 81 (compared to 59) foreign nationals employed. Spain, however, was much more reliant than Italy on non-EU nationals: 44 of Spain's 81 imports were from Eastern Europe, 31 were from South America, and only four were from the EU.

Similar patterns are evident in a later survey reported by Maguire and Pearton (2000), based on the members of the 32 national squads (each one with 22 players) which took part in the finals of the 1998 World Cup tournament staged in France. This survey confirms the central position of Europe in the world football labour market. The total number of World

Cup finals places received by each of six continental regions are determined by quota, with parallel regional qualifying competitions used to determine which nations obtain places. Europe received 15 of the 32 places (47 per cent) in the 1998 tournament, while 436 of the 704 squad players (62 per cent) were employed by European clubs. Among the 704 squad players, there were 122 non-Europeans playing for European clubs. In stark contrast, there were no non-South Americans playing in South America, and no non-Africans playing in Africa. Of the 110 South American squad players, 37 per cent played outside South America and of these 83 per cent played in Europe. Italy and Spain were the most popular destinations for South American players. Of the 110 African squad players, 67 per cent played outside Africa and of these 96 per cent played in Europe. France and Spain were the most popular destinations for African players.

Within Europe, Italy, Spain and England were the biggest importers of World Cup players, ahead of Belgium, Germany and France, whose clubs employed the highest proportions of foreign nationals in Maguire and Stead's (1998) earlier survey (based on 1995 data on all first-division players). Maguire and Pearton attribute the discrepancy partly to the higher preponderance in the World Cup survey of elite players, who naturally tend to gravitate towards the leagues with the highest spending power. Any changes in patterns of intra-European migration between 1995 and 1998 are also likely to reflect the impact of the Bosman ruling (see chapter 2). By 1998 France appears to have replaced Holland as the most popular recruiting ground within the EU for the leading Italian clubs. The tendency for Spain to recruit principally from Eastern Europe and South America rather than from the EU remained evident, however, as did the imbalance between the magnitudes of north–south and south–north intra-European migration flows described above.

Section 4.2 concludes by reporting an analysis of the home and destination countries of the members of the 16 national squads which took part in the finals of the 2000 European National Championships (Euro 2000) staged in Belgium and Holland. The analysis, along the same lines as that of the 1998 World Cup reported by Maguire and Stead (2000), provides a more recent snapshot of patterns of intra-European player migration at the highest level. As in the World Cup, 22 players are permitted in each squad, or 352 players in total. A notable feature of Euro 2000 was that just over half of those selected, 177 players or 50.3 per cent of the total, were foreign-based players.

The full data are shown in table 4.13. The columns of table 4.13 show the 16 participating nations, arranged from left to right in ascending order of the numbers of foreign-based players included in their squads,

Table 4.13. *Analysis of home countries and countries of employment, Euro 2000 squad players*

Destination country	Home country																
	Ita	Spa	Eng	Tur	Ger	Por	Bel	Cze	Rom	Nor	Fra	Slov	Swe	Hol	Yug	Den	All
England			*21*	1	2	1	2	3	1	9	6		4	5		5	39
Spain		*22*	1	1		4		1	6		2		3	7	7	4	33
Italy	*22*				1	4	1	2	1		5	3	3	3	5	4	29
Germany					*18*		4	5	1	1	2		2		1	3	22
Holland							3	1	2					*5*	2		10
Belgium						1	*10*		1	1		3			1		7
France						1	1			1	*7*	1			1	1	5
Portugal						*11*	1	1									4
Turkey				*19*					3								3
Denmark										1			2			*3*	3
Norway										*7*			1				1
Yugoslavia												1			*4*		1
Czech								*8*									0
Romania									*7*								0
Sweden													*5*				0
Slovenia												*6*					0
Scotland				1						1			2	2			6
Austria								1				5					6
Greece										1		1				1	3
USA					1											1	2
Croatia												1					1
Switzerland												1					1
Japan															1		1
All	0	0	1	3	4	11	12	14	15	15	15	16	17	17	18	19	177

Source: *World Soccer* (June 2000).

shown in the final row. At one extreme, Italy and Spain selected squads consisting solely of home-based players. At the other extreme, Denmark and Yugoslavia selected 19 and 18 foreign-based players, respectively. The rows of table 4.13 show the countries of employment of the squad members of each country. The first 16 rows show players employed in the participating nations; the remaining seven rows show players employed in non-participating nations. Each group of nations is arranged in descending order of the total numbers of imported players employed, shown in the final column. The numbers of home-based players in each squad, shown in italics in the relevant cells of table 4.13, are not included in the final row and column totals.

Table 4.13 identifies England as by some distance the leading importer of players at this level, followed by Spain, Italy and Germany. England's position, together with the fact that there was only one foreign-based England squad member, undoubtedly reflects the present-day attractiveness of the English league to leading players as a result of its commercial vibrancy, despite the fact that doubts remain (fuelled partly by the England team's own performances in Euro 2000!) as to whether playing standards in England are truly comparable with the very best that can be found elsewhere in Europe. The long-standing tendency for the leading Spanish and Italian players to remain home-based has continued in 2000, though the absence of foreign-based players from the Italian squad appears to reflect a conscious policy decision rather than a complete lack of suitably skilled foreign-based talent.

England's apparent ascendancy within Europe as an importer of foreign-based players is clearly a recent phenomenon, but several longer-established features of intra-European migration patterns are also apparent in table 4.13. These include the popularity of England as a destination for Scandinavians (especially Norwegians); the ability of Scandinavians to find employment across a wide range of northern and southern European countries; the popularity of Spain (especially) and Italy as a destination for Eastern Europeans (represented here principally by Yugoslavia and Romania); and the importance of geographical proximity or historical links in determining migration flows, especially for players from nations with less economically powerful domestic leagues. In Euro 2000 these included the Czech Republic with five squad members based in Germany, and Slovenia with five Austrian-based players.

Finally it is interesting to note that the number of squad members based in either Italy or Spain provides a rather accurate predictor of eventual success in Euro 2000. Apart from these two countries themselves, the five nations with the next highest totals on this criterion (Yugoslavia, Holland, Portugal, France and Romania) all progressed beyond the first round to reach the quarter-finals. Turkey, unusually among the lesser European powers at club level, picked 19 home-based nationals, and was the only quarter-finalist without significant numbers of Italian or Spanish-based players. In the Turkish case, a policy aimed at limiting the outflow of leading players to foreign clubs in recent years appears to have paid dividends in 2000, with a successful Euro 2000 campaign for the national team following a UEFA Cup victory for Galatasaray, making them the first Turkish team to lift a European club trophy.

4.3 The earnings of professional footballers

In section 4.3, the focus shifts away from the occupational mobility of professional football players, towards the determinants of their compensation. Both the level and the rapid growth of earnings of the top professional football players are of course issues of significant popular concern. In the 1999 season, the total wages and salaries bill of the 20 English Premier League clubs was £391 million: a figure that represents an increase of more than 200 per cent over the five previous seasons for the same clubs (Deloitte and Touche, 2000). In the 2000 season, four clubs (Manchester United, Liverpool, Chelsea and Arsenal) each paid a total wages and salaries bill of more than £25 million. A survey in the spring of 2000 estimated that as many as 100 Premier League players earned a basic wage above £1 million per year or £25,000 per week (*The Independent*, 18 April 2000). The number of players breaching the £1 million annual wage barrier in England is increasing rapidly.

Public concern about football players' earnings tends to have two dimensions: one which relates to the economic or competitive implications for the football industry itself; and one which questions the appropriateness, or even the morality, of such disproportionately high rewards accruing to participants in what is seen as an essentially frivolous occupation. The first of these areas is considered at length elsewhere in this volume (see especially chapters 2 and 3). The second is the main concern of section 4.3. Even allowing for the fact that career durations at the highest level in professional sports are often brief, can it be right that the leading professional sports stars achieve earnings so obviously disproportionate to those of other occupational groups, including doctors, nurses, teachers and police officers? To most observers, of course, the contributions of these latter groups to society's well-being appear far more significant than those of even the most well-intentioned sports personalities.

Without necessarily being able to resolve the moral debate to everyone's satisfaction, economists can perhaps make a significant contribution to the discussion by proposing explanations for observed patterns of professional sports stars' earnings that are grounded in axioms of rational, optimising behaviour on the part of players and the clubs that employ them. Two of the most influential theoretical contributions by economists (Lazear and Rosen, 1981; Rosen, 1981) are reviewed in some detail in section 4.3.

One way to approach the subject of wage determination is simply to consider the market for football players in the same way as any other labour market, by analysing the interaction between the supply and demand for players. Market mechanisms allocate players to clubs by matching bids and offers for the players' services. If clubs seek to maximise profits, the highest wage that a club is prepared to offer a player is the amount he would add to the club's revenue if he were signed: his Marginal Revenue Product (*MRP*). If the player were paid more than his *MRP*, the club's profit would be lower than if it had not signed him. If the club can get away with paying the player less than his *MRP*, the club's profit is higher than if it had not signed him.

As already seen, the question as to whether a player is paid his *MRP* depends partly on the institutional characteristics of the players' labour market. In the theoretical models described in section 3.1, under a reserve clause players do not generally receive a wage equal to their *MRP*. Because the player can negotiate only with the club that owns his contract, effectively there is only one bidder for the player's services and the market structure is monopsonistic. The player's reservation wage is the next highest that he can achieve in alternative employment outside the sport. Provided the wage on offer is equal to or higher than the reservation wage, the theoretical models predict that the player will accept this wage. Wages therefore tend to be held down, and players' compensation may capture only a small proportion of the clubs' total revenues. Nevertheless, if there is trade in players between clubs, the player is still expected to end up playing for the club with which his *MRP* is the highest: the club to which he is most valuable.

Under free agency the player's wage should lie between his *MRP* with that club and the next highest *MRP* that would be attainable if he were to sign for another club. The club to which the player is most valuable can outbid other clubs for his services, and still increase its profit by signing him. The theoretical models predict that under free agency each player should capture at least his *MRP* with the club that would place the second-highest value upon him out of all clubs in the league. Wages tend to be bid up to the point where most of the clubs' revenues end up contributing to players' compensation (Quirk and Fort, 1992).

One possible objection to this type of analysis when applied to football clubs arises from its reliance on the profit maximisation assumption. As seen in chapter 1, Sloane (1971) argues that it is more appropriate to model the club's objectives using a utility maximising framework. Football clubs seek to maximise utility, subject to a financial solvency constraint. Arguments in the utility function include playing success, attendance and profit. In this case, even under a reserve clause clubs that attach high value to playing success relative to profit may choose to sign players for wages higher than their *MRP*, even though it is not profitable to do so.

Nevertheless, departures on the part of some clubs from profit maximisation hardly seem likely to account for the highly skewed patterns observed in the distribution of earnings, especially since in some cases where the profit maximisation assumption seems reasonable, very high wages are still paid to leading players. Several floated English football clubs, as well as the leading teams in a number of North American professional sports, spring readily to mind.

If the earnings of star players are to be explained using marginal productivity theory within a traditional supply-and-demand framework, it therefore seems necessary to confront head-on the question of whether the *MRP*s of leading football players could conceivably be so high as to justify annual wages of £1 million or more. Rosen (1981) provides an influential explanation as to how not only sports stars, but also superstars in other fields such as acting, publishing and music can indeed generate extremely high *MRP*s when they reach the pinnacle of their respective professions. Although Rosen's analysis is presented in terms of professionals selling their services directly to the public, most of the insights are relevant at a general level in the case of professional team sports, in which individual sellers contract with one another (or with a club) to form a team before their services are sold collectively to the public. It is important to note at the outset, however, that when the superstars model is applied to team sports, a further set of complexities that arise in explaining intra-team earnings distributions are not addressed. This issue will be pursued later in section 4.3.

The economics of superstars

Rosen (1981) seeks to explain not only the highly skewed distribution of earnings within certain professions, but also the unusually high levels of seller concentration that appear to coexist with skewed earnings. In other words it is important to explain not only the high levels of earnings, but also why employment in the fields concerned often tends to be restricted to relatively small numbers of individuals. Professional football in England, for example, has an annual turnover of around £1 billion, but employs only just over 3,000 professionals in its core activity of playing football matches. Rosen's account of these phenomena rests on two key aspects of consumer tastes and production technology:

- *Imperfect substitution* between sellers of certain services. The very best talent is in scarce supply. For consumers lesser talent is not perfectly substitutable for greater talent, even if there is compensation in terms of quantity. For example, Manchester United might be three times more talented than Birmingham City, but watching Birmingham City on three occasions is not equivalent to watching Manchester United once.
- *Scale economies in joint consumption* of certain services. The technology of production enables very large audiences to be serviced at the same time. The effort and therefore the production costs incurred by Manchester United's players are much the same if they are playing in a half-empty stadium, or in front of a capacity crowd, or additionally before a large television audience. The technology, in other words, has characteristics similar to that employed to supply certain public goods like street lighting and national defence: production costs depend only slightly, or not at all, on the number of people consuming the service. But in contrast to these examples, in football there are no free rider problems preventing the seller from appropriating a charge for providing the service. Would-be audience members who are unwilling to pay (by purchasing a match ticket or a pay-television subscription) can easily be excluded from consumption.

The implications of these attributes of tastes and technology for the distribution of earnings and employment opportunities depend on the precise nature of the relationship between production costs and audience size. Rosen suggests two reasons why marginal costs of production may eventually start to increase as the audience size increases. First, *internal diseconomies* include all the usual reasons why marginal costs rise as output increases. In professional football, marginal costs start to rise when players become tired or injured as the number of matches played increases, or perhaps as a result of increased stress or psychological pressure in matches played before a large audience. Second, *external diseconomies* are factors that reduce the quality of the product as the audience size increases. A stadium with a capacity of 50,000, for example, might provide a better viewing experience than one twice that size, owing to excessive distance from the pitch in the latter case. Beyond the stadium capacity, the television audience consumes a product that is presumably inferior to that obtained by 'live' spectators, though one whose characteristics do not vary further as the television audience size increases.

Rosen demonstrates first that imperfect substitution between sellers, combined with internal diseconomies, induces a skewed distribution of earnings, even if there are no joint consumption economies. The more talented sellers charge each consumer a higher price and capture a larger share of the market than their less talented counterparts. But in the absence of joint consumption economies, talent differentials do not lead to extremely high seller concentration: all sellers are able to capture some market share. Under certain simplifying assumptions, both the price paid by each consumer and each seller's audience share can be shown to be linear functions of the seller's talent. This implies that sellers' total earnings, the product of price and audience, are quadratic in talent. The distribution of earnings is therefore more skewed than the distribution of talent.

To account for high seller concentration as well as a skewed earnings distribution, joint consumption economies are also required in the model. Suppose initially that there are no internal or external diseconomies at all, so joint consumption economies are not limited by the size of the audience. In other words, the audience size can be expanded indefinitely, without imposing additional costs upon the seller, and without causing any deterioration in the quality of the product obtained by the consumer. In this extreme case, the market has the characteristics of a natural monopoly. The most talented seller is able to drive all other sellers out of business, and in the long run services the entire market. The equilibrium price, however, is constrained by the threat of entry. The rent element in the equilibrium price, which is proportional to the talent differential between the most and second most talented sellers, is modest. But crucially, the total rent obtained by the most talented seller is very large indeed, because the latter captures the entire audience. As Rosen and Sanderson (2000) observe, superstars achieve high earnings by operating at high volume (by servicing very large audiences) but at low margins (by charging each audience member only a modest mark-up relative to less talented suppliers).

The 'zero diseconomies' case described above is somewhat unrealistic, but useful because it illustrates the main insight of the Rosen model. The most talented seller captures the entire market because the production technology permits limitless expansion of the audience at zero cost to the seller. This is in stark contrast to the experience of doctors, nurses, teachers and police officers, who find that the number of patients they can treat, schoolchildren they can teach and criminals they can catch on any one day is strictly finite. The key to the high earnings of superstars, in other words, lies in the vast extent of the audience they can reach at any one time, afforded by the existence of scale economies in joint consumption (Rosen and Sanderson, 2000).

In practice, of course, one football team does not dominate the entire market. The Rosen model suggests that this is not solely due to considerations of jointness in production or competitive balance (see chapters 1 and 3). It is also to be expected if joint scale economies in consumption are eventually limited by internal or external diseconomies of the kind described above. In this case several sellers obtain market shares in long-run equilibrium. The price each seller charges is again constrained by the (actual not potential) presence in the market of other sellers with less talent, and the rent element in the price is dependent on the talent differential. If the rate at which internal or external diseconomies increase varies inversely with talent, audience share and price both increase with talent, but audience share increases at a faster rate than does price. As before the high earnings of the most talented sellers derive principally from the vast size of their audiences, rather than from the modest price differential paid by each audience member.

An extension of Rosen's superstars model is discussed by MacDonald (1988), who considers the career progression of performers who eventually become superstars in their fields, despite the fact that in the early stages of their careers they may have imperfect information about their future performance and future earnings. Aspiring stars enter the profession at a young age and perform cheaply. The audience feedback they receive provides useful but incomplete information about their probable future performance. Those who receive negative feedback are persuaded to withdraw from the profession. Those who receive positive feedback are encouraged to continue, and as the favourable notices accumulate their audience rapidly expands. So, too, do their earnings, and as in the Rosen model at a faster rate than the talent gradient would suggest. Although MacDonald seems to have in mind primarily groups such as actors or musicians, the notion of a professional sports apprenticeship as an information-gathering process, enabling individuals to take rational decisions at various stages as to whether to continue in pursuit of a career as a professional, seems an appropriate description of the path followed by many aspiring youngsters in professional sports.

In summary, the contrast between the configurations of high earnings–low utility achieved by sports stars, and low earnings–high utility achieved by groups such as nurses and teachers is explained mainly by the technologies under which the former operate, which enable them to provide services, albeit of modest value, to very large audiences (Rosen, 1981; Rosen and Sanderson, 2000). The latter groups provide services of much higher value, but to a very finite number of users. The same technological conditions explain the high levels of seller concentration found in professional sports. Internal and external diseconomies of scale, however, impose limits on the audience share of the most talented sellers, enabling the less talented to capture some share of the market. The road from apprenticeship to stardom can be viewed as a type of sequential information-gathering process, in which cumulative feedback on performance enables the individual to take rational decisions on whether to continue or withdraw from the profession (MacDonald, 1988).

Rosen's essentially technological explanation for the high earnings of superstars is clearly relevant in explaining wage inflation in professional football during the 1990s. Before the introduction of pay-television, English football reached large television audiences via free-to-air services provided by the BBC and ITV. But constrained by this type of 'public goods' production technology, football was unable to appropriate the full economic price for providing the service to individual audience members. Since the late 1980s, however, technological innovation in broadcasting has transformed this situation. Television has unquestionably made the single most important contribution to recent growth in football revenues. Meanwhile, with further moves in the direction of free agency taking place in the footballers' labour market at the same time, the leading players' bargaining position in wage negotiations has strengthened appreciably. This has enabled them to capture a large proportion of the rent element in the additional revenues that are being generated, resulting in rampant wage inflation.

Rank-order tournaments and intra-team earnings distributions

As noted previously, Rosen's insights on the economics of superstars do not address the complexities of intra-team earnings distributions. Yet at first sight, these can seem as puzzling as the disparities between the earnings of sports stars in general and those of other groups. In the English Premier League, for example, the highest paid players can earn many times as much as the average first-team player, even though it seems doubtful whether this differential could be explained by a corresponding differential in *MRP*.

In a competitive labour market, the intra-team wage structure is equivalent to a piece-rate system, since each player receives a wage equivalent to his *MRP*. Differences in wages between players in the same club should reflect the fact that those contributing most to club revenues get paid the most. Casual observation, however, suggests that some players receive large wage increases even when there is no noticeable improvement in performance. Often, players who might be judged only a small fraction better than others appear to earn significantly more. In these cases, the intra-team wage structure seems to be hierarchical. The models outlined above are unable to explain why top stars can earn n times more than other players, if the talent gradient is shallower than n, and if their contribution to revenue is not n times as high.

In a highly influential paper on the determination of executive salaries in corporate business, Lazear and Rosen (1981) argue by analogy that top executives' high salaries are equivalent to the outcome of a rank-order tournament. In situations where it is costly to monitor or measure exactly the productivity of individual workers, it may be efficient for firms to rank workers according to their productivity, and then reward them according to the rankings that they achieve. In the corporate sector, the salaries of vice-presidents are typically much lower than those of presidents. Yet presidents are often promoted from the ranks of vice-presidents. On the particular day an individual is promoted, his salary might triple, but it is difficult to argue that his productivity has also suddenly increased by an equivalent amount on the same day.

According to the Lazear and Rosen model, the individual who achieves promotion to president is like the winner of a contest for which there is a very large first prize. The president's salary does not reflect his or her current productivity, but it does induce all junior employees (from the rank of vice-president downwards) to perform appropriately, in the hope that one day they too will win the prize and achieve promotion to president. In other words, the president earns a high salary not because he is highly productive as president, but because this type of salary structure provides incentives for all employees to be more productive over their entire working lives.

Scully (1995) adapts this type of analysis in order to examine player wage determination in a number of North American sports. It is worth noting that in contrast to the situation in the corporate sector, the productivity of each player or 'worker' is relatively easy to measure (baseball being perhaps the most obvious case in point). Both the employer *and* the customer observe the joint output of the team, and have ample opportunity to form their own subjective assessments of the individual contributions of each team member. With reference to English football, this relationship is aptly described as follows. 'The first team player faces over forty public examinations a year before an attendance of thousands of spectators. He will be talked about, shouted at, criticised or praised, given extensive coverage in the press and radio . . . he is in the limelight and must be seen to behave as befits his profession' (PEP, 1966, p. 134).

Even so, professional team sports players do not seem to be paid on a piece-rate basis. Scully (1995) argues that the rank-order tournament model may provide a more convincing explanation of compensation scales than the traditional supply-and-demand model. Clubs that are motivated either by playing success or by profit need players to develop their skills to their maximum potential, and to exert the maximum effort on behalf of the team. A compensation structure in which wages depend upon each player's ranking relative to others within the same club provides suitable incentives for all players to compete (effectively against one another) in pursuit of these aims. Even in sports such as football, where there is high input complementarity and individual outputs are less easily identified, the rank-order tournament model may still be applicable.

In English football, there are no restrictions on the number of players a club can register. A typical league club may have a first team squad of 25–30 full-time professional players, while some Premier League clubs have squads twice as large as this. Each club's professionals compete against one another for a place in the first team. At the start of each game the manager selects one goalkeeper, 10 outfield players and five substitutes, three of whom can be used to replace any of the 11 players on the field of play at any time during the game, either for tactical reasons or because of injury. The numbers of defenders, midfield players and forwards among the outfield players depends upon the tactical choices of the manager. Typical formations include 4-3-3 (four defenders, three midfielders and three forwards), 4-4-2, 5-3-2 and 3-5-2. For each playing position, the squad will include several players who can provide cover. Especially useful in this respect are utility players, who are able to play in more than one outfield position. Performance is related to athletic endowment such as speed, strength, agility, balance and co-ordination; intangible attributes of talent such as determination and concentration; and player and team investments in enhancing skill through coaching, tactical awareness and practice at passing, shooting, heading and tackling.

Theoretical and empirical models of rank-order tournaments have been applied extensively to individual sports such as tennis and golf. Competitors face a fixed prize structure and achieve the next-higher reward by moving up by one place in the ranking of competitors. Scully (1995) argues, however, that competition among team sports players for a first-team place is not entirely dissimilar. Those in the first team are always threatened explicitly by the performance of lower-ranked reserve players, and implicitly by the possibility that the club might sign a replacement player for the same position from outside. If a first-team player experiences a slump in form, a reserve is substituted into the team or the club acquires a new player. Injury or suspension for disciplinary transgressions can also lead to the replacement of one player by another. A replacement that performs well can often capture a first-team place, until he in turn eventually drops out owing to loss of form, injury or suspension.

The rest of this sub-section contains an exposition of the rank-order tournament model using mathematical notation. Apart from minor changes of notation, the model is the one presented by Scully (1995). It is assumed that two players ($i=1,2$) are competing for one first team place. The performance of player i, denoted Q_i, is determined by his athletic endowment and his investment in playing skill, denoted t_i, plus a number of exogenous factors that affect performance randomly, denoted ε_i. Random factors include temporary fluctuations in form, fitness and fortune. The probability that player 1 defeats player 2 in the contest for a first-team place, denoted p, is the probability that player 1's performance exceeds that of player 2:

$$p = p(Q_1 > Q_2) = p(t_1 - t_2 > \varepsilon_2 - \varepsilon_1) = F(t_1 - t_2) \qquad (4.1)$$

where $Q_i = t_i + \varepsilon_i$ for $i = 1, 2$; $E(\varepsilon_2 - \varepsilon_1) = 0$; and $F(\ )$ is the cumulative distribution function of $\varepsilon_2 - \varepsilon_1$.

The intra-team wage structure pays S_F to the first-choice player and S_R to the reserve player, with $S_F > S_R$. The expected wages of the two players, S_1 and S_2, are determined by the probability that player 1 beats player 2 for the first team place (p) and the wages for the two positions (S_F, S_R):

$$S_1 = pS_F + (1-p)S_R; \qquad S_2 = (1-p)S_F + pS_R \qquad (4.2)$$

Players can improve their skills by means of investment. Because some attributes of playing talent are natural, the cost of investment, $C_i(t_i)$, is assumed to vary between players. It is assumed that the marginal cost of investment in further skill increases with the level of skill already acquired, so $\dfrac{\partial C_i}{\partial t_i} > 0$, and that marginal cost increases at a faster rate as the level of skill increases, so $\dfrac{\partial^2 C_i}{\partial t_i^2} > 0$. If player 1 has more natural ability than player 2, player 1's marginal cost of further investment in playing skill (starting at any given level of skill) is lower than that of player 2, so $\dfrac{\partial C_1}{\partial t_1} < \dfrac{\partial C_2}{\partial t_2}$. Players are assumed to invest in the development of playing skills to maximise expected net income, $Y_i = S_i - C_i(t_i)$. The first-order conditions are:

$$\frac{\partial Y_i}{\partial t_i} = (S_F - S_R)f(t_1 - t_2) - C_i'(t_i) = 0 \qquad \text{(for } i = 1, 2) \qquad (4.3)$$

where $f = F'$ is the probability density function of $\varepsilon_2 - \varepsilon_1$. Equation (4.3) provides the Cournot–Nash solution for each player's level of investment in skill (based on the assumption that the investment of the competitor is fixed at its current level) in terms of the wage levels, S_F and S_R. The

Marginal cost and
benefit to players
of investment in
talent

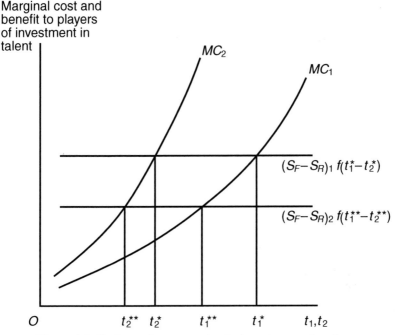

Figure 4.1 Optimum investment in playing talent, rank-order tournament model

equilibrium is illustrated in figure 4.1. Player 1 has more natural ability than player 2, so $MC_1 = \dfrac{\partial C_1}{\partial t_1} < MC_2 = \dfrac{\partial C_2}{\partial t_2}$. If the wage differential is $(S_F - S_R)_1$, t_1^* and t_2^* represent the optimal investments in playing talent for each player.

The greater the level of playing skill at the club's disposal, the more valuable is each match to the club. By varying the intra-team wage structure (S_F, S_R), the club can influence the level of investment by both players in their playing skills. Increased player investment adds to the value of the club's matches, but there are lower and upper bounds to the range within which the club can vary the wages. First, S_R has a lower bound because player 2 has the option to earn a living outside the sport. If player 2's potential earnings outside the sport are $\overline{C}$, this constraint implies that the lower bound of player 2's expected earnings is equal to outside earnings plus player 2's cost of investment in playing skill:

$$(1 - p)S_F + pS_R = C_2(t_2) + \overline{C} \tag{4.4}$$

Second, assuming that the club has a financial constraint which prohibits it from making a loss, there is an upper bound to the total wage bill, equal to the club's total revenue.

Scully simplifies the derivation of the equilibrium intra-team wage structure by introducing a parameter c $(0 < c \leq 1)$, which reflects the degree of competitiveness in the players' labour market. c is the total wage bill expressed as a proportion of total revenue, as follows:

$$S_F + S_R = cTR \tag{4.5}$$

At the maximum value of $c = 1$, the players' wages capture all of the club's revenue. This would apply with free agency in the players' labour market, so the players' bargaining power is maximised.[2] The distance by which c falls below one is a measure of the degree of monopsony power held by the club as a buyer of players.

Equations (4.4) and (4.5) can be used to derive the following expressions for the wage levels, S_F and S_R:

$$S_F = cTR[p/(2p-1)] - [(C_2(t_2) + \bar{C})/(2p-1)]$$
$$S_R = [(C_2(t_2) + \bar{C})/(2p-1)] - cTR[(1-p)/(2p-1)] \tag{4.6}$$

Scully points out two important implications of the model:

- The greater the degree of monopsony power in the players' labour market, the narrower is the intra-team wage structure. This follows from (4.6), because $S_F - S_R = [cTR - 2(C_2(t_2) + \bar{C})]/(2p-1)$. Conversely, a move towards free agency should increase the differential between the wages of the top players and the rest.
- A reduction in the differential between S_F and S_R reduces the level of investment in playing skills by both players, and narrows the differential in playing skills between the first-team and the reserve team player. This is illustrated by the move from (t_1^*, t_2^*) to (t_1^{**}, t_2^{**}) in figure 4.1. Conversely, a move towards free agency should increase the level of investment in playing skills generally, and increase the differential between the playing skills of the top players and the rest.

Clearly, the rank-order tournament model of wage determination generates a number of propositions which seem relevant in the case of English football. In contrast to the traditional supply-and-demand model, the rank-order tournament model is capable of decoupling players' wages from their MRPs, thereby explaining highly unequal and hierarchical intra-team wage distributions (Lazear and Rosen, 1981; Scully, 1995).

---

[2] Implicitly, for $c = 1$ there is also an assumption that the club seeks to maximise revenue or playing success, subject to a zero profit constraint.

The model also predicts that moves towards free agency should lead to a widening of the gap in compensation between top players and the rest, and should lead to an increase in investment in playing skills all round. There is no doubt that the former has occurred in English football since movement towards free agency first started in the early 1960s. The latter is more difficult to verify conclusively, but there is overwhelming anecdotal evidence: video footage suggests, and most commentators agree, that modern-day players are much fitter, faster and stronger than their counterparts from earlier eras.[3] More tentatively, it is possible to speculate that increased investment in human capital by players could account for the increase over the past 20 years in the average age of the players appearing most regularly in the league (see section 4.1). If as seems likely, the full benefits of such investment take time to materialise, players' performance may tend to peak later, and careers may tend to last longer, under a high-investment than under a low-investment regime. This would be consistent with the shift in the age distribution identified in table 4.1.

4.4 Determinants of players' compensation: empirical evidence

Empirical evidence on the links between competitive conditions in the players' labour market, wage structures and performance in football is virtually non-existent at the microeconomic level, because in most countries individual players' wage details are not disclosed. For a number of North American professional team sports, however, there is sufficient individual disclosure to permit empirical investigation of these relationships at the micro level. An influential early contribution to this literature was made by Scully (1974), who developed a framework for making comparisons between estimated $MRPs$ for different categories of player in Major League Baseball (MLB), and the average wages of players in the same categories. Scully's study dates from the pre-free-agency period when the reserve clause was still effective, so systematic divergence between wages and $MRPs$ is to be expected.

Scully obtains estimated marginal productivities for baseball hitters and pitchers using the slope coefficients in a regression of team win ratios on team slugging averages (for hitters) and team strikeout-to-walk ratios (for pitchers). Dummy variables are also included in the regression to

---

[3] It is not at all clear, however, that modern-day players are more skilful on average than players of earlier periods. Natural skill is, of course, mainly an endowed rather than an acquired attribute, and is therefore not sensitive to changes in the structure of players' compensation.

control for differences between the National League (NL) and the American League (AL), and to differentiate teams according to the extent to which they were in contention to be divisional winners in the season concerned. Gross *MRP*s for hitters and for pitchers are imputed by multiplying the marginal productivity estimates by the slope coefficient obtained from a second regression of team revenues on win ratios. Various additional controls used in the second regression include a NL–AL dummy, home-town population and a variable reflecting underlying differences between teams in intensity of support. Net *MRP*s are calculated by deducting allowances for player training and other factor costs from the gross *MRP*s.

Scully then estimates wage equations for hitters and pitchers, using individual data. Among the explanatory variables are personal career slugging averages and strikeout-to-walk ratios, career durations and variables (such as population and intensity of support) that are also used in the revenue regression to control for demand factors contributing to monopoly rent. The latter are mainly insignificant in the wages equations, suggesting that players failed to capture any share of monopoly rents under the reserve clause. The comparisons between *MRP*s and wages are drawn by substituting sets of explanatory variables describing representative hitters and pitchers of mediocre, average and star quality into the various estimated equations. The *MRP*–talent gradient is found to be much steeper than the wage-talent gradient. Consequently, while mediocre players earned more than their net *MRP*s, the wages of average players and star players were around only 20 per cent and 15 per cent of their net *MRP*s, respectively. This constitutes evidence that before free agency there was substantial monopsony exploitation in the players' labour market.

Using an empirical framework similar to that employed by Scully 20 years earlier, MacDonald and Reynolds (1994) use data on player performance and earnings in MLB in the 1987 season to show that after the introduction of free agency, players' wages matched their estimated career *MRP* more closely than in the pre-free-agency period. But there were still some anomalies: young players were paid less than their *MRP*, perhaps because of institutional restrictions on their mobility within the labour market, and senior pitchers (but not senior hitters) were over-paid. MacDonald and Reynolds also present evidence that differences between the wages of top and middle-rank players are consistent with Rosen's model of superstars.

Scully (1995) uses data on the individual performance and wages of baseball and basketball players before and after the introduction of free agency in both sports to examine the impact of this change. There is of course no doubt that the wage–talent gradient has become much steeper during the free-agency period, and for both sports the sensitivity of wages to performance in the current season and to measures of past experience (included in the regressions to control for talent, investment and effort) is higher than it was before free agency. For baseball, an average individual performance index exceeds an average individual wage index for up to 547 career games; thereafter, the wage index exceeds the performance index. This finding seems consistent with the time-profile of wages predicted by the rank-order tournament model. For the pre-free-agency period, in contrast, the wage index is higher than the performance index both for inexperienced players (less than 405 games) and for players nearing the end of their careers (1,550 games).

On the other hand, some empirical research has suggested that there are limits to the applicability of the rank-order tournament model to team sports. An intra-team wage distribution that is *too* unequal may be divisive, perhaps damaging team cohesion and spirit to an extent that outweighs the incentive benefit described above. It is certainly common enough for English football clubs to explain failure to reach agreement with a player they are seeking to sign in terms of a reluctance or refusal to overturn existing internal wage structures. Richards and Guell (1998) argue on similar lines that a high intra-team variance in wages may have a negative effect on performance, since it implies a dispersed level of talent and an inability to function effectively as a team. One or two star players do not necessarily carry a team. In their empirical results for MLB over the period 1992–5, the mean wage has a positive effect on the win ratio and the propensity to win championships, but an increase in the variance of wages reduces the win ratio (with a coefficient that is significant at the 10 per cent level). A greater dispersion of wages does not seem to affect the probability of winning the championship, however.

The investigation of discrimination in professional team sports has motivated many empirical studies of the determinants of player compensation, especially in the USA. This issue has been of particular interest in North American sports because before the Second World War there was complete racial segregation at professional level in a number of sports: the teams in the top leagues employed only white players. The colour bar was lifted for the first time in both baseball and basketball during the late 1940s, but there is no doubt that discriminatory practices still continued for many more years afterwards.

Speaking generally, the forms that discrimination can take include inequality in the level of compensation; inequality in hiring standards; inequality in the allocation of playing positions; and inequality in the availability of opportunities for endorsements or sponsorship. Possible perpetrators of discrimination are employers, co-workers or customers. Although in principle it is possible to distinguish between the different forms and sources of discrimination, in practice the boundaries may be blurred. A derisory wage offer, for example, may be tantamount to a refusal to hire. An employer practising discrimination may seek to blame the attitudes of customers.

In the present context, Becker's (1971) argument would suggest that eventually, economic competition between teams as employers should eliminate employer discrimination. Teams that discriminate should be forced out of business because they are inefficient. But using once again the 'joint economies of scale in consumption' argument (see section 4.3) Rosen and Sanderson (2000) suggest that customer discrimination is likely to have especially adverse consequences for black athletes. Each customer may demonstrate only a trivial prejudice, reflected in a small reduction in the price they are willing to pay to watch a team containing black athletes. But from the team's perspective, the total loss of revenue that has to be compensated (by paying black athletes a wage that reflects customer prejudices) may be huge, because of the large audience sizes involved. In this case a feasible wage may not exist, and the black athlete is effectively forced out of the market altogether.

Kahn (1991) reviews the pre-1990s empirical literature on discrimination in professional team sports, while Kahn (2000) provides a recent update. Empirical tests for wage discrimination normally use a cross-sectional regression of individual wages on various productivity indicators, and a dummy variable for race (or any other characteristic that is thought to be the subject of discrimination). The availability of accurate productivity indicators is vital since, as Kahn points out, any correlation between race and the measurement error in the productivity component will lead to bias in the estimated discrimination effect. Direct tests for discrimination in hiring practices are rather more unusual, principally because data on players that *were not* hired is required, as well as data on those that were. Indirect testing, mostly based on comparisons between the performances of black and white players, is more common. If blacks tend to outperform whites on average this is interpreted as evidence of discrimination in hiring: on average, a black athlete needs to attain a higher standard to be hired than a white one. Similar methods can be used to test for discrimination in the allocation of specific team positions between whites and blacks. Finally, tests for discrimination on the part of customers normally focus on the relationship between match attendances or revenues and team racial composition.

Summarising broadly the pre-1990s' evidence for North American team sports, Kahn finds that evidence of wage, hiring or customer racial discrimination in baseball is relatively weak. There is, however, some evidence of discrimination in terms of the length of career durations and in the allocation of team positions. In basketball, in contrast, there is consistent evidence of both wage and customer discrimination. Apart from some evidence of positional discrimination, less evidence on other forms of discrimination is available for American football, mainly because of difficulties in defining suitable individual performance indicators.

It is also apparent that evidence of discrimination in North American team sports is becoming weaker over time (Kahn, 2000; Rosen and Sanderson, 2000). Given that most of the evidence of discrimination during the 1980s was stronger for basketball than for other sports, it is unsurprising that basketball was the main focus for several discrimination studies during the 1990s. Using NBA data for the 1995 season, Hamilton (1997) finds evidence of a 1 per cent across-the-board wage differential between white and black players. At the lower end of the wage range, whites earned less than blacks; though when the number of matches is included in the regressions as a control, the effect reverses. At the upper end of the wage range, whites earned more than equally qualified blacks. The premium was the same regardless of the race of the team's manager, and so is attributed by Hamilton to customer rather than employer discrimination.

Bodvarsson and Brastow (1999) use wage regressions to test for employer discrimination in the NBA in the 1986 and 1991 seasons. Again the race of the team's manager is assumed to convey information about team owners' attitudes: owners that employ black managers are assumed to be non-discriminators. The test therefore examines whether black players working for white managers experienced discrimination. The wage regressions include the percentages of team members and of the local population that were black, as controls for co-worker and customer discrimination, respectively. Wage discrimination, present in 1986, is found to have disappeared by 1991. This finding is consistent with the hypothesis that two important structural changes in the interim increased competition between teams as employers, and therefore reduced the discretion for team owners to exercise discrimination as monopsony purchasers in the labour market. These were the 1988 NBA Collective Bargaining Agreement which introduced free agency, and the addition of four new teams which stimulated competition between teams as employers of players.

Szymanski (2000b) has presented the first test for employer discrimination against black players in English football. Although football has never operated a formal colour bar, instances of black players appearing in the Football League before the 1970s were isolated. There is abundant anecdotal or circumstantial evidence of widespread discrimination against black players throughout the 1970s and 1980s, on the part of certain club officials as well as significant numbers of spectators.[4] As Szymanski reports, the rate at which first team opportunities opened up for black players appears to have varied between different clubs, to a degree that seems difficult to attribute purely to chance. During the 1990s the situation appears to have improved markedly, with black players now accounting for roughly 10 per cent of the total workforce and with routine crowd abuse of black players a much rarer phenomenon than it was at times in the past. But even now, there is circumstantial evidence that primitive attitudes still prevail within football to some extent. One could cite, for example, the very small proportions of black former players that go on to pursue careers in coaching or management.

In the Szymanski study, the difficulties caused by the non-availability of individual wages data for football players are circumvented by testing for discrimination using data at team rather than at individual level. Team wages and salaries data are available from annual football club company accounts. Using data on 39 clubs for which complete data were available for the period 1978-93, Szymanski finds that teams that used a below-average proportion of black players achieved inferior playing performance (measured by league position) after controlling for wages and for the total number of players used in each season (a proxy for the disruptive effect on performance of high player turnover resulting from injuries). Perhaps surprisingly, this finding is stronger for the period 1986-93 than it is for 1978-85. The test, however, is more powerful for the later period because by then more black players were employed. The evidence of discrimination is also stronger for the larger clubs (measured by stadium capacity) than for the smaller ones.

How is the finding that teams that under-recruited black players also under-performed on the pitch to be interpreted? It appears that by refraining from recruiting the most talented players available for a given wage spend, team owners or managers with a taste for discrimination indulged their preferences by accepting a lower standard of team performance than they could otherwise have achieved. The proportion of black players used turns out to be insignificant in attendance and revenue regressions reported in a separate study by Preston and Szymanski (2000), suggesting that discrimination originates with the teams as employers rather than with spectators as customers. A crucial assumption underlying the test is that the market for playing talent is efficient, so all teams recruit from the same pool of players. This may rest uneasily with

---

[4] See for example Brown (1998); Moran (2000).

the evidence that player recruitment is, in practice, geographically segmented (see section 4.1). Szymanski suggests that the fact that the market
for corporate control of football teams has been relatively weak and
inefficient may explain why the more efficient, non-discriminating teams
did not drive the less efficient, discriminating ones out of business
through economic competition between clubs as employers.

4.5 The football transfer market

In contrast to major team sports in North America, the trading of players
for cash is common in professional football. In any football season the
large majority of player transfers go almost unnoticed by the public, yet
there are a few deals that make headlines, on the front as well as the back
pages of newspapers, simply because of the enormous sums of money
involved. These big-money transfers help to raise the public profile of the
football transfer market across Europe; but recently they have also
attracted the critical scrutiny of the European Commission who, at the
time of writing, are proposing to enforce major changes to the transfer
system. Nevertheless, the production and circulation of rumours of
impending big-money moves has clearly developed into a highly lucrative
cottage industry in its own right. Such rumours enable players (or their
agents) to send signals of availability to prospective buyers and, as a side-
effect, help to fuel wage inflation. During the summer months in particular, the same rumours generate welcome publicity for clubs attempting to
sell season tickets for the coming season. And of course they also help to
fill the sports sections of newspapers starved of match action to report.

Not so many years ago a world record transfer fee would be set every
few years, and typically the players involved would be great names like
Johan Cruyff, Diego Maradona, Ruud Gullit and Roberto Baggio. Today
it is not unusual for the world record fee to be broken several times in the
same year. As of summer 2000, the world record transfer fee stands at
£37 million, paid by Real Madrid to Barcelona for Luis Figo (see section
2.1). Yet having also acquired exclusive rights to sell merchandise bearing
Figo's name and image, Real believe that they will easily be able to recoup
the fee paid. To put recent fees into perspective, in 1990 Baggio moved
from Fiorentina to Juventus for a fee of just £8 million. And by today's
standards, the fee of £5 million paid in 1984 by Napoli to Barcelona for
the signature of Maradona looks very small indeed.

Although transfer inflation has become a matter of significant public
debate and concern, until recently relatively little academic analysis of the
football transfer market has been undertaken by economists. Section 4.5
begins by reviewing a small number of empirical studies of the English

transfer market. In all of these studies, the attributes of the player and the characteristics of the buying and selling clubs determine the transfer fee. Section 4.5 then presents an empirical analysis of the determinants of transfer fees in English football.

In the first empirical study of the transfer market in English football, Carmichael and Thomas (1993) assume that the transfer fee is determined by characteristics of the player concerned and by the relative bargaining power of the buying and selling clubs. Using a similar methodology, Reilly and Witt (1995) investigate the degree to which there is racial discrimination in the transfer market. No evidence of discrimination is found. Speight and Thomas (1997) analyse the determination of transfer fees settled through the arbitration process for disputed fees for out-of-contract players, under the system that operated from 1978 until the late 1990s (see section 2.7). Speight and Thomas find that fees are determined mainly by player and club characteristics, rather than by compromise between the final offers of the buying and selling clubs.

An innovative feature of the paper by Carmichael, Forrest and Simmons (1999) is that the propensity of players to be transferred, and the transfer fees of players that are transferred, is modelled separately in a two-stage estimation process. The first stage involves the estimation of a discrete choice model of the propensity for a player to be transferred. The second stage involves the estimation of a model of the transfer fee, which incorporates a sample selection bias correction. The latter is derived from the first stage, and allows for the fact that the characteristics of players who are transferred may differ systematically from the characteristics of players in general. Dobson and Gerrard (2000) point out a difficulty that arises because the propensity to be transferred has to be modelled excluding information about actual or potential buying clubs. The buying club is observed for players who are transferred, but the potential buyers of non-transferred players are not observed. Excluding information on the characteristics of the actual and potential buyers may create a misspecification problem at the first stage, which is carried over into the transfer fee equation via the sample selection bias correction.

In contrast to some of the earlier studies, the empirical analysis of Dobson and Gerrard (1999, 2000) is based explicitly on a theoretical model of the transfer market. The starting point is Sloane's (1971) assumption that the football club is a utility maximiser subject to a financial solvency constraint (see also chapter 1). The club's utility function is assumed to have two arguments: team performance and club profits. The relative weightings of these arguments in the utility function depend on, among other things, the ownership and control structure of the club. Each club's valuation of a player depends upon his expected impact on team performance and club profits, and on the relative importance attached to the two arguments. The decision to be involved in the transfer of a player (either as seller or buyer) is interpreted as an attempt on the part of the club to move towards its optimal position on the performance–profit frontier. Clubs that are net sellers of players need to raise revenue and reduce costs in order to increase profits or (in many cases) reduce losses. In contrast, clubs that are net buyers of players are motivated by the need to improve playing success, having already satisfied their profit requirements.

The determination of transfer fees: a theoretical model

The model of the player transfer market described in this sub-section is based on that of Dobson and Gerrard (1999). Consider the trade of player k from selling club m to buying club n. The purchase of the player is expected to improve team performance and the buying club's revenue. In essence, the buying club's valuation function represents a money measure of the increase in utility from the expected change in team performance $(\Delta_k^e Q_n)$ and club revenue $(\Delta_k^e R_n)$. Formally, the buying-club valuation function $(V_{n,k}^B)$ over the period of the contract can be written:

$$V_{n,k}^B = V_{n,k}^B(\Delta_k^e Q_n, \Delta_k^e R_n) \qquad (4.7)$$

The expected change in team performance depends on the quality of the player relative to the existing quality of the team. The expected change in revenue depends on the increases in gate revenue and other revenue expected to accrue from improved team performance, as well as any expected non-performance-related revenue gains arising, for example, from the star quality of the player. Given the buying club's valuation function, the maximum price that buying club n is prepared to pay in order to acquire player k $(T_{n,k}^B)$ is as follows:

$$T_{n,k}^B = V_{n,k}^B - W_{n,k} - S_{n,k} + {}^e T_{n,k} \qquad (4.8)$$

In equation (4.8) $W_{n,k}$ is the wage costs of the player during the period of the contract, $S_{n,k}$ is the signing-on fee paid to the player when the contract is agreed and ${}^e T_{n,k}$ is the expected proceeds (if any) from selling the player before his contract legally expires. Each component of the maximum bid price is a present value at the time of the transfer. Assuming the club to be rational, the maximum bid price sets the upper limit for the observed transfer fee.

Selling-club m's valuation of player k depends on the expected difference between the team's current level of performance $(\Delta_k^e Q_m)$ and revenue ($\Delta_k{}^e R_m$) and the post-transfer levels over the remaining period of the player's current contract. The selling club's valuation function ($V_{m,k}^S$) is as follows:

$$V_{m,k}^S = V_{m,k}^S (\Delta_k{}^e Q_m, \Delta_k{}^e R_m) \tag{4.9}$$

If the selling club is rational, its minimum acceptable transfer fee is the current net present value of the player to the club. The minimum price that selling-club m is prepared to accept for player k or player k's reservation price ($T_{m,k}^S$) is as follows:

$$T_{m,k}^S = V_{m,k}^S - W_{m,k} + {}^e T_{m,k} \tag{4.10}$$

In (4.10) $W_{m,k}$ is the present value of the wage costs for the remainder of the player's contract with club m, and ${}^e T_{m,k}$ is the present value of the expected transfer fee if player k were to be sold at a later stage in his contract.

The observed transfer fee for player k, (TF_k) should lie somewhere between the upper and lower limits, $T_{n,k}^B$ and $T_{m,k}^S$. If the observed fee lies above the lower limit, there is a monopoly rent: the selling club is able to extract some of the excess of the buying club's net valuation over the reservation price. The monopoly rent is $\lambda = (TF_k - T_{m,k}^S)/(T_{n,k}^B - T_{m,k}^S)$. For simplicity, it is assumed that λ is determined exogenously, and remains constant for all transfers. The observed transfer fee for player k can be written:

$$TF_k = \lambda T_{n,k}^B + (1 - \lambda) T_{m,k}^S, \quad T_{n,k}^B \geq T_{m,k}^S, \quad 0 \leq \lambda \leq 1 \tag{4.11}$$

The observed transfer fee is therefore a weighted average of the buying club's maximum bid price and the selling club's reservation price. In order to estimate (4.11), it is necessary to specify the observable determinants of $T_{n,k}^B$ and $T_{m,k}^S$. It is assumed that the buying club's maximum bid price depends on a vector of player characteristics, P_k, and a vector of buying-club characteristics, $B_{n,k}$. Similarly, the selling-club's reservation price is assumed to depend on P_k, and a vector of selling-club characteristics, $S_{m,k}$. Substituting these terms into (4.11) yields:

$$TF_k = \lambda T_{n,k}^B (P_k, B_{n,k}) + (1 - \lambda) T_{m,k}^S (P_k, S_{m,k}) \tag{4.12}$$

Equation (4.12) suggests a simple empirical test for the existence of monopoly rents in the transfer market. If there are no rents ($\lambda = 0$), observed transfer fees depend only upon player and selling club characteristics. If there are rents ($0 < \lambda \leq 1$), observed transfer fees depend upon player, selling-club and buying-club characteristics. A test of the joint significance of buying-club characteristics as determinants of observed transfer fees is therefore a test for the existence of monopoly rents in the transfer market. Assuming a linear functional form, the specification of the empirical model is as follows:

$$TF_k = \alpha_0 + \alpha_1' P_k + \alpha_2' S_{m,k} + \alpha_3' B_{n,k} + u_k \qquad (4.13)$$

In (4.13) α_1, α_2 and α_3 are vectors of regression coefficients, and u_k is a normally distributed random error term. In the next sub-section, equation (4.13) is estimated using the data set analysed by Dobson and Gerrard (1999, 2000). The empirical model retains the flavour of the original, but contains a significantly smaller number of explanatory variables.

The determination of transfer fees: data and empirical results

The data used for the estimation contains 1,350 fees from a sample of transfers that took place between 1 June 1990 and 31 August 1996. All the data were obtained from various editions of *Rothmans Football Yearbook*. Prior to June 1990, there is no publicly available comprehensive listing of transfer fees. The data set is terminated in August 1996 so that the estimated model is uncontaminated by the effects of institutional change in the transfer market following the Bosman ruling. The data include only permanent transfers involving two league clubs located in England and Wales, for which the fee is disclosed. Transfers involving non-league clubs, or clubs from Scotland, Northern Ireland or overseas, as either buyer or seller, are excluded since the use of comparable data on buying- and selling-club characteristics is precluded in these cases. Transfers involving players whose previous career includes spells with professional clubs outside England and Scotland are also excluded, because complete and consistent career playing records are not available in these cases. The data set also excludes free (or nominal fee) transfers; player exchanges which did not involve any cash payment between the two clubs; and transfers involving combined fees (when two or more players were sold jointly). Transfers involving player-exchanges are included if an agreed valuation has been disclosed. The sample of 1,350 transfers represents 60.9 per cent of all permanent transfers that took place between English league clubs within the sample period.

A lack of information on the length of transferred players' remaining contracts creates a significant gap in the data set. Since the Bosman ruling, the expiry date of a player's contract is likely to be a key determinant of the transfer fee. Players nearing the end of their contracts will become free agents, whose transfer fee should converge to zero as the expiry date approaches. A similar point also applies, to a lesser extent, to the pre-Bosman period. Then, an out-of-contract player could insist on a transfer, at a fee to be determined by arbitration if the two clubs involved failed to reach agreement (see section 2.7). An in-contract player could (and still can) be transferred only at the discretion of his present club, but the fee would naturally tend to converge towards its expected out-of-contract level as the expiry date approached. Since the mechanisms for instigating a transfer and settling the fee differed between in-contract and out-of-contract players, it is likely that the underlying model for the determination of the fee also differed between the two cases. Nevertheless, the empirical model reported below relies on a simplifying assumption that during the pre-Bosman period the difference between the in-contract and the out-of-contract fee was negligible.

The degree of player mobility within English league football is shown in table 4.14, which charts the number of permanent and temporary transfers between league clubs between the 1973 and 1996 seasons. There were just over 12,000 transfers during this period, 56 per cent of which were permanent. Before the introduction of freedom-of-contract in 1978, the average number of permanent transfers per season was 238. Between 1978 and 1996 the average number of permanent transfers per season was 294. This represents around 15 per cent of all full-time professionals registered at any one time.[5] Not all of the permanent transfers listed in table 4.14 involved the payment of a fee; some were free transfers and some involved player-exchanges. It is not possible to give an accurate picture of the proportion of permanent moves involving the payment of a fee for the entire period covered by table 4.14, because Rothmans provides a complete record only from the 1991 season onwards. During the six seasons 1991 to 1996 inclusive, however, there were 1,918 permanent transfers between league clubs, of which 1,350 (70.4 per cent) involved the payment of a fee.

In the empirical model, the dependent variable is *LRLFEE*, the natural logarithm of the real transfer fee (in June 1990 prices). The nominal transfer fee is deflated by the monthly retail price index for entertainment and other leisure goods.[6] The independent variables measure characteristics of the player (P_k), the buying club ($B_{n,k}$) and the selling club ($S_{m,k}$). The information set on player characteristics includes personal and career details such as the player's age, number of previous clubs, career

---

[5] The number of registered players with the 92 league clubs has remained relatively stable since the 1970s at around 2,000. The number declined temporarily to around 1,600 during the period of financial retrenchment in the sport in the early 1980s.

[6] The entertainment and other leisure goods' retail price index is used as the best available proxy for the football industry's own price index. Constraints such as the partial availability of gate price data and the non-disclosure of individual player wage data prevent the construction of a more specific football price index.

Table 4.14. *Permanent and temporary transfers, 1973–1996*

Seasons	Permanent			Temporary			Total	Permanent as per cent of total
	Close season	In season	Total	Close season	In season	Total		
1973–1975	261	503	764	37	401	438	1,202	64
1976–1978	190	476	666	29	351	380	1,046	64
1979–1981	363	471	834	25	160	185	1,019	82
1982–1984	267	367	634	23	479	502	1,136	56
1985–1987	331	495	826	54	622	676	1,502	55
1988–1990	427	655	1,082	50	672	722	1,804	60
1991–1993	343	492	835	71	840	911	1,746	48
1994–1996	410	673	1,083	124	1,375	1,499	2,582	42
Totals	2,592	4,132	6,724	413	4,900	5,313	12,037	56

Sources: Rothmans, Dobson and Gerrard (1999).

league appearances, career league scoring record, international recognition, current form (measured by league appearances), goals scored in the previous season and positional dummy variables. Buying- and selling-club characteristics include league position, goal difference and average gate attendance in league matches. The definitions of the independent variables and the expected signs of their coefficients are detailed in table 4.15. A number of statistically significant quadratic terms are included in the estimations to allow for non-linear effects.

Table 4.16 shows summary statistics for selected variables. The mean transfer fee in nominal terms is £418,334 with fees ranging from a minimum of £5,000 to a maximum of £15 million. The sample includes players aged from 17 years 2 months to 36 years 2 months; players with no league experience to players with nearly 600 career league appearances; and players with no full or Under-21 international appearances to 86 full international appearances and 18 Under-21 appearances. The sample also includes buying and selling clubs covering the full spectrum of performance and attendance levels.

The estimation results are presented in table 4.17. The estimated model explains almost 77 per cent of the variation in real transfer fees, suggesting that there is a considerable degree of systematic variation in transfer fees. The estimated model also provides evidence of the existence of a monopoly rent element in transfer fees. The buying-club's characteristics are jointly significant as determinants of transfer fees. Observed transfer fees therefore appear to exceed the reservation price of the selling club. The selling club is able to extract a share of the non-negative differential between its reservation price and the buying-club's maximum bid price. These findings lend support to the claim of Carmichael and Thomas (1993) that observed transfer fees are the outcome of a bargaining process.[7]

Dobson and Gerrard (1999) report that the average nominal transfer fee increased at an annual rate of around 25 per cent between the 1991 and 1996 seasons. This figure may tend to over-state the underlying rate of inflation in transfer fees, however, for two reasons. First, owing to skewness in the distribution of transfer fees, the average fee may be misleading as a representation of the sample as a whole. Average logarithmic growth in transfer fees can be used as a measure of transfer inflation that avoids this problem. This transformation yields an average annual rate of transfer inflation of 19.4 per cent.

The second difficulty in measuring the underlying rate of transfer inflation is that average inflation is affected by any change in the mix of players being transferred. The transfer fees model can be used to control

---

[7] In contrast, Szymanski and Smith (1997) assume that the transfer fee is established at the reservation price of the selling club.

Table 4.15. *Variable definitions*

Variable	Definition	Expected sign	Quadratic term (expected sign in parentheses)
LRLFEE	Log of transfer fee deflated by RPI for entertainment and other leisure goods	n/a	n/a
AGE	Age of player; rescaled by 10^{-1}	+	AGESQ $(-)$
PRCLUB	Number of previous of clubs	?	n/a
LGTOT	Total number of career league appearances; rescaled by 10^{-1}	+	LTOTSQ $(-)$
GLRATE	Career league scoring rate (i.e. career average of goals scored per league match played)	+	n/a
CAPS	Number of full international appearances; rescaled by 10^{-1}	+	CAPSSQ $(-)$
U21CAP	Number of Under-21 international appearances; rescaled by 10^{-1}	+	U21SQ $(-)$
LEAG	Number of league appearances in previous season; rescaled by 10^{-1}	+	n/a
GOALS	Number of league goals scored in previous season; rescaled by 10^{-1}	+	n/a
DEF1	Dummy variable = 1 if player is defender multiplied by GLRATE	?	DEF1SQ (?)
FOR1	Dummy variable = 1 if player is forward multiplied by GLRATE	?	FOR1SQ (?)
SELPOS	League position of selling club; top position in top division = 1; bottom position in lowest division = 92; rescaled by 10^{-1}	—	n/a
SELAST	League position of selling club in previous season; rescaled by 10^{-1}	—	SLSTSQ (?)
SELGD	Goal difference of selling club in previous season; rescaled by 10^{-1}	+	n/a
SELGAT	Average league attendance of selling club in previous season; rescaled by 10^{-4}	+	n/a
DSELGD	Dummy variable = 1 if player is defender multiplied by SELGD	—	n/a
FSELGD	Dummy variable = 1 if player is forward multiplied by SELGD	—	n/a
BUYPOS	League position of buying club; rescaled by 10^{-1}	—	n/a
BUYLST	League position of buying club in previous season; rescaled by 10^{-1}	—	BUYLSTSQ (?)
BUYGD	Goal difference of buying club in previous season; rescaled by 10^{-1}	+	n/a
BUYGAT	Average league attendance of buying club in previous season; rescaled by 10^{-4}	+	n/a
DBUYGD	Dummy variable = 1 if player is defender multiplied by BUYGD	—	n/a
FBUYGD	Dummy variable = 1 if player is forward multiplied by BUYGD	—	n/a

Table 4.16. *Summary statistics for selected variables*

Variable	Mean	St. dev.	Minimum	Maximum
FEE	418,334	819,845	5,000	15,000,000
RLFEE	306,435	560,699	3,212	9,461,756
AGE	25.97	3.57	17.17	36.16
LGTOT	172.93	126.67	0	589
LEAG	24.82	14.88	0	46
GOALS	3.74	5.45	0	42
GLRATE	0.134	0.129	0.000	1.392
CAPS	1.41	6.53	0	86
U21CAP	0.75	2.24	0	18
SELGD	1.20	18.90	-57	56
SELGAT	12,546.92	9,079.93	1,450	44,984
BUYGD	1.75	18.83	-53	56
BUYGAT	12,088.21	8,361.08	1,532	44,984

for the changing mix of transferred players, however, to produce a quality-adjusted transfer inflation rate. Between 1991 and 1996, Dobson and Gerrard's estimate of the average annual quality-adjusted inflation rate is 11.6 per cent.

Quality-adjusted transfer inflation rates may be calculated for different categories of transfers. Transfers can be classified, for example, by the age of the player, the divisional status of the buying club and the international experience of the player. On these criteria, the underlying transfer inflation rate is estimated to have been highest for players in mid-career (aged 24–28); players bought by clubs in the top two divisions; and players with international experience. Lower inflation rates for players with no international experience and for those bought by clubs in the lower two divisions seem likely to reflect the existence of more competitive conditions in these segments of the players' labour market. The market for star players is relatively thin, because both the supply of top-quality talent and the number of potential buyers of such talent are limited. Consequently transfer fees should provide substantial monopoly rents to the selling clubs. For lower-division transfers, both the supply of equivalent talent and the number of potential buyers are much higher. Consequently there is less scope for selling clubs to earn monopoly rents.

4.6 Conclusion

Spiralling wages, especially for superstar players, transfer fee inflation and the globalisation of the transfer market are some of the more dramatic

Table 4.17. *Estimated model for determinants of transfer fees*

CONST	6.1887[a] (1.0975)	LEAG	0.1736[a] (0.0189)	DSELGD	−0.0776[a] (0.0261)
AGE	4.8381[a] (0.8518)	GOALS	0.2109[a] (0.0585)	FSELGD	−0.0864[a] (0.0235)
AGESQ	−1.0591[a] (0.1630)	DEF1	4.0062[a] (0.9206)	BUYPOS	−0.1637[a] (0.0220)
PRCLUB	−0.06449[a] (0.0165)	DEF1SQ	−10.6374[a] (3.2181)	BUYLST	−0.0997[a] (0.0387)
LGTOT	0.0301[a] (0.0067)	FOR1	0.6854[c] (0.3557)	BUYLSTSQ	0.0035 (0.0035)
LTOTSQ	−0.000416[a] (0.0001)	FOR1SQ	−1.2445[a] (0.4848)	BUYGAT	0.3615[a] (0.0421)
GLRATE	1.0365[a] (0.3939)	SELPOS	−0.0656[a] (0.0216)	BUYGD	0.0523[a] (0.0189)
CAPS	0.1677 (0.0726)[b]	SELAST	−0.1375[a] (0.0399)	DBUYGD	−0.0420 (0.0260)
CAPSSQ	−0.0242[c] (0.0127)	SLSTSQ	0.0061[c] (0.0035)	FBUYGD	−0.0788[a] (0.0243)
U21CAP	0.625[a] (0.2373)	SELGD	0.0816[a] (0.0177)	obs. = 1350	s.e. of regression = 0.6934
U21SQ	−0.4922[b] (0.2166)	SELGAT	0.0659 (0.0404)	R^2 = 0.77	$F(B_{n,k})$ = 170.97[a]

Notes:
[a] = significantly different from zero, two-tail test, 1% level;
[b] = 5% level;
[c] = 10% level.
Standard errors of estimated coefficients are shown in parentheses.
Dependent variable is LRLFEE.
$F(B_{n,k})$ is an F-statistic for the joint significance of the buying club characteristics.

changes that have affected football, both in England and worldwide, in recent years. Chapter 4 has considered the effects of these and other developments in the players' labour market.

Using a data set that records a number of key personal and professional characteristics of the 12 players who made the most league appearances for each of the league's 92 member clubs in the 1979 and 1999 seasons, a number of changes to the structure and composition of English football's regular workforce have been identified. Players born outside Britain and Ireland accounted for over 14 per cent of those who appeared most regularly for their clubs in the 1999 season. France, Italy and the

Scandinavian countries were among those which were not represented at all in 1979, but which contributed significant numbers of players in 1999. The average age of regular professionals has increased by about 18 months over the past 20 years. There were more regular players born in southern regions of England, the West Midlands and the Irish Republic in 1999 than in 1979, but many fewer from the northern regions of England and from Wales, Scotland and Northern Ireland. Over the same period, player mobility between clubs has increased significantly. Mobility is higher at the bottom than at the top end of the league, but the difference has narrowed somewhat over time. It has become less common for players to jump between the top and bottom divisions in a single transfer. In a review of international evidence on patterns of migration among football players, the high concentrations of Irish and Scandinavian players employed by English clubs, and the smaller numbers of outstanding French, Dutch and Italian players who have arrived more recently, represent a part of a larger and more complex model of international mobility on the part of professional footballers throughout (and beyond) Europe.

The theoretical analysis of the economics of superstars addresses the apparent paradox between the high earnings achieved by sports stars whose contribution to society's well-being is perhaps rather modest (despite the adulation they receive), and the low earnings achieved by groups such as nurses and teachers, whose contribution is far more important. The discrepancy is explained by the fact that especially since the advent of pay-television, sports stars are capable of servicing very large paying audiences simultaneously, incurring little or no incremental cost as the audience size increases. Nurses and teachers, in contrast, service strictly finite numbers of users.

The potential for high wage inflation in football is therefore created by changes in the level and composition of effective demand, in turn caused primarily by technological change in broadcasting. Meanwhile successive moves towards free agency in the players' labour market have increased players' bargaining power in their wage negotiations, enabling them to capture a large proportion of the rent element in the extra revenues that are being generated. Consequently, the potential for high wage inflation has materialised into reality.

Another feature of footballers' compensation is explained by the rank-order tournament model, which examines intra-team wage distributions. Clubs have an interest in providing incentives for footballers to maximise investment in their playing skills, and to maximise their level of effort. High performance arises from innate ability and from investment in skills and effort. According to the rank-order tournament model, large wage differentials provide all players with the incentive to invest in the development of their skills, in the hope of securing a first-team place and a higher wage. Individual players' wages therefore tend to differ systematically from their marginal revenue products.

Empirical research has quantified the relationships between players' characteristics, performance and compensation, especially in the case of North American team sports. In many studies there is significant evidence of discrimination against blacks during the post-war period, though the situation has improved markedly during the last decade. During the 1970s and 1980s English football does not appear to have been completely innocent of similar tendencies. In the final empirical section of chapter 4, the English transfer market has been modelled by assuming that transfer fees depend on attributes of the player concerned, as well as characteristics of both the buying and selling clubs. The model has been used to test for the existence of a monopoly rent element in transfer fees. The evidence is consistent with transfer fees settled through a bargaining process, in which the selling club captures some of the non-negative differential between its own reservation price and the buying club's maximum bid price.

5   The contribution of the football manager

For many years economists have recognised the importance of the manager in the production process. In classical and neoclassical theory, individual firms and consumers are the fundamental building blocks of the market economy. The theoretical distinction between the owners, entrepreneurs and managers of firms tends to be rather blurred, because all are assumed to pursue the same objective of profit maximisation. In Austrian theory the manager is distinct from the entrepreneur who supplies the ideas and spots new and potentially profitable business opportunities, and from the owner or capitalist who advances the finance needed to implement the entrepreneur's ideas. The manager is regarded primarily as an employee, hired to carry out the day-to-day running of the firm (von Mises, 1966; Kirzner, 1973).

In a highly influential contribution Coase (1937) reinvented the theoretical role of the firm, by asking why it is that in a free-market economy, certain transactions take place outside the domain of the market, within centrally planned and hierarchical organisations known as firms. Coase's answer was that for certain types of transaction, the costs of gathering information and negotiating contracts prohibit the use of market mechanisms; instead it is more efficient for such transactions to be planned and co-ordinated consciously. The manager is the individual within the firm who takes responsibility for this co-ordinating function. In the context of team sports, whatever the outcome of the debate as to whether the league or the individual club is the relevant unit of observation (Neale, 1964; Sloane, 1971; see also chapter 1), it is clear that the Coasian story has some merit in explaining why sports team production is organised outside the market domain. One can easily imagine that transactions costs would be prohibitive if each football player had to enter into a network of bilateral contracts with 10 other players to form a team, and each team (or each set of individuals) had to contract bilaterally with the individuals in other teams to formulate a set of rules and produce a series of fixtures. Consequently these matters are more efficiently resolved by means of centralised planning, either at league or at individual club level.

240

The historical development and the present-day characteristics of the football manager's role as the principal planner and co-ordinator of team affairs are discussed in section 5.1.

In behavioural theories of the firm, the separation of ownership from control is crucial to understanding the way modern corporations operate (Berle and Means, 1932). Here the key insight is that the interests of the owner and the manager may diverge, with implications for the behaviour and performance of the firm. While the owner is concerned with profit maximisation, the manager may pursue other objectives such as sales revenue or utility maximisation (Baumol, 1959; Simon, 1959; Cyert and March, 1963; Williamson, 1963; Marris, 1964). In businesses generally, this conflict of interest is important because once hired, the manager cannot necessarily be monitored effectively. If monitoring is imperfect, the manager may devote less than the maximum level of effort towards attainment of the owner's objectives: there is a moral hazard problem (Alchian and Demsetz, 1972; Jensen and Meckling, 1976). One way to alleviate this problem is to create incentive structures that align the objectives of the manager more closely with those of the owner. But so-called 'agency problems' (in this case, managerial shirking) are perhaps unlikely to be as serious a problem in football as elsewhere. The club's owners are able to observe the performance of the team each time a match is played, at least once a week. Monitoring is direct and regular, and performance is transparent and easy to measure.

In professional football, if the output of the team (measured by its win ratio) is below the maximum that should be attainable given the playing and financial resources at the manager's disposal, it could be because the manager is not exerting maximum effort. Perhaps more likely, it could simply reflect a bad job match, caused by the owner not having full information about the manager's characteristics prior to hiring, or by the manager sending misleading signals during the hiring process, overstating his true abilities. To determine whether a football manager is operating at the maximum level of performance, an objective way of measuring his performance relative to best practice is required. Production frontier estimation is a suitable empirical technique, which attempts to measure the manager's performance while controlling for team quality. In section 5.2 the production frontier approach to measuring the managerial input is described, and the literature on production frontier estimation in US team sports is reviewed. In section 5.3 some recent estimates of managerial performance in English football are reported. This section draws on research by Peter Dawson (2000), who uses production frontier estimations to obtain a set of efficiency scores for a panel of English football managers.

5.1 The role of the football manager

The football manager needs to perform some of the functions typically attributed in the management literature to his business counterpart. According to Mintzberg (1973), for example, there are three broad managerial functions: interpersonal relations, information processing and decision making. Interpersonal relations include the roles of leadership and motivation, perhaps the most important managerial attributes. The way in which the football manager treats his players can affect not only the performance of the individual player, but also the performance of the team. In the information-processing role the manager will use match reports and videos to analyse and assess the performance of players, in order to formulate plans and strategies. It is also likely that the manager will delegate responsibility, by employing coaches and scouts, to help disseminate information. Finally, the decision making role involves determining the organisation of the team (team formation) and the role of individual players both before and during the game (pre-match and half-time team talk and strategic substitutions). The manager's ability to respond rapidly to situations such as a player suffering a loss of form or an injury can of course make the all the difference between the team achieving success or failure.

In a more recent management text, Robbins (1994) identifies four main managerial functions: planning, organising, leading and controlling. Planning involves formulating broad strategies to achieve organisational objectives; in many clubs the chairman and board of directors are likely to play a major role in the planning function. Organising involves assigning responsibilities to players and other subordinates (such as assistants and coaches) for both on-field and off-field tasks. Leading involves inspiring and motivating players and other subordinates to contribute maximum effort in pursuit of team and club objectives. Finally, controlling involves assessing how effectively the organisation is meeting its objectives, and taking remedial action wherever it is required.

Most football managers are ex-professional players. A playing career is the only source of previous work experience for many managers, although some enter management having previously been employed as a coach or assistant manager. There are very few managers who come into the job without some previous professional involvement in the sport. The careers of most professional players start at age 16. Many players therefore have only limited educational attainment, and relatively few study in further or higher education. There is a marked contrast with the typical educational attainment of managers in other business sectors. Furthermore, while the majority of managers in industry or commerce are likely to have had some formal training, only limited training opportunities exist for the football manager. The Football Association organises coaching courses, but most managers still rely primarily on their playing experience as preparation for a career in football management.

The role of the modern-day football manager as the person responsible for team affairs first started to evolve during the inter-war period. Previously, in the nineteenth and the early part of the twentieth centuries, responsibility for team affairs rested primarily with the club's directors and chairman. Throughout this period, it was quite common for a manager to see his players on match days only. During the rest of the week, the manager would undertake scouting missions, watch other teams play and carry out administrative duties. Walvin (1994) identifies the growth of a stronger ethos of professionalism within football during the 1920s and 1930s as instrumental in encouraging directors to begin shifting responsibility for performance on the pitch towards the professional manager.

Two individuals from the inter-war period, Herbert Chapman (Huddersfield Town 1921–5, Arsenal 1925–34) and Major Frank Buckley (Wolverhampton Wanderers 1927–44) typify the new breed of professional, hands-on team manager. Before Chapman's arrival, Huddersfield and Arsenal were both under-achieving clubs. Having enjoyed only a modest career as a player himself, Chapman steered Huddersfield to the first two of three consecutive championships in 1924 and 1925, and then won further titles with Arsenal in 1931 and 1933. The latter was also the first of three consecutive championships; tragically, however, Chapman died during the course of the 1934 season, aged 55. Chapman's success at Arsenal (in particular) was based on a regime of physical fitness, strength and skill previously unseen in the English game. Chapman's tactical acumen was also impressive: Arsenal are widely credited as the first team to adapt tactically to the introduction of the present-day offside law in 1925:[1]

Arsenal came in with the idea of a stopper centre-half. Previously centre-halfs were allowed to wander, and it now became a pendulum. The stopper centre-halves stayed there and then the two full-backs were like pendulums on a clock. If play was on one wing, one full-back would take it and the other one came back to cover behind the centre-half. You had three forwards up front, two in the 'V' point of the 'W' with a lot of alternatives. One of those men had two men in front of him and one at the side. He'd got three alternatives with the ball. (Jack Curtis, quoted in Taylor and Ward, 1995, pp. 27–8)

---

[1] A player is offside if, when the ball is played forward to him, fewer than two opposing players stand between him and the goal line. Before 1925 a player was offside if there were fewer than three opposing players.

Although he won no major honours with any of the seven sides he managed,[2] Major Frank Buckley is one of the best-known managers of all time. His military background, disciplined approach and personal demeanour[3] seem to belong to a bygone era, but other aspects of his style, including his dealings in the transfer market and his astute handling of the media, mark him clearly as an early prototype of the modern-day football manager:

> I soon realised that Major Buckley was one out of the top drawer. He didn't suffer fools gladly . . . his style of management in football was very similar to his attitude in the army . . . Major Buckley implanted into my mind the direct method of playing which did away with close interpassing and square-ball play. If you didn't like his style you'd very soon be on your bicycle to another club. He didn't like defenders overelaborating in their defensive positions . . . Major Buckley also knew how to deal with the press. (Stan Cullis, quoted in Taylor and Ward, 1995, pp. 31–2)

In modern-day professional football, the remit of most managers is the selection, supervision and coaching of playing staff, and devising the team's tactics and strategies (King and Kelly, 1997; Lambert, 1997). During the post-war period, most managers have also taken responsibility for the buying and selling of players, wage negotiations and a wide range of administrative duties. This multi-functional role of the manager still predominates in many clubs in the lower divisions of the league. Among a number of leading clubs, however, as the scale and complexity of the financial and administrative aspects of club management has increased, there has been a shift towards the division of responsibility between teams of specialists in the various functional areas of management. The modern-day manager of a large club typically takes full responsibility for playing matters only. The extent of the manager's influence over player transfers and contract negotiations seems to vary quite considerably from club to club at present. Even within the remit of playing affairs, the manager is likely to delegate duties among a team of subordinate coaches and assistants, responsible for first-team, reserve-team and youth-team affairs, as well as specialised positions such as goalkeeper.

[2] Under Buckley's management Wolverhampton Wanderers finished runners-up in both the league and FA Cup in 1939.
[3] Buckley characteristically wore 'plus-fours' and brogue shoes, and could easily be mistaken for a farmer. His military record included service in the Boer War (Turner and White, 1993).

5.2 Measuring the managerial contribution: the production frontier approach

'Production' in professional team sports

As discussed in chapter 1, 'production' in team sports is unlike that in other business sectors because it cannot take place at all without the co-operation of at least two teams. The requirement that clubs simultaneously co-operate and compete with one another is almost unique to team sports industries, and has led to extensive debate regarding the status of the sports team as a firm in the economist's sense (Neale, 1964). For some commentators the objective of a sports team is simply to win as many matches as possible. Elsewhere, much of the US sports literature assumes an objective of profit or wealth maximisation. While many North American professional team sports clubs consistently make operating profits, in English football historically the story is very different. Sloane (1971) argues that it is more appropriate to think of English football clubs as utility maximisers. Arguments for the utility function might include playing success, attendance, media recognition and sponsorship, as well as profit.

Rottenberg (1956) first proposed the notion of a sporting production function.

[T]he product is the game, weighted by the revenues derived from its play. With game admission prices given, the product is the game, weighted by the number of paying customers who attend. A baseball team, like any other firm, produces its product by combining factors of production. Consider the two teams engaged in a contest to be collapsed into a single firm, producing as output games, weighted by the revenue derived from admission fees. Let the players of one team be one factor and all the others (management, transportation, ball parks, and the players of the other team) another . . . Given the quantity of the other factors, the total product curve of the factor – players of one team – will have the conventional shape; it will slope upward as the 'quantity' of this factor is increased, reach a peak and then fall. (Rottenberg, 1956, p. 255)

In subsequent literature, however, attendance is generally used as a measure of demand. If it is believed that the players and the manager are the key factor inputs, then the measure of output ought to relate directly to their performance. It therefore seems appropriate to derive the output measure from match results.

Managers of professional sports teams can influence performance in two ways. First, taking the collection of playing inputs at his disposal as given in the short term, the manager seeks to maximise the level of performance achieved using these inputs. The manager's direct contribution depends partly on the quality of his strategic input: the effectiveness of his team selections and tactics. The direct contribution also depends to some extent on the manager's ability to inspire and motivate players. Second, the manager can attempt to improve the level of skill of his existing players over the longer term, or strengthen his squad by dealing in the transfer market. The manager's indirect contribution depends partly on his effectiveness as a coach in training and developing his existing players, and partly on his skill and astuteness in deciding which players he should buy and sell.

In theoretical terms, one can think of each team as facing a production set, comprising all technologically feasible means of transforming a given set of playing inputs into a given level of output (measured by the team's win ratio). Within the production set there is a maximum level of output that corresponds to a particular combination of inputs, or there is a minimum combination of inputs that can be used to produce a particular level of output. Both of these define the limit of technological possibility. A production function defined using the maximum efficiency assumption is known as a frontier production function or a production frontier. The quality of the managerial contribution, or the level of managerial efficiency, can be measured by examining the team's actual performance relative to the maximum attainable performance (given the quality of its inputs) that would be predicted by the production frontier.

If several different teams (or managers) are observed, it is likely that some will be found not to operate on the technologically feasible boundary (too many inputs are being used to produce the boundary level of output; or output is below the maximum that should be attainable). Compared to best-practice these managers are technically inefficient. They use a greater quantity of inputs to produce the same output as the best-practice managers, or they produce a smaller output level than the best practice managers with the same level of inputs. Neoclassical production functions do not allow for sub-optimal solutions, and so exclude the notion of inefficiency. In contrast, the production frontier approach acknowledges that most managers are inefficient to some extent, relative to best practice. The production frontier approach identifies the frontier, and locates the position of each manager relative to it.

Figure 5.1 illustrates the concept of a frontier production function in input orientation. It is assumed that there is a single output measure (Y), which can be produced using various combinations of two inputs (X_1 and X_2). Constant returns to scale are assumed: if X_1 and X_2 are increased in a given proportion, Y will increase by the same proportion. The axes of Figure 5.1 can therefore be labelled X_1/Y and X_2/Y, allowing the line QQ to represent the unit isoquant. For a given value of Y, QQ shows the combinations of X_1/Y and X_2/Y that would allow the most efficient firm to

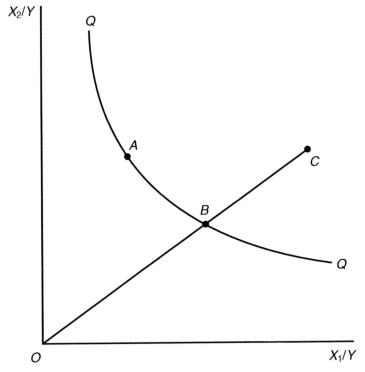

Figure 5.1 Deterministic production frontier

produce Y. QQ is also known as the production frontier. The manager located at point A is technically efficient, as A is on the unit isoquant. The efficiency of different managers can be compared by constructing a ray through the origin that extends beyond the frontier to locate the manager in question. For example, the manager at C is inefficient because he uses greater quantities of X_1 and X_2 than is required to produce the unit output (at B). His technical efficiency is measured as the ratio of the amount of X_1 and X_2 that should be needed to produce Y to the amount of X_1 and X_2 actually used to produce Y (or the distance OB/OC). If this ratio were 0.5, then the manager at C would be using twice as many inputs as he should if he were operating efficiently.

Estimation techniques for production frontiers have been developed by Aigner, Lovell and Schmidt (1977) and Jondrow *et al.* (1982). In the empirical literature production frontiers can be deterministic or stochastic. With a deterministic frontier the entire deviation from the frontier is caused by technical inefficiency. With a stochastic frontier part of the deviation from the frontier is attributed to technical inefficiency, and part is considered to be random. The deterministic frontier takes the following form:

$$y_{i,t} = \beta' x_{i,t} - u_{i,t} \tag{5.1}$$

where $y_{i,t}$ is the output of the ith team in the tth season (for $i = 1 \ldots N$; $t = 1 \ldots T$); $x_{i,t}$ is a vector of inputs used by the ith team (including an intercept term); β is a vector of unknown parameters to be estimated; and $u_{i,t}$ is a one-sided (non-negative) error term that reflects managerial inefficiency. $y_{i,t}$ is therefore bounded from above.

In the stochastic production frontier model, the error term consists of two parts: a one-sided component (to capture technical inefficiency, as before) and a two-sided component (to capture random influences on performance). The stochastic frontier takes the following form:

$$y_{i,t} = \beta' x_{i,t} + (v_{i,t} - u_{i,t}) \tag{5.2}$$

In (5.2) the variables are defined as before, with the addition of a symmetrical component $(v_{i,t})$ in the error term that captures the effects of all random influences on the performance of the ith team.

Effectively, the inclusion of the random component $(v_{i,t})$ in the error term produces a different efficient frontier for each team, incorporating the effects of luck or other random influences on the team's performance. Managerial efficiency is then measured by comparing actual performance with the efficient performance implied by the team-specific frontier. Intuitively, this approach is appealing since deviations from the average frontier might be partly the result of events beyond the manager's control. In figure 5.2, QQ represents a deterministic frontier. Good fortune results in the stochastic frontier for team A being placed below the deterministic frontier ($Q'Q'$, for which the random error is positive). Bad fortune results in the stochastic frontier for team C being placed above the deterministic frontier ($Q''Q''$, for which the random error is negative). Although A is closer to the deterministic frontier than C in figure 5.2, C turns out to be more efficient than A when efficiency is measured relative to each team's stochastic frontier, because $OD/OC > OB/OA$.

In order to make this approach operational, certain assumptions have to be introduced. With cross-sectional data, and sometimes with panel data, it is necessary to make a specific distributional assumption about the inefficiency term $u_{i,t}$. The theoretical literature suggests half-normal, exponential, gamma or truncated normal distributions. A weakness of the production frontier approach is that different assumptions about the distribution of $u_{i,t}$ can sometimes produce widely differing results. Recently, the increasing availability of panel data has increased the scope of frontier

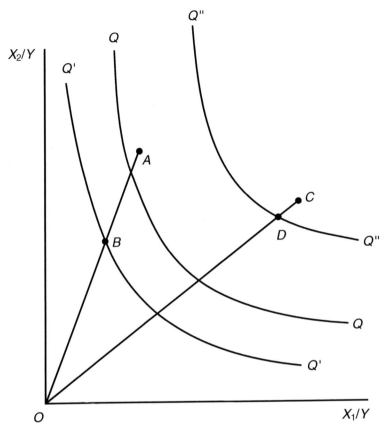

Figure 5.2 Stochastic production frontier

estimation procedures. Using panel data there is no need to specify a particular distribution for the one-sided team-specific error term. With several observations on each team, it is possible to obtain estimates of this term directly, using either fixed-effects (FE) or random-effects (RE) specifications. Alternatively, if assumptions about the distribution of the inefficiency term are retained, maximum likelihood estimation can be used to locate the efficient frontier and obtain the managerial efficiency scores.

Estimation of team production functions

Scully's (1974) study of baseball, already reviewed in some detail in chapter 4, was the first to estimate a team production function with team performance as an output measure. Using an average production function rather than a production frontier, Scully modelled team output (percentage of matches won) as a function of playing and non-playing (management, capital and team spirit) inputs. This method of modelling the sporting production process soon became the norm in production function studies. In Zech's (1981) study of baseball, output is a function of the following playing skills: hitting, running, defence and pitching. Similar approaches have been used to measure output in basketball (Scott, Long and Somppi, 1985) and American football (Atkinson, Stanley and Tschirhart, 1988). In Schofield's (1988) study of English county cricket and Carmichael and Thomas's (1995) study of English rugby league, a single-equation model is estimated, treating the player inputs as exogenous in the same way as the US studies. The production function is determined through a system of recursive equations, thus endogenising playing performance.

None of the above studies uses the production frontier approach, so all of them assume implicitly that team production takes place at maximum efficiency. Very little consideration is given to the contribution of the manager to team output. In some cases, one or two managerial variables are included on the right-hand side of the estimated equation. Zech (1981), for example, includes the number of years spent managing in major league baseball and the manager's lifetime win-loss ratio, but neither variable is found to be a statistically significant determinant of current performance. Carmichael and Thomas (1995) include the number of years' coaching experience to capture the managerial contribution.

Surprisingly, production frontier analysis has been used in relatively few professional team sports studies. Zak, Huang and Siegfried (1979) estimate a deterministic frontier using match data for the 1976–7 National Basketball Association (NBA) season. The efficiency of each team is found to be close to 100 per cent (the lowest efficiency rating is 99.7 per cent). This is somewhat surprising since in a deterministic model, all of the deviation from the optimum is the result of inefficiency. The highly competitive nature of the sport and the extensive data coverage might account for the findings. Porter and Scully (1982) also use a deterministic specification to estimate a baseball production frontier. There are two measures of team quality: team slugging percentage (a measure of hitting skill) and team strikeout-to-walk ratio (a measure of pitching quality). Managerial efficiency and job tenure are found to be positively correlated. The contribution made by the manager to team output is found to compare favourably with that of the superstar players.

In subsequent research, Scully (1994, 1995) compares efficiency in baseball, basketball and American football. Scully finds that efficiency in all three sports improved over time, with baseball having the highest mean efficiency and football the lowest. One possible reason why efficiency varies between sports is that greater demands are placed on managers in sports where team strategies are important. Scully considers both a deterministic and a stochastic specification but tends to favour the deterministic model. Scully's estimated managerial efficiency scores are used subsequently as a covariate in a model that seeks to identify the determinants of managerial turnover (see chapter 6).

Hofler and Payne (1996) use stochastic frontier analysis to examine managerial efficiency in the National Football League (NFL). Using panel data they find an overall mean efficiency score over a five-year period of 96 per cent. Their lowest individual efficiency score is 81 per cent. Mean efficiency falls slightly over the sample period. In tests, however, none of the efficiency scores is found to be significantly different from 100 per cent. Hofler and Payne (1997) study managerial efficiency in the NBA, also using stochastic frontier estimation. The dependent variable is the team's seasonal win ratio. Average efficiency is significantly lower than in the NFL study, at 89 per cent. Some caution is required, however, when comparing the results. Not only is there a difference of nearly 20 years between the two sample periods, but a number of significant institutional changes occurred in both sports in the meantime (see chapter 3).

Ruggiero *et al.* (1996) use both deterministic and stochastic frontier models to compare efficiency estimates in baseball for the period 1982–93. As in most other sports studies, a Cobb–Douglas specification is used for the team production function. Playing quality measures include slugging percentage, batting average, number of stolen bases, fielding percentage and earned run average. Although the alternative estimation methods produce almost identical efficiency rankings, Ruggiero *et al.* argue in favour of the stochastic version because it allows for random influences on performance.

In studies that investigate the managerial contribution specifically, player performance is usually measured at the end of the season under review. Horowitz (1994) and Scully (1995) measure team quality in terms of the team's scoring relative to opponents' scoring. Under this approach, the direct role of the manager can be seen as turning a given input (the scoring ratio) into team wins. The definitions of the input measures are, however, dangerously similar to that of the output measure (Ruggiero *et al.*, 1997).

In contrast, in studies using measurable aspects of player performance, an ability to turn the inputs into team scoring (or conceding) is regarded as an important part of the managerial contribution. Clement and McCormick (1989) measure managerial performance in terms of the allocation of playing time: the better managers make better decisions regarding the team's line up. The coefficient of determination from a regression of minutes played per season as a function of measurable player performance is used to measure the managerial contribution.

Kahn (1993) and Singell (1993) both attempt to separate the direct contribution of the manager to team performance (through team selection and tactics) from the indirect contribution (through enhancement of player quality by effective coaching). To measure the direct effect they use a conventional production function. Kahn proxies for managerial performance using the predicted salary, while Singell uses managerial experience. The indirect managerial effect is then captured by running separate regressions that compare individual player performance for the season under review with the historical performance of the player. Kahn focuses on the effect of a new manager on player performance, while Singell concentrates on the performance of players once they have moved to a new club.

Although both studies find a significant managerial effect, it is unclear as to whether the improvements in player performance are due to the manager. An improvement in performance in the first season with a new club or a new manager may be a result of job matching: the player is now with the right club. It is also possible to estimate the indirect and direct effects together. To do this it is necessary to use player input measures that are unaffected by performance during the period over which the manager's contribution is being assessed. For college basketball, Fizel and D'Itri (1996) measure both the direct and indirect effects using a deterministic frontier model. Their average managerial efficiency score is substantially lower than those found in most other studies.

5.3 Measuring managerial efficiency in English football

As noted above, team sports are well suited to the evaluation of performance because output (the results of matches) is completely transparent and well documented, while extensive data on inputs (the attributes of players and the manager) are readily available. In football, all clubs compete under the same rules and share a common technology. Each club employs playing and non-playing (managerial) inputs in similar numbers and proportions. The manager is the key decision maker in the production process: his role is to transform a given set of playing resources into the maximum number of team wins.

This section reviews some recent research by Peter Dawson (2000). His study is the first to quantify efficiency or inefficiency in the performance of managers in English football. It is perhaps worth commenting at the outset that many of the issues involved in measuring managerial efficiency in football seem even more problematic than in the main North American team sports. In baseball, for example, scoring depends heavily on the skills of the individual pitcher and hitters, whose individual performances are easily quantified. In football, goals scored and conceded are very much dependent on the efforts of the entire team, from which it is difficult to disentangle either the contributions of individual players, or the manager's team selection, choice of tactics and powers of motivation. By assuming responsibility for matters including transfers and signings, negotiation of player contracts and remuneration, training and fitness, scouting and youth development, the English football manager is also involved in a whole swathe of activities which contribute directly or indirectly to team performance. In North America in contrast, many of these matters are the responsibility of individuals other than the team manager or coach, who concentrates mainly on team selection and tactics, and whose contribution is therefore easier to isolate.

The reverse-order-of-finish draft system for allocating new players between league members in baseball, basketball and American football is another feature of North American sports that is absent from English football. The draft is intended to level standards by allocating the best new players to the least successful teams, though whether this is the actual outcome is a matter of some debate (see chapter 3). In contrast, given the squad he inherited at the start of his appointment, the quality of the players at the English football manager's disposal subsequently depends mainly on his own dexterity in dealing in the transfer market, and his (and his subordinates') ability to motivate, organise and develop players (Audas, Dobson and Goddard, 1999). In effect, all of these features make it more difficult to isolate the manager's specific contribution to team performance.

In Dawson's study, the full playing season is the basic unit of observation. But provided at least 10 matches were completed, managerial spells which either start or terminate within the season are treated as separate observations, and assigned a weight in the estimation process equal to the proportion of the full season's matches that was completed during the spell. In general, other professional team sports studies have eliminated observations that include mid-season changes of coach or manager. For the purposes of calculating managerial efficiency scores, a single score is assigned to each complete spell. The same efficiency score therefore applies to all annual observations in the data set which comprise a single spell. This is known as the time-invariant model, for which (5.2) is re-specified as follows:

$$y_{i,t} = \beta' x_{i,t} + (v_{i,t} - u_i) \tag{5.3}$$

The manager's efficiency within each spell is assumed not to vary over time (i.e. $u_{i,t} = u_i$). Each spell is treated separately, however, so a manager can obtain several efficiency scores from separate spells.[4]

In order to exploit both the cross-sectional and time-series dimensions of his panel data set, Dawson estimates efficiency scores using both fixed-effects (FE) and random-effects (RE) specifications. For purposes of comparison, Dawson also estimates another set of efficiency scores using maximum likelihood. The FE model is estimated using the within estimation procedure (Hallam and Machado, 1996); the RE model is estimated as a generalised least squares (GLS) regression. The team production function, which converts playing and managerial inputs into output measured by win ratio data, is assumed to be the same for all teams, because each team plays to a given set of rules and uses the same production technology. It is also assumed to satisfy the standard properties of any neoclassical production function.

Associated with each player is a certain level of playing skill, reflecting the player's ability to pass, shoot and head the ball, speed, agility, strength, awareness, concentration, determination, and so on. These attributes may be intrinsic or acquired through investment in training and development (by either the player or the club). Although it is difficult to evaluate the quality of a player independently of his team-mates and manager, for simplicity Dawson assumes that team quality is the linear sum of the skills of the individual players. In other words, the inputs are treated as separable. This approach is standard in the US literature. It may cause the manager's performance to be over- or under-stated, however, depending on whether team synergy effects are positive or negative.

In contrast to North American sports like baseball, in football little data is recorded systematically on different aspects of the contributions made by individual players to team performance.[5] This clearly poses a

---

[4] If the performance of the manager is believed to vary over time, perhaps because the value of the manager's human capital increases as he gains experience, it may seem rather restrictive to measure efficiency assuming time invariance. For this reason Dawson also estimates managerial efficiency using a number of time-varying models based on (5.2), but each with its own temporal structure. The interested reader is referred to Dawson, Dobson and Gerrard (2000a, 2000b).

[5] The Carling Opta Index of playing performance in the Premier League has been compiled in recent seasons (Carling Opta, 1999, 2000). This is constructed from data measuring a variety of contributions made by players during each match: passes, tackles, shots on goal, and so on. Carmichael, Thomas and Ward (2000) have recently presented an analysis of the relationship between team performance and a variety of player contribution measures of this kind. It seems likely that the Carling Opta Index will provide a valuable source of data for future studies of the type described in this chapter.

problem in a study of this nature because without a measure of player and team quality it is impossible to estimate managerial efficiency. Consequently, a different approach is needed in controlling for the quality of the players' contribution to team performance. One solution is to examine the existing empirical evidence on the transfer market in English football. As described in chapter 4, empirical studies show that the transfer value of players is systematically related to a number of factors that are correlated with player quality, including age, experience, international recognition and goal scoring records (see below). The fact that a systematic relationship exists between these player characteristics and transfer values suggests that transfer values may serve as a suitable proxy for unobservable player quality attributes. Furthermore, if the transfer values of players who have been transferred can be modelled using observable characteristics of these players as covariates, the estimated model can be used subsequently to generate estimated transfer values of players who have not been transferred, based on their observable characteristics.

Dawson therefore measures player quality using the fitted transfer value of each player in each team at the start of each season, obtained from an estimated model similar to the one described in chapter 4 (see also Dawson, Dobson and Gerrard, 2000b; Dobson and Gerrard, 2000). The model is as follows:

$$VALUE = \beta_0 + \beta_1 LGTOT + \beta_2 GLSTOT + \beta_3 PRCLUB + \beta_4 AGE$$
$$+ \beta_5 LEAG + \beta_6 GOALS + \beta_7 INT + \beta_8 DIVSTAT_{-1} + ERROR$$

$$(5.4)$$

where $LGTOT$ and $GLSTOT$ are player's career league appearances and career goals scored; $PRCLUB$ is the number of previous clubs played for (including loan spells); AGE is the player's age in years and months; $LEAG$ and $GOALS$ are league appearances and league goals scored in the previous season; INT measures whether the player is a current international; and $DIVSTAT_{-1}$ is the divisional status of the player in the previous season. The model is estimated using data on all players transferred between the 1991 and 1996 seasons inclusive.[6]

---

[6] As a way of independently checking the validity of the transfer value approach, Dawson also measures team quality using a 'raw characteristics' approach. This defines team quality as a vector of the means of the player variables (described above) for the team. In this approach the coefficients are estimated as part of the team production function. In contrast, the transfer value approach defines the mean of player quality as the weighted sum of the player variables for each individual player, with the weights being derived from a parsimonious version of the model of transfer fees in Dobson and Gerrard (1999, 2000) based on 1,350 transfers. In the results reported below team quality is measured using the transfer value approach only.

As discussed in chapter 4, it is an empirical fact that transfer fees are correlated not only with the characteristics of the players, but also with the divisional status of the two clubs involved in each transfer (see also Dobson and Gerrard, 2000). The valuations obtained from (5.4) are therefore adjusted to reflect the divisional status of the player's current club, or the selling club in the original model. The buying club in the original model is simply assumed to be situated in the middle of the same division as the player's current club. The player valuations vary by season owing to variation in the player characteristic variables as defined. The aggregate playing quality measure for team i in season t, $q_{i,t}$, is the mean of the estimated transfer values of all players who featured in a minimum number of first-team matches.

Naturally, the use of estimated transfer values to measure the quality of the playing input does raise some problems. First, there is an implicit assumption that the relationship between player characteristics and value is the same for non-transferred players as for those who were transferred. It is therefore assumed that there are no unobserved characteristics which might affect both the propensity to be transferred and the valuation of the player concerned. Second, by relying solely on quantifiable characteristics (such as age, appearances or goals scored), (5.4) may fail to capture fully some of the most important determinants of a player's true value (such as natural talent). Third, the data requirements for estimation of (5.4) are highly intensive. Finally, with an increasing proportion of transfers taking place at a zero fee during the post-Bosman period, it is doubtful whether the value approach will continue to be useful or operational in the future.

Another important issue concerns the most appropriate time to measure team quality. Some US researchers have measured team quality at the end of the season under review. Dawson adopts a prior measure of playing talent, based on the players' estimated values at the start of the season. By using an *ex ante* player input measure, Dawson seeks to minimise the problems of simultaneity inherent in *ex post* player quality measures based on performance during the season under consideration. These arise because player performance is affected in part by the manager's decisions taken during the course of the season. Under Dawson's specification, efficiency is evaluated in terms of how effectively the manager can turn a set of playing resources allocated at each start of the season into wins during the same season. There is, however, still an element of simultaneity, because efficiency is measured over the manager's entire spell. If the indirect component of the manager's contribution is important (see above), the quality of the players under the manager's control at the start of season t may be determined in part by his own efforts during previous seasons.

Table 5.1. *Fixed effects, random effects and maximum likelihood estimates of production frontier, Premier League, 1993–1998*

	Estimation method		
	FE	RE	ML
Constant	-1.005^a	-1.125^a	-0.801^a
	(0.211)	(0.159)	(0.129)
$\ln(q_{i,t})$	1.362^a	1.352^a	1.345^a
	(0.108)	(0.082)	(0.081)
t	-0.048^a	-0.009	-0.011
	(0.015)	(0.100)	(0.021)
obs.	147	147	147
R^2	0.623	0.672	n/a

Notes:
[a] = significantly different from zero, two-tail test, 1% level.
Standard errors of estimated coefficients are shown in parentheses.
Dependent variable is $\ln(W_{i,t})$ where $W_{i,t}$ = win ratio.
n/a = not available.
Source: Dawson (2000).

Respecifying (5.3), the empirical model becomes:

$$\ln(W_{i,t}) = \beta_1 + \beta_2 \ln(q_{i,t}) + \beta_3 t + (v_{i,t} - u_i) \tag{5.5}$$

where $W_{i,t}$ is team i's win ratio in season t; $q_{i,t}$ is the mean of the estimated transfer values of all players who featured in a minimum number of first-team matches; t is a linear time trend, included to allow for possible changes in the position of the efficient production frontier over time; and u_i and $v_{i,t}$ are the inefficiency and random components of the error term, as before.

Dawson generates manager efficiency scores using English football league data covering the 1993 to 1998 seasons inclusive. For purposes of illustration, some results for the Premier League only are presented, assuming efficiency to be time invariant. Table 5.1 shows the results obtained from the FE and RE estimations obtained by pooling the data over the six seasons; and from a maximum likelihood (ML) estimation in which u_i are distributed half-normal, obtained from separate cross-sectional estimations for each of the six seasons individually. The coefficient for the team quality measure $(q_{i,t})$ in each of the estimated models is positive and statistically significant. The time trend is insignificant in all models except FE, indicating that the position of the efficient frontier does not change over time. The overall explanatory power of the models

Table 5.2. *Summary statistics for manager efficiency scores*

	FE	RE	ML
Mean	0.549	0.633	0.825
Standard deviation	0.163	0.103	0.059
Maximum	1.000	1.000	0.915
Minimum	0.071	0.391	0.561
Correlations:			
FE	1		
RE	0.983	1	
ML	0.926	0.878	1
Win ratio	0.709	0.733	0.614
Frequencies:			
0.901–1.000	1	1	4
0.801–0.900	2	2	50
0.701–0.800	8	11	15
0.601–0.700	15	33	2
0.501–0.600	24	18	1
0.401–0.500	12	5	0
0.301–0.400	4	2	0
0.201–0.300	3	0	0
0.101–0.200	1	0	0
0.001–0.100	2	0	0

Source: Dawson (2000).

suggests that roughly two-thirds of the variation in the win ratio is explained by team quality. The remaining one-third is attributable to random factors and the contribution of the manager.

A comparison of the efficiency scores generated by the four models is shown in table 5.2. Just as the efficient frontier parameter estimates vary according to the estimation procedure, so too do the efficiency scores. The average efficiency scores are 55 per cent for FE, 63 per cent for RE and 83 per cent for ML. The efficiency scores for both panel models are more widely dispersed than those generated by ML estimation. In both FE and RE, only three managers have an efficiency score above 80 per cent. For the ML model, the corresponding number is 54. All Pearson correlation coefficients between the scores produced by the three models are above 0.87. These values suggest that the three estimation procedures provide very similar managerial efficiency rankings.

The most efficient managers according to each estimation procedure are reported in table 5.3. Overall, Arsène Wenger (Arsenal), Kevin Keegan (Newcastle United), John Gregory (Aston Villa) and Gianluca Vialli (Chelsea) emerge as the most efficient managers across the three estimation methods. Managers at some of the smaller clubs, with more limited resources and fewer household names among their playing staffs, including Martin O'Neill (Leicester City), Mike Walker (Norwich City) and Gerry Francis (Queens Park Rangers), also figure prominently.

One apparent anomaly is that despite being the most successful club manager throughout this period, Alex Ferguson (Manchester United) does not register at all in the top 25 places in either the FE and RE models.[7] Even though Ferguson won four of the six Premier League championships available during the sample period, the estimated models suggest that he should have won even more games, given the quality of the playing resources that were available to him! Of course, the dependent variable in the stochastic frontier estimations is win ratio, not league position. Differences in the distributional properties of win ratios and league positions may have implications for the ranking and distribution of the managerial efficiency scores. It should also be noted that Dawson is measuring only one dimension of managerial performance: the ability to turn a given quality of playing resources into wins. The estimated models therefore capture only partially the manager's abilities in developing and motivating players, qualities for which Ferguson is justly renowned. Finally, there is perhaps a strong case for regarding Manchester United as a special case: there is no basis for comparing the efficiency of Ferguson's performance with that of managers of other English clubs of similar means, simply because there are no other clubs of similar means!

Dawson also investigates the causes of variation in efficiency between managers. It is suggested that variations in managerial efficiency arise principally from two main sources. First, managers have varying levels of experience, powers of motivation and leadership qualities; in other words, they have different amounts of accumulated human capital and different levels of inherent managerial ability. Second, football clubs differ in terms of their policies regarding the level and incentive structure of compensation for players and manager, and according to the frequency with which they tend to change their managers. Both types of factor (manager-specific and club-specific) may help to explain variations in managerial efficiency.

---

[7] Ferguson does perform better according to specifications that use the raw player characteristics as frontier inputs: he is assigned rankings of 7th and 1st respectively in the RE and ML versions of this model (see Dawson, Dobson and Gerrard, 2000b).

Table 5.3. *Managers with highest efficiency scores in production frontier estimations*

Rank	Manager (club)	Efficiency (FE)	Rank	Manager (club)	Efficiency (RE)	Rank	Manager (club)	Efficiency (ML)
1	J. Gregory (Aston Villa)	1.000	1	J. Gregory (Aston Villa)	1.000	1	A. Wenger (Arsenal)	0.915
2	A. Wenger (Arsenal)	0.852	2	A. Wenger (Arsenal)	0.862	2	K. Keegan (Newcastle)	0.911
3	G. Vialli (Chelsea)	0.812	3	G. Vialli (Chelsea)	0.829	3=	J. Gregory (Aston Villa)	0.902
4	P. Reid (Sunderland)	0.779	4	R. Gullitt (Chelsea)	0.799	3=	R. Gullitt (Chelsea)	0.902
5	R. Gullitt (Chelsea)	0.777	5	P. Reid (Sunderland)	0.796	5	M. O'Neill (Leicester)	0.891
6	W. Bonds (West Ham)	0.773	6	W. Bonds (West Ham)	0.771	6	R. Wilkins (QPR)	0.887
7=	D. Webb (Chelsea)	0.729	7	M. O'Neill (Leicester)	0.761	7	M. Walker (Norwich)	0.885
7=	M. O'Neill (Leicester)	0.729	8	R. Wilkins (QPR)	0.742	8	A. Ferguson (Man Utd)	0.881
9	R. Wilkins (QPR)	0.721	9	D. Jones (Southampton)	0.739	9	G. Vialli (Chelsea)	0.879
10	M. Walker (Norwich)	0.720	10	K. Keegan (Newcastle)	0.732	10	K. Dalglish (Blackburn)	0.876
11	K. Keegan (Newcastle)	0.706	11	D. Webb (Chelsea)	0.730	11	P. Reid (Sunderland)	0.874
12	D. Jones (Southampton)	0.693	12	M. Walker (Norwich)	0.729	12=	P. Neal (Coventry)	0.873
13	P. Neal (Coventry)	0.674	13	C. Todd (Bolton)	0.709	12=	C. Todd (Bolton)	0.873
14	C. Todd (Bolton)	0.663	14	P. Neal (Coventry)	0.701	14	W. Bonds (West Ham)	0.871
15	R. Gould (Coventry)	0.661	15	D. Wilson (Barnsley)	0.695	15=	R. Gould (Coventry)	0.867
16	O. Ardiles (Tottenham)	0.645	16	G. Graham (Leeds)	0.694	15=	G. Graham (Leeds)	0.867
17	K. Dalglish (Blackburn)	0.643	17	J. Smith (Derby)	0.686	17=	O. Ardiles (Tottenham)	0.864
18	G. Graham (Leeds)	0.635	18	R. Gould (Coventry)	0.685	17=	G. Francis (QPR)	0.864
19	D. Wilson (Barnsley)	0.633	19	C. Gross (Tottenham)	0.684	19=	J. Kinnear (Wimbledon)	0.863
20	G. Souness (Liverpool)	0.629	20	O. Ardiles (Tottenham)	0.681	19=	J. Smith (Derby)	0.863
21	J. Smith (Derby)	0.623	21	K. Dalglish (Blackburn)	0.679	21	D. Webb (Chelsea)	0.862
22=	G. Francis (QPR)	0.618	22	R. Atkinson (Sheff Wed)	0.672	22	D. Jones (Southampton)	0.861
22=	C. Gross (Tottenham)	0.618	23	B. Rioch (Arsenal)	0.668	23	G. Souness (Liverpool)	0.859
24	B. Rioch (Arsenal)	0.610	24	G. Souness (Liverpool)	0.666	24	H. Redknapp (West Ham)	0.855
25	D. Livermore (Tottenham)	0.609	25	R. Hodgson (Blackburn)	0.664	25	H. Kendall (Everton)	0.854

Source: Dawson (2000).

Included among the manager human capital measures are the amount of experience the manager gained as a player (number of league games played and number of clubs played for); the quality of that experience (number of international caps); and a number of measures reflecting managerial experience. These include the number of previous clubs managed; the number of months spent managing before the current job; the total number of months spent managing in the current division; the total number of months spent managing the current club; and dummy variables reflecting whether or not the manager had a prior affiliation with the club, either as player, assistant manager or manager. The club-specific factors include the total wage bill of the club and the average managerial tenure at the club over the past 10 and 25 seasons.

Dawson finds that most of the manager human capital measures are significant in explaining variations in managerial efficiency. The number of clubs the manager played for and the number of international caps both improve efficiency. The latter finding reflects an important difference between football (worldwide), and North American team sports in which there is little or no competition at international level. Football players apparently do gain valuable experience while on international duty, both by playing under the guidance of the national team manager, and by gaining experience of different playing styles and tactics adopted by opposition teams. This experience provides tangible benefits subsequently, when a former international player pursues a career in management.

Elsewhere, Dawson's empirical results suggest that older managers are more efficient than their younger counterparts. Managerial experience is important, and efficiency increases if there was a previous association with the manager's current club. Contrary to expectation, however, the number of months spent managing in the current division and the total number of months spent managing before the present job are both inversely related to efficiency. All of the club-specific factors are significant. Managerial efficiency increases with the absolute level of wages paid relative to the average. Assuming that the manager's relative pay is correlated with the relative value of the club's overall wages and salaries bill, this is consistent with the notion that higher managerial pay induces higher performance. Managers at clubs with high average tenure levels are found to be less efficient than those employed by clubs where the threat of dismissal is higher.

Dawson's study is the first systematic empirical investigation of the efficiency of managers in English professional football, using a novel way of measuring the quality of the playing input based on predicted transfer values. The results appear to be robust over a variety of estimation procedures. The most efficient managers are not necessarily those that manage the most successful teams. Managers that gain honours or keep a team afloat with relatively limited playing resources feature prominently towards the top of the estimated efficiency rankings, as of course they should.

5.4 Conclusion

The contribution of the football manager to team performance can be broken down into a direct and an indirect component. Taking the collection of players at his disposal as given, the manager's direct contribution is to maximise performance through astute team selection, superior tactics and powers of motivation. Over the longer term, the manager's indirect contribution is to enhance his existing squad, by coaching players so as to improve their skills, and by effective dealings in the transfer market. Despite the fact that the output of the professional sports team is easily measured by win ratios or league standings, and much data on the characteristics of the major inputs (players and manager) is easily available and in the public domain, the indivisibility of the team effort which ultimately determines performance poses a major challenge for any researcher seeking to isolate and measure precisely the contribution made by the manager to the effectiveness of the team's performance.

A realistic assessment of the quality of the managerial contribution can be made only if the quality of the playing resources that were at the manager's disposal is measured and taken into account. In the case of North American professional team sports, considerable academic effort has been invested in separating the managerial from the playing input to team production, using sophisticated econometric techniques such as stochastic frontier analysis. In this literature, it is clear that empirical results can depend heavily on the way in which the inputs are measured; on the specification of the production function and the distributional assumptions concerning the inefficiency and random components of the error term; and on the estimation method employed. Clearly it is important to be able to demonstrate that any set of empirical results is reasonably consistent over a range of definitions, model specifications and estimation procedures.

The recent work of Peter Dawson, which has been reviewed in some detail in this chapter, represents a promising first attempt at bringing similar methods to bear on English professional football. The lack of adequate historical data on most aspects of player performance apart from goals scored and conceded, and the fact that the playing and managerial inputs are in any case less easily separable than in North American sports such as baseball, make this task a formidable challenge. The valuation of players using a model created from player transfer data offers a novel way round some of the problems, though not without presenting some further difficulties of its own. The inclusion of financial data in the measurement of inputs also acknowledges the critical fact that the quality of the resources at the English football manager's disposal depends, to a large and ever-increasing extent, on the strength of his club's financial muscle.

6   Managerial change and team performance

Chapter 5 has focused on measuring the football manager's contribution to the performance of his team. Using production frontier analysis it is possible to rank managers by their estimated efficiency scores, which measure performance relative to the quality of the playing resources each manager had at his disposal. But while the measurement of managerial efficiency is an interesting exercise, it does not necessarily capture every aspect of a manager's performance. Many times, a manager who was deemed a hero yesterday has been transformed into a villain today, and all football followers know that one of the most enduring characteristics of the football manager's position is its chronic insecurity. Chapter 6 therefore investigates the relationship between managerial change and team performance.

The chapter begins in section 6.1 with some tabulations, which describe a number of features of this relationship. The factors that are critical in triggering the decision, taken either by the club or by the manager himself, to terminate a manager's appointment are then investigated more systematically in sections 6.2–6.5. Previous findings from the US literature are reviewed in section 6.2, while technical issues involved in specifying managerial job-departure hazard functions, which identify the probabilities of involuntary or voluntary job departure, are covered in section 6.3. Empirical managerial job-departure hazard functions for English football are presented in sections 6.4–6.5. These show the extent to which team performance, both in the short term and in the long term, tends to influence the decision to terminate a manager's appointment. They also show the extent to which human capital attributes of the manager, such as age and previous managerial and playing experience, are important in influencing his survival prospects. Hazard functions for both involuntary and voluntary managerial departures are estimated, based on season-level data (in section 6.4) and match-level data (in section 6.5).

Sections 6.6–6.8 examine the relationship between managerial change and team performance from the opposite direction, by considering the

264

extent to which the removal of a manager influences the team's performance subsequently. According to one view, it is simple common sense for a manager to be replaced when his team is performing badly. Assuming that a more effective replacement can be appointed, team performance should improve post-succession. An alternative view is that a change of leadership is usually disruptive, especially if it occurs while the season is in progress, and tends to make matters worse rather than better. A third view suggests that on average, the appointment of a new manager has no effect whatever on team performance, because performance depends primarily on the playing talent available to the team, and not on the managerial input. Managerial dismissal is a form of scapegoating: during a poor run of results team owners can appease disgruntled spectators by removing the manager, even if doing so is not expected to have any real effect on team performance. The US evidence on these matters is considered in section 6.6. Some new results for English football are then presented in sections 6.7–6.8. These seek to identify managerial succession effects, using season-level data (in section 6.7) and match-level data (in section 6.8).

6.1 Patterns of managerial change in English football

The analysis of managerial change and team performance draws on data for 1,092 managerial spells with English clubs that were recorded between the 1973 and 1999 seasons (inclusive). Exactly 1,000 of these spells began after the start of the 1973 season, while 1,010 terminated before the start of the 2000 season. In total, the data set includes 918 complete spells that both began after the start of the 1973 season and terminated before the start of the 2000 season.

For the 1,000 spells that began after the start of the 1973 season, table 6.1 shows the top 50 ranked in descending order of duration, measured in matches completed. Of course, in view of the notorious insecurity of the English football manager's job tenure, the longevity of a spell is itself often a meaningful measure of its success. In some cases it may also reflect attributes or attitudes of the club's owners, which influence their willingness either to stick with or dismiss a manager during a lean spell. Among the longest-serving managers shown in table 6.1, Brian Clough (Nottingham Forest), Dario Gradi (Crewe Alexandra), John Rudge (Port Vale), Joe Royle (Oldham Athletic) and Graham Taylor (Watford) all steered their clubs through one or more promotion campaigns, and then consolidated and achieved further success at a higher level. In a slightly different category, Alex Ferguson (Manchester United), Bob Paisley (Liverpool) and George Graham (Arsenal) all achieved lasting success

Table 6.1. *Managerial spells ranked by duration in matches: top 50*

Rank	Manager	Team	Dates	Matches	Win ratio
1	Brian Clough	Nottingham Forest	1975–93	758	0.574
2	Dario Gradi	Crewe Alexandra	1983–	726	0.518
3	John Rudge	Port Vale	1984–99	679	0.497
4	John Lyall	West Ham United	1974–89	621	0.507
5	Joe Royle	Oldham Athletic	1982–94	534	0.504
6	Alex Ferguson	Manchester United	1986–	503	0.669
7	Lawrie McMenemy	Southampton	1973–85	488	0.550
8	Brian Flynn	Wrexham	1989–	439	0.502
9	Graham Taylor	Watford	1977–87	434	0.568
10	John King	Tranmere Rovers	1987–96	415	0.564
11	Harry Redknapp	Bournemouth	1983–92	401	0.510
12	Arthur Cox	Derby County	1984–93	397	0.524
13	Bob Paisley	Liverpool	1974–83	378	0.692
14	Steve Coppell	Crystal Palace	1984–93	376	0.535
15	Mike Buxton	Huddersfield Town	1978–86	374	0.537
16	Frank Clark	Leyton Orient	1982–91	368	0.507
17	George Graham	Arsenal	1986–95	363	0.606
18	Alan Curbishley	Charlton Athletic	1991–	360	0.517
19	Lennie Lawrence	Charlton Athletic	1982–91	358	0.443
20	Graham Turner	Wolverhampton Wandrs	1986–94	355	0.569
21	David Pleat	Luton Town	1978–86	352	0.523
22	Dave Bassett	Sheffield United	1988–95	339	0.506
23	Keith Burkinshaw	Tottenham Hotspur	1976–84	336	0.531
24	Howard Wilkinson	Leeds United	1988–96	335	0.584
25	Harry McNally	Chester City	1985–92	333	0.482
26	Dave Smith	Southend United	1976–83	322	0.550
27=	Sam Ellis	Blackpool	1982–9	320	0.517
27=	Bobby Roberts	Colchester United	1975–82	320	0.527
29	Terry Neill	Arsenal	1976–83	318	0.563
30	Ron Saunders	Aston Villa	1974–82	317	0.576
31	Billy Bremner	Doncaster Rovers	1978–85	316	0.494
32	Barry Lloyd	Brighton	1987–93	312	0.466
33	Colin Murphy	Lincoln City	1978–85	311	0.532
34=	Phil Neal	Bolton Wanderers	1985–92	302	0.527
34=	Billy Horner	Hartlepool United	1976–83	302	0.440
36	Maurice Evans	Reading	1977–84	301	0.542
37	Ken Brown	Norwich City	1980–7	299	0.517
38	Keith Peacock	Gillingham	1981–7	297	0.571
39	Terry Dolan	Hull City	1991–7	296	0.458
40=	Jimmy McGuigan	Rotherham United	1973–9	295	0.517
40=	Joe Kinnear	Wimbledon	1992–9	295	0.483
42=	Alan Buckley	Grimsby Town	1988–94	288	0.531
42=	John Bond	Norwich City	1973–80	288	0.476
44=	John Duncan	Chesterfield	1993–	284	0.560
44=	Dave Bassett	Wimbledon	1981–7	284	0.600
46	Alan Little	York City	1993–9	277	0.487
47	Ian Greaves	Mansfield Town	1983–9	276	0.495
48	Danny Bergera	Stockport County	1989–95	274	0.582
49	Terry Cooper	Bristol City	1982–8	270	0.574
50	Len Walker	Aldershot	1985–91	267	0.412

Source: Managers' data set.

with big-market clubs at the very highest level. Of course, managerial spells that survive for durations of 250 matches or more are very much the exception and not the rule. In fact, 50 per cent of all spells that both started and finished within the sample period survived for just 75 matches or less.

Using a measure of success that would perhaps be recognised more readily by most spectators, table 6.2 shows rankings of the same 1,000 spells by win ratio. Win ratios are calculated (as in previous chapters) by awarding 1 point for a win, 0.5 points for a draw and 0 points for a defeat, and dividing the total by the number of league matches played in each spell. Table 6.2 shows the top 50 spells according to these rankings. The most successful spell of all on this criterion is Kevin Keegan's brief reign at Fulham during the 1999 season, which ended with promotion from Division Two to Division One. Three of the remaining top five places are occupied by successive Liverpool managers from the 1970s and 1980s: Bob Paisley, Joe Fagan and Kenny Dalglish. Manchester United's Alex Ferguson finishes slightly lower, in 7th place, mainly because United's eventual successes were preceded by several seasons of more modest achievement between Ferguson's appointment in the 1987 season and his first championship in 1993. Keegan and Dalglish also achieve top-50 rankings with other clubs (Newcastle United and Blackburn Rovers, respectively); others who appear twice in the top 50 are Graham Taylor (Lincoln City and Watford), David Webb (Southend United and Bournemouth) and Barry Fry (Barnet and Southend United). Howard Kendall's achievement in achieving top-50 rankings with three different clubs (Blackburn Rovers, Sheffield United and his first spell at Everton) is unique, though Kendall's two later spells with Everton, ranked 445th and 784th, respectively, were rather less successful.

As a method of comparing the success of managerial spells, rankings by win ratio are crude for several reasons. Most fundamentally, rankings of this kind do not take account of the separate contributions of the manager and the players. But even ignoring the difficulties involved in identifying the manager's individual contribution to team performance, the rankings reported in table 6.2 are still contentious. One problem is that they often tend to penalise success or reward failure: a manager who achieves promotion to a higher division, for example, is likely to suffer a reduction in his win ratio during the following season, simply because his team is playing at a higher level. This is why the top end of table 6.2 is dominated by managers of top-level teams (for whom success is not rewarded by promotion), as well as several managers who, having achieved promotion, left their jobs very soon afterwards. Keegan's spell at Fulham is one case in point; Jim Smith's spell at Oxford United, which

Table 6.2. *Managerial spells ranked by win ratio: top 50*

Rank	Manager	Team	Dates	Matches	Win ratio
1	Kevin Keegan	Fulham	1998–9	46	0.761
2	Kenny Dalglish	Liverpool	1985–91	224	0.732
3	Arsène Wenger	Arsenal	1996–	114	0.702
4	Bob Paisley	Liverpool	1974–83	378	0.692
5	Joe Fagan	Liverpool	1983–5	84	0.673
6	Colin Appleton	Hull City	1982–4	111	0.671
7	Alex Ferguson	Manchester United	1986–	503	0.669
8	Ray Graydon	Walsall	1998–	46	0.663
9	Kenny Dalglish	Blackburn Rovers	1991–5	169	0.663
10	Jim Smith	Oxford United	1982–5	160	0.663
11	Gianluca Vialli	Chelsea	1998	51	0.657
12	Kevin Keegan	Newcastle United	1992–7	205	0.656
13	Graham Taylor	Watford	1997–	92	0.652
14	David Webb	Southend United	1986–7	33	0.652
15	Peter Reid	Sunderland	1995–	183	0.650
16	David O'Leary	Leeds United	1998–	31	0.645
17	Roy McFarland	Bradford City	1981–2	70	0.643
18	Steve Thompson	Southend United	1995	14	0.643
19	Ron Noades	Brentford	1998–	46	0.641
20	Osvaldo Ardiles	West Bromwich	1992–3	46	0.641
21	Barry Fry	Barnet	1991–3	82	0.640
22	Howard Kendall	Everton	1981–7	252	0.637
23	Colin Lee	Wolverhampton Wandrs	1998–	30	0.633
24	Nigel Spackman	Sheffield United	1997–8	34	0.632
25	Ron Atkinson	Manchester United	1981–6	225	0.629
26	Barry Fry	Southend United	1993	28	0.625
27	Bryan Hamilton	Wigan Athletic	1985–6	60	0.625
28	Richie Barker	Shrewsbury Town	1978	33	0.621
29	Chris Turner	Peterborough United	1991–2	87	0.621
30	Howard Kendall	Blackburn Rovers	1979–81	88	0.619
31	Lou Macari	Swindon Town	1984–9	228	0.618
32	Dave Bassett	Crystal Palace	1996–7	52	0.615
33	Martin O'Neill	Wycombe Wandrs	1993–5	88	0.614
34	Micky Adams	Fulham	1996–7	71	0.613
35	Terry Venables	Queens Park Rangers	1980–4	157	0.612
36	David Williams	Bristol Rovers	1983–5	90	0.611
37	John Beck	Cambridge United	1990–2	128	0.609
38	Roy Evans	Liverpool	1994–8	184	0.609
39	Joe Royle	Manchester City	1998–	60	0.608
40	Graham Taylor	Lincoln City	1972–7	209	0.608
41	Ron Atkinson	Cambridge United	1974–8	149	0.607
42	Cyril Knowles	Hartlepool United	1989–91	75	0.607
43	George Graham	Arsenal	1986–95	363	0.606
44	Howard Kendall	Sheffield United	1995–7	71	0.606
45	George Burley	Colchester United	1994	19	0.605
46	Bobby Campbell	Chelsea	1988–91	129	0.605
47	David Webb	Bournemouth	1980–2	87	0.603
48	Don Howe	Arsenal	1984–6	97	0.603
49	Ian Porterfield	Rotherham United	1979–81	73	0.603
50	Joe Jordan	Bristol City	1988–90	108	0.602

Source: Managers' data set.

ended at the close of the 1985 season following two consecutive promotions, is another.

Table 6.3 shows an alternative set of rankings, which make adjustments to the points awarded for wins, draws and losses during the two seasons following promotion or relegation. In calculating the adjusted win ratios, 0.2 extra points are awarded per match played during the season following promotion, and 0.1 extra points per match are awarded during the second season following promotion. Similarly, negative adjustments of -0.2 and -0.1 points per match are made during the first and second seasons following relegation. The precise numerical adjustments are arbitrary, but they do address the problems discussed in the previous paragraph in a straightforward manner. Naturally, managers whose spells included one or more seasons following promotion are beneficiaries of the adjustment: notably, John Beck (Cambridge United), George Kerr (Grimsby Town) and Chris Turner (Peterborough United), who occupy the top three positions, each having achieved two promotions. In the process of taking Wimbledon from Division 4 to Division 1, Dave Bassett achieved no fewer than four promotions and one relegation. Accordingly, the ranking of Bassett's spell with Wimbledon jumps from just outside the top 50 (52nd) in table 6.2 to 11th in table 6.3.

Audas, Dobson and Goddard (1999) discuss a number of factors contributing to the chronic insecurity of the English football manager's position. On the one hand, match results (the manager's most important performance measure) are completely transparent, easily interpreted and instantly in the public domain.[1] On the other hand, the manager's ability to influence results is constrained by uncertainty concerning the fitness, performance and motivation of players. Whether or not a group of players will combine to form a successful team has always depended on a mixture of luck and judgement, in proportions which ultimately are impossible to fathom. In any event, each match and each season's league programme are by their very nature zero-sum affairs, in which failure for some participants is inevitable. As characteristics of the manager's position, the combination of direct accountability for outcomes that are transparent and public, and imperfect control over the processes which determine the same outcomes, could not be better designed to minimise job security.

Whereas inadequate performance in business tends to lead to the loss of customers followed by events such as internal restructuring, acquisition by new owners or liquidation, football clubs are highly resilient, even

---

[1] In contrast, the types of performance measure on which business managers are judged, such as sales, growth or profits, are relatively opaque and subject to interpretation.

Table 6.3. *Managerial spells ranked by adjusted win ratio: top 50*

Rank	Manager	Team	Dates	Matches	Adj win ratio
1	John Beck	Cambridge United	1990–2	128	0.798
2	George Kerr	Grimsby Town	1979–82	105	0.795
3	Chris Turner	Peterborough United	1991–2	87	0.789
4	Kevin Keegan	Fulham	1998–9	46	0.761
5	Colin Appleton	Hull City	1982–4	111	0.754
6	Graham Taylor	Watford	1997–	92	0.752
7	Stan Ternent	Bury	1995–8	133	0.752
8	Kenny Dalglish	Blackburn Rovers	1991–5	169	0.737
9	Lou Macari	Swindon Town	1984–9	228	0.737
10	Kenny Dalglish	Liverpool	1985–91	224	0.732
11	Dave Bassett	Wimbledon	1981–7	284	0.722
12	Martin O'Neill	Wycombe Wandrs	1993–5	88	0.718
13	Kevin Keegan	Newcastle United	1992–7	205	0.718
14	Jim Smith	Oxford United	1982–5	160	0.715
15	Arsène Wenger	Arsenal	1996–	114	0.702
16	Chris Nicholl	Walsall	1994–7	130	0.695
17	Bobby Saxton	Exeter City	1977–9	95	0.693
18	Bob Paisley	Liverpool	1974–83	378	0.692
19	Bruce Rioch	Bolton Wandrs	1992–5	138	0.691
20	Alan Mullery	Brighton and Hove Albion	1976–81	214	0.690
21	Roy McFarland	Bradford City	1981–2	70	0.689
22	Johnny Giles	West Bromwich	1975–7	86	0.680
23	Dave Smith	Mansfield Town	1974–6	103	0.674
24	John McGrath	Port Vale	1980–3	195	0.673
25	Joe Fagan	Liverpool	1983–5	84	0.673
26	Alex Ferguson	Manchester United	1986–	503	0.669
27	Alan Murray	Hartlepool United	1991–3	74	0.669
28	Terry Venables	Crystal Palace	1976–80	182	0.668
29	Tony Pulis	Gillingham	1995–9	184	0.667
30	Allan Clarke	Barnsley	1978–80	108	0.667
31	Terry Venables	Queens Park Rangers	1980–4	157	0.665
32	Jack Charlton	Newcastle United	1996–7	42	0.664
33	Ray Graydon	Walsall	1998–	46	0.663
34	Larry Lloyd	Wigan Athletic	1981–3	96	0.663
35	Gianluca Vialli	Chelsea	1998	51	0.657
36	Graham Taylor	Watford	1977–87	434	0.657
37	Emlyn Hughes	Rotherham United	1981–3	74	0.657
38	Alan Mullery	Charlton Athletic	1981–2	42	0.652
39	Gary Peters	Preston North End	1994–8	143	0.652
40	Jack Charlton	Middlesbrough	1973–7	178	0.652
41	Graham Taylor	Lincoln City	1972–7	209	0.652
42	David Webb	Southend United	1986–7	33	0.652
43	John Deehan	Wigan Athletic	1995–8	127	0.647
44	David Webb	Bournemouth	1980–2	87	0.647
45	David O'Leary	Leeds United	1998–	31	0.645
46	Norman Hunter	Barnsley	1980–4	142	0.645
47	John Ward	Bristol City	1997–8	71	0.644
48	Ken Knighton	Sunderland	1979–81	112	0.644
49	Steve Thompson	Southend United	1995	14	0.643
50	Ron Atkinson	Cambridge United	1974–8	149	0.642

Source: Managers' data set.

in the face of catastrophic failure on the field of play or on the balance sheet. This is due mainly to the highly loyal or fanatical nature of their customer base. Relegation to a lower division, or even to non-league status, usually requires some restructuring of finances and personnel, but is invariably accepted by regular spectators in sufficient numbers to ensure that clubs remain viable as going concerns. In accounting terms, all clubs benefit from significant (but intangible) goodwill.[2] But such fierce customer loyalty can generate extreme pressure for the scapegoating of an unsuccessful manager. The intensity of the clamour is scarcely imaginable in any other business, except perhaps in the case of certain high-profile privatised utilities.

Finally, the specialised nature of the football manager's contribution usually makes it difficult for an unsuccessful manager to be accommodated elsewhere within the club by means of an upward, sideways or downward move (as often happens elsewhere in business). The uniformity of football's 'production technology', however, makes the team manager's function highly transferable between clubs, since the relevant skills tend to be job-specific and not firm-specific. There are perhaps a few rigidities within the managerial labour market that should be considered. At times, many club owners have shown a preference for appointing individuals with a current or past association with the club to the manager's position. This may be because lower transactions costs are associated with the appointment of an individual who is already known to the owner; or it may be because an ex-player often brings advantages of credibility or popularity with supporters. Either way, however, it seems unlikely that the occasional propensity for clubs to show preference towards insiders (of one kind or another) seriously undermines the conclusion that the managerial labour market is highly flexible and competitive.

For the purposes of the empirical analyses reported below in sections 6.4 and 6.5, each of the 1,010 managerial departures recorded in the data set has been classified by the authors as either 'involuntary' or 'voluntary'. This is necessary in order to study the relationship between team performance and the manager's job security. While it seems reasonable to expect that poor team performance would lead to involuntary departure, voluntary departure could well be a consequence of good performance resulting in the manager receiving a more attractive job offer from another club. In making the distinction between involuntary and voluntary departures, it seems unwise to rely too heavily on the club's original

---

[2] In the past 30 years, many clubs (including big names such as Bristol City, Crystal Palace, Middlesbrough and Wolverhampton Wanderers) have teetered on the edge of bankruptcy but only two (Aldershot and Maidstone United) have gone out of business while members of the league.

explanation of the reason for the change as either a 'dismissal' or a 'resignation'. To do so would probably lead to significant over-counting of the number of voluntary departures, since many 'resignations' actually occur in response to behind-the-scenes pressure from the chairman or directors. *In extremis* this can take the form of an ultimatum to resign or be sacked (Audas, Dobson and Goddard, 1999).

In classifying managerial departures as either involuntary or voluntary, any information available on the circumstances at the time of the departure was assessed. Particularly relevant criteria were the team's performance prior to termination; the nature of any new appointment accepted by the manager immediately after his departure; and the reasons given by the club or the manager for the latter's departure. Involuntary departures (the majority) include those that were at the club's instigation, as well as resignations for which there was no obvious reason other than disappointing results or other pressures emanating from the manager's current appointment. Voluntary departures include those for which there is clear and tangible evidence that the manager instigated the move willingly. Such evidence is usually in the form of an immediate or imminent move to another job at a club (at home or overseas) of comparable or higher status, or a move to a national team manager's position.

A couple of recent examples will illustrate the method of classification. First, of the 10 close season departures during the summer of 1999, only Kevin Keegan's move from Fulham to the England manager's post is classified unambiguously as voluntary. Although Steve Bruce (Sheffield United) and Brian Little (Stoke City) both subsequently obtained managerial appointments at Huddersfield Town and West Bromwich Albion, respectively, these appointments do not appear to have motivated their departures. Bruce's move from Sheffield United was attributed to instability and disputes at boardroom level, while Little was dismissed after a disappointing campaign and an especially poor run of results towards the end of the 1999 season.[3]

Second, after a successful spell at Reading, Mark McGhee made two voluntary moves in quick succession, first to Leicester City (in December 1994) and then Wolverhampton Wanderers (December 1995). Three campaigns in which promotion to the Premier League failed to materialise resulted in McGhee's involuntary removal from Wolverhampton in November 1998. McGhee's move from Leicester triggered Martin

---

[3] At the time of writing it remains to be seen whether Ron Atkinson (Nottingham Forest) will eventually accept a new appointment or retire permanently from management. Other departures during the summer of 1999 included Nigel Pearson (Carlisle United), Peter Jackson (Huddersfield Town), Dennis Smith (West Bromwich Albion), Ray Mathias (Wigan Athletic) and Joe Kinnear (Wimbledon).

O'Neill's switch from Norwich City as his successor. This move is also classified as voluntary; but it is a borderline case, since at the time O'Neill was facing significant spectator discontent only six months into his appointment at Norwich. Ironically, while Wolverhampton and Norwich have both remained firmly rooted in Division One, Leicester gained promotion at the end of O'Neill's first season in 1996, and have since become an established Premier League team. Recently O'Neill has once again moved voluntarily, from Leicester to Celtic; though this move took place in the summer of 2000, after the end of the sample period for the data set used in this chapter.

Table 6.4 shows the numbers of involuntary and voluntary managerial departures per season. The data suggest that the level of job insecurity of football managers has increased over time. Although there is considerable year-on-year variation in the total number of departures, the long-term trend is clearly upward. The nine-year averages for the total number of departures increase from 33.8 per year (for seasons 1973–1981 inclusive) through 35.6 (1982–1990) to 42.9 (1991–1999). Significantly the increase in the total is driven by a rise in the number of involuntary departures, while the number of voluntary departures remains roughly constant. In recent seasons an increasing tendency for senior clubs to appoint current or recently retired players directly into managerial posts, or to recruit managers from overseas, may account for the pattern.[4] With no fewer than 61 managerial departures, the 1995 season established what is presumably an all-time record for managerial turnover. Although this figure looks like an outlier, it is perhaps significant that at the end of this season, the league structure was changed from 22-24-24-22 to 20-24-24-24 teams in the four divisions. The change meant there was one less promotion berth and one more relegation berth than usual in each division. This seems to have created sufficient panic at boardroom level to have cost many managers their jobs during the course of the 1995 season.

Table 6.5 summarises some other features of the managers' data set. There is a high level of monthly variation in the incidence of managerial departure. 705 of the 1,010 departures (69.8 per cent) took place during the course of the season, and only 305 (30.2 per cent) during the close

---

[4] There has been no tendency, however, for the average age of football managers to decline over time. For the league as a whole, the average age of managers in post at the start of the 1973 season was 43.4 years. The average age fell slightly to 42.2 at the start of the 1986 season, but then increased to 44.8 by the start of the 1999 season. For Division 1/Premier League managers, the corresponding figures were slightly higher: 46.5 (1973), 44.1 (1986) and 47.7 (1999). These averages are based on all managers for whom date-of-birth information was available; a very small number of managers (at most two out of 92) are excluded from these calculations for certain seasons.

Table 6.4. *Managerial departures, by season,*
1973–1999

| Season | Managerial departures | | |
	Involuntary	Voluntary	Total
1973	27	4	31
1974	20	13	33
1975	25	7	32
1976	23	4	27
1977	30	6	36
1978	37	8	45
1979	23	9	32
1980	20	1	21
1981	34	13	47
Average (1973–1981)	26.6	7.2	33.8
1982	33	4	37
1983	32	4	36
1984	32	6	38
1985	32	3	35
1986	34	6	40
1987	30	8	38
1988	25	3	28
1989	23	8	31
1990	33	4	37
Average (1982–1990)	30.4	5.1	35.6
1991	35	12	47
1992	31	2	33
1993	34	6	40
1994	30	6	36
1995	50	11	61
1996	34	5	39
1997	38	10	48
1998	41	7	48
1999	28	6	34
Average (1991–1999)	35.7	7.2	42.9

Source: Managers' data set.

Table 6.5. *Managerial departures, by month and by division, 1973–1999*

| | Managerial departures | | |
	Involuntary	Voluntary	Total
Month			
August	18	2	20
September	51	9	60
October	82	16	98
November	86	12	98
December	70	18	88
January	77	14	91
February	69	6	75
March	79	8	87
April/May	82	6	88
Close season	220	85	305
Division			
D1/Prem	156	43	199
D2/One	198	48	246
D3/Two	219	54	273
D4/Three	261	31	292
Total	834	176	1,010

Source: Managers' data set.

season. Of the 705 within-season departures, 91 (12.9 per cent) were voluntary, whereas of the 305 close season departures, 85 (27.9 per cent) were voluntary. Departure within the season is therefore relatively more likely to be at the club's behest, while departure during the close season (when most managerial contracts tend to expire) is more likely to be at the manager's behest. October and November, when failure to realise over-optimistic pre-season aspirations first becomes inevitable for many clubs, are the peak months for within-season departures. January, perhaps the latest time at which a new appointment might reasonably be expected to bring about a change of fortune within the current season, is another peak period; while March–May, when many clubs begin planning for the next season, are also periods of high turnover. There appear to be (slight) lulls in the rate of turnover during the months of December and February.

Table 6.5 also shows that managerial insecurity is greater in the lower than in the higher divisions. Both the number of involuntary departures and the total number of departures vary inversely with divisional status. If

Table 6.6. *Complete managerial spells, by duration (matches):*
summary statistics

	All divs	D1/Prem	D2/One	D3/Two	D4/Three
All departures					
No.	918	176	222	247	273
Mean duration	99.4	119.7	105.8	102.2	78.6
1st quartile	42	43.5	44	46	38
Median	75	86.5	82.5	78	64
3rd quartile	132	161.5	138	143	107
Involuntary departures					
No.	765	136	183	199	247
Mean duration	94.9	110.4	99.1	99.3	79.9
1st quartile	41	42	41	45	39
Median	72	82.5	75	75	63
3rd quartile	127	141	133	137	112
Voluntary departures					
No.	153	40	39	48	26
Mean duration	121.6	151.5	137.5	114.0	65.9
1st quartile	58	61	58	61.5	33
Median	92	136	114	92	66
3rd quartile	165	198	177	147.5	92

Source: Managers' data set.

as seems likely recent relegation often triggers managerial departure, the pattern may be explained by the fact that while no team can be relegated to Division 1/Premier League, most teams (with the exception of a small number of sides elected or promoted from non-league) enter Division 4/Three as a result of relegation. In contrast, the incidence of voluntary departure is highest in Division 3/Two, which appears to be the most effective launch pad for a successful manager seeking another post at a higher level.

Figures 6.1–6.3 show the distributions of spells that ended involuntarily and voluntarily by duration, measured in terms of matches played. Durations are tabulated in bands of 30 matches. On this basis the modal duration band for spells that ended involuntary is 31–60 matches, and the modal band for spells that ended voluntarily is 61–90 matches. Table 6.6 reports summary statistics for the distributions of spells by duration, disaggregated by mode of departure and by the team's division at the time of departure. Table 6.6 shows that the mean duration of spells that ended voluntarily was significantly higher than the mean duration of spells that ended involuntarily. The mean duration of spells ending in the higher

All departures

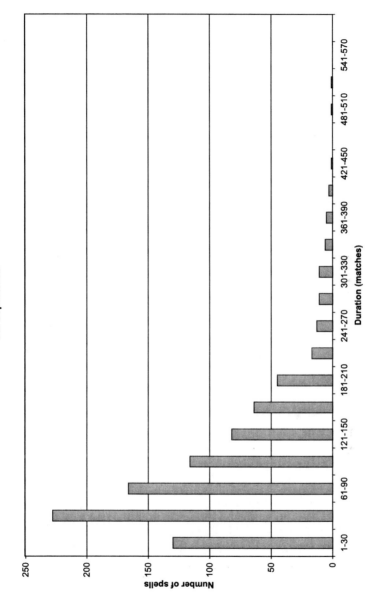

Figure 6.1 Distribution of complete managerial spells, by duration, 1973–1999, all departures
Source: Managers' data set.

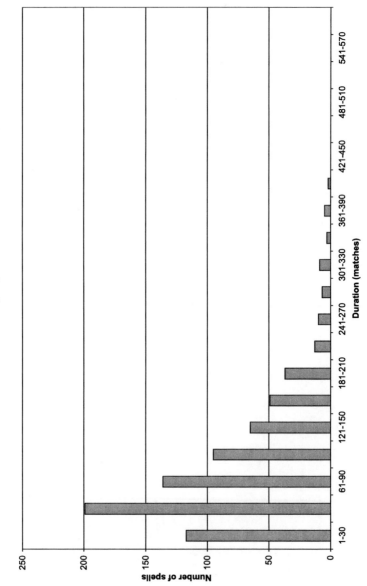

Figure 6.2 Distribution of complete managerial spells, by duration, 1973–1999, involuntary departures
Source: Managers' data set.

Voluntary departures

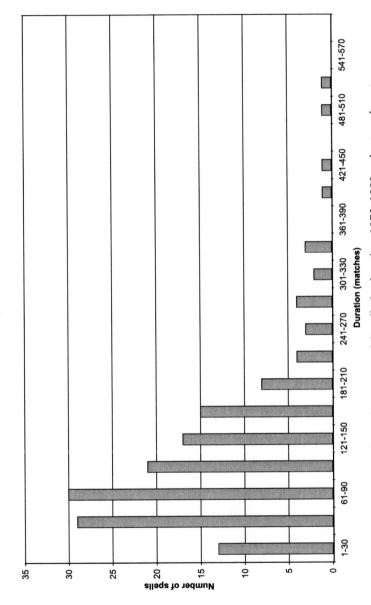

Figure 6.3 Distribution of complete managerial spells, by duration, 1973–1999, voluntary departures
Source: Managers' data set.

divisions was higher than the mean duration of spells that ended in the lower divisions. Finally, the shape of the distribution by duration differs between spells that ended involuntarily and those that ended voluntarily. For the latter the inverse relationship between mean duration and divisional status holds uniformly across all four divisions. For the former there is little or no difference between the mean and median duration of spells that ended in Divisions 2/One and 3/Two. Although spells that ended involuntarily in Division 1/Premier League were longer on average, and those that ended in Division 4/Three were shorter, the difference in mean duration (about 30 matches) is much smaller than the corresponding difference for spells that ended voluntarily (about 85 matches).

6.2 Determinants of managerial change: evidence from North American team sports

Grusky's (1963) investigation of managerial succession in North American baseball appears to have been the first academic study to consider the possibility of a bidirectional link between managerial change and team performance. For 16 professional baseball teams, Grusky obtains a negative correlation between the number of managerial changes and the average standing of each team, for both of the periods 1921–41 and 1951–8. In other words, teams that made the most managerial changes tended to perform badly. Grusky also obtains a negative correlation between the change in the average duration of managerial tenure between these two periods, and the change in average standing. The teams that increased their rate of managerial turnover the fastest therefore tended to experience a decline in average standing. Grusky (1963) and Gamson and Scotch (1964), in a comment on the Grusky paper, go on to identify three possible theories of managerial turnover:

- The *common sense* theory. When a team is under-performing, the manager is held accountable and is likely to be replaced. If a more effective replacement is hired, or if the incoming manager can learn from the mistakes of his predecessor, team performance should improve post-succession. This would be sufficient to explain Grusky's finding of negative correlation between managerial turnover and team performance.
- The *vicious circle* theory. Again, poor performance tends to trigger managerial change. But the disruptive effect of a change of leadership, particularly if it occurs within-season, tends to make matters worse rather than better. Faltering teams can become trapped in a vicious circle of high managerial turnover and declining performance. Grusky's empirical results therefore reflect a bi-directional relationship between turnover and performance.

- The *ritual scapegoating* theory. On average, the appointment of a new manager makes no difference to team performance. The latter depends primarily on the supply of playing talent and not on the managerial input. A change of manager is not and cannot be expected to improve matters overnight. The supply of playing talent is determined primarily by the effectiveness of scouting and player development programmes, for which club owners are ultimately responsible. Grusky's inverse relationship between turnover and performance is an effect of scapegoating: during a poor spell, owners can appease disgruntled spectators and perhaps deflect attention from any shortcomings in their own contribution, by offering the manager's head in ritual sacrifice.

Grusky himself argues in favour of the vicious circle, bi-directional causality theory, on the grounds that it captures a wider range of possible interactions between performance and succession than the common sense theory, in which causality is unidirectional. Gamson and Scotch are more hesitant to discard the latter, but in the absence of any clear evidence as to whether a change of manager actually does affect team performance, argue that the ritual scapegoating explanation should be adopted as a working hypothesis. This debate provided sufficient motivation for a number of other researchers to whether or not a change of manager affected team performance after the change took place. These studies are reviewed in section 6.6.

More recently, there has been a renewal of interest in quantifying the relationship expressed in the common sense theory, in which managerial change is primarily a response to poor team performance. Scully (1992, 1994, 1995) and Fizel and D'Itri (1997) investigate this link for several North American professional team sports, using more sophisticated empirical techniques than were available to the first-generation researchers whose findings are outlined above. In developing a model of managerial departure in baseball, basketball and American football, Scully adopts a neoclassical economics perspective, viewing the manager's function primarily as one of resource allocation. The role of the manager is twofold. First, he seeks to maximise points scored subject to the quality of his team's offensive skills relative to his opponents' defensive skills, and to minimise points conceded subject to the quality of his team's defensive skills relative to his opponents' offensive skills. 'Scoring is maximised and opponent scoring is minimised by allocating offensive and defensive skills in such a manner that not one extra run or point can be produced or an opponent's one extra run or point avoided by redistribution of playing assignments at any moment of time' (Scully, 1995, p. 148).

Second, the manager seeks to convert the realised points scored and conceded into the maximum attainable win ratio. Scully assumes that all managers perform the first of these tasks with equal efficiency, so all teams achieve the maximum attainable points scored and the minimum attainable points conceded given their playing resources. But there are differences between managers in terms of the efficiency with which points scored and conceded are converted into win ratios. Each manager achieves an efficiency score based on the residuals, ε, from a regression of the form:

$$\ln(W) = \beta_0 + \beta_1 \ln(S/OS) + \varepsilon \tag{6.1}$$

where W is the win ratio and S and OS are points scored and conceded, respectively.

Scully (1995) obtains ε from OLS estimation of (6.1). It is shown that career efficiency is positively related to career length, demonstrating (indirectly) that efficiency does influence the decision to terminate the manager's appointment. Evidence is also found that in baseball and basketball, player-managers are less efficient than their non-playing counterparts, and that average efficiency increased over time in all three sports.

Scully (1995) models the decision to terminate the manager's appointment directly. In principle the decision to terminate or retain should be based on a comparison between the actual and the maximum attainable win ratio, given the quality of playing resources at the manager's disposal. In practice, however, many other factors also come into play: owners' subjective judgements about the quality of their own and their opponents' players; the manager's relationships with both the owner and the players; the manager's past experience; the possibility that the owner may wish to sacrifice the manager primarily in order to send signals to players, supporters or the media; and last but not least, the influence of luck on team performance.

In Scully's empirical estimations, the dependent variable is a 0-1 dummy that indicates either continuation or termination of the manager's position within or at the end of each season. The independent variable is the team's league standing at the end of the season (or at the time of departure for within-season departures). Although this measure is crude because it takes no account of either playing strengths or managerial efficiency (as defined above), it is justified on the grounds that '[f]or both owner and manager, [the club's standing] is the bottom line' (Scully, 1995, p.161). No distinction is made between involuntary and voluntary managerial departures. The linear probability model and logit and probit models are used for estimation. The main finding, that in both sports the decision to terminate is highly sensitive to league standing, is robust across all specifications.

Scully's (1994) study provides a number of (mainly technical) improvements and refinements in both the estimation of managerial efficiency and the modelling of the decision to terminate the manager's appointment. Deterministic and stochastic frontier estimation methods (rather than OLS) are applied to (6.1) to estimate managerial efficiency scores. The latter (rather than league standings) are then used as the main explanatory variable in regressions that seek to model the decision to terminate the manager's appointment. This seems preferable, because it makes this decision dependent directly on the manager's own performance, rather than factors largely beyond his control such as player quality. Regressions are estimated in the form of survivor functions (see section 6.3). This specification seems preferable to the linear probability model or a discrete choice model on theoretical grounds. The main finding is that efficiency exerts a strong positive influence on average managerial survival time in all three sports.

Using college basketball data, Fizel and D'Itri (1997) investigate the extent to which the decision to terminate the manager's appointment is influenced by managerial efficiency, a measure of the team's playing talent (to proxy for the manager's success in player recruitment), the season's win ratio and a measure of the extent of the manager's past experience. Managerial efficiency scores are generated by comparing win ratios with standardised measures of own-team playing talent and opponent strength. Instead of (parametric) deterministic or stochastic frontier estimation methods, Fizel and D'Itri use data envelopment analysis, a non-parametric method for fitting the efficient frontier based on linear programming.[5] A major strength of Fizel and D'Itri's approach is that playing talent is measured *ex ante* and independently of team performance, using a 'talent index' compiled from expert assessments of each player's talent when he first entered college. The index is upgraded automatically as a player accumulates experience and there is discretion to upgrade players who improve dramatically while in college. *Ex ante* measurement of inputs avoids most of the simultaneity problems inherent in the usual *ex post* measures based on observed performance (except perhaps to the extent that dramatic player improvement might be a consequence of good coaching, or the manager's indirect contribution as

---

[5] Parametric estimation of a deterministic or stochastic frontier assumes that the efficient frontier is described by an equation containing a number of unknown parameters, which describe the relationship between the inputs and output, and which can be estimated from the data given a set of assumptions about the distribution of the error term. Non-parametric estimation using data envelopment analysis identifies directly from the data those managers who employ the fewest inputs to produce a given level of output. The efficient frontier is constructed by connecting these points in input–output space with a series of linear segments. No assumptions concerning the functional form of the production function or the distribution of error term are required.

discussed in chapter 5). Simultaneity problems normally arise because player performance depends partly on the manager's contribution, which the model seeks to capture in the error term and not in the input measures.

In probit regressions using a 0-1 dependent variable indicating either continuation or termination of the manager's position, and estimated separately for involuntary and voluntary departures, Fizel and D'Itri find that managerial efficiency and playing talent both affect the probability of involuntary departure in the expected direction. The number of years' service is found to be positively related to the probability of departure: Fizel and D'Itri's interpretation is that longer-tenured coaches are held more accountable for performance than their shorter-tenured counter-parts. The significance of the managerial efficiency and playing talent var-iables disappears, however, if the win ratio is also included among the covariates. This might suggest that a lack of adequate playing resources is an ineffective mitigating plea for a manager failing to achieve a sufficient proportion of wins. But as managerial efficiency is measured by compar-ing the win ratio with the level of playing talent, it is perhaps unsurprising that the model is incapable of identifying separate effects for all three of these covariates. There does appear to be an element of collinearity between them.

While the complete season is the unit of observation in the US studies reviewed above, Audas, Dobson and Goddard (1999) report estimations of job-departure hazard functions for English football managers using, for the first time, match-level duration data. Below, two sets of hazard function estimations are presented, based on the data set described in section 6.1. In section 6.4 durations are measured season-by-season, pro-ducing results that are comparable to those of the US studies described above. In section 6.5 durations are measured match-by-match. These latter results update those reported by Audas, Dobson and Goddard (1999). But before presenting the hazard function estimation results, it is first necessary to outline the specification of job-departure hazard func-tions. This is the subject of section 6.3.

6.3 Specification of job-departure hazard functions

Section 6.3 describes the essentials of duration analysis, including the specification of hazard functions for events such as job departure. Keifer (1988) provides a more comprehensive review of this topic. In order to describe how a hazard function is specified, some new notation is required. For simplicity, suppose there is a cohort of managers whose spells all start at the same time, but which subsequently terminate at different times. The following functions can be defined to describe the proportions of spells that have survived or terminated after various durations:

$S_t =$ the proportion of spells that survive to time t

$F_t = 1 - S_t =$ the proportion of spells that fail to survive to time t

$f_t = S_t - S_{t+1} =$ the probability that any one of the original cohort terminates between time t and $t+1$, so $S_{t+1} = S_t - f_t$

$h_t = f_t/S_t =$ the probability that a spell that has lasted until time t terminates between time t and $t+1$, so $S_{t+1} = S_t(1 - h_t)$.

S_t is known as the survivor function, and F_t is the distribution function of duration. f_t is the probability function of duration, which shows the unconditional probability that the spell of any member of the original cohort will terminate between time t and $t+1$. h_t is the hazard function, which shows the conditional probability that a spell that has lasted until time t will terminate between time t and $t+1$. For any durations data set, crude numerical estimates of S_t, F_t, f_t and h_t can be obtained from tabulations of the distribution of spells by duration (see sections 6.4 and 6.5). This type of estimation is really only a way of describing the data, however, and is not a way of modelling it. For the latter, one seeks to explain variations in these functions (especially the hazard function, h_t) using other explanatory variables or covariates.

When extending this simple framework in order to model the football manager's job-departure hazard, a complication arises because it is necessary to distinguish between the two modes of departure: involuntary and voluntary. This means that effectively there are two separate hazards at work depleting the number of survivors among any initial cohort of managers, and two separate hazard functions to be estimated. Extending the previous notation, f_t^1 and f_t^2 are defined as the unconditional probabilities that any one of the original spells terminates between time t and $t+1$ involuntarily and voluntarily, respectively. h_t^1 and h_t^2 are the corresponding hazards, measuring the conditional involuntary and voluntary departure probabilities for spells that have already survived to time t. Then $S_{t+1} = S_t - f_t^1 - f_t^2$, and $F_t = 1 - S_t$ as before.

A further extension necessitates making the hazards specific not only to the duration, but also to the spell in question. This means replacing h_t^d with $h_{i,t}^d$, the conditional probability that, having survived to time t, managerial spell i terminates between time t and $t+1$, either involuntarily ($d=1$) or voluntarily ($d=2$). $h_{i,t}^d$ can then be made dependent on a number of covariates, reflecting the performance of the manager and the team to which spell i belongs, as well as human capital attributes of the manager (such as his age or previous managerial or playing experience). One way of expressing the dependence of $h^d_{i,t}$ on other covariates is by using Cox's (1972) proportional hazards specification:

$$h^d_{i,t} = \tilde{h}^d_t \exp(\beta'_d x_{i,t}) \tag{6.2}$$

The terms in (6.2) are as follows:

$\tilde{h}^d_t =$ the baseline hazard of departure by mode d (involuntarily if $d=1$, voluntarily if $d=2$)

$x_{i,t} =$ a vector of covariates reflecting the performance and characteristics of the team and manager at time t within the ith managerial spell

$\beta_d =$ a vector of coefficients to be estimated; the cross-product $\beta'_d x_{i,t}$ determines whether the actual hazard of departure by mode d is above or below the baseline hazard.

Maximum likelihood methods can be used to obtain estimates of the coefficients β_d. The estimated coefficients can be interpreted in a manner similar to those obtained from other types of regression: each coefficient reflects the sensitivity of the hazard to variation in the covariate concerned.

6.4 Hazard functions for English managers: duration measured in seasons

Section 6.4 reports the estimation results for involuntary and voluntary managerial job-departure hazard functions with durations measured in seasons. In view of the discussion in chapter 5, the manager's own efficiency is probably an important covariate influencing these hazards. It is therefore necessary to obtain a set of managerial efficiency scores before the job-departure hazard functions can be estimated. The first sub-section of section 6.4 describes the estimation of managerial efficiency scores, while the second describes the estimation of the hazard functions.

Estimation of managerial efficiency scores

As already seen, the separation of the managerial and playing contribution to team performance has been an important issue in the US literature on managerial turnover. Although the work of Dawson (2000) reviewed in chapter 5 represents important and promising progress towards addressing this question for English football, the data requirements of the player valuation model used by Dawson seem prohibitive for an empirical study of 27 years' duration, as reported in this section. For these reasons, the approach used to measure the contribution of the manager's own performance to the decision to terminate his appointment differs from those adopted in both the US studies reviewed above, and in the Dawson study. In the estimations reported below, managerial efficiency scores are obtained by comparing team performance (measured by league position) with the club's average gate revenues over the previous three seasons, which provide a crude proxy measure of the financial resources the manager had at his disposal. The efficiency scores obtained from this comparison are used subsequently as a covariate in an estimated hazard function for managerial departure.

Experimentation indicated that the efficient frontier can be represented by a fourth-order polynomial, giving rise to the following model:

$$P_{i,t} = (\beta_0 + \delta_0 t) + \sum_{m=1}^{4} (\beta_m + \delta_m t)\, \bar{R}^m_{i,t-3\ldots t-1} + v_{i,t} - u_{i,t} \qquad (6.3)$$

The terms in (6.3) are as follows:

$P_{i,t} =$ league position of team i in season t ($92 =$ top of first division, $91 = $2nd, and so on)

$\bar{R}_{i,t-3\ldots t-1} =$ mean over seasons $t-3$, $t-2$ and $t-1$ of team i's shares of aggregate league gate revenue in each season, rescaled by multiplying by 10^3

$t =$ linear time trend ($t=1$ in the 1973 season, $t=2$ in the 1974 season, and so on)

$v_{i,t} =$ random error term

$u_{i,t} =$ efficiency score.[6]

In (6.3) the efficiency scores are time-varying: there is a separate score for each team in each season. For the purpose of defining variables for the hazard function estimations, the indices i and t refer to teams and seasons, respectively, from here on. Figure 6.4 illustrates the shape of the estimated efficient frontier for the 1973 and 1999 seasons, over a realistic range of values for $\bar{R}_{i,t-3\ldots t-1}$ of up to 4 per cent. The frontier becomes

---

[6] The distributional assumptions for the random error terms and the efficiency scores are $v_{i,t} \sim N(0, \sigma_v^2)$ and $u_{i,t} = |\tilde{u}_{i,t}|$ where $\tilde{u}_{i,t} \sim N(0, \sigma_u^2)$.

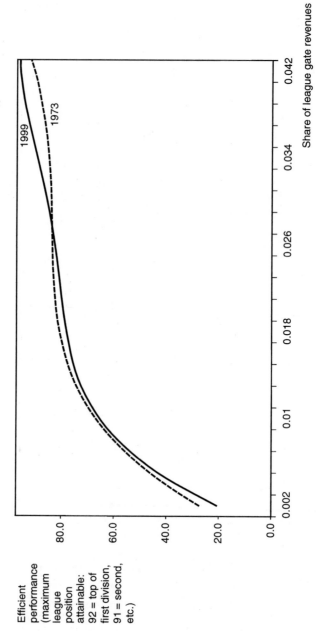

Figure 6.4 Estimated stochastic production frontiers, 1973 and 1999 seasons

Source: Managers' data set.

shallower over time because the distribution of revenues between league clubs becomes more unequal (see chapter 2).[7]

Table 6.7 shows the top 50 and bottom 10 estimated manager- and season-specific efficiency scores obtained from the estimation of (6.3). In contrast to tables 6.1–6.3, the unit of observation in table 6.7 is the playing season and not the complete managerial spell. Responsibility for each season's performance is attributed to the manager who was in charge for the first match played on or after 1 October of the season in question (see below).

Naturally, measuring managerial efficiency by comparing team performance with gate revenues tends to reward managers of teams operating at a relatively high level in the league on slender financial resources, particularly in the season or seasons immediately following one or more successful promotion campaigns. For example, Wimbledon are rewarded prolifically, with seven separate placings in the top 50, for defying football's laws of gravity by surviving at the top level for many years despite very modest home attendances. Since entering the league in the 1971 season, Cambridge United has enjoyed two very rapid ascents from Division 4 to Division 2, also on small attendances. Cambridge appears six times in the top 50. The achievements of Barnsley, Carlisle United, Charlton Athletic and Notts County in reaching Division1/Premier League for brief spells are also reflected in table 6.7. Conversely, the lowest places include several big-market teams, which at some point experienced a rapid decline in performance despite being relatively well resourced. Wolverhampton Wanderers in the mid-1980s, and the two Sheffield teams in the late 1970s and early 1980s, are cases in point.

---

[7] The full expression for the estimated frontier, with standard errors of estimated coefficients shown in parentheses, is as follows:

$$P_{i,t} = [0.0079 + 0.4415^a t] + [11.35^a - 0.10^a t]\bar{R}_{i,t-3...t-1} - [0.6205^a - 0.0092^a t]\bar{R}^2_{i,t-3...t-1}$$
$$\quad (2.283)\ (0.109)\qquad (0.68)\quad (0.03)\qquad\qquad (0.0602)\quad (0.0029)$$

$$\quad + [0.0152^a - 0.0003^a t]\bar{R}^3_{i,t-3...t-1} - [0.000133^a - 0.000003^a t]\bar{R}^4_{i,t-3...t-1} + \hat{v}_{i,t} - \hat{u}_{i,t}$$
$$\quad (0.0019)\quad (0.0001)\qquad\qquad (0.000019)\quad (0.000001)$$

$$obs = 2,450 \qquad \hat{\sigma}^2_v = 121.8 \qquad \hat{\sigma}^2_u = 70.2$$
a = significantly different from zero, two-tail test, 1 per cent level.

The inclusion of the interactions between each coefficient and the time trend allow the position of the efficient frontier to shift progressively over time. This is necessary, because while the distribution of the output variable, $P_{i,t}$, does not change over time, the distribution of the inputs, $\bar{R}_{i,t-3...t-1}$ does change with variation over time in the distribution of revenues between clubs. In 1999 it was possible to attain a relatively high position in the lower divisions with a smaller share of total revenue than would have been possible in 1973. Conversely, the teams occupying the highest positions in the top division in 1999 tended to have a higher revenue share than their counterparts in 1973.

Table 6.7. *Playing seasons ranked by efficiency score obtained from estimation of (6.3): top 50 and bottom 10*

Rank	Manager	Team	Season	League position	Efficiency score
1	Dave Bassett	Wimbledon	1987	6, D1	2.224
2	Dario Gradi	Crewe Alexandra	1998	11, Div One	2.667
3	Dave Bassett	Wimbledon	1986	3, D2	2.679
4	John Docherty	Cambridge United	1979	12, D2	2.706
5	Gary Megson	Stockport County	1998	8, Div One	2.729
6	John Beck	Cambridge United	1992	5, D2	2.748
7	Dave Bassett	Wimbledon	1985	12, D2	2.766
8	Stan Ternent	Bury	1998	17, Div One	2.813
9	Mark McGhee	Reading	1995	2, Div One	2.862
10	Bobby Gould	Wimbledon	1988	7, D1	2.901
11	John Docherty	Millwall	1989	10, D1	2.936
12	John Docherty	Cambridge United	1980	8, D2	2.971
13	Kenny Dalglish	Blackburn Rovers	1993	4, Prem	3.023
14	Bob Stokoe	Carlisle United	1984	7, D2	3.078
15	Dave Bassett	Wimbledon	1984	2, D3	3.089
16	Ron Atkinson	Cambridge United	1978	2, D3	3.092
17	Dario Gradi	Crewe Alexandra	1999	18, Div One	3.103
18	Graham Turner	Shrewsbury Town	1980	13, D2	3.106
19	Joe Kinnear	Wimbledon	1994	6, Prem	3.107
20	Jimmy Sirrell	Notts County	1982	15, D1	3.107
21	Stan Ternent	Bury	1997	1, Div Two	3.112
22	Emlyn Hughes	Rotherham United	1982	7, D2	3.121
23	Bob Stokoe	Carlisle United	1983	14, D2	3.153
24	Alan Ashman	Carlisle United	1975	22, D1	3.170
25	Brian Clough	Nottingham Forest	1978	1, D1	3.176
26	Jimmy Adamson	Burnley	1974	6, D1	3.177
27	Tom Johnston	York City	1975	15, D2	3.181
28	Joe Royle	Oldham Athletic	1987	3, D2	3.239
29	Gary Megson	Stockport County	1999	16, Div One	3.266
30	Alan Buckley	Grimsby Town	1999	11, Div One	3.323
31	Neil Warnock	Bury	1999	22, Div One	3.336
32	Alan Nelson	Charlton Athletic	1976	2, D2	3.339
33	Chic Bates	Shrewsbury Town	1985	8, D2	3.345
34	Joe Kinnear	Wimbledon	1995	9, Prem	3.362
35	George Kerr	Grimsby Town	1981	7, D2	3.364
36	Jim Smith	Oxford United	1985	1, D2	3.365
37	Graham Turner	Shrewsbury Town	1984	8, D2	3.385
38	Kenny Dalglish	Blackburn Rovers	1994	2, Prem	3.408
39	Chris Turner	Cambridge United	1991	1, D3	3.433
40	John Docherty	Cambridge United	1983	12, D2	3.451
41	Jimmy McGuigan	Rotherham United	1977	4, D3	3.458
42	Dennis Smith	Oxford United	1998	12, Div One	3.462
43	Richie Barker	Shrewsbury Town	1979	1, D3	3.464
44	Neil Warnock	Notts County	1992	21, D1	3.465
45	Jimmy Sirrell	Notts County	1981	2, D2	3.470
46	Danny Wilson	Barnsley	1998	2, Div One	3.473
47	Neil Warnock	Notts County	1991	4, D2	3.478
48	Danny Wilson	Barnsley	1997	19, Prem	3.479
49	Alan Durban	Shrewsbury Town	1976	9, D3	3.482
50	Alan Curbishley	Charlton Athletic	1999	18, Prem	3.484

Table 6.7. (*cont.*)

Rank	Manager	Team	Season	League position	Efficiency score
2441	Jimmy Dickinson	Portsmouth	1979	7, D4	15.609
2442	Steve Gritt	Brighton and Hove Albion	1997	23, Div Three	15.648
2443	Steve Burkinshaw	Sheffield Wednesday	1976	20, D3	15.726
2444	Mike Everitt	Brentford	1974	19, D4	16.251
2445	Harry Haslam	Sheffield United	1981	21, D3	16.682
2446	Bill McGarry	Wolverhampton	1986	23, D3	16.699
2447	Colin Appleton	Swansea City	1985	20, D3	17.615
2448	Ian Porterfield	Sheffield United	1982	1, D4	17.843
2449	Bobby Houghton	Bristol City	1982	21, D2	18.331
2450	Terry Cooper	Bristol City	1983	23, D3	19.670

Estimation of hazard functions

In the estimations of the involuntary and voluntary job-departure hazard functions, indicator variables are used to identify observations at which a managerial change took place (involuntarily or voluntarily). When more than one manager was in charge of a team (team i) during a season (season t), responsibility for team i's performance is always attributed solely to the manager who was in control for the first league match played on or after 1 October of season t. Season t is identified as containing a managerial change if the manager in charge on 1st October was no longer in charge on 1 October of season $t+1$.[8]

The variable definitions for the hazard function covariates are as follows:

$\hat{u}_{i,t} =$ estimated efficiency score based on team i's performance in season t and revenues in seasons $t-3 \ldots t-1$, obtained from stochastic frontier estimation of (6.3) as described above

$P_{i,t} =$ league position achieved by team i in season t (92 = top of first division, 91 = 2nd, as before)

$\tilde{P}_i =$ league position achieved by team i in the season preceding the current manager's initial appointment

[8] These definitions imply that appointments terminated very early in a season (during August or September) are attributed by the model to performance indicators (or other covariates) from the previous season, while appointments terminated subsequently are attributed to current-season performance. A new manager appointed after October does not take the blame (or the credit) for performance during the season of appointment, and starts to appear in the estimations only in the season after appointment (if he is still in post in October of that season). Managers appointed after October and terminated before the following October do not appear in the estimations at all.

$C_{i,t} =$ number of wins achieved by team i in season t's FA Cup competition if the manager who is in post on 1 October was still in post when the FA Cup started, or in season $t-1$'s FA Cup competition if this manager's appointment was terminated before season t's FA Cup competition started

$A_{i,t} =$ manager's age (in years) on 1 October of season t

$M_i =$ number of months of managerial experience in English league football acquired by the manager prior to his current appointment

$S_i =$ number of seasons of playing experience in English league football acquired by the manager as a player

$O_i =$ dummy variable indicating a manager whose playing or previous managerial experience was gained mainly in Scotland or overseas

$I_i =$ dummy variable indicating a manager who gained international caps as a player

$Y_{i,t} =$ time trend ($1 = 1973$ season, $2 = 1974$, and so on).

The data set used in the estimations comprises 843 managerial spells as defined above, including 62 that were right-censored (live on 1 October 1999, and still live 12 months later). Left-censored spells (that commenced before 1 October 1972) are not used in the estimations. Table 6.8 describes the distribution of the 843 spells by duration and reports the crude estimates of S_t, F_t, f_t and h_t, as defined in section 6.3. These show that 32 per cent of managerial spells failed to last for a full season, and 58.7 per cent failed to last for two full seasons. Fewer than 10 per cent of spells lasted for five or more complete seasons. The job-departure hazard appears to achieve peak values between three and four seasons and again between eight and nine seasons, though the estimates become quite volatile at high durations because there are relatively few observations. For this reason, table 6.8 is truncated beyond durations of 10 seasons.

Table 6.9 reports the estimates of the hazard function coefficients β_d for $d=1$ (involuntary departures) and $d=2$ (voluntary departures) as defined in (6.2). Column (1) and column (2) show estimates of the involuntary departure hazard function. Column (1) includes all of the covariates; column (2) omits two, O_i and I_i, whose estimated coefficients in column (1) are close to zero. This suggests that having overseas or international experience does not affect the manager's involuntary departure

Table 6.8. *Distribution of complete and right-censored managerial spells, by duration (in seasons) and crude estimates of the survivor, distribution, probability and hazard functions*

Duration in seasons, t	Spells of duration t live on 1/10 in any season	Departures before 1/10 of following season	Right-censored spells, live on 1/10/99 at duration t, and still live on 1/10/2000	Survivor function, S_t	Distribution function, F_t	Probability function, f_t	Hazard function, h_t
0	843	270	23	1.000	0.000	0.320	0.320
1	550	216	14	0.680	0.320	0.267	0.393
2	320	119	9	0.413	0.587	0.154	0.372
3	192	91	8	0.259	0.741	0.123	0.474
4	93	30	3	0.136	0.864	0.044	0.323
5	60	20	1	0.092	0.908	0.030	0.333
6	39	12	0	0.062	0.938	0.019	0.308
7	27	10	1	0.043	0.957	0.016	0.370
8	16	7	1	0.027	0.973	0.012	0.438
9	8	1	0	0.015	0.985	0.002	0.125
10	7	—	—	0.013	0.987	—	—

Source: Managers' data set.

Table 6.9. *Involuntary and voluntary managerial job-departure hazard functions: duration in seasons*

Covariates	Mode of departure			
	Inv. (1)	Inv. (2)	Vol. (3)	Vol. (4)
$\hat{u}_{i,t}$	0.0604^a	0.0600^a	-0.1497^a	-0.1500^a
	(0.0189)	(0.0189)	(0.0585)	(0.0583)
$(P_{i,t}-\tilde{P}_i)$	-0.0277^a	-0.0278^a	0.0121^c	0.0122^c
	(0.0036)	(0.0036)	(0.0071)	(0.0071)
$C_{i,t}$	-0.1106^a	-0.1112^a	-0.0006	—
	(0.0337)	(0.0337)	(0.0640)	
$A_{i,t}$	-0.0867	-0.0887	0.2592	0.2660
	(0.0640)	(0.0639)	(0.1910)	(0.1897)
$A_{i,t}^2$	0.0012^c	0.0012^c	-0.0033	-0.0033
	(0.0007)	(0.0007)	(0.0022)	(0.0022)
M_i	-0.0012	-0.0012	0.0045^b	0.0044^b
	(0.0009)	(0.0009)	(0.0021)	(0.0021)
S_i	0.0126	0.0143^b	-0.0011	—
	(0.0079)	(0.0073)	(0.0176)	
O_i	-0.1999	—	0.7741	0.8138
	(0.3705)		(0.5685)	(0.5260)
I_i	0.0298	—	0.2909	0.2928
	(0.0896)		(0.1944)	(0.1831)
$Y_{i,t}$	0.0125^b	0.0123^b	0.0061	—
	(0.0057)	(0.0057)	(0.0130)	
obs.	2,157	2,157	2,157	2,157
departures	649	649	132	132

Notes:
^{a} = significantly different from zero, two-tail test, 1% level;
^{b} = 5% level;
^{c} = 10% level.
Standard errors of estimated coefficients are shown in parentheses.

Key:
$\hat{u}_{i,t}$ = managerial efficiency score, obtained from (6.3)
$P_{i,t}$ = league position
$\tilde{P}_i$ = league position achieved in the season preceding the manager's appointment
$C_{i,t}$ = victories achieved in most recent FA Cup campaign
$A_{i,t}$ = manager's age (years)
M_i = manager's previous managerial experience in English league football (months)
S_i = manager's playing experience in English league football (seasons)
O_i = Scottish/overseas managerial experience dummy
I_i = international playing experience dummy
$Y_{i,t}$ = time trend (1 = 1973 season, 2 = 1974, and so on).

hazard directly. As expected, the involuntary departure hazard increases with an increase in managerial inefficiency; decreases if the team's league position has improved since the manager was appointed; and decreases with the amount of progress the team made in its most recent FA Cup campaign. All of these effects are strongly significant, at the 1 per cent level. The coefficients on the age variables are individually insignificant, but are jointly significant at the 5 per cent level, and are therefore retained in column (2). These suggest that the probability of involuntary departure increases with age over most realistic age ranges.[9] The coefficient on managerial experience is also insignificant but only marginally so, and is retained in column (2). The negative sign suggests that experienced managers are less likely to depart involuntarily than their inexperienced counterparts. A long playing career is found to have a positive effect on the involuntary departure hazard, with a coefficient which is significant at the 5 per cent level in column (2). Finally, the positive and significant estimated coefficient on the time trend confirms that the involuntary departure hazard has increased over time (see table 6.4).

Columns (3) and (4) of table 6.9 report the voluntary job-departure hazard function estimates. Column (4) omits the coefficients on $C_{i,t}$, S_i and $Y_{i,t}$, which are all close to zero in column (3), indicating that cup performance and the manager's playing experience are insignificant determinants of the voluntary departure hazard, which is also untrended.[10] The most notable feature of columns (3) and (4) is that the coefficients on managerial inefficiency and the change in league position are of opposite sign to their counterparts in columns (1) and (2). The estimations therefore succeed in confirming the intuition that highly efficient managers or managers of rapidly improving teams are those most likely to receive alternative job offers which will cause them to leave their current jobs voluntarily.

As before, the coefficients on the age variables are individually insignificant but jointly significant. The signs are the opposite of those in the involuntary departure hazard function. The coefficients suggest that the voluntary departure hazard increases up to about age 39 and decreases thereafter; so relatively young managers are the most likely to receive job offers causing them to leave voluntarily. Managerial experience, however,

---

[9] The hazard is minimised at about age 32; most managerial careers start later than this.

[10] The FA Cup variable, although significant in the involuntary departure hazard, does not seem to affect the voluntary departure hazard. If cup success is largely a matter of chance (often depending heavily on luck in the draw) it is unsurprising that cup success typically does not tend to attract job offers from other clubs. A cup run may nevertheless be useful to an incumbent manager in mollifying supporters and helping to stave off the threat of involuntary departure.

has a positive and significant coefficient, indicating that managers with a long track record are also more likely to depart voluntarily. Finally, although not quite significant (on two-tail tests), the coefficients on the overseas dummy and on international playing experience are retained in column (4). Positive coefficients on these two variables seem intuitively plausible. The fact that they fall just short of being significant may reflect the relatively small number of voluntary departures (132 out of 781) in the data set.

6.5 Hazard functions for English managers: duration measured in matches

Section 6.5 reports the estimation results for involuntary and voluntary managerial job-departure hazard functions with durations measured in matches. Audas, Dobson and Goddard (1999) advocate match-level measurement of durations on the grounds that if owners tend to react to short-term pressures, a run of poor results over a short period within a season may exert a greater influence on the owner's decision to terminate the manager's appointment than would be apparent from the contribution such a run makes to the full season's win ratio or efficiency score. Disaggregating the measurement of durations to match level should therefore permit identification of short-term influences on the decision to terminate that are obscured when durations are measured by season.

Estimations of job-departure hazard functions using match-level data covering the 1973 to 1997 seasons inclusive are reported in Audas, Dobson and Goddard (1999). In this section, these estimations are updated by extending the data set to the end of the 1999 season. A few minor changes are also made to the variable definitions and model specification. For simplicity, most of the notation used above is retained, but the t-subscript now refers to matches and not seasons. The job-departure indicator variables show, for each match t, whether the manager's appointment was terminated (involuntarily or voluntarily) between the completion of match t and match $t+1$.

Job-departure hazards in the match-level model are calculated over sequences of match results for each team. This implies that each match generates two observations, one for each team, and therefore appears in the data set twice. The model does not allow the probability that a manager departs between matches t and $t+1$ of his reign to be influenced by the standard of opposition his team met in match t (or in preceding matches). Involuntary departure is usually triggered by a run of several poor results, over which the standard of opposition rapidly tends to converge towards the divisional average. The model also does not allow for cross-sectional interdependence between the probabilities of simultaneous departure for managers of different clubs. In practice, however, one can think of instances when, having just lost the services of its manager to Club A, Club B has offered the post to the manager of Club C, which in turn has attempted to secure Club D's manager as his successor. Nevertheless, the incidence of chain-reactions of this kind is probably lower today than it has been in the past, thanks partly to an increased tendency for clubs to appoint foreign managers, as well as serious attempts that have been made by the football authorities (including the League Managers' Association) to discourage unauthorised poaching of managers under contract with other clubs.

Most of the covariates in the match-level hazard function model are similar to those in the season-level model, with the exception of the managerial efficiency scores, for which no obvious match-level equivalent is available, and which are therefore omitted. In their place, to capture the short-term effect of match results on the job-departure hazard, the match-level model includes the individual results of the last few league matches as additional covariates. The full set of covariate definitions is as follows:

$R_{i,t-k} =$ result of the kth match before match t for team i, defined for $k = 0 \ldots 17$, $R_{i,t-k} = 1$ denotes a win, 0.5 denotes a draw, 0 denotes a defeat

$P_{i,t} =$ league position of team i going into match t ($92 =$ top of first division, $91 =$ 2nd, as before)

$\tilde{P}_i =$ league position of team i going into the first match of the current manager's spell

$C1_{i,t} =$ 1 if team i has played at least one match in the FA Cup in the current season and is not eliminated at the time of the current league match, 0 otherwise

$C2_{i,t} =$ 1 if team i has played at least one match in the FA Cup in the current season and is eliminated at the time of the current league match, 0 otherwise; $C1_{i,t}$ and $C2_{i,t}$ are both reset to zero if a managerial change takes place after a cup campaign has begun, any subsequent cup matches under a new manager are treated as a new campaign.

$A_{i,t} =$ age of manager of team i in years at the time of match t

M_i, S_i, O_i, I_i and $Y_{i,t}$ are the same as in previous definitions (see p. 292).

$X_{j,i,t}$ =   month-within-season dummy variables for $j = 8$ (August), 9 (September) ... 12, 1 ... 5; $X_{j,i,t} = 1$ if match t took place in month j, 0 otherwise, except when match t is the final match of the season, in which case $X_{j,i,t} = 0$ for all $_p$, close season departures are therefore the base, and the coefficient on $X_{j,i,t}$ represents the difference between the month j hazard and the close season hazard.

Table 6.10 shows the crude estimates of the functions S_t, F_t, f_t and h_t for the 981 managerial spells included in the match-level model. The definitions of the survivor function S_t and the distribution function F_t are the same as before (see section 6.3), but with 't' now denoting durations in matches. The probability and hazard functions show total job-departure probabilities within duration bands 30 matches in width. With durations measured in matches, the peaks in the hazard are located around durations 180 and 360 matches.

Table 6.11 reports the estimates of the hazard function coefficients in the match-level model. Columns (1) and (2) show estimates of the involuntary departure hazard function. Column (1) includes all of the covariates; column (2) omits those with estimated coefficients in column (1) that are close to zero. The importance of current and recent match results is reflected in coefficients on $R_{i,t-k}$ that are negative and significant being obtained for up to 16 matches prior to the current match. The absolute magnitude of the effect diminishes quite regularly as the number of lagged matches increases. The most recent matches therefore have a greater effect on the hazard than the more distant ones, as expected. In general, the coefficients on $R_{i,t-k}$ confirm that the decision to terminate a manager's appointment involuntarily tends to be heavily influenced by very short-term considerations.

Elsewhere the results are mostly consistent with those for the season-level involuntary departure hazard function. The change in league position since the start of the manager's spell is a highly significant determinant of the involuntary hazard. Dummy variables indicating the team's position in the current season's FA Cup competition did not produce significant estimated coefficients; nor did FA Cup dummies created using various alternative definitions. The failure to show that a manager's job is more secure before elimination from the cup and less secure after elimination may reflect difficulties in disentangling the cup effect from other month-within-season variation in the hazard, captured by the dummies $X_{j,i,t}$. The

Table 6.10. *Distribution of complete and right-censored managerial spells, by duration (in matches) and crude estimates of the survivor, distribution, probability and hazard functions*

Duration in matches, t	Spells that survived to duration t	Departures between durations t and $t+30$	Right-censored spells, live at duration t, and still live at duration $t+30$	Survivor function, S_t	Distribution function, F_t	Hazard function for departure between durations t and $t+30$	Probability function for departure between durations t and $t+30$
0	981	124	13	1.000	0.000	0.128	0.128
30	844	228	20	0.872	0.128	0.243	0.279
60	596	166	7	0.629	0.371	0.179	0.285
90	423	117	11	0.450	0.550	0.132	0.294
120	295	84	10	0.317	0.683	0.099	0.311
150	201	64	3	0.218	0.782	0.072	0.331
180	134	46	8	0.146	0.854	0.058	0.398
210	80	19	1	0.088	0.912	0.022	0.249
240	60	12	0	0.066	0.934	0.013	0.200
270	48	12	1	0.053	0.947	0.014	0.270
300	35	11	0	0.039	0.961	0.012	0.314
330	24	6	0	0.026	0.974	0.007	0.250
360	18	5	1	0.020	0.980	0.007	0.333
390	12	3	0	0.013	0.987	0.004	0.307
420	9	—	—	0.009	0.991	—	—

Source: Managers' data set.

Table 6.11. *Involuntary and voluntary managerial job-departure hazard functions: duration in matches*

Mode of departure

Covariates	Inv. (1)	Inv. (2)	Vol. (3)	Vol. (4)
$R_{i,t}$	-1.05^a	-1.05^a	-0.166	-0.137
	(0.10)	(0.10)	(0.202)	(0.200)
$R_{i,t-1}$	-1.03^a	-1.04^a	-0.024	-0.013
	(0.10)	(0.10)	(0.199)	(0.197)
$R_{i,t-2}$	-0.492^a	-0.493^a	-0.396^b	-0.376^c
	(0.091)	(0.091)	(0.200)	(0.198)
$R_{i,t-3}$	-0.503^a	-0.508^a	-0.530^a	-0.507^b
	(0.092)	(0.092)	(0.202)	(0.199)
$R_{i,t-4}$	-0.670^a	-0.674^a	-0.147	—
	(0.093)	(0.093)	(0.199)	
$R_{i,t-5}$	-0.440^a	-0.441^a	0.160	—
	(0.090)	(0.090)	(0.202)	
$R_{i,t-6}$	-0.604^a	-0.604^a	-0.028	—
	(0.092)	(0.092)	(0.203)	
$R_{i,t-7}$	-0.405^a	-0.407^a	-0.075	—
	(0.091)	(0.091)	(0.203)	
$R_{i,t-8}$	-0.350^a	-0.350^a	-0.054	—
	(0.090)	(0.090)	(0.201)	
$R_{i,t-9}$	-0.396^a	-0.395^a	0.172	—
	(0.091)	(0.091)	(0.206)	
$R_{i,t-10}$	-0.203^b	-0.202^b	-0.022	—
	(0.090)	(0.090)	(0.204)	
$R_{i,t-11}$	-0.235^a	-0.233^a	-0.396	—
	(0.090)	(0.090)	(0.207)	
$R_{i,t-12}$	-0.217^b	-0.217^b	0.321	—
	(0.090)	(0.090)	(0.208)	
$R_{i,t-13}$	-0.217^b	-0.222^b	0.211	—
	(0.091)	(0.091)	(0.206)	

Mode of departure

Covariates	Inv. (1)	Inv. (2)	Vol. (3)	Vol. (4)
$(P_{i,t}-\hat{P}_{i,t})$	-0.027^a	-0.028^a	0.018^a	0.021^a
	(0.003)	(0.003)	(0.006)	(0.006)
$C1_{i,t}$	0.169	—	-0.292	—
	(0.148)		(0.353)	
$C2_{i,t}$	-0.158	—	-0.826	—
	(0.209)		(0.517)	
$A_{i,t}$	-0.222^a	-0.221^a	0.371^b	0.387^b
	(0.061)	(0.060)	(0.182)	(0.178)
$A^2_{i,t}$	0.003^a	0.003^a	-0.004^b	-0.004^b
	(0.001)	(0.001)	(0.002)	(0.002)
$M_{i,t}$	-0.001	—	0.004^c	0.003^c
	(0.001)		(0.002)	(0.002)
$S_{i,t}$	0.006	—	-0.033^b	-0.038^b
	(0.007)		(0.016)	(0.016)
$O_{i,t}$	0.251	—	0.563	—
	(0.322)		(0.570)	
$I_{i,t}$	0.064	—	0.451^b	0.479^b
	(0.086)		(0.190)	(0.189)
$Y_{i,t}$	0.022^a	0.023^a	0.014	—
	(0.005)	(0.005)	(0.012)	
$X_{8,i,t}$	-3.37^a	-3.51^a	-5.04^a	-4.75^a
	(0.30)	(0.27)	(0.79)	(0.72)
$X_{9,i,t}$	-2.96^a	-3.10^a	-4.50^a	-4.26^a
	(0.22)	(0.18)	(0.54)	(0.43)
$X_{10,i,t}$	-2.38^a	-2.53^a	-3.78^a	-3.52^a
	(0.20)	(0.14)	(0.45)	(0.32)
$X_{11,i,t}$	-2.12^a	-2.26^a	-3.83^a	-3.63^a
	(0.18)	(0.14)	(0.47)	(0.36)

	(1)	(2)	(3)	(4)
$R_{i,t-14}$	-0.207^b (0.091)	-0.212^b (0.091)	0.369^c (0.210)	—
$R_{i,t-15}$	-0.162^c (0.091)	-0.168^c (0.091)	0.172 (0.209)	—
$R_{i,t-16}$	-0.231^b (0.091)	0.233^b (0.091)	-0.183 (0.204)	—
$R_{i,t-17}$	-0.127 (0.091)	—	0.549^a (0.213)	—
$X_{12,i,t}$	-2.45^a (0.17)	-2.57^a (0.15)	-3.33^a (0.37)	-3.24^a (0.29)
$X_{1,i,t}$	-2.06^a (0.15)	-2.12^a (0.14)	-3.25^a (0.35)	-3.29^a (0.34)
$X_{2,i,t}$	-2.32^a (0.15)	-2.33^a (0.15)	-3.88^a (0.43)	-3.97^a (0.43)
$X_{3,i,t}$	-2.66^a (0.14)	-2.66^a (0.14)	-4.24^a (0.40)	-4.28^a (0.40)
$X_{4,i,t}$	-2.98^a (0.15)	-2.97^a (0.15)	-5.28^a (0.60)	-5.29^a (0.60)
$X_{5,i,t}$	-2.67^a (0.27)	-2.65^a (0.27)	-3.89^a (0.72)	-3.93^a (0.72)
obs.	98,799	98,799	98,799	98,799
departures	765	765	153	153

Notes:

[a] = significantly different from zero, two-tail test, 1% level;

[b] = 5% level;

[c] = 10% level.

standard errors of estimated coefficients are shown in parentheses.

Key:

$R_{i,t-k}$ = result of the kth match before match t, defined for $k = 0 \ldots 17$ (1 = win, 0.5 = draw, 0 = defeat)

$P_{i,t}$ = league position going into match t

$\hat{P}_{i,t}$ = league position going into first match of current manager's spell

$C1_{i,t}$ = 1 if team's FA Cup campaign is underway and incomplete, 0 otherwise

$C2_{i,t}$ = 1 if team's FA Cup campaign has finished, 0 otherwise

A_i = age of manager (years)

M_i = manager's previous managerial experience in English league football (months)

S_i = manager's playing experience in English league football (seasons)

O_i = Scottish/overseas managerial experience dummy

I_i = international playing experience dummy

$Y_{i,t}$ = time trend (1 = 1973 season, 2 = 1974, and so on)

$X_{j,i,t}$ = calendar month dummies.

coefficients on the age variables suggest that the probability of involuntary departure increases with age above age 37. The other manager human capital variables are all insignificant in the involuntary hazard function. The coefficient on the time trend is highly significant, as are the coefficients on the month-within-season dummies. The negative signs on the latter reflect the fact that the probability of departure during the close season is significantly higher than the probability during any particular month within the season (even though the total probability of within-season departure is much higher than the close season probability).

Columns (3) and (4) report the voluntary departure hazard functions estimated, respectively, using all covariates and significant covariates only. The few most recent match results appear to play a much less important role in determining the voluntary departure hazard than they do in determining the involuntary hazard. Nevertheless, the coefficients for the current and four previous match results are all negative, and two of these five coefficients are significant at the 5 per cent level. For more than four matches prior to departure, there is a mix of positive and negative coefficients, very few of which are significant.[11] $R_{i,t-k}$ are therefore omitted from column (4) for $k \geq 4$. The finding that the voluntary departure hazard increases if recent results are poor is perhaps counterintuitive, given that voluntary departure occurs when a manager accepts a better job offer from elsewhere. Audas, Dobson and Goddard (1999) suggest that while a run of poor results might not be helpful in attracting alternative job offers, it might influence a manager's willingness to accept rather than turn down such an offer if one is forthcoming. If so, this could account for the observed pattern.

The change in league position since the start of the manager's appointment is again a highly significant determinant of the voluntary departure hazard: managers who have achieved an improvement in league position are more likely to leave voluntarily. The maximum hazard with respect to age is estimated to occur rather later (at around age 48) than in the season-level model. The signs of the estimated coefficients on previous managerial, playing, overseas and international experience in column (3) are all the same as their counterparts in the season-level model. The first, second and fourth of these coefficients are significant and are retained in column (4). The time trend is insignificant, while the coefficients on the month-within-season dummies are all highly significant and larger in absolute terms than their counterparts in the involuntary departure hazard function.

---

[11] The highly significant coefficient on $R_{i,t-17}$ in column (3) appears to be a statistical quirk, and this covariate is not retained in column (4).

6.6 The effect of managerial change on team performance: evidence from North American team sports

Sections 6.6–6.8 investigate whether, on average, a change of manager tends to lead to an improvement in team performance. In a comment on Grusky's (1963) article (see section 6.2), Gamson and Scotch (1964) identify a key issue that must be addressed by any empirical investigation of this question, by means of an analogy.

'If we compared average rainfall in the month preceding and the month following the performance of the Hopi rain dance, we would find more rain in the period after. The dance is not performed unless there is a drought, so such a comparison would be misleading. Nevertheless, this 'slump-ending' effect may help to account for the tenacity of belief in the effectiveness of the ritual' (Gamson and Scotch, 1964, p. 71).

Team performance, like rainfall and many other natural and man-made phenomena, exhibits a tendency for *mean-reversion* or regression towards the mean over time. Successful teams do not remain successful forever; and teams that are unsuccessful eventually find the wherewithal to improve. This means that on average, the performance of the most successful teams at time t will tend to deteriorate at time $t+1$, and the performance of the least successful teams will tend to improve. If teams that change their manager are predominantly teams that are unsuccessful at the time they make the change, some improvement in their average performance in the season following the change is to expected as a result of the mean-reversion effect. This is the case even if the manager is just a figurehead, who makes no contribution whatever to his team's performance. Any investigation of the relationship between managerial change and subsequent team performance must therefore control for this mean-reversion effect.

Gamson and Scotch attempt to control for mean-reversion in a relatively crude but straightforward manner. In their comparison of the win ratios before and after 22 mid-season managerial changes in Major League Baseball (MLB) which took place between 1954 and 1961, match results during the two weeks prior to each change are excluded from the calculations. In 13 of the 22 cases, the team performed better under the new manager than it did up to two weeks before the removal of the old manager. This finding could be consistent with either the common sense or the ritual scapegoating theories of managerial succession (see section 6.2), but it does not support the vicious circle theory, which would anticipate deterioration in post-succession performance. Of course, the assumption that the omission of two weeks' results is sufficient to exclude the mean-reversion effect is rather arbitrary.

Using the same data, Grusky (1964) tackles the mean-reversion problem by comparing the post-succession win ratio for the remainder of the season with the win ratio from the previous season. Grusky also distinguishes between inside succession, involving promotion of one of the club's existing coaches or players to the manager's position, and outside succession, involving the appointment of an outsider. Whereas inside succession was associated with an improvement in performance on average, outside succession tended to be followed by further decline.

Allen, Panian and Lotz (1979) apply more sophisticated statistical techniques to an investigation of the same issues, using a more extensive MLB data set, covering the period 1920–73. Analyses of variance and covariance are employed to identify the proportion of the variation in per-season win ratios that can be explained by managerial succession. The mean-reversion effect is controlled by including the previous season's win ratio in the analysis of covariance. Allen, Panian and Lotz distinguish between insider and outsider succession and between within-season and close season succession. Succession effects are found to be relatively small, but statistically significant. Whereas close season succession tended to produce an improvement in performance in the following season, within-season succession had the opposite effect. Teams tended to perform better following insider succession than they did following outsider succession. Multiple succession (two or more changes of manager within the same season) had a particularly damaging effect on team performance. By attributing the entire season's performance of teams experiencing a within-season change of manager to the successor, however, the methodology seems to be biased in favour of identifying deterioration in performance (relative to the previous season) in such cases.

In a study of managerial succession effects in American football for the period 1970–8, Brown (1982) uses panel techniques to estimate a multiple regression model, in which current-season performance depends on lagged performance and a managerial succession dummy. All (unspecified) cross-sectional variation in organisational structure between clubs, which might affect both performance and the decision whether or not to terminate the manager's appointment, is controlled in the error structure. As in other studies, teams that changed their manager within-season are found to have under-performed during the same season. But more importantly, a match-level comparison between the win ratios of teams that experienced an early-season slump and changed their manager within-season, and the win ratios of a control group that experienced a similar slump but did not change manager, shows that the recovery pattern following the initial slump was very similar between the two groups. In other words, changing the manager made very little difference to the subsequent performance of the teams concerned. This conclusion seems most consistent with the ritual sacrifice theory of managerial succession.

Jacobs and Singell (1993) shift the emphasis away from succession effects, to address the question as to whether managers generally make a difference to the performance of the organisations they work for. Observing organisational performance immediately after a managerial departure might not be the best way of tackling this question, since a change of leadership suggests that (presumably) atypically, the organisation is experiencing a period of crisis. Using MLB data covering the period 1945–65, Jacobs and Singell model team win ratios using a variety of measures of playing and managerial inputs. In common with a number of other studies, managerial change is found to have a damaging impact on the team's win ratio post-succession. More importantly, however, a set of individual manager dummies, as well as measures of managerial experience, are significant in the regressions that model win ratios. Managerial effects are also found to have influenced changes in the individual performance of players who were traded between teams. Jacobs and Singell's overall conclusion is that managers do have a significant effect on team performance.

Fizel and D'Itri's (1997) study of performance and managerial turnover in basketball (see also section 6.2) reports panel estimates of regressions that investigate the separate effects of involuntary and voluntary managerial departure on performance, measured by win ratios. Among the covariates, the previous season's win ratio controls for mean-reversion. Interactions between the manager change dummies and the team's playing talent index, the incoming manager's past experience and his efficiency score from the preceding season are also included. The latter two variables allow for the possibility that not only the succession event itself, but also the human capital attributes of the incoming manager, influence team performance. Playing talent and managerial efficiency (but not experience) are found to be highly significant determinants of post-departure performance. It is unclear, however, why performance should be influenced by the new manager's attributes only in the season immediately after his appointment, and not thereafter. Involuntary and voluntary managerial departure are both found to have a significant and similar negative impact on subsequent performance.

Sections 6.7 and 6.8 report estimates of regressions that investigate the effects of managerial change on subsequent team performance in English football. In line with the approach used for the estimation of managerial job-departure hazard functions in sections 6.4 and 6.5, two sets of results are reported. In section 6.7, the complete season is the unit of observation for team performance. These regressions are comparable to those reported in the more recent of the US studies reviewed above. In section 6.8, post-succession team performance is measured on a match-level basis, using an adapted version of the match results forecasting model that was developed in chapter 3. Dummy variables indicating the timing of within-season managerial departures are added to the forecasting model, to determine whether managerial change has a discernible impact on individual match results immediately after the change takes place.

6.7 Managerial succession effects in English football: performance measured by season

Section 6.7 reports estimations of the effect of managerial departure on team performance during the season after the change takes place. The variable definitions for the estimations are as follows:

$P_{i,t} =$ league position achieved by team i in season t (92 = top of first division, 91 = 2nd, as before)

$pr_{i,t-1} =$ 1 if team i was promoted at the end of season $t-1$, 0 otherwise

$re_{i,t-1} =$ 1 if team i was relegated at the end of season $t-1$, 0 otherwise

$w_{i,t-1}^1 =$ 1 if the manager of team i at the start of season $t-1$ departed involuntarily within (during the course of) season $t-1$, 0 otherwise

$c_{i,t-1}^1 =$ 1 if the manager of team i at the start of season $t-1$ departed involuntarily during the close season following season $t-1$, 0 otherwise

$w_{i,t-1}^2 =$ 1 if the manager of team i at the start of season $t-1$ departed voluntarily within season $t-1$, 0 otherwise

$c_{i,t-1}^2 =$ 1 if the manager of team i at the start of season $t-1$ departed voluntarily during the close season following season $t-1$, 0 otherwise.

The dependent variable in the estimations is $\Delta P_{i,t} = P_{i,t} - P_{i,t-1}$, the change in league position between seasons $t-1$ and t. For most teams in most seasons, mean-reversion is controlled by including $P_{i,t-1}$ among the covariates, though some additional controls are also required. If a team is promoted, its league position in the following season can only improve, and if it is relegated, its position can only worsen. The promotion and relegation dummies are therefore used to control for this feature of the data. The managerial departure dummies distinguish between within-season and close season departures and between involuntary and voluntary departures (as before). Measuring performance in the season following succession offers the advantage that the dependent variable is not contaminated by any match results which accrued during the latter stages of the outgoing manager's spell in charge. A price is paid, however, for this benefit: performance immediately following a within-season departure (until the end of the same season) is excluded from the definition of the dependent variable.

Both ordinary least squares (OLS) and fixed-effects (FE) panel estimates of the season-level succession effects model are reported in table 6.12. The FE estimator allows for the presence of club-specific influences on performance, referred to more generally as individual effects. These are modelled using a full set of club-specific dummy variables; their estimated coefficients are not reported in table 6.12. Columns (1) and (3) show the OLS and FE estimates of a model that uses just one dummy variable for all four types of managerial change, obtained by summing the four dummies defined above

$$\sum_{j=1}^{2} (w_{i,t-1}^j + c_{i,t-1}^j)$$

Columns (2) and (4) show the results for the model that includes the four dummies as separate covariates.[12]

The coefficients on the lagged managerial change dummy in columns (1) and (3) of table 6.12 are both positive and significant at the 1 per cent level. When this dummy variable is disaggregated into its four constituent components in columns (2) and (4), the coefficients on the involuntary departure dummies are positive (involuntary departure leads to an improvement in the following season), but only the coefficient on the within-season involuntary departure dummy is statistically significant. Conversely the coefficients on the voluntary departure dummies are negative (voluntary departure leads to a decline in the following season). In this case, the coefficient on the close season voluntary departure dummy is significant at the 5 per cent level in the OLS estimation, but not in the (preferred) FE estimation. The fact that the coefficients on the involuntary departure dummies are positive and those on the voluntary dummies negative, does at least tend to support the common sense theory of

---

[12] Although the coefficients on the promotion and relegation dummies are quite similar in both sets of estimations, the estimated coefficients on lagged league position are considerably lower in the FE models than in the OLS versions. This reflects the fact that this coefficient is upward biased if OLS is used on a panel data set when individual effects are in fact present.

Table 6.12. *Relationship between managerial succession and performance, measured by season*

	Estimation method			
	OLS	OLS	FE	FE
Covariates:	(1)	(2)	(3)	(4)
Constant	1.465^a	1.250^a	—	—
	(0.336)	(0.337)		
$P_{i,t-1}$	-0.0434^a	-0.0392^a	-0.1853^a	-0.1789^a
	(0.0055)	(0.0055)	(0.0103)	(0.0104)
$pr_{i,t-1}$	12.87^a	13.09^a	12.38^a	12.53^a
	(0.47)	(0.47)	(0.46)	(0.47)
$re_{i,t-1}$	-12.26^a	-12.62^a	-11.97^a	-12.22^a
	(0.47)	(0.47)	(0.46)	(0.46)
$\sum_{j=1}^{2} (w_{i,t-1}^j + c_{i,t-1}^j)$	1.111^a	—	0.861^a	—
	(0.307)		(0.302)	
$w^1_{i,t-1}$	—	2.029^a	—	1.553^a
		(0.364)		(0.361)
$c^1_{i,t-1}$	—	0.770	—	0.299
		(0.567)		(0.559)
$w^2_{i,t-1}$	—	-0.617	—	-0.178
		(0.749)		(0.737)
$c^2_{i,t-1}$	—	-1.748^b	—	-0.868
		(0.821)		(0.806)
obs	2,238	2,238	2,238	2,238
R^2	0.43	0.44	0.49	0.50

Note:
[a] = significantly different from zero, two-tail test, 1% level;
[b] = 5% level.
Standard errors of estimated coefficients are shown in parentheses.
Dependent variable is $\Delta P_{i,t} = P_{i,t} - P_{i,t-1}$.

Key

$P_{i,t-1}$ = league position achieved in previous season
$pr_{i,t-1}$ = 1 if team was promoted at the end of previous season, 0 otherwise
$re_{i,t-1}$ = 1 if team was relegated at the end of previous season, 0 otherwise
$w^1_{i,t-1}$ = 1 if the manager departed involuntarily within the previous season, 0 otherwise
$c^1_{i,t-1}$ = 1 if the manager departed involuntarily in the previous close season, 0 otherwise
$w^2_{i,t-1}$ = 1 if the manager departed voluntarily within the previous season, 0 otherwise
$c^2_{i,t-1}$ = 1 if the manager departed voluntarily in the previous close season, 0 otherwise.

managerial succession. Poor managers tend to depart involuntarily, and performance improves after they have gone; good managers tend to get alternative job offers causing them to depart voluntarily, and performance deteriorates after they have gone. But on conventional statistical criteria, only one of the four estimated effects can be regarded as reliable.

The main finding from the season-level investigation of managerial succession effects is that involuntary managerial departure during the course of a season tends to be associated with an improvement in performance during the following season, over and above what would be expected in view of the natural tendency for performance to revert towards the mean. Other types of managerial departure appear to make little or no difference to performance. So do these results contradict those of several US studies reviewed above, in which involuntary managerial departure is associated with a decline in performance? Probably not because, as discussed above, in most of these cases performance was measured partly or wholly in the same season as the change of manager took place. Consequently the tendency for managerial departure to be associated with relatively poor team performance is hardly surprising.

The reliability of the finding that managerial departure leads to an improvement in performance the following season depends crucially on whether the automatic tendency for mean-reversion in performance is controlled adequately by the inclusion in the estimations of the lagged performance variable. And here, there is still some reason for caution. Consider for example two teams, both of which have suffered an early-season slump in performance. In the previous summer, one manager spent heavily on talented new players, while the other had no money to spend. Accordingly, the first manager is dismissed for failing to fulfil pre-season expectations, while the second is exonerated and retained because his team was expected to struggle anyway. In this situation, the first team might recover more rapidly than the second, not because of the managerial change, but simply because it has a more talented squad. This type of story could account for the pattern of results shown in table 6.12, but it would not necessarily be correct to attribute the first team's faster recovery to its decision to change its manager. It does suggest, however, that some care needs to be exercised in interpreting empirical results of the kind described in section 6.6 and presented in section 6.7.

6.8 Managerial succession effects in English football: performance measured by match

Section 6.8 reports estimations of the effect of managerial departure on team performance in the matches played immediately after the change takes place. As discussed in section 6.6, Brown (1982) attempts to isolate the effect of a change of manager on team performance by drawing comparisons between the post-departure results of a group of teams that changed manager, and the corresponding results of a control group that experienced a similar run of poor results, but retained their current manager. Brown finds that the recovery pattern was very similar in both groups. Audas, Dobson and Goddard (1997) perform a similar exercise, also using non-parametric methods, on a somewhat larger English football data set. There was some evidence that the teams that changed manager tended to recover less quickly than the teams in a control group. This suggests that on average, managerial change had a disruptive effect, which was damaging to performance in the matches played immediately after a change took place.

Controlling adequately for mean-reversion, which in the context of these studies means identifying a control group of clubs whose characteristics match accurately those of the group that changed manager, is once again an issue of vital importance. Despite the difficulties that this creates, studying succession effects using individual matches (rather than entire seasons) as the unit of measurement appears to represent a promising line of inquiry. In this section, for the first time, match-level succession effects are investigated using a parametric model.

The model in question is an adapted version of the one developed in chapter 3 for the purpose of generating match result forecasts. With this kind of specification, the tendency for mean-reversion is controlled, probably more comprehensively than in the other specifications described above, by the inclusion of a multitude of lagged match result and win ratio measures, which reflect information on team performance over the past 48 months. Using a match-level performance measure, it seems reasonable to restrict the investigation to within-season managerial changes only. Close season changes, which can allow players up to three months' opportunity to adapt to the methods of the incoming manager, seem unlikely to be disruptive to the same extent as within-season changes.

The model developed in section 3.3 is modified by adding a set of suitably defined managerial change dummy variables. The effects of a change of manager on the results of the next 20 matches (within the same season) following the change are investigated. The dummy variables are defined as follows:

> $D_i^k = 1$ if team i changed its manager between the kth and $k-1$th matches before the current match and if both these matches were played within the same season as the current match for $k = 1 \ldots 20$, and 0 otherwise.[13]

---

[13] For consistency with the notation used in chapter 3, the 't'-subscript for match t is suppressed.

Preliminary inspection of the data suggested that it was not feasible to identify a separate effect for involuntary and voluntary departures, as there were too few of the latter for reliable estimated effects to be obtained. As the managerial change dummy variables are operative only for matches played within the same season as the change, the maximum value of k is restricted to 20. The number of managerial changes after which more than 20 matches were still to be played within the same season is also too small for reliable estimated effects to be obtained for $k > 20$.

In chapter 3, the match results forecasting model generates a score, $y_{i,j}^*$, for the match between home team i and away team j, whose sign and magnitude indicate the direction and the extent to which the relative strengths of the two teams should influence the match result (see (3.10)). Since the effect on $y_{i,j}^*$ of a recent change of manager by the away team should be roughly equal but opposite in sign to the effect of a change by the home team, it is possible to combine D_i^k and D_j^k into a single dummy, $Z_{i,j}^k = (D_i^k - D_j^k)$. The coefficient on $Z_{i,j}^k$ reflects the combined effect of recent managerial changes (if any) by either team on the match result. This procedure reduces the number of separate coefficients to be estimated, and increases the reliability of the estimates that are obtained. The expression for $y_{i,j}^*$ is as follows:

$$y_{i,j}^* = (3.10) + \sum_{k=1}^{20} \phi_k Z_{i,j}^k \qquad (6.4)$$

Table 6.13 reports the estimated version of (6.4), obtained using all match observations for which complete data are available, between the 1973 and 1999 seasons inclusive. Apart from minor numerical variations, the estimated coefficients and standard errors on all covariates that were included in the previous version of this model are virtually unchanged (see table 3.14, columns (1), (2), (5) and (6)). The estimates of the additional coefficients on the manager change dummy variables, $Z_{i,j}^k$, and their standard errors, are reported in columns (5) and (6) of table 6.13. The estimated coefficient for the match immediately following a change of manager is negative and significant at the 1 per cent level. This suggests that a within-season managerial change is disruptive in the very short term: a team that changes its manager tends to under-perform, to an extent that is discernible on conventional statistical criteria, in the match after the change takes place.

Among the other results in column (5), only the negative coefficient on $Z_{i,j}^{11}$ is significant at the 5 per cent level. While there is a mix of positive and negative estimated coefficients, overall the preponderance is negative. It can be argued, however, the impact of a managerial change on any individual result is of less interest than the cumulative impact on results over

Table 6.13. *Relationship between managerial succession and performance, measured by match*

	(1) Coeff.	(2) s.e.		(3) Coeff.	(4) s.e.		(5) Coeff.	(6) s.e.	(7) Cum. coeff.	(8) s.e.
$P^0_{i,0,0}$	1.545[a]	0.111	$R^H_{i,1}$	0.065[a]	0.013	$Z^1_{i,j}$	-0.122[a]	0.045	-0.122[a]	0.045
$P^{+1}_{i,0,1}$	1.525[a]	0.179	$R^H_{i,2}$	0.031[b]	0.013	$Z^2_{i,j}$	-0.051	0.045	-0.173[a]	0.064
$P^0_{i,0,1}$	1.129[a]	0.100	$R^H_{i,3}$	0.074[a]	0.013	$Z^3_{i,j}$	0.023	0.045	-0.150[c]	0.079
$P^{-1}_{i,0,1}$	0.832[a]	0.091	$R^H_{i,4}$	0.008	0.013	$Z^4_{i,j}$	0.015	0.046	-0.135	0.092
$P^{+1}_{i,1,1}$	0.601[a]	0.154	$R^H_{i,5}$	0.018	0.013	$Z^5_{i,j}$	0.032	0.046	-0.104	0.105
$P^0_{i,1,1}$	0.546[a]	0.096	$R^H_{i,6}$	-0.002	0.013	$Z^6_{i,j}$	-0.072	0.047	-0.176	0.116
$P^{-1}_{i,1,1}$	0.461[a]	0.085	$R^H_{i,7}$	0.015	0.013	$Z^7_{i,j}$	-0.038	0.047	-0.214[c]	0.126
$P^{+2}_{i,1,2}$	0.165	0.350	$R^H_{i,8}$	0.027[b]	0.013	$Z^8_{i,j}$	-0.039	0.048	-0.253[c]	0.136
$P^{+1}_{i,1,2}$	0.712[a]	0.142	$R^H_{i,9}$	0.042[a]	0.013	$Z^9_{i,j}$	0.016	0.048	-0.237	0.146
$P^0_{i,1,2}$	0.401[a]	0.094	$R^A_{i,1}$	0.019	0.013	$Z^{10}_{i,j}$	-0.010	0.049	-0.248	0.156
$P^{-1}_{i,1,2}$	0.313[a]	0.080	$R^A_{i,2}$	0.037[a]	0.013	$Z^{11}_{i,j}$	-0.105[b]	0.049	-0.353[b]	0.165
$P^{-2}_{i,1,2}$	-0.115	0.158	$R^A_{i,3}$	0.047[a]	0.013	$Z^{12}_{i,j}$	-0.002	0.050	-0.355[b]	0.175
$P^0_{j,0,0}$	-1.278[a]	0.110	$R^A_{i,4}$	0.006	0.013	$Z^{13}_{i,j}$	-0.031	0.051	-0.386[b]	0.184
$P^{+1}_{j,0,1}$	-1.329[a]	0.177	$R^H_{j,1}$	-0.031[b]	0.013	$Z^{14}_{i,j}$	0.070	0.052	-0.316	0.193
$P^0_{j,0,1}$	-0.912[a]	0.099	$R^H_{j,2}$	-0.031[b]	0.013	$Z^{15}_{i,j}$	-0.049	0.053	-0.365[c]	0.202
$P^{-1}_{j,0,1}$	-0.618[a]	0.091	$R^H_{j,3}$	-0.031[b]	0.013	$Z^{16}_{i,j}$	-0.008	0.054	-0.373[c]	0.212
$P^{+1}_{j,1,1}$	-0.857[a]	0.154	$R^H_{j,4}$	-0.036[a]	0.013	$Z^{17}_{i,j}$	0.041	0.055	-0.332	0.221
$P^0_{j,1,1}$	-0.612[a]	0.096	$R^A_{j,1}$	-0.044[a]	0.013	$Z^{18}_{i,j}$	-0.021	0.056	-0.352	0.230
$P^{-1}_{j,1,1}$	-0.472[a]	0.086	$R^A_{j,2}$	-0.045[a]	0.013	$Z^{19}_{i,j}$	0.015	0.057	-0.338	0.240
$P^{+2}_{j,1,2}$	-0.405	0.354	$R^A_{j,3}$	-0.043[a]	0.013	$Z^{20}_{i,j}$	0.048	0.059	-0.290	0.250
$P^{+1}_{j,1,2}$	-0.718[a]	0.142	$R^A_{j,4}$	-0.046[a]	0.013					

$P^0_{j,i,1,2}$	-0.468^a	0.093	$R^A_{j,5}$	-0.028^b	0.013
$P^{-1}_{j,i,1,2}$	-0.282^a	0.080	$R^A_{j,6}$	-0.037^a	0.013
$P^{-2}_{j,i,1,2}$	-0.412^a	0.161	$R^A_{j,7}$	-0.030^b	0.013
$S^H_{i,j}$	0.148^a	0.027	$R^A_{j,8}$	-0.030^b	0.013
$S^A_{i,j}$	-0.114^a	0.027	$R^A_{j,9}$	-0.020	0.013
μ_1	-0.631	0.055			
μ_2	0.143	0.055			
obs.	53,820				

Notes:

[a] = significantly different from zero, two-tail test, 1% level;

[b] = 5% level;

[c] = 10% level.

Estimation period is 1973–99

Key:

$Z^k_{i,j} = D^k_i - D^k_j$

$D^k_i = 1$ if home team i changed manager between the kth and $k-1$th matches before the current match (within the current season) for $k = 1 \ldots 20$, 0 otherwise

D^k_j is the same for away team j

Key to all other variables is the same as in table 3.14.

the remaining weeks or months of the season. Column (7) therefore reports the cumulative values of the $\hat{\phi}_k$'s in column (5); and column (8) reports the corresponding standard errors. For example, row 1 of column (7) is $\hat{\phi}_1 = -0.122$, row 2 is $\hat{\phi}_1 + \hat{\phi}_2 = -0.173$, and so on. The estimated cumulative effect of a managerial change on subsequent results is uniformly negative, and a number of the estimated cumulative values are statistically significant. For up to 16 matches following a change, the cumulative effect is significant at the 10 per cent level; and for up to 13 matches, the effect is significant at the 5 per cent level. For the first two matches, the effect is significant at the 1 per cent level. Overall, these results show that, on average, a change of manager that takes place within-season tends to have an adverse effect on the results of matches played during the remaining weeks or months of the same season.

6.9 Conclusion

In the first part of chapter 6, a number of simple indicators of managerial achievement were presented, each of which captures different aspects of the profile of the successful English football manager. In a profession notorious for its insecurity of tenure, survival in one post for more than just a handful of seasons may in itself be a meaningful measure of success. The top placings in the league table of managerial spells ranked by duration (table 6.1) include several managers who, by popular consent, would rate prominently among the greats of the past three decades. On the other hand, if winning as many matches as possible is the ultimate aim of any football club, then the league table of managerial spells by win ratio (table 6.2) is a more appropriate indicator of success. The top of this table also includes several all-time great managers, together with some interlopers who achieved significant success over a shorter period with lower-division teams before moving on, often to more prestigious appointments elsewhere. If ranking managerial spells according to win ratios tends to create a table biased in favour of successful top-level managers, whose winning percentages cannot subsequently be blighted following promotion to a higher level, the rankings by adjusted win ratios (table 6.3) have a pleasingly more democratic flavour. Finally, the rankings by league position relative to a simple measure of the club's financial resources (table 6.7) highlight yet another aspect of managerial performance. In this case, the top places are dominated by managers who have achieved success that is spectacular, though sometimes very short-lived, with relatively slender financial backing.

In chapter 6 the relationship between managerial change and team performance has been investigated from two different angles. Sections

6.2–6.5 have investigated the causes of managerial departure, and sections 6.6–6.8 have examined succession effects, of managerial change on subsequent team performance. The extent to which poor team performance tends to trigger managerial change has been examined using both season-level and match-level data. In the season-level estimations, the likelihood of involuntary departure is higher for inefficient managers; is lower if there has been an improvement in the team's league position since the manager was appointed; and is lower if the team made progress in the FA Cup. The involuntary departure hazard has increased over time. The voluntary departure hazard tends to be higher for efficient managers and managers who have improved their team's league position. Experienced managers are also found to be more likely to depart voluntarily.

The virtue of estimating the job-departure hazard with match-level data is that it permits identification of short-term influences on the departure decision, which tend to be obscured when durations are measured by season. A statistically significant link between individual match results and the involuntary departure hazard is found for up to 16 matches prior to the current match. The involuntary departure hazard decreases with an improvement in league position; decreases with the age of the manager; but does not seem to depend on the manager's other human capital attributes. The few most recent match results are also significant in the voluntary departure hazard function, but the effect is weaker. Perhaps surprisingly, a run of poor results is more likely to trigger a voluntary departure than a run of good results; this may be because managers are more inclined to accept alternative employment offers when their current team is struggling than when it is doing well. Managers that have improved their team's position are more likely to leave voluntarily, and previous managerial experience and international recognition as a player both increase the likelihood of voluntary departure.

The effect of a change of manager on team performance after the change takes place has also been considered in chapter 6. In order to measure managerial succession effects correctly, it is necessary to control for a natural tendency for mean-reversion in team performance. No team carries on losing forever, so a team that has recently experienced a poor spell should be expected to improve, whether it changes its manager or not. To measure the average effect of a change of manager on post-succession performance, this natural tendency to improve should not be attributed to the decision to terminate the previous manager's appointment. Only if teams tend to improve by more than the expected amount is it correct to infer that removing the manager has a beneficial average effect.

In estimations of the managerial succession effect using match-level data, it is found that a within-season managerial departure tends to be disruptive in the short term. On average, and after controlling for the mean-reversion effect, a team that changes its manager tends to under-perform in its next few matches. In the longer term, however, estimations using season-level data suggest that involuntary within-season manage-rial departure tends to lead to an improvement in performance in the fol-lowing season. The improvement is greater than would be expected given the mean-reversion effect. Ironically these results suggest that club owners, who are often accused of short-termism and myopia when taking the decision to terminate an under-performing manager's appointment, may actually be incurring short-term pain in order to realise long-term gains by so doing.

7 The demand for football attendance

A number of broad trends in league match attendances in English football at the aggregate level have been identified in chapter 2. During the post-Second World War boom, league attendances surged, reaching an all-time high of 41.0 million in the 1949 season. The boom, however, was relatively short-lived. It was followed by a period of sustained decline that continued, almost uninterrupted, until the 1986 season, when attendances fell to 16.5 million. The period since the late 1980s has seen a gradual but significant improvement. By the 1999 season, total attendances had risen to 25.4 million. The recent growth in attendance actually under-states the growth in demand because of ground-capacity constraints, with many leading clubs currently experiencing demand for tickets far in excess of existing capacities.

Chapter 2 has also reviewed the academic debate about the causes of the long post-war decline in football attendances, and its recent reversal. Social and demographic change, increasing material affluence, the option to watch football on television rather than in person, crowd misbehaviour, the deteriorating physical state of many of football's stadia and the dubious quality of the some of the 'entertainment' on offer on the field of play are among the factors considered to have contributed to the decline in the popularity of attending live football. More recently, improved facilities in all-seated stadia, together with the near-eradication of the hooligan problem, have helped strengthen football's appeal as a middle-class spectator sport. In addition, a sport so heavily steeped in history and tradition could hardly have failed to benefit from the 1990s 'heritage' fad. Improved standards of entertainment on the field of play, boosted by a large influx of talented overseas players, have also contributed much to football's recent popular resurgence.

Social history and sociology provide many useful insights into the causes of fluctuating football attendances. In section 7.1, however, an alternative approach to the analysis of attendances is pursued. The statistical or econometric analysis of attendances at the micro level forms the subject matter. Statistical modelling of variations in the attendances of

317

individual sports clubs, both season-by-season and match-by-match, has been a topic of considerable interest to sports economists since the 1970s, and especially in the UK. Section 7.1 provides an extensive, non-technical review of the empirical literature. It discusses the main problems of variable definition, model specification, estimation and interpretation that researchers in this area have faced.

The emphasis in the literature reviewed in section 7.1 is on the economic, demographic and sporting determinants of football attendances. In part this is because broader social, cultural, political and historical traditions seem to have been relatively unimportant in shaping the size and composition of the audiences for individual English football clubs. But the same cannot be said for certain clubs in a number of other countries. Although a comprehensive survey of the voluminous literature on the history and sociology of football audiences would be far beyond the scope of this volume, section 7.2 takes the opportunity to dip into this literature by describing two extensively documented cases. The first concerns the role of FC Barcelona as an outlet for expressions of Catalan national and cultural identity at various times during Spain's turbulent and often troubled twentieth-century history. The second concerns the relationship between the competitive rivalries of the two Glasgow football giants, Celtic and Rangers, and deep-rooted protestant–catholic, unionist–republican cleavages within Scottish society. In both cases, it can be shown that social and cultural identities have played a crucial part in shaping the support the clubs attract.

Section 7.3 returns to a predominantly econometric method of enquiry. Using the match attendance and revenues data set described in earlier parts of this volume, an analysis is presented of variations in club-specific average season attendances during the post-Second World War period. There are two stages to the empirical analysis. At the first stage, a model of the demand for attendance is estimated, reflecting the influence of four factors upon demand: short-term loyalty, team performance, admission price and entertainment (proxied by goals scored). The model also produces rankings of all clubs according to their estimated base levels of attendance. At the second stage, the cross-sectional variation between clubs' base levels of attendance, and between their short-term loyalty, performance, price and entertainment coefficients, is explained in terms of socio-economic, demographic and football-related characteristics of each club and its home town.

7.1 Econometric analysis of football attendances

As noted in the introduction to chapter 7, statistical or econometric modelling of variations in attendances has attracted considerable attention from academics since the 1970s. Hart, Hutton and Sharot (1975) published the first econometric analysis of patterns of attendance at English football matches. At around the same time, Demmert (1973) published an investigation of US baseball attendances, while Noll (1974) compared the determinants of attendances at four US professional team sports: baseball, basketball, football and hockey. Since the appearance of these early papers, the topic has continued to receive the attentions of econometricians on a regular basis. The purpose of this section is to review critically this literature, focusing primarily on studies that have analysed attendances at English and Scottish football, but also drawing insights from others where applicable. Cairns (1990) has written a comprehensive review of the literature from the 1970s and 1980s, and parts of this section draw on his findings.

Before embarking on the review, it is worthwhile to identify a useful way of classifying attendance studies. All previous empirical analyses of attendance fall into one of two categories: first, those which model individual match attendances; and second, those which model entire season or annual attendances (either for the league as a whole or for individual clubs). As will be seen, both types of study provide useful insights, though the types of influence on attendance that they are best equipped to identify differ in each case. The first sub-section of section 7.1 discusses the use of attendance data as the dependent variable in models of spectator demand for attendance. The following four sub-sections then describe the explanatory or independent variables that have been used most commonly in match and season attendance models.

Measuring the demand for football attendance

Attendance data, usually announced by the home club while the match is in progress, published in the following day's newspapers and subsequently collected in annual statistical publications such as *Rothmans Football Yearbook*, provide the main source of data for the dependent variable in econometric models of the demand for football attendance. In general, academic researchers have not hesitated to exploit such voluminous and easily accessible data sets, while acknowledging that some difficulties can arise when interpreting attendance data as a measure of spectator demand.

Football attendance data is usually aggregated over two types of spectator: season ticket holders, who pay for an entire season's admission in advance; and purchasers of tickets for individual matches, who may have committed to attend up to one month in advance, or as late as the day of the match itself. Clearly the factors that influence the decisions of members of either group to attend will tend to differ. Once a season ticket has been purchased, the only costs arising from the decision to attend an individual match relate to time and transport. The disincentives for season ticket holders to attend are therefore small, unless the home team's performance is so bad that it becomes preferable to stay at home! Match ticket purchasers on the other hand, are likely to be more selective in their choice of fixtures and more sensitive to temporary fluctuations in recent home-team performance or the quality of the visiting team. It is regrettable that most match attendance data does not distinguish between the two groups. Becker and Suls (1983) estimate separate regressions for match attendances and season ticket sales for Major League Baseball (MLB) matches played during the 1970s. Their findings for the relationship between team performance and demand are quite similar in both cases. For football the annual attendance data set used by Simmons (1996) also distinguishes between season ticket and match ticket sales.

Published match attendance data also includes groups of ticket holders who may have paid different prices for seats of varying quality. Before the advent of all-seated stadia, match attendance data was aggregated over both seated and standing spectators. Again, the nature of the aggregation tends to restrict or preclude the investigation of a range of interesting issues, including measurement of the price and other elasticities of demand for tickets in different price categories, or in different parts of the ground. Using a survey data set which disaggregates attendances into a standing and seated component, Dobson and Goddard (1992) find some evidence that the attendance of standing spectators was more variable than that of their seated counterparts. Standing attendances were particularly sensitive to the recent performance of the home team and the extent to which the match had significance for championship issues. The data set used in this study was quite small, however, and with the subsequent elimination of terracing from the league's higher echelons, the results are now more of historical than practical interest.

Most studies analyse attendance by estimating single-equation regression models, and interpreting the resulting equations as demand functions. This is acceptable if it can be assumed that supply is perfectly elastic. If not, estimation of the coefficients of the demand equation may be problematic. Suppose, for example, attendance depends on admission price, but clubs adjust admission price in the light of the previous season's attendance. Current admission price is therefore correlated with whatever 'random' factors influenced last season's attendance. If the effect of such 'random' factors tends to persist over more than one season, current admission price is also correlated with the current 'random' element in attendance. This violates one of the key assumptions of regression analysis,[1] introducing the possibility of simultaneity bias into the estimation. Borland's (1987) study of attendance at Australian Rules Football is one of the few to address this possibility explicitly, rather than simply assume it away.

Using annual data on gate revenue and team performance, Dobson and Goddard (1998a) use Granger causality tests to investigate whether most attendance models are correct in assuming, implicitly, that there is a unidirectional relationship running from variations in team performance to variations in attendance (and therefore revenue). Alternatively, causality might also run in the reverse direction, if teams that enjoy high attendance and revenue are able to 'buy success', either through transfer dealings or by offering salary inducements to retain the best players. In this study, and in an earlier one by Davies, Downward and Jackson (1995) using a smaller English rugby league data set, causality from revenue to performance is found to be stronger than causality in the reverse direction. These findings raise some doubts as to whether the single-equation models used in most annual attendance studies capture adequately the dynamics of the attendance–team performance relationship.

The treatment of ground-capacity constraints seems to be one of the least satisfactory aspects of the empirical sports attendance literature. Table 7.1 provides an analysis of capacity utilisation for English league football over a 25-year period between the 1974 and 1999 seasons. The first panel shows average league match attendances by division and for clubs in each of the five groups defined in table 2.7, at five-season intervals during this period. The second panel shows average ground capacities, disaggregated on the same basis. The third panel shows average percentage capacity utilisation, obtained by dividing average attendance by average capacity.

During the 1970s and 1980s, towards the end of the long post-war decline in football attendances, ground capacities were already being reduced progressively, to the extent that the average capacity utilisation rate of around 35 per cent did not change much between the mid-1970s and the mid-1980s. Only in Division 1 and in Group 1 was average capacity utilisation higher than 50 per cent during this period; at the other end of the scale in Division 4 and Group 5, average capacity utilisation was below 20 per cent. For some time after attendances started to increase from the 1986 season onwards, many clubs were still continuing to reduce capacity. This trend was in fact accelerated as a result of the

---

[1] Namely, the assumption that the error term is uncorrelated with any of the independent variables.

Table 7.1. *Average capacity utilisation, 1974–1999*

	1974	1979	1984	1989	1994	1999
Average attendances						
D1/Prem	28,294	27,428	18,834	20,553	23,055	30,580
D2/One	13,693	13,303	11,601	10,558	11,738	13,605
D3/Two	6,198	6,113	4,939	5,499	5,392	7,510
D4/Three	3,925	4,182	2,817	3,245	3,423	3,794
G1	29,325	30,049	22,855	22,804	26,550	31,901
G2	18,554	16,297	13,020	13,055	15,425	19,763
G3	10,372	9,636	7,097	7,290	7,750	8,652
G4	8,736	8,298	5,777	6,314	7,520	12,160
G5	3,713	4,693	3,258	3,504	3,559	3,679
All	12,681	12,426	9,301	9,503	10,800	13,146
Average ground capacities						
D1/Prem	49,071	44,483	37,491	35,388	28,157	33,573
D2/One	43,136	37,559	32,089	27,930	20,948	21,123
D3/Two	32,041	28,629	25,583	19,664	13,716	14,202
D4/Three	24,878	24,862	20,520	13,910	9,047	10,479
G1	55,058	50,594	47,745	45,343	32,808	36,762
G2	45,747	40,698	31,684	28,390	23,049	26,166
G3	33,053	29,092	24,991	20,642	14,837	15,072
G4	36,609	33,269	26,005	19,494	16,448	18,761
G5	24,632	24,052	20,767	13,044	9,609	9,580
All	36,898	33,573	28,665	23,738	17,939	19,247
Average capacity utilisation						
D1/Prem	57.7	61.7	50.2	58.1	81.9	91.1
D2/One	31.7	35.4	36.2	37.8	56.0	64.4
D3/Two	19.3	21.4	19.3	28.0	39.3	52.9
D4/Three	15.8	16.8	13.7	23.3	37.8	36.2
G1	53.3	59.4	47.9	50.3	80.9	86.8
G2	40.6	40.0	41.1	46.0	66.9	75.5
G3	31.4	33.1	28.4	35.3	52.2	57.4
G4	23.9	24.9	22.2	32.4	45.7	64.8
G5	15.1	19.5	15.7	26.9	37.0	38.4
All	34.4	37.0	32.4	40.0	60.2	68.3

Note: See Table 2.7 for group definitions.
Source: Rothmans.

renewed emphasis on safety following the Hillsborough disaster in April 1989. Consequently, average capacity utilisation increased to reach 40 per cent by 1989, and 60 per cent by 1994. Only by the middle of the 1990s did the extensive post-Hillsborough programme of stadium reconstruction lead to a reversal of the trend for capacities to decrease, with a modest rise recorded between 1994 and 1999. Average attendances, however, have continued to increase at a faster rate. Average capacity utilisation for the league as a whole reached 68 per cent by 1999, with a corresponding rate of 91 per cent for the Premier League, reflecting the fact that all but a handful of clubs at this level now regularly attract capacity attendances. Arsenal, Everton and Southampton are among the leading English clubs currently planning to relocate to sites that will allow expansion, while several others plan to increase capacity at their existing stadia. The recent trend for ground capacities to increase is therefore likely to continue for the foreseeable future.

On the wider issue of the relationship between stadium development or reconstruction and local economic development, there has been little or no academic research carried out in the UK. In North America, however, this question has attracted considerable attention, owing mainly to the high level of municipal financial subsidy and involvement in stadium development projects (Baade and Dye, 1990; Baade, 1996; Noll and Zimbalist, 1997; Siegfried and Zimbalist, 2000). In the empirical literature there is near-unanimity that stadium construction produces no discernible wider benefits for local economic development, and that competition between municipalities to attract and retain sports franchises by offering subsidies produces a socially inefficient allocation of resources.

Returning to the academic literature on modelling the demand for attendance, some of the older US sports studies (Noll, 1974; Schoellart and Smith, 1987; Kahn and Sherer, 1988) include stadium capacity as an explanatory variable. Clearly, however, the resulting model cannot be interpreted as a demand equation, as it contains a mix of demand- and supply-side influences. In the case of British football, most researchers assume that the number of matches attracting capacity attendances is small enough for the problem to be ignored. Effectively the supply function is horizontal, and (ignoring the aggregation problems discussed above) attendance is a satisfactory measure of demand. The decision to ignore capacity limits may well have been reasonable in the past, when ground capacities were higher than at present and demand for attendance was lower. Indeed, historically there was some flexibility in the capacity constraints themselves, with spectators simply being packed into the terraces more tightly than usual for the most attractive fixtures: a crowd management philosophy which was ultimately to lead to the most catastrophic consequences.

Today, as table 7.1 suggests, many of the top clubs 'sell out' regularly for all but the most insignificant matches, and attendance data can no longer be interpreted as a meaningful measure of demand. Although estimation techniques such as tobit allow valid estimation in cases where the distribution of the dependent variable is constrained or truncated, a data set containing a reasonable mix of constrained and unconstrained attendance figures is still required. At present, the information content in a recent season's array of home-match attendances for clubs such as Arsenal, Manchester United and Newcastle United is precisely zero (unless one merely wishes to discover what the ground-capacity constraint is). While this situation continues, it is clearly not possible to estimate attendance models of the type reviewed in this section using current data for capacity-constrained clubs.

Demographic and geographic determinants of attendance

A link between the size of the market from which each club draws its support and the level of attendance at the club's matches seems to be both theoretically and intuitively obvious. Empirically, however, it is less straightforward either to define each club's catchment area, or to come up with a market-size measure that is not arbitrary to some extent. Defining the size of the market is made difficult by the progressive erosion over time of the geographical segmentation of supporters, especially of the leading clubs. Manchester United, for example, are now famous (or notorious) for drawing their support from all regions of the UK, and even from beyond.

Even if markets could be segmented geographically, measurement is made difficult by the arbitrary nature of the municipal boundaries used to compile most local population statistics, and by the need to make adjustments in cases where two or more clubs are situated in close proximity. Despite these difficulties, in principle it should be possible to identify empirically a link between local population and attendance by comparing a cross-section of clubs. It may be more difficult to do so for a single club over time, since local populations change perhaps far more slowly than other factors which influence a club's attendance. In fact, many (but not all) match-attendance studies have included cross-sectional market-size measures for either or both of the home and away teams among their explanatory variables. Where such measures are used, almost invariably they produce regression coefficients which are of the expected sign and statistically significant.

By estimating separate match-attendance equations for each home team, Hart, Hutton and Sharot (1975) and Cairns (1987) both avoid the need to include a home-team market-size measure. For the away team, Hart, Hutton and Sharot use the male populations of the parliamentary constituencies surrounding each club's ground. In common with subsequent researchers who have used population measures, they make a number of arbitrary adjustments to sub-divide the data in cases where two or more clubs are in the same or neighbouring geographical areas. Jennett (1984) and Baimbridge, Cameron and Dawson (1996) use population measures for local authority districts instead. Walker (1986), whose paper focuses specifically on city-size effects on attendance, claims to improve on previous studies by using travel-to-work-area population definitions. These are based explicitly on observed patterns of personal mobility and travel, and so are arguably more meaningful than definitions based on local authority or parliamentary boundaries.

Because of the arbitrary nature of any population indicator, Peel and Thomas (1988) abstain from using such measures in their models altogether. So too do Dobson and Goddard (1992), sidestepping the difficulties of measuring the home team's catchment area by including a complete set of home-team dummy variables. With this approach, all influences on attendance which are specific to the home team and which do not vary within the sample period (from match to match) are captured in the coefficients of the dummy variables. Such influences may include a range of socio-economic and demographic factors (population, age structure, earnings and unemployment) as well as sporting ones (the strength of the club's historical record or traditions, or its success over the long term in building up a base level of support in the local or wider community). The advantage of this approach is that all such influences are automatically taken care of in the model's specification, so the rest of the estimated coefficients are not contaminated by omitted-variable problems. The disadvantage is that after dumping all such factors into the dummy variable coefficients, their individual effects on attendance cannot subsequently be disentangled.

The geographical distance between the grounds of the home and away teams is included by Hart, Hutton and Sharot (1975), and by most other researchers, to allow for the positive 'local-derby' effect on attendances, and the negative effect of long distances on the propensity of away supporters to attend. Distance is invariably a strongly significant determinant of attendance, with a negative estimated coefficient. There are slight variations in the approaches of Jennett (1984), who divides the away-team population by distance to obtain a composite market size and distance measure, and Cairns (1987) who prefers a 0-1 dummy to indicate matches classified as local derbies. Baimbridge, Cameron and Dawson (1996) also divide the away club's local population by distance, but include the distance variable in its own right as well.

Price, income and unemployment

In general, match-attendance models tend to have difficulty in identifying a relationship between variables such as admission prices and the *per capita* income, average earnings or unemployment rate among the population in the area in which clubs are located, and attendances. Cross-sectionally, the relationship tends to be ambiguous, partly because some of the most keenly supported clubs (such as Liverpool, Everton, Newcastle United and Sunderland) are located in cities or regions of low *per capita* income and high unemployment. Consequently, such clubs have often tended to charge lower admission prices than clubs of similar status in more affluent locations. This does not mean, however, that a reduction in *per capita* income or an increase in unemployment would be likely to increase attendance. Indeed, economic theory would suggest the opposite. Most match-attendance studies, however, lack an adequate time dimension to be capable of identifying the relationship between variations in price, income or unemployment over time, and variations in attendance.

Among the match-attendance studies that have used explanatory variables in this category, Jennett (1984) finds that the unemployment rates of the home and away team's local area are both negatively related to attendances at Scottish Premier League matches. However, the model was estimated with data for a period (1975–81) when Scottish attendances were falling, while unemployment was rising sharply. Under these circumstances, a negative and significant regression coefficient does not necessarily mean that there is a causal link between unemployment and attendance. The problems involved in interpreting regression models estimated using time-series data which is non-stationary or trended are discussed in greater detail below. In the absence of cross-sectional data on club admission prices, Jennett includes the league's stipulated minimum admission price as an explanatory variable, but does not obtain a significant coefficient.

Baimbridge, Cameron and Dawson (1996) include regional unemployment, and linear and quadratic terms in earnings and admission price in an English Premier League match-attendance equation for the 1994 season. Counter-intuitively (but possibly for the reasons discussed above) the coefficient on unemployment is positive and significant. The coefficients on earnings seem reasonable, and suggest that attendances increase with average earnings whenever the latter are above about £400 per week. The signs of the estimated coefficients on price, however, suggest a positive relationship between price and attendance over a realistic range of prices, so the model fails to identify an economically meaningful price effect.

Annual attendance models, using data with a longer time dimension, have been more successful in identifying relationships between price, income and unemployment variables and football attendances. Bird's (1982) study, which reports equations for attendance aggregated across the entire league and by division, was the first of its kind for English football, and is perhaps still the most widely quoted empirical attendance study. In an attempt to capture the full cost of attending, Bird's price measure combines the leagues's minimum admission price with an implicit price index for motoring and other transport costs, taken from the UK's national income accounts. Total consumer expenditure is used as an income measure. The results suggest a price elasticity of demand for football attendance of -0.22, and an income elasticity of -0.62.

Bird's negative income elasticity implies that attending football is an inferior good. As incomes increase, consumers tend to give up attending football, and follow other, perhaps more expensive or 'up-market' leisure activities instead. As a description of what actually occurred between the 1950s and 1970s, this seems plausible and consistent with the historical account given in chapter 2. However, developments in time-series econometrics since Bird's paper was published raise doubts about the statistical validity of some of the relationships which he identifies. Specifically, although it is correct to say that incomes rose and football attendances fell between the 1950s and the 1970s, nothing more than this can be inferred from a negative and significant coefficient obtained in a crude regression of attendance on income. It is not possible to infer that the rise in income 'caused' or even 'influenced' the decline in attendance in any sense. All that can really be said is that income and attendance were trended in opposite directions during the period in question.

Szymanski and Smith (1997) estimate attendance and revenue equations as part of a larger model, which attempts to capture both demand- and supply-side influences on the trade-off between team performance and profit faced by club owners. In an attendance estimation pooled over 48 clubs using data for the period 1974–89, an estimated price elasticity of -0.76 is obtained. When a set of time dummy variables is included, this estimate drops to -0.34. No income or unemployment measure is included among the explanatory variables. In this paper, the estimation period is too short for the full battery of modern time-series econometric techniques to be deployed, and in any case the attendance equation is not the main focus of Szymanski and Smith's analysis. Nevertheless, although the time dummies do make some adjustment for the trended nature of the attendance and price data, the interpretation of their results still seems likely to be subject to difficulties similar to those described in the previous paragraph.

Under what circumstances can inferences be drawn from estimations involving trended or non-stationary time-series variables,[2] which are not subject to the kind of critique outlined above? Using data on the annual attendances of individual clubs, Dobson and Goddard (1995) suggest de-trending the data prior to estimation, by expressing all variables as deviations from their annual averages across clubs. A model estimated using this approach, which eliminates the possibility that the estimated coefficients will identify spurious relationships between trended variables, is presented in section 7.2. Other papers by Simmons (1996) and Dobson and Goddard (1996) tackle the same problem using cointegration techniques. In this case, the idea is that if there is a genuine relationship between two or more non-stationary time-series variables, one or both of the following features should be apparent in the data:

- A statistical relationship should be discernible between the year-on-year changes (the first differences) in the same variables. In other words, if income really does influence attendance, it should be possible to identify a link between (say) an above-average rise in income in a particular year, and an above-average fall in attendance in the same year (or perhaps in the following year). If apart from both being trended or non-stationary, income and attendance are otherwise unrelated, no short-run relationship will be identifiable between their first differences.
- Some consistent patterns and linkages should also be discernible between the long-term movements in the variables. If for example, the rate at which incomes are increasing slows down for a few years, other things being equal there should also be a corresponding reduction in the rate at which attendances are declining, if the income effect is negative as Bird claims. The fact that soon after Bird's study was published, incomes continued to increase while attendances started to rise, suggests that this kind of pattern might have been lacking had the estimation included later data. Without a full statistical investigation, however,

---

[2] A time series is stationary if its mean and variance are constant with respect to time, and non-stationary if its mean and variance are changing with respect to time. An untrended series can be stationary or non-stationary: a non-stationary untrended series is one that tends to wander over time. A trended series is, by definition, non-stationary because the trend causes its mean to change with respect to time. Some trended series, however, can be made stationary by de-trending. Other trended series remain non-stationary even after any deterministic trend component is removed.

it is not possible to be certain. Perhaps there was another factor which also exerted a downward influence on attendance between the 1950s and 1970s, but which began to work in the opposite direction in the 1980s, to an extent sufficient to outweigh the continuing downward pull of income. Hooliganism, though difficult to quantify empirically, could be one such factor. If a group of variables can be identified, each of whose long-term movements can be adequately accounted for by co-movements in the others, then a cointegrating relationship is said to hold between the group of variables. Again, variables which are trended or non-stationary but otherwise unrelated, will not satisfy the statistical criteria for a cointegrating relationship to hold.

Dobson and Goddard (1996) report an estimated model for annual attendances based on data from the mid-1950s to the early 1990s. The data for individual clubs is pooled across all clubs located in each standard region for purposes of estimation of a set of regional attendance equations. Regional unemployment rates are used as an explanatory variable, in place of income or consumer expenditure. There is evidence of a long-term, cointegrating relationship between variations in regional unemployment and annual attendances, but no evidence of a long-term price effect. Conversely, price changes are found to have a negative short-term impact on changes in attendance, while movements in unemployment have no short-term effect. Overall, there is little evidence to suggest that the coefficients of the attendance equation vary significantly from region to region.

In a set of club-specific time series estimations for 19 leading clubs, using data from the 1960s to the early 1990s, Simmons (1996) finds evidence of a negative price effect on attendance in the long term, and limited evidence of a long-term income effect which, where apparent, tends to be positive rather than negative. To obtain economically meaningful and statistically significant estimated coefficients in the long-term part of the model the sets of variables included in the cointegration tests are permitted to vary between clubs. While expedient from a statistical perspective, this procedure does not have any obvious theoretical justification. Nevertheless, the evidence of a negative price effect is consistent, and the estimated long-term price elasticities are higher in absolute terms than in other studies: above -0.5 for 10 clubs, and above -1.0 for two. There is some evidence of a negative price effect in the short term, while the short-term income coefficients include both positive and negative signs.

Team quality and uncertainty of outcome

Match-attendance models seem to offer greater scope than season attendance models for investigating team quality influences on attendance.

Hart, Hutton and Sharot (1975) use the current league positions of the home and away teams as explanatory variables, and find that while highly placed away teams attract higher attendances, the home-position coefficients are generally insignificant. The latter finding may reflect the fact that after the first few weeks of the season (during which spectators may in any case tend to disregard the embryonic league table), there is often little further variation in the home-position variable in a club-specific equation until (perhaps) the start of the next season.

By estimating club-specific equations over a longer period, thereby obtaining greater variation into the home-position variable, Cairns (1987) obtains significant coefficients on both the home- and away-position variables, and by pooling their data across clubs Walker (1986), Peel and Thomas (1988) and Dobson and Goddard (1992) find the same. Baimbridge, Cameron and Dawson (1996) find linear and quadratic terms in the absolute difference between the positions of the two teams to be insignificant, possibly because various other team-quality measures (such as the previous season's finishing position, and the number of international and overseas players in each team) are also included. In addition to league position variables, Walker (1986), Cairns (1987) and Dobson and Goddard (1992) include the number of points gained from the three, four or five most recent matches played by either or both teams. A recent run of good results is usually found to have a significant and positive effect on attendance.

Incorporating team-quality information into a match-attendance model naturally raises questions about the link between uncertainty of outcome and attendance (see also chapter 3). Hart, Hutton and Sharot (1975) and Peel and Thomas (1988, 1992) focus on uncertainty of individual match outcomes as a determinant of attendance, while Jennett (1984) and Cairns (1987) are concerned with uncertainty of season outcomes: the impact on attendance of the importance (if any) of the match for championship, promotion or relegation issues.

Hart, Hutton and Sharot try including the absolute value of the difference between home and away positions as an explanatory variable in their attendance equation, but fail to obtain the negative coefficient that would suggest that the more evenly balanced the teams and uncertain the match outcome, the higher the attendance. This procedure ignores the influence of home advantage on outcome uncertainty. Peel and Thomas (1988) use home-win probabilities calculated from bookmakers' posted betting odds, and find that attendance is positively related to the probability of a home win. However, by incorporating this variable in linear (rather than quadratic) form, they effectively measure relative team quality and not uncertainty of outcome directly. Matches at opposite ends of the home-win probability scale (at 0.05 and 0.95, for example) should rate as roughly equal (i.e. very low) in terms of uncertainty of outcome. Nevertheless, from their results Peel and Thomas argue that measures to increase uncertainty of outcome might have a detrimental effect on attendance, if they reduce home-win probabilities. They therefore question the empirical validity of the hypothesis that uncertainty of outcome has a positive effect on attendance.

Jennett (1984) constructs dummy variables to indicate the degree of championship significance of each match for the home and away teams. While it remains mathematically possible for a team to achieve the points total observed (after the event) to be required to win the championship, the dummy is set equal to the reciprocal of the number of games that remain to be played. The dummy therefore increases progressively for teams that remain in contention as the prospect of winning the championship draws near, reflecting the heightened significance of the final few matches for such teams. For teams that drop out of contention after reaching a point from which the points required are no longer attainable, the dummy is re-set to zero for the season's remaining matches. In the estimations, the championship significance dummies are found to be highly significant for both the home and away teams, though similarly designed relegation significance dummies are insignificant.

Jennett's championship significance variable has been widely, and perhaps excessively, criticised (Cairns, Jennett and Sloane, 1986; Cairns, 1987; Peel and Thomas, 1988) on the grounds that its computation requires knowledge of the ultimate championship-winning points total. Of course, such knowledge is unavailable to spectators at the time they take their decisions whether or not to attend. The Jennett measure does nevertheless succeed in distinguishing quite accurately between matches that (on any reasonable criteria) would be regarded as having championship significance, and those that would not. If the purpose is to model attendances *ex post*, rather than forecast them *ex ante*, Jennett's measure achieves its objective. Presumably, data on changes throughout the season in bookmakers' odds on the championship outcome would provide a more widely acceptable measure, although to our knowledge no researchers have exploited this possibility as yet. Instead, Cairns (1987) defines a team to be in contention if it could still win the championship by gaining 80 per cent of the points available from its remaining matches, assuming that the current leader gains only 50 per cent. While the percentages are arbitrary, Cairns also demonstrates that matches with championship significance on this measure attract significantly higher attendances.

On the whole, the issues involved in incorporating team-quality measures into a season attendance model are relatively straightforward. The estimations of Dobson and Goddard (1995, 1996), Simmons (1996) and Syzmanski and Smith (1997) using club-level data, control for team performance by including the team's final league position as an explanatory variable in its own attendance equation. While the team's final position is unknown at the time when decisions to attend are actually taken, as the league competition unfolds potential and actual spectators are able to form increasingly reliable estimates. Unsurprisingly, final league position turns out to be a highly significant determinant of annual attendance in all of these studies. Simmons (1996) and Dobson and Goddard (1995, 1996) also include suitably standardised measures of goals scored as a crude proxy for each team's entertainment value. Various dummy variables for promotion or relegation in the previous season, or for finishes in the top three positions in each division are also used. Over each season, the average quality of opposing teams depends only on the division in which the team plays (already reflected in the league position variable), and therefore does not enter the attendance equation.

No empirical study based on UK football data has tried to capture uncertainty of outcome effects in an annual attendance model. Borland (1987), however, attempts to do so in a study using aggregate attendance data for Australian Rules Football over the period 1950–87. Uncertainty of championship outcome in each season is captured by various measures of the dispersion of points across teams within the league at various points in each season. Limited evidence is found that annual attendances may be sensitive to uncertainty of championship outcome. The extent of long-term dominance is reflected in the number of different teams which had qualified for places in the end-of-season finals over the previous three seasons. But in the empirical results there is no indication that long-term dominance, as measured, has any effect on attendance. Earlier North American evidence reported in studies by Demmert (1973), Noll (1974) and Hunt and Lewis (1976) also casts doubt on the assertion that enhanced uncertainty of match or season outcome leads to a measureable increase in spectator demand, reflected in match attendances or revenues.

Other influences on attendance

The three previous sub-sections have described the main categories of explanatory variable which have been used in attendance models. In addition, most match-attendance studies allow for systematic variations in attendance through the course of the season, or at the start and end of each season, or between weekdays, weekends and Bank Holidays, using various time trends or dummy variables. Bird (1982), Cairns (1987) and Baimbridge, Cameron and Dawson (1996) all attempt to allow for

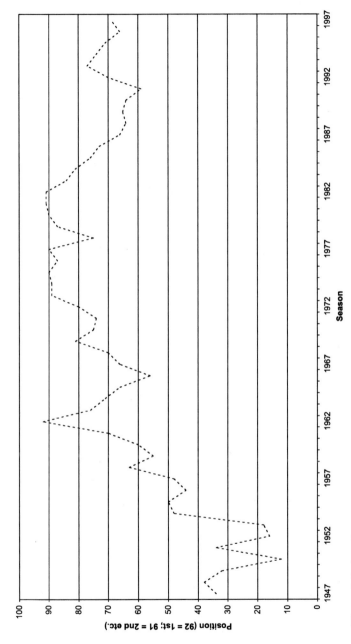

Figure 7.1 (cont.)

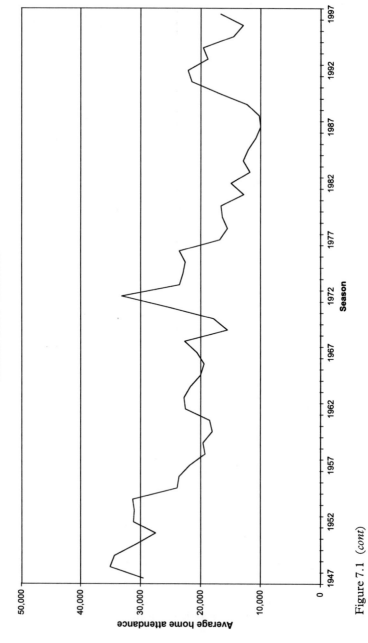

Figure 7.1 (*cont*)

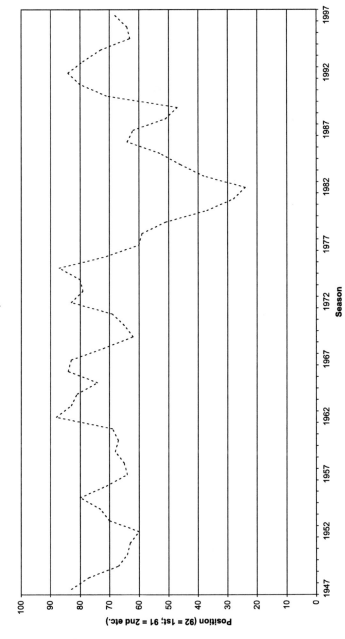

Figure 7.1 (cont)

a single census introduces a large element of imprecision. There appears to be no alternative, however, since town-specific data are unavailable (even at 10-year intervals) on a consistent definitional basis. In any event, the intention in the second-stage estimations is to use variables that capture broadly defined demographic and socio-economic characteristics of the towns in which clubs are based. Even with a 50-year observation period, it seems reasonable to assume that for most towns, such characteristics are sufficiently stable for an exercise of this type to be meaningful. The use of the 1981 Census for all demographic and socio-economic variables may seem somewhat arbitrary. It can be justified, however, on the grounds that this census was conducted at the depth of the most severe recession of the post-war period, and is therefore the census in which the differences between the socio-economic characteristics of towns located in different parts of England and Wales are likely to be most pronounced.

Table 7.3 reports the results of a set of weighted least squares (WLS) estimations of five equations, in which the estimated values of α_i, β_{1i}, δ_{1i}, δ_{2i} and δ_{3i} obtained from the previous section are used in turn as the dependent variable, and H_p, X_p, C_p, F_p, I_i and U_p, as defined above, are used as explanatory variables. For each equation there are 96 observations on each variable: one for each club included in the estimations in the previous sub-section.[9]

Column (1) of table 7.3 reports the regression which seeks to identify the determinants of base attendance, using each club's estimated alpha coefficient, $\hat{\alpha}_p$, as the explanatory variable. All of the explanatory variables, with the exception of the industrial structure variables F_i and I_p are found to be significantly different from zero at the 5 per cent level on two-tail tests. As expected, home-town population, H_p and the number of years since the club entered the league, X_p both have positive and highly significant estimated coefficients, with t-statistics of 4.08 and 4.35, respectively.

H_i is found to be a significant determinant of base attendance, despite the fact that the proportion of spectators who live in the immediate vicinity of their club's stadium has almost certainly declined over time, owing to factors such as demographic change and improved transport links (Bale, 1993; see also chapter 2). The strength of the coefficient on X_i in

---

[9] Following Saxonhouse (1976), in each equation each observation is weighted by the inverse of the estimated variance of the dependent variable obtained from the earlier estimations. Intuitively, the weights reflect the degree of confidence which can be placed in each observation. The weighting procedure takes account of the fact that the dependent variables are themselves estimated coefficients obtained from the first-stage estimations, and not (as is usually the case) hard data.

Table 7.3. *Attendance model: second-stage estimation results*

Independent variables and definition	Dependent variable and *definition*				
	$\hat{\alpha}_i$ Base attendance (1)	$\hat{\beta}_{1i}$ Short-term loyalty (2)	$\hat{\delta}_{1i}$ League position (3)	$\hat{\delta}_{2i}$ Price (4)	$\hat{\delta}_{3i}$ Goals scored (5)
Constant	-2.4978^a	-0.1791	0.01358	0.3460	0.3341
	(-0.3750)	(0.3796)	(0.01547)	(0.2428)	(0.2144)
H_i Home-town population	0.0748^a	0.0168	0.00019	-0.0150	-0.0268^c
	(0.0183)	(0.0201)	(0.00100)	(0.0147)	(0.0137)
X_i Duration of league membership	0.2841^a	0.1429^b	-0.00012	-0.0773^c	0.0393
	(0.0653)	(0.0681)	(0.00217)	(0.0445)	(0.0268)
C_i Local competition	-0.0095^b	-0.0008	0.00027	0.0037	-0.0002
	(0.0042)	(0.0051)	(0.00024)	(0.0039)	(0.0031)
F_i Agricultural employment	-0.016	-0.0035	0.0001	0.0055	0.0021
	(0.0198)	(0.0117)	(0.00063)	(0.0098)	(0.0075)
I_i Industrial employment	-0.003	-0.003	-0.00004	0.0009	-0.0018
	(0.0021)	(0.0026)	(0.00013)	(0.0013)	(0.0016)
U_i Unemployment	0.0132^a	0.0042	0.00008	0.0063^b	-0.0058^b
	(0.0044)	(0.0057)	(0.00017)	(0.0028)	(0.0027)
obs.	96	96	96	96	96
R^2	0.83	0.94	0.86	0.27	0.19
s.e. of regression	4.94	1.31	1.50	1.26	1.26

Notes:
[a] = significantly different from zero, two-tail test, 1% level;
[b] = 5% level;
[c] = 10% level.
standard errors of estimated coefficients are shown in parentheses.

particular justifies the previous comments concerning the first-mover advantages enjoyed by clubs that entered the league early. Bearing in mind the fact that 87 of the 96 clubs included in the data set first entered the league before the Second World War (before the period covered by the estimations) it seems remarkable that this effect is so strong. Clearly, this finding testifies to the importance of tradition, and loyalties which persist across generations, in shaping patterns of demand. An important policy implication for the game's governing bodies appears to be that the rules governing entry and exit to and from the league should be relatively cautious in terms of the criteria laid down by which new clubs are able to replace established ones (Dobson and Goddard, 1995). Of course, this does not preclude the possibility that other considerations in favour of admitting a new club may outweigh the tradition factor. Other things being equal, however, the results suggest that historical tradition does have a major bearing on spectator demand, and should be an important consideration when framing rules governing promotion and relegation to and from the league.

As expected from elementary economic theory, the number of clubs located within close geographical proximity (a crude measure of the level of competition facing each club), C_i, has a negative and significant association with base attendance. On the other hand, the rate of unemployment, U_i, is found to have a positive association. This finding perhaps runs counter to theoretical expectations, but is in line with the results of the cross-sectional attendance model of Baimbridge, Cameron and Dawson (1996). As discussed earlier in this chapter, it may simply reflect the fact that for various sociological and historical reasons, many of the most keenly supported clubs are located in cities or regions which tend to suffer from high structural unemployment.

In contrast to the results for the alpha coefficients, few of the explanatory variables are significant in the regressions which use the short-term loyalty, league position, price and goals scored coefficients (in turn) as the dependent variable, reported in columns (2)–(5) of table 7.3. To some extent this is to be expected. While there are strong reasons to expect factors such as population, age or the strength of local competition to influence the average or base level of a club's attendance, there seems less reason to expect such factors to influence the sensitivity of attendances to variations in league position, price, and so on.

The only explanatory variable which is significant in the regression with the estimated short-term loyalty coefficient, $\hat{\beta}_{1i}$, as dependent variable, is the number of years since the club entered the league, X_i. Clubs which entered early are found to have a higher short-term loyalty coefficient, a finding which seems to emphasise the importance of this factor in shaping attendance patterns. None of the explanatory variables is significant in the regression for the estimated steady-state league position coefficient, $\hat{\delta}_{1i}$. In the regression for the estimated steady-state price coefficient, $\hat{\delta}_{2i}$, the coefficient on the rate of unemployment, U_i, is positive and significant at the 5 per cent level, and the coefficient on the duration of league membership, X_i, is negative and significant at the 10 per cent level. The former suggests that attendances in towns with high unemployment are more sensitive to variations in price than attendances elsewhere:

a result which seems intuitively plausible. The latter reinforces the notion that the supporters of first-movers (early entrants) are more loyal, as their attendance appears to be less price-sensitive. Finally, although in the regression for the estimated steady-state goals scored coefficient, $\hat{\delta}_{3i}$, home-town population, H_i, and the rate of unemployment, U_i, are both significant, no obvious explanation suggests itself. These results could be a statistical quirk, rather than indicative of any genuine association.

7.4 Conclusion

Since the 1970s, modelling match-by-match and season-by-season variations in attendances has been a popular topic in the empirical sports economics literature. A large proportion of this work has been devoted to English and Scottish football attendances, and in chapter 7 this literature has been reviewed in some detail. Economists are naturally inclined to interpret attendance data as a measure of demand. Published attendances, however, are aggregated over various spectator groups, including season ticket holders and purchasers of tickets (at various prices) for individual matches. The nature of the aggregation tends to make the estimation of price and other elasticities of demand problematic. The possibility of multi-directional causality between variables such as price, team performance and attendance, and the fact that published attendances increasingly tend to reflect ground-capacity constraints, also present difficulties, both in the estimation of attendance equations, and in their interpretation as demand functions.

Despite precise measurement being somewhat arbitrary, market size is usually found to be a significant determinant of match attendances, as is the geographical distance separating the two teams contesting each match. Models of season attendances are better equipped to detect price, income and unemployment effects, and a number of recent studies have quantified a relatively small but statistically significant price elasticity. Some care needs to be exercised, however, in interpreting the results of regressions estimated using non-stationary or trended time series data. In any event, team performance appears to exert a much greater influence on individual club attendances than price, though there is less consensus among researchers as to whether genuine uncertainty of match outcome, or simply a high probability that the home team will win, is the more likely to generate a high match attendance. Unsurprisingly, matches which are relevant for championship outcomes are consistently found to attract higher attendances.

If not in England then elsewhere, broader social, cultural, ethnic and religious influences also play an important part in determining the size and composition of the crowds that watch certain clubs, as the histories of FC Barcelona in Spain and Celtic and Rangers in Scotland make abundantly clear. There are signs, however, that as the relevant historical divisions in society tend to fade (and as the playing staffs of the respective clubs tend to become increasingly cosmopolitan) fixtures such as Celtic–Rangers are increasingly becoming spectacles played out in stadia full of relatively orderly seated spectators, whose displays of the paraphernalia of sectarianism (flags, banners and songs) are mainly symbolic or nostalgic. The time may be not too far distant when Old Firm derbies, while still supercharged in terms of competitive intensity, are not fundamentally different from other fixtures involving leading teams in other countries, that lack the same historical associations.

In the empirical section of chapter 7, a two-stage econometric model of variation in English annual average club-specific league attendances during the post-Second World War period is presented. At the first stage, an attendance model is estimated, which ranks all clubs according to their estimated base attendance, and which examines the effect on attendance of short-term loyalty, team performance, admission price and goals scored. At the second stage, the cross-sectional variation between clubs' base levels of attendance, and their short-term loyalty, performance, price and entertainment coefficients, is explained in terms of socio-economic, demographic and football-related characteristics of each club and its home town. Home-town population, the amount of competition from other local football clubs and the duration of each club's league membership are all highly significant determinants of base attendances. Duration of membership is also a significant determinant of the short-term loyalty coefficient. These results suggest that clubs which joined the league early continue to enjoy significant first-mover advantages, in many cases more than a century after they first gained membership! It is evident that sporting history and tradition remain important factors in shaping patterns of demand for attendance at English football, even in the modern era.

8   Information transmission and efficiency: share prices and fixed-odds betting

One of the most influential and durable propositions of neoclassical economics is the idea that the interactions between large numbers of buyers and sellers operating in free, unregulated markets, each taking spontaneous and uncoordinated decisions in pursuit of their own self-interest, can normally be relied upon to deliver an efficient allocation of scarce resources. The originator of this notion was Adam Smith, whose 'invisible hand' metaphor, first articulated *The Wealth of Nations* published in 1776, represents one of the most spectacular intellectual achievements of the late-eighteenth-century Scottish enlightenment. A key assumption of the many theoretical models that have since been developed to formalise Smith's brilliant insight is that all relevant information about the prices and characteristics of tradeable commodities is transmitted rapidly and accurately among buyers and sellers. Otherwise, trade that takes place on the basis of incomplete or inaccurate information may well lead to a misallocation of resources.

Unsurprisingly, therefore, investigating the speed and efficiency with which relevant information is impounded into the prices at which trade takes place in markets is of considerable interest to economists and others. Its importance is not purely theoretical, for the reasons outlined above, but also highly practical. If relevant information is available to some traders but not to others, the well informed can exploit their informational advantage to trade with the uninformed at prices which the latter would not accept if they had access to the same information. In other words, access to privileged information confers the opportunity to profit at the expense of the informationally disadvantaged.

Chapter 8 investigates two cases in which information about the performance of football teams on the field of play is relevant to the formation of prices at which trade takes place in particular markets. In both cases, the focus is on the efficiency with which useful information is impounded into the relevant prices. The first case, considered in sections 8.1 and 8.2, is the secondary market for trade in the shares of football clubs that are quoted on the London Stock Exchange (LSE). Rapid changes in football's financial structure during the 1990s have encouraged clubs to innovate and diversify their methods of raising finance. Some clubs have moved further than others in reducing their reliance on traditional sources such as bank borrowing and loans or donations from wealthy benefactors. Developments concerning the ownership and governance of football clubs, together with recent developments including English football's mid-1990s stock market boom, are examined in section 8.1.

It is obvious that major events that take place on the field of play, such as European qualification and elimination or domestic promotion and relegation, carry implications for a football club's ability to earn gate, television and sponsorship revenues. If each club's share price reflects the market's collective assessment of its prospects for future profitability, and if new information about team performance is rapidly transmitted and absorbed by the markets, a direct link between fluctuatons in fortunes on the field of play and variations in share prices should be discernible. Section 8.2 reports the results of an empirical investigation of this link.

The match results forecasting model that was developed and presented in chapter 3 has a role to play in this investigation. Efficient markets theory suggests that only *unanticipated* news about team performance should lead to reappraisal of a club's profitability prospects and a change in the price of its shares. News about performance that was *anticipated* should already be impounded into the share price, and the event concerned should not have any effect when it eventually occurs. In an empirical investigation of the market efficiency hypothesis, the forecasting model provides a convenient decomposition of actual team performance into its anticipated and unanticipated components, allowing the latter to be compared directly with share price movements.

The second case, considered in section 8.3, is professional football's fixed-odds betting market. Here, bettors place bets on the outcomes of matches, at odds that are set by bookmakers a few days in advance of the match concerned. The main objective of section 8.3 is to establish whether the bookmaker's odds reflect all relevant, publicly available information that might help to predict the match outcome, or whether there are opportunities for profitable betting on matches for which the quoted odds and the available data are misaligned. The forecasting model of chapter 3 is used to generate predicted match results, which in turn enable bettors to calculate expected returns for bets placed on alternative outcomes.

8.1 Ownership, finance and English football's stock market boom

At the origins of professional football in England in the 1880s, football clubs were voluntary organisations, administered by committees elected by voting members. The development of professionalism led naturally to growth in gate revenues, and in the costs of player compensation and stadium construction. This in turn created pressures for clubs to acquire limited liability status. According to Russell (1997), Small Heath (which later changed its name to Birmingham City) was probably the first club to become a private company in 1888. By 1921, all but two of the league's 86 member clubs had followed suit. From then until recently, professional football's traditional methods of commercial and financial management seemed virtually impervious to pressures for modernisation emanating from a multitude of social and economic changes. For most of the twentieth century, the ownership structure and numerous aspects of the financing and administration of the average football club retained many of the features originally acquired during the late Victorian era.

Traditionally, the major shareholders and the majority of directors of football clubs were individuals drawn from the local business community. Although share ownership sometimes did extend beyond the well-heeled middle classes, working-class shareholdings were usually too small to confer much influence over the running of the club, and seem to have existed primarily as a token of loyalty (Russell, 1997). There has been much debate among academic economists and sociologists about the 'true' motives of those wealthy individuals who injected large amounts of personal finance into the local football club, often in return for little more than a seat on the board of directors. The economist's usual profit maximising assumption seems untenable given the woeful financial performance of most football clubs, and in view of the fact that directors were prohibited by FA regulations from receiving dividends, until this rule lapsed in the 1980s (Conn, 1997, 1999). No doubt a few individuals have attempted to exploit their influence in football for ends such as political advancement, or to win contracts for their own businesses. But in the vast majority of cases, the simplest explanation seems the most plausible. Success in business later on in life creates both the means and the opportunity to intervene in the running of the local football club, in an (often futile) attempt to realise the unfulfilled sporting aspirations of childhood.

In the nineteenth and the early part of the twentieth centuries, responsibility for team affairs and selection rested primarily with the club's directors and chairman. It was only during the inter-war period that the present-day role of the professional football manager first started to evolve. Walvin (1994) identifies the growth of a stronger ethos of professionalism within football during the 1920s and 1930s as instrumental in encouraging directors to begin shifting responsibility for performance on the pitch towards the team manager (see chapters 5 and 6).

Morrow (1999) identifies a number of characteristics of the financial structure of the typical English football club prior to recent changes in the financing of football. Traditionally, clubs were small, privately owned companies, which tended to be under-capitalised, and to raise little or no finance from retained profit. Under-capitalisation (in other words, a relatively low ratio of equity to total financing) seems to have been a consequence of the reluctance of many club owners to dilute or jeopardise their personal control by using new equity issues as a means of raising finance. In many cases, however, club owners or major shareholders provided significant additional long-term finance in the form of personal loans. Although these are technically distinct from equity finance, the practical implications of the distinction may often be minimal (Deloitte and Touche, 1999). Borrowing from banks, often on a short-term basis through overdraft facilities, was (and in many cases still is) another major source of finance for clubs whose outgoings are in excess of their revenues, either temporarily or in the longer term.

With hindsight, the flotation of Tottenham Hotspur on the LSE Official List in October 1983 might appear to have been a groundbreaking development. The issue, which was four times over-subscribed, raised £3.3 million, a sum considerably more substantial at the time than it seems by present-day standards. But for a number of years Tottenham remained the only club with a Stock Exchange quotation, perhaps because the company's subsequent performance did not offer strong encouragement to others who might have been considering making the same move. By the end of 1990, a series of unsuccessful diversification ventures, implemented through the creation of subsidiary companies, left Tottenham shares trading slightly below their opening price seven years earlier.[1]

Nevertheless, other clubs did eventually follow suit. Millwall raised £4.8 million in a flotation in October 1989, and Manchester United £6.7 million in June 1991. Again, the early experiences of the quoted companies were not encouraging. Within two years, Millwall shares were trading at around one-tenth of their original value. The team's relegation from Division 1 in May 1990, followed by a further decline in its fortunes within Division 2, led investors to scale back drastically their assessment

---

[1] In December 1990, trading was suspended for a year, until the club's principal shareholder, Irving Scholar, was eventually bought out by consumer electronics entrepreneur Alan Sugar and team manager Terry Venables.

of the company's value, before trading in the shares was eventually suspended. Manchester United shares were more than 50 per cent undersubscribed at the time of flotation in June 1991, and were still trading below their original offer price more than 18 months later.

At the start of the 1990s, other clubs were experimenting with alternative methods of raising external finance. Highly controversial at the time was Arsenal's 'Highbury Bond' issue, targeted at the club's own supporters. Bond purchasers were guaranteed the right (effectively in perpetuity) to purchase a season ticket for a specific seat in return for an investment of £1,500 or £1,100 (Campbell and Shields, 1993). Despite a slow initial take-up, the bond eventually raised about £14 million towards the construction of a £22.5 million new stand. A handful of other clubs launched similar bond schemes in the early 1990s, with varying degrees of success. West Ham United's 'Hammers Bond', launched in 1991, succeeded only in triggering a large-scale supporters' revolt, and by mid-1992 the club were admitting defeat. By the end of the 1990s, Newcastle United were finding that long-term guarantees of the right to a specific seat made to bond purchasers several years earlier were an inconvenient and embarrassing (temporary) impediment to the further redevelopment of their stadium.

As described in chapter 2, the first BSkyB–Premier League television contract, covering the five seasons from 1993 to 1997, injected television revenues on a scale previously unimagined into football. But almost as soon as this contract was underway, it was realised that potential still remained for even higher television revenues to be earned in the future. By 1995 speculation concerning the possible value of the next television contract was commonplace and often hyperbolic. A surge of optimistic sentiment concerning the sector's prospects for continued revenue growth led to massive appreciation in the prices of Tottenham Hotspur and Manchester United shares; by the end of December 1996, the increases over the previous 18 months were 368 per cent and 336 per cent, respectively. The circumstances were clearly favourable for a spate of 15 further flotations, all of which took place between September 1995 and October 1997. The costs of stadium redevelopment, and spiralling player salaries and transfer fees, were both creating significant pressure for football clubs to find new sources of finance. Needless to say, in the eyes of institutional investors the former was a more acceptable justification for flotation than the latter. The desire of current club owners to realise gains from past investments may also have been a factor motivating the decision to float in certain cases.

It is worth describing briefly some of the mechanics of flotation. Table 8.1 provides some of the details, and charts the six-monthly percentage

Table 8.1. *Date and method of flotation and share price returns from flotation to December 1999, floated English clubs*

Company	Date of flotation, and list		Method	Proceeds (£m)	Percentage returns over previous six months									
					6.95	12.95	6.96	12.96	6.97	12.97	6.98	12.98	6.99	12.99
Tottenham Hotspur	12/10/83	O	O	3.3	−10	68	119	28	−20	−25	−12	10	−12	1
Manchester United	07/06/91	O	PO	6.7	19	28	121	54	−9	4	0	41	−11	3
Preston North End	29/09/95	A	PO	6.7		0	35	9	−8	−18	−3	−21	−16	−6
Chelsea Village	29/03/96	A	I	—			*13*	69	−4	4	−38	14	−18	−11
Leeds Sporting	01/08/96	O	T/PO	17.1				23	−45	−7	−35	11	−7	28
Loftus Road (Queens Park Rangers)	23/10/96	A	PO	12				*18*	−32	−45	−43	11	−50	33
Sunderland	23/12/96	O	PO	10.7				28	−51	−7	29	42	−30	42
Sheffield United	01/01/97	O	T/PO	1.4					−35	15	−46	−16	−22	−8
West Bromwich Albion	02/01/97	A	P	20.5					−41	−12	−14	−8	−9	0
Birmingham City	14/01/97	A	P	7.5					−24	−21	−10	−40	−1	4
Charlton Athletic	06/03/97	A	PO	5.5					−31	−4	−10	0	−8	−20
Burnden Leisure (Bolton)	20/03/97	O	RT	—					−17	−6	18	−20	−24	16
Newcastle United	01/04/97	O	O	50.4					1	−31	−21	30	−16	−15
Southampton Leisure	22/04/97	O	RT	—					7	−40	−30	−5	5	5
Aston Villa	06/05/97	O	PO	15.2					−24	−14	−32	42	−36	−15
Nottingham Forest	09/10/97	A	O	3						−26	2	−48	22	−36
Leicester City	24/10/97	O	I	—						−35	−40	9	−9	−9
FTSE 100	—		—	—	8	11	1	11	12	12	14	1	7	10

Notes: Lists are Official LSE (O) and AIM (A).
Methods of flotation are offer (O), placing (P), introduction (I), takeover (T) and reverse takeover (RT).
Percentage returns in italics are from flotation to the end of the period shown at the top of the column.
Sources: Deloitte and Touche (1999), Datastream.

changes in the share prices of all quoted football clubs between December 1994 (or the date of flotation, if later) and December 1999. Most quoted clubs are listed on the Stock Exchange Official List, while some are listed on the Alternative Investment Market (AIM). The Official List includes the large majority of major UK companies, while AIM is designed for smaller, younger or rapidly expanding companies. Both are regulated by the Stock Exchange, but the criteria for acceptance onto the Official List are more stringent than those for AIM. Significantly for many football clubs considering flotation, neither list requires a company to demonstrate a historical record of profitability prior to acceptance.[2]

There are a number of methods by which a new listing can be implemented. In an Offer for Sale, shares are offered to the general public through an Issuing House. In a Placing, the Issuing House seeks to place the shares directly with its own clients (usually financial institutions). In an Introduction, if an unlisted company's shares are already sufficiently dispersed to satisfy Stock Exchange marketability requirements, the company can be listed with no new shares being issued. In a takeover, the bidding company acquires the target company's shares, either for cash or by issuing target company shareholders with new equity in the bidding company. A reverse takeover occurs if the bidding company needs to increase its existing share capital by more than 100 per cent in order to acquire the target company. Table 8.1 shows that all of these methods were used, sometimes in combination, by football clubs floating between 1995 and 1997 (Morrow, 1999).

It is clear that the £50.4 million raised by the flotation of Newcastle United in April 1997 was quite exceptional in terms of its magnitude. Timed just as the inevitable market correction was beginning to take effect, the Newcastle flotation appears to have maximised to the full the benefit to the club of football's short-lived stock market boom.[3] But it is important not to exaggerate the extent to which Stock Exchange flotations have changed the ownership and financial structure of English

---

[2] Companies seeking acceptance onto the Official List must be able to produce audited accounts for the previous three years, must satisfy a minimum capitalisation requirement and must make some shares available to the general public. None of these criteria applies to companies joining AIM. The absence of the need to demonstrate a historical record of profitability is in contrast to the rules of several European exchanges. This fact has encouraged some leading European clubs to consider the possibility of acquiring a listing in London (Morrow, 1999).

[3] The timing was also fortuitous with regard to Newcastle United's on-field performance. Newcastle finished 2nd to Manchester United in the Premier League in both the 1996 and 1997 seasons, and Newcastle was seen widely as one of the two or three leading English teams. Finishes in 13th position in both the 1998 and 1999 seasons, however, rather belied this impression. By December 1999, Newcastle shares were trading at just over 50 per cent of their April 1997 opening price.

professional football as a whole. According to Morrow (1999), more than 40 per cent of the equity of only three quoted clubs (Manchester United, Leeds United and Tottenham Hotspur) was in the hands of financial institutions by December 1997. In some cases, effective control of quoted clubs remains firmly in the hands of individuals who might have been easily recognisable as stereotypical club owners in an earlier era: Doug Ellis (Aston Villa) and Ken Bates (Chelsea) are both perhaps cases in point.[4]

Meanwhile, many privately owned clubs have also benefited from significant injections of equity or long-term lending in recent years. By the end of the 1998 season, for example, Sir Jack Walker had advanced £30.9 million to Blackburn Rovers; Sir Jack Hayward, £25.2 million to Wolverhampton Wanderers; and Mohamed Al-Fayed, £12.4 million to Fulham. After flotation, Chelsea raised another £73.2 million on the capital markets through a 'Eurobond' issue in 1998 (Deloitte and Touche, 1999). One major effect of flotation and the use of other sources of finance, however, has been a significant reduction in the reliance of the clubs concerned on bank borrowing. Deloitte and Touche (1998) estimate that £262 million of new equity finance raised by all league members during the 1997 season was partly offset by £132 million of debt repayment to banks. As a group, the floated clubs dominated both of these totals.

A statistical analysis of the determinants of short-term movements in football share prices is presented in section 8.2. At this stage, however, a few general observations can be made about the patterns indicated by the data in table 8.1. Clearly the share price boom of 1996, and the subsequent reaction that occurred during 1997 and the first half of 1998, have many of the hallmarks of a classic stock market 'bubble'. By the end of June 1998, all football shares were trading at prices lower than 18 months before (or at the time of flotation within the previous 18 months). The 5 per cent reduction in the price of Manchester United shares was modest, but all other club share prices were marked down by at least 25 per cent over this period, and in eight cases (Aston Villa, Bolton Wanderers, Leicester City, Leeds United, Queens Park Rangers, Sheffield United, Southampton, West Bromwich Albion) by more than 50 per cent. More cautious assessment of the potential for further growth in television revenues arising from developments such as pay-per-view was undoubtedly a major contributory factor.

Since mid-1998 share price performance has been more mixed, but

---

[4] Morrow (1999) suggests that, in some cases, the presence of a dominant chairman may act as a deterrent to the acquisition of shareholdings by institutional investors.

26	Stoke City	19,230	23.5	−0.182	0.412[a]	0.017[a]	−0.047	0.102
27	Portsmouth	17,499	33.0	−0.186	0.533[a]	0.013[b]	0.091	0.189
28	Bristol City	14,689	44.5	−0.188	0.571[a]	0.013[a]	−0.085	0.041
29	Brighton and Hove Albion	13,367	49.0	−0.209	0.533[a]	0.019[a]	0.056	0.024
30	Ipswich Town	17,028	26.7	−0.250	0.654[a]	0.028[a]	−0.295[a]	−0.072
31	Burnley	16,667	30.6	−0.259	0.723[a]	0.006	−0.205	0.043
32	Bolton Wandrs	17,063	30.1	−0.259	0.567[a]	0.025[a]	0.107	0.085
33	Preston North End	14,686	40.1	−0.272	0.627[a]	0.013[b]	−0.176	0.280[b]
34	Plymouth Argyle	12,500	47.4	−0.275	0.605[a]	0.021[b]	−0.086	0.064
35	Fulham	14,895	37.5	−0.278	0.581[a]	0.019[a]	−0.211[b]	0.130[c]
36	Blackburn Rovers	16,068	27.2	−0.281	0.698[a]	0.022[a]	0.275[c]	0.187
37	Queens Park Rangers	14,240	32.8	−0.298	0.600[a]	0.027[a]	−0.079	0.046
38	Swindon Town	10,656	53.8	−0.307	0.501[a]	0.020[a]	−0.120[c]	0.134[c]
39	Watford	11,015	49.7	−0.312	0.738[a]	0.018[a]	−0.060	0.152
40	Huddersfield Town	13,108	38.7	−0.326	0.017	0.025[a]	0.077	0.217[a]
41	Millwall	11,495	47.8	−0.327	0.565[a]	0.009[b]	−0.174[a]	0.016
42	Cardiff City	14,454	41.6	−0.329	0.604[a]	0.028[a]	−0.613[b]	0.043
43	Charlton Athletic	14,689	30.3	−0.331	0.543[a]	0.028[a]	−0.156[a]	−0.030
44	Hull City	12,549	46.5	−0.344	0.697[a]	0.010	0.060	−0.023
45	Bristol Rovers	11,044	48.0	−0.352	0.859[a]	0.016	−0.449	0.744[b]
46	Brentford	9,897	57.4	−0.353	0.503[a]	0.015[a]	−0.058	−0.035
47	Blackpool	13,613	34.5	−0.356	0.413[a]	0.022[a]	0.032	−0.108[c]
48	Notts County	11,507	47.6	−0.364	0.741[a]	0.007	−0.242	0.385[c]
49	Luton Town	12,382	32.0	−0.365	0.458[a]	0.016[a]	−0.071[b]	0.013
50	Oldham Athletic	9,574	50.8	−0.391	0.512[a]	0.011[b]	−0.218[c]	0.188[c]
51	Swansea City	10,212	52.2	−0.400	0.676[a]	0.025[a]	−0.188	0.199
52	Bradford City	7,475	64.1	−0.406	0.257	0.029[a]	−0.068	0.060
53	Peterborough United	6,215	66.1	−0.413	0.315[c]	0.018[a]	0.054	0.054
54	Bournemouth	7,848	59.9	−0.421	0.528[a]	0.012[b]	−0.053	0.311[a]
55	Reading	8,200	57.6	−0.421	0.437[a]	0.020[a]	0.058	−0.012
56	Barnsley	9,560	49.2	−0.424	0.585[a]	0.010	0.272	0.366[b]

Table 7.2. (cont.)

Rank	Team	Average attendance (1)	Average position (2)	$\hat{\alpha}_i$ (3)	$\hat{\beta}_{1i}$ (4)	$\hat{\delta}_{1i}$ (5)	$\hat{\delta}_{2i}$ (6)	$\hat{\delta}_{3i}$ (7)
57	Grimsby Town	8,881	50.6	−0.434	0.569[a]	0.011[a]	0.017	0.175[b]
58	Northampton Town	6,969	69.8	−0.437	0.455[a]	0.015[b]	−0.094	−0.011
59	Oxford United	7,521	45.3	−0.444	0.612[a]	0.015[a]	0.017	0.103
60	Southend United	7,187	61.1	−0.449	0.498[a]	0.006	−0.181[a]	0.145[c]
61	Port Vale	7,926	59.7	−0.453	0.517[a]	0.022[a]	0.113	−0.070
62	Leyton Orient	8,400	53.5	−0.460	0.533[a]	0.013[a]	−0.121	0.086
63	Gillingham	6,298	67.1	−0.472	0.568[a]	0.011[c]	0.024	0.109
64	Walsall	6,975	63.3	−0.473	0.497[a]	0.011[a]	−0.169[b]	0.055
65	Bradford Park Avenue	8,851	69.9	−0.476	0.206	0.019[a]	0.048	0.000[c]
66	Rotherham United	8,414	49.6	−0.495	0.407[c]	0.023[a]	−0.162	−0.047
67	Lincoln City	6,770	65.5	−0.501	0.447[a]	0.013[a]	0.072	0.134[c]
68	Wrexham	6,572	65.5	−0.505	0.658[a]	0.015	−0.210[c]	0.144
69	Chesterfield	6,658	63.1	−0.507	0.400[a]	0.013[a]	−0.105	0.179[c]
70	Carlisle United	7,211	58.5	−0.507	0.463[a]	0.018[a]	0.086	0.029
71	Exeter City	5,391	75.1	−0.517	0.285[c]	0.007[c]	−0.083	0.071
72	Doncaster Rovers	7,165	68.2	−0.525	0.464[a]	0.024[a]	0.198	0.233
73	Mansfield Town	6,194	66.7	−0.531	0.449[a]	0.013[b]	−0.061	0.124
74	Tranmere Rovers	6,188	64.4	−0.535	0.783[a]	0.009	−0.115	0.277
75	Stockport County	5,580	72.4	−0.540	0.367[a]	0.012[b]	−0.188[a]	0.122
76	Wimbledon	6,608	31.7	−0.553	0.830[a]	0.075	−0.994	0.918
77	Hereford United	3,832	77.5	−0.553	0.328[a]	0.022[a]	0.196[a]	0.046
78	Bury	7,276	54.9	−0.555	0.582[a]	0.021[a]	0.145[b]	0.027
79	York City	5,340	70.2	−0.566	0.308[b]	0.014[a]	−0.025	0.154[b]
80	Aldershot	4,638	77.8	−0.580	0.711[a]	0.008	−0.061	0.259[c]
81	Colchester United	4,917	70.6	−0.588	0.463[a]	−0.006	−0.084	0.131

82	Scunthorpe United	5,024	68.9	−0.589	0.328[b]	0.015[a]	0.114[c]	0.013
83	Cambridge United	4,190	61.2	−0.590	0.228	0.014[a]	−0.047	0.041
84	Shrewsbury Town	5,599	57.4	−0.599	0.610[a]	0.014[a]	0.050	−0.009
85	Newport County	5,435	73.0	−0.607	0.638[a]	0.004	−0.173	0.238
86	Wigan Athletic	3,713	65.5	−0.614	0.753[a]	−0.028	−0.849	0.530
87	Torquay United	4,691	73.2	−0.617	0.604[a]	0.022[a]	−0.093	0.100
88	Chester City	4,481	74.3	−0.621	0.651[a]	−0.002	−0.173	0.331[b]
89	Crewe Alexandra	4,292	76.5	−0.628	0.611[a]	0.006	−0.090	0.132
90	Hartlepool United	4,283	79.5	−0.638	0.379[b]	0.019[c]	0.027	0.111
91	Darlington	4,022	80.0	−0.655	0.169	0.019[a]	−0.059	0.060
92	Halifax Town	4,010	76.9	−0.714	0.346[b]	0.011[a]	0.004	0.030
93	Barrow	5,099	76.1	−0.729	0.184	0.007	−0.114[b]	0.099
94	Rochdale	3,665	77.5	−0.742	0.444[a]	0.010	0.026	0.095
95	Southport	4,169	76.3	−0.801	0.164	0.001	0.115	0.212[a]
96	Workington Town	3,970	77.7	−0.845	0.564[b]	0.004	0.829[a]	−0.264

Notes:

[a] = significantly different from zero, two-tail test, 1% level;

[b] = 5% level;

[c] = 10% level.

Statistically significant $\hat{\alpha}_i$s are not indicated.

between Everton and Liverpool is instructive in illustrating how the alpha coefficient works. Although Liverpool's average post-war attendance (40,289) is higher than Everton's (36,082), the difference is more than explained by the fact that Liverpool's average finishing position of 7.8 is about three places higher than Everton's of 10.9 (and by the fact that up to 1997, Liverpool had won 14 post-war league championships to Everton's four). After adjusting for the differences in the league position variable (and in all other variables) Everton (ranked 4th) turn out to have a higher alpha coefficient and therefore a higher base attendance than Liverpool (ranked 6th). Similarly, the high placings of clubs like Newcastle United (5th), Manchester City (7th) and Sunderland (9th) reflect the high levels of support which these clubs have maintained, despite long barren periods when their supporters have been starved of success.

Towards the top of the list, it is noticeable that all of the 20 highest-ranked clubs are from cities with large populations (above 250,000 in the 1981 Census). Only two of the top 20 (West Ham United at 13th and Coventry City at 20th) entered the league after the First World War (in both cases in the 1920 season). The other 18 clubs were all pre-1914 entrants, and four of the top 20 (Everton, Aston Villa, Wolverhampton Wanderers and West Bromwich Albion) were among the league's 12 founder members in 1888. The highest-ranked clubs among the 22 original members of Division 3 (South) in the 1921 season are Norwich City (21st) and Crystal Palace (22nd), while Wrexham (68th) are the highest-placed of the 20 original Division 3 (North) clubs admitted in the 1922 season.

Of the nine clubs included in the analysis that were admitted to the league for the first time after the Second World War, seven (including the most spectacularly successful post-war entrant, Wimbledon) can be found in the bottom 21 places, with only Peterborough United (53rd) and Oxford United (59th) achieving mid-table rankings. Of the seven clubs which had left the league (and were not re-admitted) by the end of the 1997 season, three (Workington, Southport and Barrow) can be found in the bottom four places, and only Bradford Park Avenue (65th) are placed outside the bottom 20. The alpha coefficients therefore seem to suggest that while clubs with low base attendances (unsurprisingly) find it difficult to survive, their replacements also experience difficulty in building up their attendances after entering the league. Early (pre-1914) entry to the league, on the other hand, together with a big-city location, appears to have conferred significant first-mover advantages, allowing the clubs concerned to achieve high base levels of attendance. Further statistical investigation of these features of the data is reported below.

The estimates of the coefficients β_1 to β_{10} reported in (7.3) all have the expected signs. All are significantly different from zero at the 5 per cent level except the estimate of β_5 (the coefficient on $g_{i,t}$, goals scored), which is insignificant at any conventional significance level. The estimates of β_1 (the short-term loyalty coefficient on $a_{i,t-1}$, lagged attendance) and β_2 and β_3 (the coefficients on $l_{i,t}$ and $l_{i,t-1}$, currrent and lagged league position) have particularly high t-statistics, indicating that these variables are the strongest determinants of attendance according to the estimated model. The estimate of β_4 (the coefficient on $p_{i,t}$, admission price), while also significant at the 1 per cent level, nevertheless has a much smaller t-statistic.

In the steady-state equation (7.4), the estimates of δ_1 (the steady-state league position coefficient) and δ_2 (the steady-state price coefficient) are significantly different from zero at the 1 per cent level, and the estimate of δ_3 (the steady-state goals scored coefficient) is significantly different from zero at the 5 per cent level. Using data for the 1997 season for Premier League clubs, (7.4) implies that an improvement of one place in a club's final league position would add 1.68 per cent to its average attendance. A £1 increase in admission price would lead to a loss of attendance of 0.81 per cent, implying a price elasticity of -0.114 for a club charging the divisional average admission price. These estimates are similar to those for the period 1926–92 reported in Dobson and Goddard (1995).

It is also possible to estimate a set of club-specific attendance equations, in which the slope coefficients $(\beta_1 - \beta_{10})$ are allowed to vary between clubs in the same way as the intercept coefficient (α_i) in (7.1) and (7.3).[7] The model specification, shown below as equation (7.5), is essentially the same as (7.1), except that i-subscripts are attached to each slope coefficient to indicate that these coefficients are now specific to each club. Following the same procedures as before, it is also possible to obtain the steady-state equivalent, (7.6).

$$a_{i,t} = \alpha_i + \beta_{1i} a_{i,t-1} + \beta_{2i} l_{i,t} + \beta_{3i} l_{i,t-1} + \beta_{4i} p_{i,t} + \beta_{5i} g_{i,t} + \beta_{6i} D_{1,i,t}$$

$$+ \beta_{7i} D_{2,i,t} + \beta_{8i} D_{3,i,t} + \beta_{9i} pr_{i,t-1} + \beta_{10i} re_{i,t-1} + u_{i,t} \qquad (7.5)$$

$$a_i^s = \gamma_i + \delta_{1i} l_i^s + \delta_{2i} p_i^s + \delta_{3i} g_i^s \qquad (7.6)$$

The estimation results are summarised in columns (4)–(7) of table 7.2, which report for each club the estimates of the coefficients β_{1i} (the short-term loyalty coefficient), δ_{1i} (the steady-state league position coefficient),

---

[7] Downward and Dawson (1999) have pointed out that the estimates of the coefficient on the lagged dependent variable $a_{i,t-1}$ in the pooled model ((7.3)) are downward biased and inconsistent, owing to the presence in the model of the individual club fixed effects or alpha coefficients. This problem disappears in the club-specific estimations. The fact that the estimated β_1 (equal to 0.5125) in (7.3) is smaller than 61 of the 96 estimated β_{1i}s in table 7.2 reflects the bias in the pooled model.

δ_{2i} (the steady-state price coefficient) and δ_{3i} (the steady-state goals scored coefficient).[8] There is considerable variation between clubs in the estimates of these coefficients, as would be expected given the relatively small number of time-series observations for each club. Nevertheless, the general pattern is the same as before. The estimates of β_{1i} are signed as expected in all 96 cases, and are significantly different from zero at the 5 per cent level on a two-tail test in 86 cases. The estimates of δ_{1i} are signed as expected in 89 out of 96 cases, and significant in 58 of these cases. Price and goals scored are found to exert a less powerful effect on attendance, as before. The estimates of δ_{2i} and δ_{3i} are signed as expected in 59 and 80 cases, respectively. The numbers of these coefficients that are significant at the 5 per cent level are 13 and 10, respectively.

The results indicate, unsurprisingly, that variations in league position are by far the strongest determinant of variations in attendance. Figure 7.1 shows plots of (unadjusted) average league attendances and league position (measured, as above, on a scale of 92 to 1) for six selected clubs: Arsenal, Blackpool, Bolton Wanderers, Derby County, Ipswich Town and Sheffield United. In most of these cases, there is obvious similarity between the shapes of the two plots. Arsenal, however, whose $\hat{\delta}_{1i}$ in table 7.2 is not statistically significant, are an exception. Relative to other clubs, there is little variation in Arsenal's performance, as they remained in the top division throughout the period. Variations in Arsenal's attendance do not appear to be closely correlated with movements in their position within the top division. Blackpool and Ipswich Town are included in figure 7.1 as representatives of the downwardly mobile northern and upwardly mobile southern contingents, respectively (see chapter 2). For Derby County, one of six clubs whose $\hat{\delta}_{1i}$ in table 7.2 is negative (though not significant), the attendance and performance plots appear to correspond in the early 1970s, when the team surged from relative obscurity to win the Division 1 title twice in four seasons. There seems to be little similarity elsewhere, however.

Bolton Wanderers ($\hat{\delta}_{1i}=0.25$) and Sheffield United ($\hat{\delta}_{1i}=0.15$) form an interesting contrast. Changes in Bolton's performance are tracked closely throughout by changes in their attendance. Several seasons spent near the foot of Division 3 followed by one season in Division 4 in 1988 saw average attendances fall to around 20 per cent of their immediate post-war

---

[8] With a maximum of 50 time series observations per club, diagnostic tests show little evidence of serial correlation in the residuals in the club-level estimations. The estimations of (7.5) are therefore carried out using ordinary least squares (OLS), without incorporating an autoregressive error structure. There is, however, some evidence of heteroscedasticity, so the standard errors and significance tests are again based on White's (1980) adjustment.

levels. For Sheffield United, the link between performance and attendance is also apparent, but less pronounced. When the club dropped into Division 4 in the 1982 season, average attendances still held up to around 35 per cent of their immediate post-war levels.

Explaining base attendances, and the loyalty, league position, price and goals scored coefficients

The second stage of the empirical analysis investigates whether there are observable characteristics of the clubs or their home towns that are important in determining the estimated values of α_i (the alpha coefficients), β_{1i} (the short-term loyalty coefficients), δ_{1i} (the steady-state league position coefficients), δ_{2i} (the steady-state price coefficients) and δ_{3i} (the steady-state goals scored coefficients) reported in table 7.2. At the second stage, estimations are carried out of five cross-sectional regressions, in which the estimated coefficients listed above are used as dependent variables, to be explained by a set of variables which measure club or home town characteristics. The full list of explanatory variables used in the second-stage regressions is as follows:

H_i = natural logarithm of the population of the local authority district in which club i is located, recorded in the 1981 Census of Population

X_i = the natural logarithm of the number of years since club i first entered the league, measured at the end of the observation period in 1997

C_i = the number of other clubs that were members of the league for at least 18 seasons during the post-Second World War period, located within a 30 mile radius of club i's stadium

F_i = the percentage of employed residents working in agriculture in club i's local authority district, 1981 Census of Population

I_i = the percentage of employed residents working in energy and water, manufacturing and construction in club i's local authority district, 1981 Census of Population

U_i = Males aged 16–64 out of employment as a percentage of those classed as economically active in club i's local authority district, 1981 Census of Population.

Where several clubs are located in the same town, all have the same H_i, F_i, I_i and U_i based on the town's census data. Inevitably, the use of data from

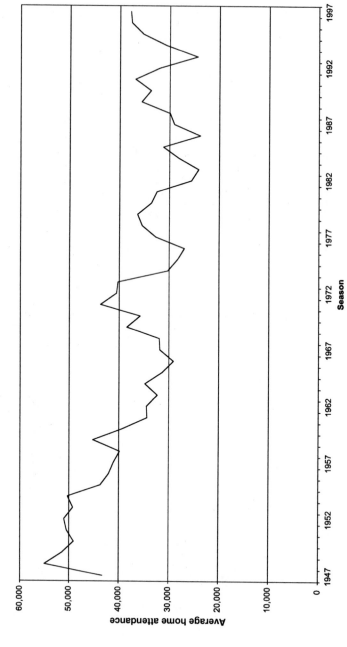

Figure 7.1   Trends in league attendance and performance, selected English clubs
Sources: Butler (1987), Smailes (1992), Tabner (1992), Rothmans.

Arsenal - performance

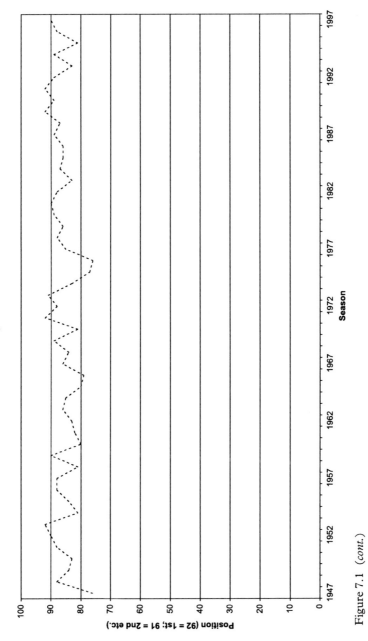

Figure 7.1 *(cont.)*

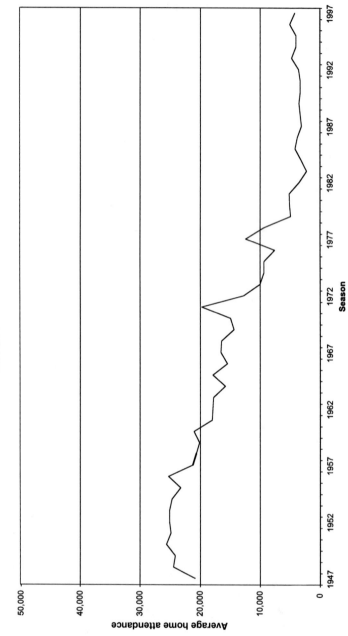

Blackpool - attendance

Average home attendance

Season

Figure 7.1 (*cont*)

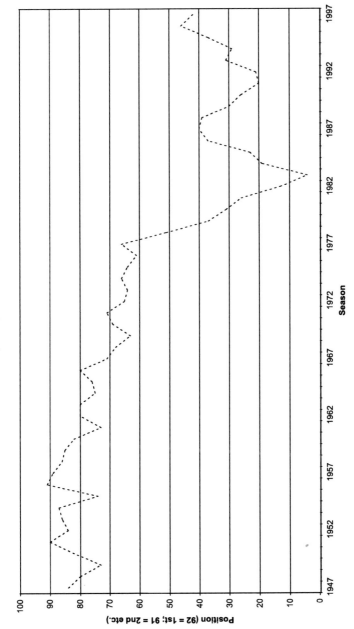

Figure 7.1 (*cont.*)

Bolton Wanderers - attendance

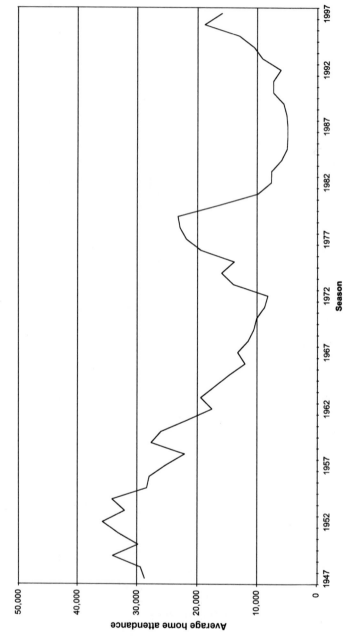

Figure 7.1 (*cont*)

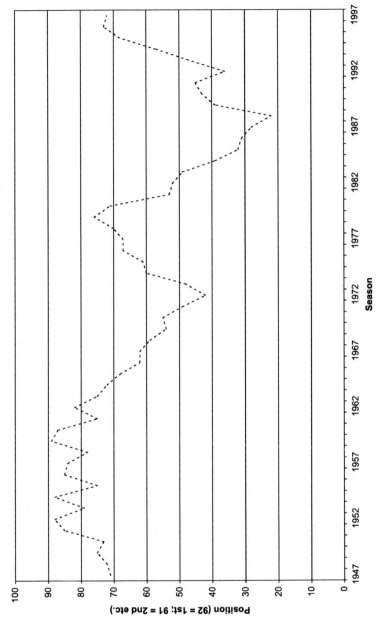

Figure 7.1 (*cont.*)

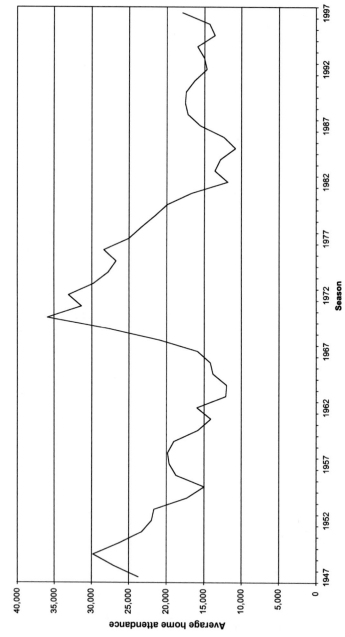

Derby County - attendance

Figure 7.1 *(cont)*

Derby County - performance

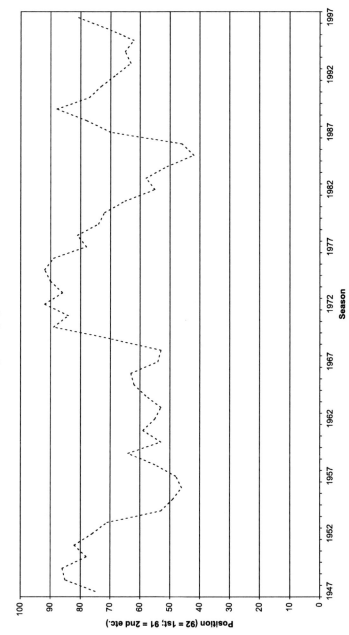

Figure 7.1 *(cont.)*

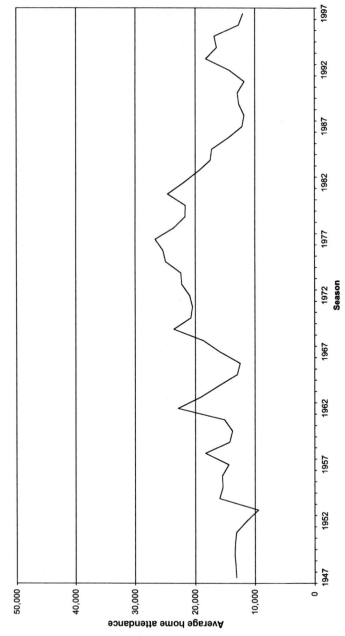

Ipswich Town - attendance

Average home attendance

Season

Figure 7.1 *(cont)*

still heavily dependent on fluctuating sentiment concerning the future of football's relationship with the media, and with television in particular. When the BSkyB bid for Manchester United was announced in September 1998, the price of shares in the latter immediately increased by 25 per cent. There was a corresponding downward adjustment when the bid was eventually blocked by the MMC in April 1999 (see chapter 2). The failure of the OFT's action through the RPC to outlaw the collective negotiaton (by the Premier League on behalf of its member clubs) of television contracts may also have dampened some of the long-term optimism, though there was little discernible share price reaction when the RPC's decision was announced in July 1999. Meanwhile, the acquisition by several media groups of small stakes (of up to 10 per cent) in a number of leading clubs helped keep the market in football shares reasonably buoyant during the course of 1999 (see chapters 2 and 9). A return to the boom conditions of 1996, however, seems unlikely for the foreseeable future.

8.2 Football team performance and share price movements: an event study

Event study methodology provides a simple but widely used and accepted means of measuring the impact of a specific event on the value of a firm. Assuming that information about the event is impounded rapidly into the company's share price, the relevant effect can be deduced from movements in the share price immediately after the event occurs. It is of course likely that movements in the share price are to some extent correlated with general fluctuations in the stock market. If so, event study methodology provides a means of controlling for the latter, so as to separate the price change attributable to the event itself from the price change that probably would have occurred anyway as a result of market movements that took place on the same day.

An investigation of the effects on share prices of stock splits by Dolley (1933) was possibly the first event study. Development of the econometric methodology in use today is usually credited to Ball and Brown (1968), who studied the information content of company earnings announcements, and Fama et al. (1969) who also studied the effect of stock splits. Since the late 1960s event studies have been used widely to analyse the effects on share prices or company valuations of events such as mergers and acquisitions, earnings announcements, bankruptcies of competitors and macroeconomic shocks. Practical applications include assessment of the impact on firms of changes in the regulatory environment, and assessment of damages in legal liability cases

(Campbell, Lo and MacKinlay, 1997). Various technical aspects of event study methodology have been reviewed by MacKinlay (1997) and Binder (1998).

For football, Morrow (1999) reports an informal analysis of the relationship between match results and share price movements for two clubs (Manchester United and Sunderland) during the latter stages of the 1997 season. In both cases, there appears to be an association between the results of matches and the movement in the share price on the next trading day. Furthermore, the association appears to have strengthened markedly towards the end of the 1997 season, as the importance of each individual match for championship (Manchester United) or relegation (Sunderland) outcomes increased. The event study reported below provides a more comprehensive and formal statistical analysis of these and other relationships, for the quoted football clubs' sector as a whole.

The data set comprises the daily closing prices of the shares of 13 football clubs listed on the LSE Official List or AIM (see section 8.1 and table 8.1), during the two-year estimation period from Monday 28 July 1997 to Friday 30 July 1999 (inclusive). The 13 clubs are Tottenham Hotspur, Manchester United, Chelsea, Leeds United, Queens Park Rangers, Sunderland, Sheffield United, Birmingham City, Charlton Athletic, Bolton Wanderers, Newcastle United, Southampton and Aston Villa. The estimation period is chosen because it is one of relative price stability (at least in comparison with the boom–bust conditions of 1996 and early 1997) and because the majority of clubs that have floated so far had already done so before mid-1997. Nottingham Forest and Leicester City, both of which floated in October 1997, are excluded because two years' complete data up to July 1999 were not available. Preston North End and West Bromwich Albion are also excluded, because it was found that there was insufficient daily variation in the share prices of these two clubs.[5]

The dependent variable in the empirical model is the daily logarithmic return in each club's share price, denoted $r_{i,t} = \log_e(P_{i,t}) - \log_e(P_{i,t-1})$, where $P_{i,t}$ is club i's share price on trading day t. Among the independent variables, movements in the FTSE-100 share index are used to proxy for

---

[5] If a substantial proportion of shares remain more or less permanently in the hands of a small number of shareholders, then a market in the shares cannot really be said to exist, and the econometric techniques employed in this section do not provide an appropriate means of modelling whatever share price movements do take place. In fact, the share price data of several of the clubs included in the analysis also bear some of the hallmarks of thin trading, though to a lesser extent than in the case of Preston North End and West Bromwich Albion. The difficulties which this creates are acknowledged, but otherwise disregarded, in the empirical analysis that follows.

general market movements, which are expected to influence football share prices to some extent. The daily logarithmic return on the FTSE-100 index is denoted $r_{m,t} = \log_e(P_{m,t}) - \log_e(P_{m,t-1})$, where $P_{m,t}$ is the index value on day t. The other independent variables are event dummy variables, defined as follows.

League match results

Following earlier definitions, the win ratio for the league match between home team i and away team j is $W_{i,j} = 1$ if team i won, 0.5 if team i drew and 0 if team i lost. Using the match results forecasting model's computed probabilities for the same match (see section 3.3 and (3.12)), it is also possible to define the expected win ratio, $\hat{W}_{i,j} = p_{i,j}^H + 0.5 p_{i,j}^D$. The actual and expected win ratios can be used to define two alternative league match result event dummies:

$$X_{i,t} = \quad W_{i,j} - 0.5 \text{ if team } i \text{ played team } j \text{ at home between trading day } t-1 \text{ and trading day } t$$

$$0.5 - W_{j,i} \text{ if team } i \text{ played team } j \text{ away between trading day } t-1 \text{ and trading day } t$$

$$0 \text{ if team } i \text{ did not play a match between trading day } t-1 \text{ and trading day } t.$$

$$Y_{i,t} = \quad W_{i,j} - \hat{W}_{i,j} \text{ if team } i \text{ played team } j \text{ at home between trading day } t-1 \text{ and trading day } t$$

$$\hat{W}_{j,i} - W_{j,i} \text{ if team } i \text{ played team } j \text{ away between trading day } t-1 \text{ and trading day } t$$

$$0 \text{ if team } i \text{ did not play a match between trading day } t-1 \text{ and trading day } t.$$

$X_{i,t}$ produces a score of $+0.5$, 0 and -0.5 for wins, draws and losses, respectively, and makes no allowance for prior expectations concerning the match result. In contrast, $Y_{i,t}$ takes account of prior expectations. For a completely unexpected win (for which the expected win ratio is zero) $Y_{i,t}$ takes a value of 1. For a fully expected win (for which the expected win ratio is one) $Y_{i,t}$ takes a value of 0. Similarly, $Y_{i,t}$ takes values of 0 and -1 for defeats that were completely expected and completely unexpected, respectively. The value of $Y_{i,t}$ between $+1$ and -1 is therefore a measure of *unanticipated* performance, where $Y_{i,t} > 0$ indicates good news (better than expected performance), and $Y_{i,t} < 0$ indicates bad news (worse than expected performance).

Promotion and relegation

It is expected that events such as promotion and relegation, or (equally important) narrowly missing promotion and avoiding relegation, will affect investors' assessment of the club's future profitability, to a far greater extent than would normally be expected from the result of the individual match that finally determines the team's fate. Finance theory suggests that in the days leading up to the decisive match, the share price should be a probability-weighted average of the prices that would apply if the team ends up either in the higher or in the lower division. When the final outcome is known, the price should then adjust, up or down, to one of these two prices as appropriate. For quoted clubs whose fate rested on the outcome of the final match of the regular league season or on the outcome of play-off matches, the following event dummy variables are defined:

> $U_{i,k,t}$ = 1 on trading day t if team i gained promotion or avoided relegation as a result of a match played between trading days $t-k$ and $t-k+1$, for $k = 1 \ldots 5$, and 0 elsewhere
>
> $D_{i,k,t}$ = 1 on trading day t if team i was relegated or failed to win promotion as a result of a match played between trading days $t-k$ and $t-k+1$, for $k = 1 \ldots 5$, and 0 elsewhere.

Of the quoted clubs included in the estimations, the following were involved in promotion and relegation issues at the end of the 1998 and 1999 seasons:

> *Queens Park Rangers*: avoided relegation from Division One, 1999
>
> *Sunderland*[6]: missed promotion from Division One, 1998
>
> *Sheffield United*: missed promotion from Division One, 1998
>
> *Birmingham City*: missed promotion from Division One, 1998
>
> *Charlton Athletic*: promoted from Division One, 1998 and relegated from the Premier League, 1999
>
> *Bolton Wanderers*: relegated from the Premier League, 1998 and missed promotion from Division One, 1999

---

[6] Sunderland's eventual promotion from Division One was confirmed several matches before the end of the following (1999) season, and had been recognised as a forgone conclusion for weeks or months in advance. Little or no share price reaction is discernible on the trading days immediately after promotion was confirmed.

Southampton: avoided relegation from the Premier League, 1999.

For these and the other events described below, dummy variables are included for up to five days after each event, to allow for the possibility that it takes several days for reappraisal of a club's future profit potential to be completed.

FA Cup and European elimination

In principle, matches played in the FA Cup or in European competition could be dealt with in the same way as league matches in the estimations. In practice, however, an equivalent method of calculating match result probabilities to assess the expected outcomes of these matches is not available. The approach adopted is therefore simpler, but also realistic in that it recognises that *elimination* from one of these tournaments is the event most likely to cause a discernible share price reaction.[7] Event dummies are included to capture the share price reaction on each of the five trading days immediately following elimination from the FA Cup or from any of the European tournaments, as follows:

$F_{i,k,t} = 1$ on trading day t if team i was eliminated from the FA Cup between trading days $t - k$ and $t - k + 1$, for $k = 1 \ldots 5$, and 0 elsewhere

$E_{i,k,t} = 1$ on trading day t if team i was eliminated from European competition between trading days $t - k$ and $t - k + 1$, for $k = 1 \ldots 5$, and 0 elsewhere.

All quoted clubs participated in the FA Cup in the 1998 and 1999 seasons. Manchester United won the FA Cup in the 1999 season. Manchester United (1998 season), Chelsea (1999), Leeds United (1999), Newcastle United (1998 and 1999) and Aston Villa (1998) were all eliminated from European tournaments during the 1998 and 1999 seasons, while Chelsea (1998 Cup-Winners' Cup) and Manchester United (1999 European Cup) both won European tournaments. While cup elimination does appear to cause a discernible share price reaction

---

[7] Winning a cup tie merely guarantees that the team will play another tie in the same tournament, with the prospect of further ties (and more revenue), but only for as long as the team avoids defeat. Winning either the FA Cup or a European tournament outright guarantees lucrative admission to one of the next season's European tournaments. Losing a cup tie, on the other hand, guarantees immediately that no further revenue will be earned from that season's cup competition, and closes off a possible route into Europe for the following season.

(see below), the victories achieved by Chelsea and Manchester United appear to have had little effect, perhaps because at the time, entry into the following season's European competitions had already been secured by both teams.

The BSkyB bid for Manchester United

As noted in chapter 2, BSkyB's £623 million takeover bid for Manchester United, which valued the company around 25 per cent higher than the market value implied by its share price at the time, naturally had an immediate effect on Manchester United's share price, and on the prices of the shares of other quoted clubs. The initial bid was announced on 9 September 1998, and the Manchester United board recommended acceptance of BSkyB's improved offer two days later. Stories that the MMC were recommending prevention of the takeover appeared in the press on 17 March 1999. Trade Secretary Stephen Byers announced his formal acceptance of the MMC's recommendations on 4 April 1999. The relevant event dummies are as follows:

$B_{1,k,t}$ = 1 on the $k-1$th trading day after 9 September 1998 for
$k = 1 \ldots 5$, and 0 elsewhere

$B_{2,k,t}$ = 1 on the $k-1$th trading day after 17 March 1999 for
$k = 1 \ldots 5$, and 0 elsewhere

$B_{3,k,t}$ = 1 on the $k-1$th trading day after 4 April 1999 for
$k = 1 \ldots 5$, and 0 elsewhere.

Two sets of estimation results are reported below. In the first set, the data for all 13 clubs is pooled, producing a single set of estimated coefficients common to all clubs. In the second set, separate estimations are carried out for each club individually. Pooling the data confers benefits of large numbers, allowing more precise estimates of the coefficients to be obtained. But pooling also entails the imposition of an assumption, which may or may not be justified. The assumption is that the coefficient on each dummy variable is the same for all clubs. This assumption is removed in the second set of club-specific estimations.

Table 8.2 reports the results of the pooled estimation of the model for the determinants of share price returns. This model is estimated using ordinary least squares (OLS). All estimated coefficients are common to all clubs, with the exception of those on the event dummies $B_{j,k,t}$. It seems likely that the effect of news about the BSkyB takeover bid on Manchester United's share price would differ from its effect on other clubs' share prices. For this reason, in the estimations reported in table 8.2, one set of

Table 8.2. *Estimation results for determinants of share price returns, pooled model*

Market returns and league match results		FA Cup/Europe		BSkyB bid: Man Utd		BSkyB bid: other clubs	
Constant	-0.11^a (0.03)	$F_{i,1,t}$	-1.62^a (0.50)	$B_{1,1,t}$	25.57^a (2.51)	$B_{1,1,t}$	5.33^a (0.73)
$r_{m,t}$	0.20^a (0.03)	$F_{i,2,t}$	-0.91^c (0.50)	$B_{1,2,t}$	-3.08 (2.51)	$B_{1,2,t}$	1.28^c (0.73)
$Y_{i,t}$	1.96^a (0.20)	$F_{i,3,t}$	0.21 (0.50)	$B_{1,3,t}$	7.13^a (2.51)	$B_{1,3,t}$	2.46^a (0.73)
Promotion/relegation		$F_{i,4,t}$	0.40 (0.51)	$B_{1,4,t}$	3.75 (2.51)	$B_{1,4,t}$	3.72^a (0.73)
$U_{i,1,t}$	22.48^a (1.45)	$F_{i,5,t}$	0.18 (0.51)	$B_{1,5,t}$	-0.04 (2.51)	$B_{1,5,t}$	7.19^a (0.73)
$U_{i,2,t}$	-2.20 (1.45)	$E_{i,1,t}$	-1.97^b (0.95)	$B_{2,1,t}$	-8.85^a (2.51)	$B_{2,1,t}$	-2.45^a (0.73)
$U_{i,3,t}$	-1.27 (1.45)	$E_{i,2,t}$	-3.19^a (0.95)	$B_{2,2,t}$	0.65 (2.51)	$B_{2,2,t}$	0.90 (0.73)
$U_{i,4,t}$	-1.18 (1.45)	$E_{i,3,t}$	-1.43 (0.95)	$B_{2,3,t}$	1.31 (2.51)	$B_{2,3,t}$	-0.11 (0.73)
$U_{i,5,t}$	-2.91 (1.45)	$E_{i,4,t}$	0.31 (0.95)	$B_{2,4,t}$	-0.13 (2.51)	$B_{2,4,t}$	0.70 (0.73)
$D_{i,1,t}$	-15.59^a (0.95)	$E_{i,5,t}$	0.17 (0.95)	$B_{2,5,t}$	0.41 (2.51)	$B_{2,5,t}$	0.05 (0.73)
$D_{i,2,t}$	2.59^a (0.95)			$B_{3,1,t}$	-16.10^a (2.51)	$B_{3,1,t}$	-3.87^a (0.73)
$D_{i,3,t}$	-0.11 (0.95)			$B_{3,2,t}$	-0.06 (2.51)	$B_{3,2,t}$	-0.19 (0.73)
$D_{i,4,t}$	-2.49^a (0.95)			$B_{3,3,t}$	0.43 (2.51)	$B_{3,3,t}$	-0.16 (0.73)
$D_{i,5,t}$	-0.62^c (0.95)			$B_{3,4,t}$	2.82 (2.51)	$B_{3,4,t}$	-1.41^c (0.73)
obs. = 6,604				$B_{3,5,t}$	6.03^b (2.51)	$B_{3,5,t}$	0.50 (0.73)
s.e. of regression = 2.51							
$R^2 = 0.15$							

Notes:
[a] = significantly different from zero, two-tail test, 1% level;
[b] = 5% level;
[c] = 10% level.
Standard errors of estimated coefficients are shown in parentheses.
Dependent variable is $r_{i,t}$ (daily return on club share prices).

coefficients on $B_{j,k,t}$ applies specifically to Manchester United, while a second set applies to all other clubs.

Tables 8.3 and 8.4 report separate estimations of the determinants of share price returns for each club individually. These equations are estimated using Zellner's (1962) Seemingly Unrelated Regressions (SUR) estimation method.[8] Although the results of the SUR estimation are split into two tables for presentational purposes, the contents of tables 8.3 and 8.4 in fact constitute a single estimation.

An issue to be addressed before commenting on the estimation results is the choice between $X_{i,t}$ and $Y_{i,t}$ as the most suitable league match results event dummy variable. Inclusion of $X_{i,t}$ is appropriate if the size of the share price reaction depends on the match result only; inclusion of $Y_{i,t}$ is more appropriate if the reaction depends on the unanticipated component of the result, as defined above. This issue is resolved by estimating three versions of the pooled model: M1, including $X_{i,t}$ only; M2, including both $X_{i,t}$ and $Z_{i,t} = X_{i,t} - Y_{i,t}$; and M3, including $Y_{i,t}$ only. A test for the significance of $Z_{i,t}$ in M2 assesses whether the inclusion of additional information about the anticipated match result adds to the explanatory power achieved by M1, which omits this information. The t-statistic of -7.05 implies that $Z_{i,t}$ is significant, so M2 is preferred to M1. A second test of the hypothesis that the coefficients on $X_{i,t}$ and $Z_{i,t}$ are equal but opposite in sign in M2 assesses whether it is justifiable to combine the information about the actual and anticipated match result into a single variable measuring the unanticipated component of the result, as in M3. The t-statistic of 1.18 is insignificant, so this procedure is justified and M3 is preferred to M2. Consequently, $Y_{i,t}$ is the league match results event dummy used in tables 8.2–8.4. When share prices react to league match results, the key determinant of the direction and size of the adjustment is the market's assessment of the result relative to what was expected; in other words, the unanticipated component of the result.

In the pooled model reported in table 8.2, the negative estimated constant term of -0.11 (alpha in the standard textbook treatment of finance theory) indicates that the general trend in football clubs' share prices between July 1997 and July 1999 was downward (see also table 8.1). In the individual models reported in tables 8.3 and 8.4, only Manchester United and Sunderland have positive alpha coefficients. Both companies

---

[8] SUR takes advantage of similarities in the structure of the error term across equations to provide more efficient estimates of the model's coefficients than would be available if each equation were estimated separately using OLS. The use of SUR to estimate a system of equations is advantageous if (as seems likely in the present case) there are regular or occasional shocks, other than those controlled for by the event dummies, which affect the dependent variable in all equations in a similar manner on the same day.

gained in value over the two-year period. In terms of its size, and the diversified nature and international scope of its business, it seems reasonable to consider Manchester United, whose share price does not behave in the same manner as those of other quoted clubs, as a special case. Sunderland's gains appear to reflect a period of sustained improvement on the field of play, as the club gradually constructed a team which, by the end of the 1999 season, had achieved and appeared capable of retaining Premier League status.

The estimated coefficient on $r_{m,t}$ of 0.20 (the textbook *beta*) in table 8.2 indicates a relatively weak link between general market movements and movements in the football sector. Other things being equal, a 1 per cent rise in the market index translates into an average rise of 0.2 per cent in football club share prices on the same day. Tables 8.3 and 8.4 suggest that there is considerable variation in this coefficient between clubs, though perhaps without very much discernible pattern.

In table 8.2, the pooled coefficient on $Y_{i,t}$ of 1.96, which is significant at the 1 per cent level, quantifies the link between the unanticipated component of league match results and the share price movement on the next trading day, as discussed above. If a quoted team wins a match it was expected to lose (with win/draw/lose probabilities of 0.1/0.3/0.6, say, producing an expected 'win ratio' of $\hat{W}_{i,j} = 0.25$) the model's expected share price movement is $1.96 \times (1 - 0.25)$, or just under $+1.5$ per cent. If the team wins a match it was expected to win (with probabilities of 0.6/0.3/0.1, producing $\hat{W}_{i,j} = 0.75$) the expected price movement is $1.96 \times (1 - 0.75)$, or around $+0.5$ per cent. It is interesting to note that in tables 8.3 and 8.4, Manchester United is the only club for which the coefficient on $Y_{i,t}$ is not statistically significant at the 5 per cent level. As before, this seems to indicate that Manchester United's fortunes as a business are no longer dependent on short-term fluctuations in the team's fortunes on the field of play, especially in regular domestic league competition.

Promotion or avoidance of relegation (captured by $U_{i,k,t}$) and relegation or failure to achieve promotion (captured by $D_{i,k,t}$), are both found to have a dramatic and immediate effect on the share prices of the clubs concerned in table 8.2. On average, the former produced an upward adjustment of around 22.5 per cent on the next trading day, and the latter caused a downward adjustment of around 15.6 per cent (with further smaller but statistically significant fluctuations over the next couple of trading days). Immediately before the final outcome is decided, the share price of a club involved in promotion or relegation issues should be a weighted average of the prices that would apply given either outcome (as discussed above). A next-day reaction of $+22.5$ per cent when promotion is confirmed therefore starts from a share price which already reflects

Table 8.3. *Estimation results for determinants of share price returns, individual models (1)*

	Aston Villa	Chelsea	Leeds Utd	Man Utd	Newcastle Utd	Tottenham
Market returns and league match results						
Constant	-0.08	-0.15[c]	-0.23[c]	0.01	-0.08	-0.07
$r_{m,t}$	0.06	0.27[a]	0.36[a]	0.11[b]	0.16[c]	0.13[b]
$Y_{i,t}$	1.02[b]	1.31[b]	2.01[a]	0.15	1.41[b]	1.13[a]
$F_{i,1,t}$	0.14	-3.23[a]	-3.30[c]	0.32	-4.48[a]	0.39
$F_{i,2,t}$	-1.11	-1.07	-0.16	-0.23	-0.43	-4.09[a]
$F_{i,3,t}$	0.26	0.73	-2.16	1.07	2.47	-0.99
$F_{i,4,t}$	0.11	-0.30	1.39	2.14[c]	-0.41	8.10[a]
$F_{i,5,t}$	0.12	0.16	8.41[a]	1.16	0.31	-1.96[b]
$E_{i,1,t}$	-3.75[a]	-3.51[b]	0.05	-2.37[b]	0.06	—
$E_{i,2,t}$	-4.57[a]	0.85	-9.49[a]	0.39	-5.21[a]	—
$E_{i,3,t}$	-2.01[c]	-1.34	5.90[b]	-0.06	-3.86[b]	—
$E_{i,4,t}$	-0.53	-1.35	3.28	0.04	0.98	—
$E_{i,5,t}$	-0.43	0.47	7.53[a]	-2.42[b]	0.17	—
BSkyB bid						
$B_{1,1,t}$	8.81[a]	7.93[a]	8.33[a]	25.76[a]	7.23[a]	5.25[a]
$B_{1,2,t}$	0.09	0.17	-0.41	-3.20[b]	5.85[b]	0.08
$B_{1,3,t}$	2.56	0.89	18.39[a]	7.48[a]	2.08	-0.34
$B_{1,4,t}$	4.53[a]	13.05[a]	17.92[a]	3.32[a]	-2.18	3.59[b]
$B_{1,5,t}$	3.09[c]	10.96[a]	22.92[a]	-0.19	23.44[a]	8.82[a]
$B_{2,1,t}$	-3.05[c]	-6.27[a]	-9.36[a]	-9.06[a]	-5.16[b]	-3.35[b]
$B_{2,2,t}$	2.85[c]	2.76	2.68	0.49	1.80	0.73

	(1)	(2)	(3)	(4)	(5)	(6)
$B_{2,3,t}$	0.93	-0.06	-1.21	1.26	-0.59	-0.03
$B_{2,4,t}$	1.51	-0.48	1.86	-0.01	0.03	2.47^c
$B_{2,5,t}$	0.17	0.56	0.78	0.15	-0.23	-3.91^a
$B_{3,1,t}$	-9.38^a	-2.64	-9.17^a	-16.17^a	-11.86^a	-3.95^a
$B_{3,2,t}$	-0.76	1.11	-1.51	-0.23	7.81^a	-7.15^a
$B_{3,3,t}$	0.02	-0.14	-0.18	0.41	-2.58	5.44^a
$B_{3,4,t}$	0.10	0.26	-3.43	2.67^b	-0.50	0.39
$B_{3,5,t}$	0.63	-0.40	-0.91	5.87^a	0.78	-9.41^a
obs.	508	508	508	508	508	508
s.e. of regression	1.63	1.89	2.67	1.25	2.59	1.46
R^2	0.20	0.23	0.35	0.61	0.26	0.25

Notes:

[a] = significantly different from zero, two-tail test, 1% level;

[b] = 5% level;

[c] = 10% level.

Dependent variable is $r_{i,t}$ (daily return on club share prices).

Table 8.4. *Estimation results for determinants of share price returns, individual models (2)*

	Birmingham	Bolton	Charlton	QPR	Sheff Utd	Southampton	Sunderland
Market returns and league match results							
Constant	-0.06	-0.09	-0.10	-0.20	-0.19	-0.23[a]	0.09
$r_{m,t}$	0.03	0.62[a]	0.09[c]	0.15	0.45[a]	0.15[b]	0.08
$Y_{i,t}$	1.44[a]	6.54[a]	0.98[a]	2.49[a]	2.56[a]	2.03[a]	2.13[a]
Promotion/relegation							
$U_{i,1,t}$	—	—	20.80[a]	31.66[a]	—	14.47[a]	—
$U_{i,2,t}$	—	—	0.25	-0.10	—	-6.87[a]	—
$U_{i,3,t}$	—	—	0.10	-3.44	—	0.07	—
$U_{i,4,t}$	—	—	-3.24[b]	-0.11	—	-0.25	—
$U_{i,5,t}$	—	—	-6.90[a]	-4.02	—	1.68	—
$D_{i,1,t}$	-9.82[a]	-26.46[a]	-8.47[a]	—	-7.53[b]	—	-20.96[a]
$D_{i,2,t}$	2.89[a]	6.69[b]	-1.20	—	-0.97	—	-0.02
$D_{i,3,t}$	0.15	-1.96	0.03	—	-1.54	—	2.22
$D_{i,4,t}$	-1.45	-5.29[c]	0.04	—	-5.35[c]	—	0.00
$D_{i,5,t}$	-0.26	-0.72	-1.75	—	-1.16	—	-0.45
FA Cup							
$F_{i,1,t}$	0.16	-1.54	0.47	0.24	-3.46	-0.22	-1.02
$F_{i,2,t}$	0.08	0.65	-0.20	-3.23	-5.80[a]	0.43	-0.71
$F_{i,3,t}$	1.36	-0.53	-0.45	-0.41	-0.14	0.05	-0.21
$F_{i,4,t}$	0.25	0.49	0.25	-0.19	-0.32	0.06	-4.08[a]
$F_{i,5,t}$	0.05	0.35	0.15	-4.01[c]	-0.27	0.57	-0.19

BSkyB bid

$B_{1,1,t}$	-0.56	6.42	4.30^a	-0.33	2.28	11.49^a	2.72
$B_{1,2,t}$	-0.39	-3.28	5.28^a	0.31	-0.60	3.89^b	2.06
$B_{1,3,t}$	1.65	0.47	3.75^a	0.29	0.47	0.32	-0.54
$B_{1,4,t}$	0.17	2.16	1.23	0.72	1.71	0.74	1.66
$B_{1,5,t}$	0.07	2.97	1.73	0.25	0.35	11.40^a	0.43
$B_{2,1,t}$	0.09	0.70	-0.94	0.35	-2.09	0.38	-0.44
$B_{2,2,t}$	0.07	0.35	0.14	0.27	0.38	-0.99	-0.05
$B_{2,3,t}$	0.03	-0.40	0.02	0.08	-0.17	0.11	-0.15
$B_{2,4,t}$	0.04	2.02	0.11	-0.73	-0.40	-0.59	3.16^c
$B_{2,5,t}$	0.11	1.03	0.24	0.43	0.88	0.46	0.45
$B_{3,1,t}$	-7.46^a	-0.25	1.18	0.11	-0.06	-1.18	-1.80
$B_{3,2,t}$	-0.48	-2.56	0.45	-0.77	1.52	0.99	-0.42
$B_{3,3,t}$	0.02	-2.29	-0.01	0.94	-0.31	0.06	-0.88
$B_{3,4,t}$	0.07	-5.61	0.13	0.25	0.33	0.27	-7.93^a
$B_{3,5,t}$	0.07	6.24	0.14	0.26	0.38	-3.79^b	-0.97
obs.	508	508	508	508	508	508	508
s.e. of regression	1.69	4.17	1.35	3.41	3.51	0.27	0.28
R^2	0.19	0.24	0.44	0.19	0.05	1.90	1.85

Notes:

[a] = significantly different from zero, two-tail test, 1% level;

[b] = 5% level;

[c] = 10% level.

Dependent variable is $r_{i,t}$ (daily return on club share prices).

partially anticipated promotion. The overall effect of promotion on the company's value should therefore be somewhat greater than the next-day reaction would suggest by itself.

The importance of prior expectations also seems to be reflected in the magnitudes of some of the individual promotion and relegation dummy variable coefficients reported in table 8.4. The promotion of Charlton Athletic to the Premier League in 1998 was perhaps more surprising to most football followers than their subsequent relegation in 1999. The next-day share price adjustments ($+21$ per cent and -8.5 per cent, respectively) seem to reflect this, though some of the initial euphoria following the 1998 promotion seems to have worn off quickly: the share price had fallen back by about 10 per cent a few days later. The failures of Sheffield United (1998) and Birmingham City (1999) to win promotion both occurred at the semi-final stages of the play-offs and therefore caused smaller next-day adjustments (-7.5 per cent and -10 per cent, respectively) than Sunderland's defeat by Charlton in the 1998 play-off final (-21 per cent). The defeat of Bolton Wanderers by Watford in the 1999 play-off final, and (to a lesser extent) Bolton's relegation in 1998, were perhaps quite surprising events. The average next-day adjustment for these two failures (-26.5 per cent) was therefore relatively large. Figures 8.1 and 8.2 illustrate the effects of promotion, relegation and play-off defeat on the share prices of two of these clubs: Bolton Wanderers and Charlton Athletic.

The coefficients on the dummy variables $F_{i,k,t}$ and $E_{i,k,t}$ in table 8.2 indicate that elimination from either the FA Cup or from European competition tends to cause a significant negative share price reaction. In both cases, the adjustment appears to take around two days to complete. Elimination from Europe seems to be viewed generally by the markets as a more serious setback, reducing a club's market value by about 5 per cent on average. Elimination from the FA Cup reduces a club's market value by around 2.5 per cent on average. But in the club-specific results in tables 8.3 and 8.4, it seems that the FA Cup effect does differ between clubs: the markets seem worried when a club with a realistic possibility of winning the cup is eliminated, but less concerned by the elimination of weaker contenders. The largest negative coefficient (-4.5 per cent) is for Newcastle United, who lost in both the 1998 and 1999 finals. Sheffield United's significant negative coefficient presumably reflects disappointment after this Division One club narrowly failed to reach the 1998 final, having been eliminated by Newcastle at the semi-final stage.

Finally, the estimated coefficients on the dummy variable $B_{1,1,t}$ in table 8.2 show that the effects on Manchester United's share price of the announcement of the BSkyB takeover bid were both immediate and

Bolton Wanderers

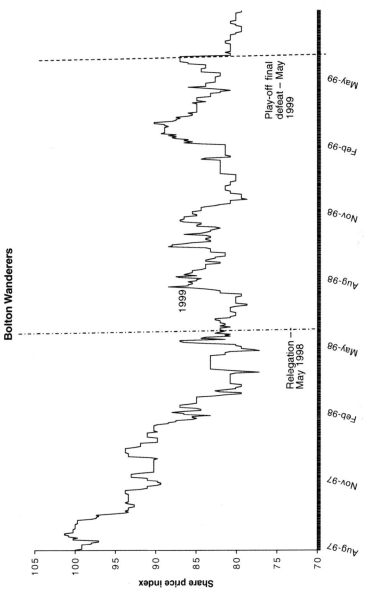

Figure 8.1 Trends in index value of logarithmic share price: Bolton Wanderers
Source: Datastream.

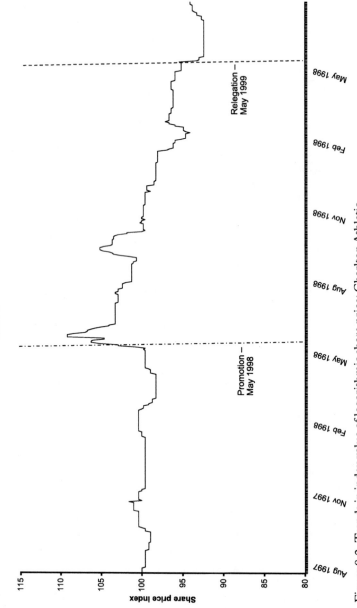

Figure 8.2   Trends in index value of logarithmic share price: Charlton Athletic
Source: Datastream.

obvious. United's shares jumped in value by around 25 per cent on the day of the announcement, and by a further 7 per cent later in the same week, as the improved bid was submitted and accepted. Overall, other clubs' share prices were marked up by around 5 per cent on average on the day of the BSkyB–Manchester United announcement. There was, however, a stark difference between the clubs that were in the Premier League at the time (all clubs in table 8.3, plus Charlton Athletic and Southampton in table 8.4), and those that were in Division One. All of the former and none of the latter recorded statistically significant gains on the day of the BSkyB announcement. Premier League club shares also continued to make strong gains later in the same week, as speculation mounted that rival media groups would seek to follow BSkyB's lead by taking over or acquiring stakes in other leading clubs.

The negative impact of the MMC's recommendation against the BSkyB bid, and Stephen Byers' eventual acceptance of the MMC's findings, are also clearly discernible in the coefficients on the dummy variables $B_{2,1,t}$ and $B_{3,1,t}$. Manchester United shares fell in value by about 9 per cent and 16 per cent on the two days in question. Other leading Premier League clubs' shares also fell sharply. In contrast, the Division One clubs' shares were left mostly unscathed by the adverse reaction to the MMC's recommendation and the Secretary of State's decision. Figures 8.3 and 8.4 show the effects on the share prices of Manchester United and Newcastle United of the BSkyB takeover bid announcement and its later rejection. Clearly the big-market clubs have most to gain and lose from fluctuations in the fortunes of football's relationship with the media. Consequently, their share prices tend to be more sensitive to developments of this kind.

8.3 Efficiency of prices in the fixed-odds betting market

Section 8.3 investigates whether the match results forecasting model that was developed in chapter 3 is capable of producing information about the likely outcomes of league matches that is not fully reflected in the fixed-odds quoted in advance by a leading firm of high street bookmakers. If so, this would suggest that the bookmaker's odds fail to meet the standard criterion for *weak-form efficiency*: that all historical information relevant to the assessment of the match outcome probabilities should be reflected in the odds quoted.[9] If the bookmaker's odds are weak-form inefficient, then

---

[9] This can be contrasted with the conditions for *semi-strong-form efficiency*, which requires that all publicly available information (not just historical information) is reflected in the price; and *strong-form efficiency*, which requires that all publicly and privately held information is reflected in the price.

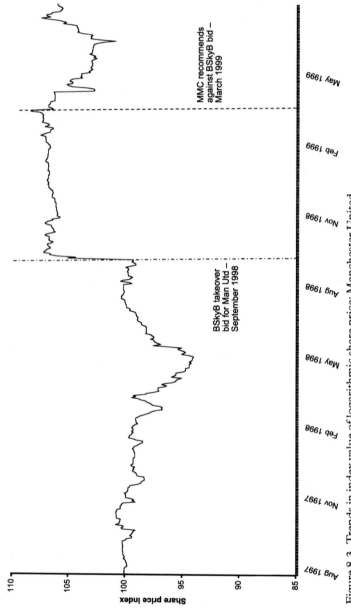

Manchester United

Figure 8.3 Trends in index value of logarithmic share price: Manchester United
Source: Datastream.

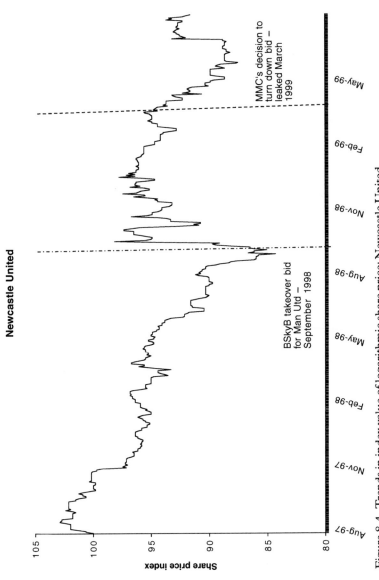

Figure 8.4 Trends in index value of logarithmic share price: Newcastle United
Source: Datastream.

it should be possible to use the forecasting model to devise betting strategies that either make a profit, or (at least) reduce the losses expected in view of the inclusion of the bookmaker's margin in the odds, and the obligation to pay betting duty. If the prices are weak-form efficient, then it is not possible to devise such strategies using historical data that is publicly available (Fama, 1970).

In the economics literature, there have been numerous studies of the efficiency of betting markets. Much of this literature focuses on racetrack betting, and only a representative selection of these papers is considered here. Several early contributions focused on the relationship between the forecast prices (FP), published in the sporting press on the race-day morning, and the starting prices (SP), at which all bets are settled, and which are compiled and published minutes before the race takes place. Dowie (1976) interpreted a finding of little or no difference between the correlations between FP and race outcomes on the one hand, and SP and race outcomes on the other, as evidence against the hypothesis that bets were being placed on the basis of inside information between the publication of FP and the start of the race. If inside information were being used, the SP correlation should exceed the FP correlation. Crafts (1985), however, demonstrated that this interpretation was not necessarily justified. Similar FP and SP correlations across all outcomes could be consistent with substantial discrepancies between FP and SP on individual outcomes, and with SP containing significantly superior information. By betting at SP on outcomes whose SP were substantially shorter than the longest prices that had previously been quoted, significantly smaller losses than average could have been realised.

More recent literature has focused on a consistent empirical regularity in racetrack betting odds known as *longshot bias*, implying that the expected return to a bet placed at longer odds is lower than at shorter odds. Several kinds of explanation have been put forward. One possibility is that bettors may be risk lovers, and are therefore willing to accept bets on longshots offering low expected returns but high variance (Weitzman, 1965; Ali, 1977). Another possibility is that bettors' subjective probabilities of losing are systematically downward biased (Henery, 1985). If so, it is straightforward to show that SP are subject to longshot bias. Golec and Tamarkin (1998) have suggested incorporating skewness, as well as the mean and variance of the return, into the bettor's utility function. They demonstrate that it may be rational for risk-averse bettors who love skewness (bets offering a high probability of losing and a low probability of a very large return) to accept bets on longshots despite the low expected returns.

An alternative kind of explanation regards longshot bias as a rational pricing response on the part of bookmakers to the presence in the market of insiders trading on the basis of private information (Shin, 1991, 1992, 1993; Vaughan Williams and Paton, 1997). Since both the average length of the odds and the opportunities for insider trading are directly proportional to the number of runners, bookmakers' margins need to be higher (and bettors' expected returns lower) at longer odds, in order to protect bookmakers from the actions of the informed traders. Terrell and Farmer (1996) have proposed a similar type of explanation that does not rely on insider trading. They consider a world of imperfect information, in which there are two distinct groups of bettors: pleasure bettors who place bets without knowing the true probabilities of the various outcomes; and informed bettors who incur costs in order to ascertain the true probabilities. Informed bettors study the actions of the pleasure bettors in order to identify and accept bets that offer a positive expected return. The interaction between the two groups produces a distribution of odds that fails to reflect the true probabilities. Moreover, since the intervention of the informed bettors always lowers the odds on the outcomes with high expected returns (and raises the odds on outcomes with low expected returns) there is a statistical association between high odds and low expected returns. This may explain the consistent tendency for empirical studies to identify longshot bias.

A number of researchers have tested the efficiency of betting markets on the outcomes of North American team sports. These markets operate on a spread betting system, whereby the bookmaker quotes a points spread, reflecting an assessment of the expected points difference between the favourite and the underdog. Bettors backing the favourite expect the latter to win by more than the spread; those backing the underdog expect the favourite to win by less than the spread, or expect the underdog to win. Once a bet is placed the payoffs are fixed, but bookmakers can adjust the spread as the time of the match approaches, in an attempt to equalise the volume of bets placed on either team. The bookmaker's margin is provided by the '11-for-10 rule', requiring a bettor to stake $11 in order to win $10. To make a profit, the bettor therefore requires more than 52.4 per cent of bets to be correct.

Pankoff (1968) developed the first regression-based test of efficiency in the National Football League (NFL) betting market, by regressing match outcomes (measured by the score differential) on bookmakers' spreads using data for the period 1956–65. Intercept and slope coefficients not significantly different from zero and one, respectively, suggest that the spread was an unbiased predictor of the match outcome (see below). Obtaining similar results using a 1980–5 NFL data set, Gandar et al. (1988) point to the low power of regression-based tests to reject the null hypothesis of efficiency. They propose a series of alternative economic tests, involving direct evaluation of the returns that would have been earned from the implementation of various trading rules. Two types of trading rule are considered: technical rules, which select bets purely on the basis of the past performance of the teams; and behavioural rules, which select bets in an attempt to exploit certain hypothesised behavioural patterns of the betting public. An example of a behavioural rule is to back underdogs against favourites in cases where the favourite covered the spread by a large margin the previous week. The behavioural hypothesis is that the public tends to over-react in such cases, creating the opportunity for a profitable contrarian strategy. Gandar *et al.* find that some behavioural rules are consistently profitable; technical rules, in contrast, fail to produce a profit.

Golec and Tamarkin (1991) test the efficiency of the spreads posted on the outcomes of NFL and college football matches, using data covering a 15-year period from 1973 to 1987. For NFL betting they find evidence of inefficiencies favouring bets on home wins and bets on underdogs. While the extent of the bias against home teams in the bookmakers' prices seems to have diminished over time, the bias against underdogs has increased. No evidence of similar bias is found in the college football betting spreads. Dare and MacDonald (1996) generalise the empirical methodology for regression-based tests, and demonstrate that a number of earlier tests were based on specifications that unknowingly imposed implicit restrictions on a more general model. Tests that search only for evidence of home–away team or favourite–underdog biases, without recognising the interdependence between these characteristics of teams, are capable of producing misleading results. Little evidence of inefficiency is found when the general model is applied to a 1980–3 NFL and college football data set.

In other recent US studies, Badarinathi and Kochmann (1996) use NFL data for the period 1984–93 to show that a strategy of betting regularly on underdogs when the spread exceeded five points and when variations in spreads among bookmakers in different cities enabled the bettor to obtain an additional two-point advantage, was systematically profitable. Investigating the question of market efficiency from a different perspective, Gandar *et al.* (1998) find that the bookmakers' closing prices provided a closer approximation to match outcomes than their opening prices using a National Basketball Association (NBA) betting market data set covering the period 1986–94. Movements in prices between the opening and close of trade tended to eliminate biases in the opening prices, suggesting that informed traders were both active and influential in this market.

Testing the efficiency of the bookmaker's prices for betting on the results of English football matches raises a slightly different set of issues. In contrast to the situation with racetrack betting, prices are fixed by the bookmakers several days before the match takes place, so both bookmaker and bettor know the price and the payoffs when the bet is placed. And in contrast to North American team sports betting, the bookmaker does not adjust the prices as bets are placed, even if new information is received as the time of the match draws near. The pricing system requires the bookmaker to quote 'odds' in the form: 'a-to-b' home win; 'c-to-d' draw; and 'e-to-f' away win. This means, for example, that if a bettor stakes b on a home win, the overall net payoffs are $+a$ (the bookmaker pays the winnings and returns the stake) if the outcome is a home win, and $-b$ (the bookmaker keeps the stake) if the outcome is anything else. Except for televised matches, bettors must place combination bets on at least five matches (if home wins are selected) or three matches (if draws or away wins are selected).

A bookmaker's quoted prices can be converted to match outcome 'probabilities' as follows: $\theta_{i,j}^H = b/(a+b)$; $\theta_{i,j}^D = d/(c+d)$; $\theta_{i,j}^A = f/(e+f)$. The sum of these expressions invariably exceeds one, because the odds contain a margin to cover the bookmaker's costs and profits. But implicit home-win, draw and away-win probabilities which sum to one can be obtained easily, by applying the adjustment: $\phi_{i,j}^H = \theta_{i,j}^H / (\theta_{i,j}^H + \theta_{i,j}^D + \theta_{i,j}^A)$, and by applying similar adjustments for $\phi_{i,j}^D$ and $\phi_{i,j}^A$. The bookmaker's total margin is $\lambda_{i,j} = \theta_{i,j}^H + \theta_{i,j}^D + \theta_{i,j}^A - 1$.

For English football, Pope and Peel (1989) investigate the efficiency of the prices set by four national high-street bookmakers for matches played during the 1982 season. A simple, though as before not necessarily a very powerful test of the weak-form efficiency hypothesis is based on regressions of match outcomes against implicit bookmaker's probabilities. For the purposes of describing these tests, the following variable definitions are used:

$H_{i,j}=$ 1 if the match between team i and team j results in a home win, and 0 otherwise

$D_{i,j}=$ 1 if the match between team i and team j results in a draw, and 0 otherwise

$A_{i,j}=$ 1 if the match between team i and team j results in an away win, and 0 otherwise.

In the linear probability model: $H_{i,j}=\rho_1 + \rho_2\phi_{i,j}^H + v_{i,j}$, a necessary condition for weak-form efficiency is $\{\rho_1=0,\ \rho_2=1\}$. Equivalent conditions apply in the corresponding regressions for $D_{i,j}$ and $A_{i,j}$. Any other combination of values for $\{\rho_1, \rho_2\}$ suggests that there may be inefficiencies. The combination $\{\rho_1 > 0, \rho_2 < 1\}$, for example, means that bookmakers overestimate the home-win probabilities for the matches least likely to produce home wins (with long odds), and under-estimate the probabilities for those most likely to produce home wins (with short odds). Noting that ordinary least squares (OLS) estimation of the linear probability model gives rise to a heteroscedastic error structure, Pope and Peel suggest using weighted least squares (WLS) estimation, using $\hat{H}_{i,j}(1 - \hat{H}_{i,j})$ as weights, where $\hat{H}_{i,j}$ are the fitted values of the dependent variable obtained from (preliminary) estimation of the model using OLS. Alternatively, the model can be estimated as a logit regression, in which case different numerical estimates of the coefficients ρ_1 and ρ_2 are expected.

In the linear probability model regressions, Pope and Peel find no significant departures from the condition $\{\rho_1 = 0, \rho_2 = 1\}$ for the odds on home- and away-win outcomes. On the other hand, the draw odds have no significant predictive content for draw outcomes, suggesting a departure from efficiency conditions. The returns achievable from two betting strategies are investigated. The first, using only information derived from bookmakers' odds, involves betting on outcomes for which the predicted probability derived from the logit regression of match outcome on bookmakers' implicit probabilities exceeds the geometric mean of the four bookmakers' implicit probabilities. The second, also exploiting extraneous information, involves betting on a consensus of the recommendations of six national newspaper tipsters. Under both strategies, there is some evidence that positive pre-tax returns could have been earned, though these would not have been sufficient to generate a profit after allowing for payment of betting duty.

Dixon and Coles (1997) use their match scores forecasting model (see chapter 3) to test the profitability of a strategy of betting on English football matches with the highest expected return according to the match outcome probabilities derived from the model. Betting on outcomes for which the ratio of the model's probability to the bookmaker's implicit probability exceeds about 20 per cent is found to produce a pre-tax return significantly greater than zero, after allowing for the bookmaker's margin.

Cain, Law and Peel (2000) report evidence of longshot bias in the fixed-odds betting market for match results and scores in English football. The odds available for bets on specific scores are dependent only on the odds posted for the three possible match results (home win, draw or away win), and it is possible to bet on the score of a single match. The poisson and the negative binomial distributions are used to model the home and away team scores independently. Estimates of the fair odds for specific scores are computed, conditional on the bookmaker's posted home-win odds. In comparisons of the estimated fair odds with the bookmaker's actual odds for specific scores, the former are generally found to be significantly longer than the latter for longshot bets, indicating longshot bias. The fair odds are sometimes shorter than the bookmaker's odds for bets on strong favourites. Direct calculations of average profitability for different categories of bet suggests that bets on strong favourites may offer limited profitable betting opportunities.

In the rest of section 8.3, the match results forecasting model developed in section 3.3 and estimated using data for the 1989 to 1998 seasons inclusive (see table 3.14) is used to test for the efficiency of the prices quoted by one of the leading high-street bookmakers for fixed-odds betting on match results during the 1999 season. To test the weak-form efficiency hypothesis, a full set of fixed-odds betting coupons for matches played over each weekend was collected throughout the season. From a total of 2,036 league matches played during the 1999 season, the forecasting model is capable of generating predictions for 1,944 matches.[10] The bookmaker's weekend coupons provided odds for 1,568 of these matches, which constitute the data set for the analysis in this section. The average value of the bookmaker's margin across the 1,568 matches included in the data set was $\lambda_{i,j} = 0.115$, or 11.5 per cent.

Probabilities and forecasts of the results of the 1,568 matches are obtained by substituting the full set of covariate values for each match into the estimated version of (3.10), as reported in columns (3)–(4) and (7)–(8) of table 3.14. This procedure is described in detail in section 3.3. For each match, a set of estimated home-win, draw and away-win probabilities is obtained. As before, these are denoted $p_{i,j}^{H}$, $p_{i,j}^{D}$ and $p_{i,j}^{A}$ (see (3.12)). Following the methods described in section 3.3, a specific forecast for the result of each match is also obtained.

Tables 8.5 and 8.6 show some of the key features of the implicit bookmaker's probabilities and the evaluated match result probabilities. When the bookmaker's and the model's probabilities are disaggregated by month and by division, there is little systematic variation in the mean probabilities for each outcome, but some significant systematic variation in the standard deviations. First, the standard deviations of both the bookmaker's probabilities and the model's probabilities increase systematically during the course of the season. Towards the end of the season, it

---

[10] Ninety-two matches involving two teams (Macclesfield Town and Halifax Town) which entered the league at the start of the 1998 and 1999 seasons respectively, had to be discarded as the forecasting model requires a full set of match results for a two-year period prior to the match in question.

Table 8.5. *Bookmakers' implicit match result probabilities, descriptive statistics*

	$\phi_{i,j}^{H}$: Home win		$\phi_{i,j}^{D}$: Draw		$\phi_{i,j}^{A}$: Away win	
	Mean	St. dev.	Mean	St. dev.	Mean	St. dev.
August	0.446	0.080	0.274	0.009	0.280	0.074
September	0.446	0.088	0.273	0.008	0.281	0.082
October	0.447	0.089	0.273	0.009	0.280	0.082
November	0.452	0.095	0.272	0.011	0.275	0.089
December	0.450	0.091	0.272	0.012	0.279	0.085
January	0.447	0.094	0.273	0.009	0.280	0.089
February	0.449	0.110	0.272	0.014	0.279	0.103
March	0.467	0.112	0.267	0.017	0.266	0.101
April/May	0.459	0.131	0.258	0.022	0.283	0.118
Premier	0.444	0.121	0.271	0.019	0.286	0.110
D1	0.453	0.101	0.270	0.014	0.277	0.093
D2	0.456	0.098	0.269	0.015	0.275	0.090
D3	0.452	0.088	0.270	0.012	0.277	0.082
All	0.452	0.102	0.270	0.015	0.279	0.093
Actual proportions	0.445		0.285		0.269	

Source: Fixed-odds betting coupons.

Table 8.6. *Match results forecasting model's evaluated match result probabilities, descriptive statistics*

	$p_{i,j}^{H}$: Home win		$p_{i,j}^{D}$: Draw		$p_{i,j}^{A}$ - Away win	
	Mean	St. dev.	Mean	St. dev.	Mean	St. dev.
August	0.457	0.068	0.283	0.013	0.260	0.057
September	0.453	0.073	0.283	0.013	0.264	0.062
October	0.461	0.083	0.280	0.017	0.258	0.068
November	0.468	0.095	0.277	0.021	0.255	0.078
December	0.464	0.089	0.279	0.020	0.257	0.072
January	0.463	0.091	0.279	0.020	0.258	0.074
February	0.469	0.108	0.275	0.025	0.256	0.088
March	0.483	0.108	0.272	0.026	0.244	0.085
April/May	0.477	0.127	0.270	0.030	0.253	0.103
Premier	0.463	0.110	0.276	0.025	0.261	0.090
D1	0.471	0.106	0.275	0.025	0.254	0.086
D2	0.473	0.090	0.277	0.020	0.250	0.072
D3	0.459	0.081	0.281	0.017	0.260	0.066
All	0.467	0.097	0.277	0.022	0.256	0.079
Actual proportions	0.445		0.285		0.269	

is possible to make a more specific assessment of the win/draw/lose probabilities based on the current season's results, than is possible at the start,
when the previous season's results provide the only available guidance.
Second, there is also some systematic variation in the standard deviations
by division: these are highest in the Premier League and lowest in
Division Three. This seems likely to reflect a greater degree of competitive
balance in the lower than in the upper divisions of the league. The forecasting model appears to be reasonably accurate in replicating the main
features of the bookmaker's implicit probabilities.

Testing for weak-form efficiency without using the forecasting model

WLS estimation results, obtained using the regression-based test procedure employed by Pope and Peel (1989) and Golec and Tamarkin (1991),
are as follows:

$$H_{i,j} = -0.0323 + 1.0572\ \phi_{i,j}^{H} + \hat{v}_{i,j} \qquad F(2,1566) = 0.28$$
$$(0.0524)\ (0.1145)$$

$$D_{i,j} = -0.1942 + 1.7779\ \phi_{i,j}^{D} + \hat{v}_{i,j} \qquad F(2,1566) = 1.48$$
$$(0.1878)\ (0.6974)$$

$$A_{i,j} = 0.0455 + 0.8055^{c}\ \phi_{i,j}^{A} + \hat{v}_{i,j} \qquad F(2,1566) = 1.52 \qquad (8.1)$$
$$(0.0319)\ (0.1154)$$

Notes: ^{c} = significantly different from zero (constant) or one
(slope), two-tail test, 10 per cent level.

Standard errors of estimated coefficients are shown in
parentheses.

In (8.1) the rejection of $H_{0}{:}\rho_{1}=0$ or $H_{0}{:}\rho_{2}=1$ in a two-tail test is denoted
in the usual manner. The F-statistics test the joint hypothesis $H_{0}{:}\{\rho_{1}=0,$
$\rho_{2}=1\}$. This is accepted in all three tests, though $H_{0}{:}\rho_{2}=1$ is rejected at
the 10 per cent level in the estimation for $A_{i,j}$. The numerical magnitudes
of the estimated coefficients in the regressions for $D_{i,j}$ and $A_{i,j}$ suggest that
the bookmakers tended to under-estimate the probability of a draw for
the matches most likely to produce draws (with short odds), and to
under-estimate the probability of an away win for the matches least likely
to produce away wins (with long odds).

The relative advantages of betting short on draws and long on away wins
are confirmed in table 8.7, which shows the average returns from £1 bets
placed on matches with long, medium and short odds for home wins,
draws and away wins. The 500 matches with the lowest values of $\phi_{i,j}^{H}$ are
classified as having long odds (for a home win); the 500 matches with the

Table 8.7. *Average returns from £1 bets, long, medium and short odds*

	Betting regime		
	R1	R2	R3
Home win			
Long odds	−0.032	−0.132	−0.232
Medium odds	0.001	−0.103	−0.203
Short odds	0.027	−0.126	−0.226
All	−0.018	−0.119	−0.219
Draw			
Long odds	0.015	−0.090	−0.190
Medium odds	0.027	−0.080	−0.180
Short odds	0.130	0.015	−0.085
All	0.056	−0.053	−0.153
Away win			
Long odds	0.204	0.080	−0.020
Medium odds	−0.122	−0.212	−0.312
Short odds	−0.090	−0.183	−0.283
All	−0.008	−0.110	−0.210
Draw, Aug–Dec			
Long odds	0.041	−0.066	−0.166
Medium odds	0.008	−0.097	−0.197
Short odds	0.091	−0.020	−0.120
All	0.045	−0.063	−0.163
Draw, Jan–May			
Long odds	−0.006	−0.109	−0.209
Medium odds	0.055	−0.054	−0.154
Short odds	0.183	0.063	−0.038
All	0.070	−0.040	−0.140
Away win, Aug–Dec			
Long odds	0.050	−0.058	−0.158
Medium odds	−0.148	−0.237	−0.337
Short odds	−0.113	−0.204	−0.304
All	−0.079	−0.174	−0.274
Away win, Jan–May			
Long odds	0.360	0.220	0.120
Medium odds	−0.081	−0.175	−0.275
Short odds	−0.064	−0.161	−0.261
All	0.079	−0.032	−0.132

Key:

R1: bets at odds consistent with bookmaker's implicit probabilities (no profit margin)

R2: bets at quoted odds inclusive of margin, but not allowing for betting duty

R3: bets at quoted odds, with betting duty of 10 pence on each £1 bet.

highest values of $\phi^H_{i,j}$ are classified as having short odds; and the remaining 568 matches are classified as having medium odds. The same classification scheme is used for draws and away wins. Three betting regimes are considered. Under $R1$, betting takes place at odds consistent with the bookmaker's implicit probabilities with no profit margin, so the bookmaker's expected return across all bets is zero. Under $R2$, betting takes place at the quoted odds inclusive of the bookmaker's margin, but not allowing for betting duty. Several high-street bookmakers offered tax-free betting via the Internet during the course of the 2000 season, (though this service was not available during the 1999 season, to which the data used in the present analysis refers). Finally, under $R3$, betting takes place at the bookmaker's quoted odds, with betting duty of 10 pence levied on each £1 bet.

The average returns across all bets under $R1$ reflect the tendency of the bookmaker's implicit probabilities to under-estimate the proportion of draws and to over-estimate the proportions of home wins and away wins (see also table 8.5). Although a strategy of betting on every match to finish drawn would produce a profit of just below 6 per cent under $R1$, this converts to losses of −5 per cent under $R2$, and −15 per cent under $R3$. Strategies of betting selectively on draws with short odds and away wins with long odds, on the other hand, are capable of producing profits under both $R1$ (13 per cent and 20 per cent, respectively) and $R2$ (2 per cent and 8 per cent, respectively). But even in these cases, payment of betting duty converts these profits into losses under $R3$ of −8 per cent and −2 per cent, respectively.

If betting duty is ignored, do these results constitute evidence of weak-form inefficiency and profitable trading opportunities? The answer depends upon whether it would have been possible at any stage to have anticipated that betting on draws with short odds and away wins with long odds was the appropriate strategy. This question is investigated in the lower rows of table 8.7. The season is split into two periods (August–December and January–May), and the average returns for the matches in each period classified previously as having long, medium and short odds for draws and away wins are reported. There appears to be some consistency over time in the results. A strategy of betting on draws with short odds could have been observed to produce a relatively high return over the period August–December. If continued subsequently, the same strategy would have produced an average return of 18 per cent under $R1$ over the period January–May. The same applies to the strategy of betting on away wins with long odds which, if continued over the period January–May, would have produced an average return under $R1$ of 36 per cent. In this case, a positive return of 12 per cent for January–May would have been realised even under $R3$. At the start of January, however, there would of course have been no guarantee that betting strategies based on outcomes for the period August–December would continue to succeed thereafter.

Testing for weak-form efficiency using the forecasting model

The availability of the evaluated probabilities obtained from the forecasting model permits an extension of the weak-form efficiency tests discussed above. It is possible to test whether the forecasting model produces useful additional information that is not impounded into the bookmaker's prices. For home wins, for example, such information (if it exists) is represented by the expression $(p_{i,j}^H - \phi_{i,j}^H)$. A test of the significance of the coefficient on this term in the linear probability model for home wins is a test of whether or not the model produces useful additional information.

In the linear probability model: $H_{i,j} = \rho_1 + \rho_2 \phi_{i,j}^H + \rho_3 (p_{i,j}^H - \phi_{i,j}^H) + v_{i,j}$, the condition for weak-form efficiency becomes $\{\rho_1 = 0, \rho_2 = 1, \rho_3 = 0\}$. $\rho_3 = 0$ is the specific condition under which the forecasting model contains no information which has not already been impounded into the bookmaker's odds. As before, equivalent tests can also be run on the models for draws and away wins. The WLS estimation results are as follows:

$$H_{i,j} = -0.0931^a + 1.1704\, \phi_{i,j}^H + 0.6411^b\, (p_{i,j}^H - \phi_{i,j}^H) + \hat{v}_{i,j}$$
$$(0.0562)\quad (0.1201)\qquad (0.2516)$$
$$F(3,1565) = 2.43^a$$

$$D_{i,j} = -0.1888 + 1.7010\, \phi_{i,j}^D + 2.0740^c\, (p_{i,j}^D - \phi_{i,j}^D) + \hat{v}_{i,j}$$
$$(0.1787)\ (0.6663)\qquad (0.6297)$$
$$F(3,1565) = 4.63^c$$

$$A_{i,j} = 0.0239 + 0.9216\phi_{i,j}^A + 0.4614^a\, (p_{i,j}^A - \phi_{i,j}^A) + \hat{v}_{i,j}$$
$$(0.0345)\ (0.1362)\qquad (0.2792)$$
$$F(3,1565) = 2.00$$

$$(8.2)$$

Notes: [a] = significantly different from zero (constant), one (slope coefficient on $\phi_{i,j}^r$), or zero (slope coefficient on $(p_{i,j}^r - \phi_{i,j}^r)$), two-tail test, 1 per cent level;
[b] = 5 per cent level;
[c] = 10 per cent level.

Standard errors of estimated coefficients are shown in parentheses.

Table 8.8. *Average returns from £1 bets placed on forecasting model's prediction for each match*

	Betting regime		
	R1	R2	R3
August	0.121	0.005	−0.095
September	−0.155	−0.242	−0.342
October	0.067	−0.043	−0.143
November	0.081	−0.031	−0.131
December	0.053	−0.055	−0.155
January	0.127	0.011	−0.089
February	0.056	−0.052	−0.152
March	0.049	−0.059	−0.159
April/May	−0.070	−0.167	−0.267
All	0.031	−0.075	−0.175

Key:
*R*1: bets at odds consistent with bookmaker's implicit probabilities (no profit margin)
*R*2: bets at quoted odds inclusive of margin, but not allowing for betting duty
*R*3: bets at quoted odds, with betting duty of 10 pence on each £1 bet.

The F-statistics test the joint hypothesis $H_0: \{\rho_1 = 0, \rho_2 = 1, \rho_3 = 0\}$. This hypothesis is rejected at the 1 per cent level in the regression for draws and at the 10 per cent level in the regression for home wins, but is accepted in the regression for away wins. t-tests for $H_0: \rho_3 = 0$ reject the null at the 5 per cent level for home wins; at the 1 per cent level for draws; and at the 10 per cent level for away wins. This seems to constitute reasonably strong and consistent evidence that the forecasting model does contain additional information not already impounded into the bookmaker's odds. The latter are therefore found to be weak-form inefficient.

Tables 8.8–8.10 investigate the extent to which the additional information available from the forecasting model might be capable of generating a trading profit, under the three (hypothetical and actual) betting regimes, *R*1–*R*3. Table 8.8 shows the average returns obtained from betting on the forecasting model's predicted result for every match. The predicted results are obtained using the procedure described in section 3.3. Under *R*1, the average return from all possible bets, placed indiscriminately, is around 1 per cent. According to table 8.8 however, the average return from bets placed only on the model's predicted outcome for each match is

Table 8.9. *Average returns from £1 bets based on the outcome of each match with the highest expected return, according to the forecasting model (bets ranked in descending order of expected return)*

	Betting regime		
	*R*1	*R*2	*R*3
August	0.165	0.045	−0.055
September	0.142	0.024	−0.076
October	0.082	−0.029	−0.129
November	0.067	−0.043	−0.143
December	0.028	−0.077	−0.177
January	0.081	−0.030	−0.130
February	0.109	−0.005	−0.105
March	0.200	0.077	−0.023
April/May	0.218	0.092	−0.008
All	0.124	0.008	−0.092

Key:
*R*1: bets at odds consistent with bookmaker's implicit probabilities (no profit margin)
*R*2: bets at quoted odds inclusive of margin, but not allowing for betting duty
*R*3: bets at quoted odds, with betting duty of 10 pence on each £1 bet.

Table 8.10. *Average returns from every possible £1 bet (bets ranked in descending order of expected return according to forecasting model)*

	Betting regime		
	*R*1	*R*2	*R*3
Best 900	0.071	−0.038	−0.138
Second-best 900	0.151	0.032	−0.068
Middle 1,104	0.048	−0.060	−0.160
Second-worst 900	−0.122	−0.213	−0.313
Worst 900	−0.106	−0.198	−0.298
All	0.010	−0.094	−0.194

Key:
*R*1: bets at odds consistent with bookmaker's implicit probabilities (no profit margin)
*R*2: bets at quoted odds inclusive of margin, but not allowing for betting duty
*R*3: bets at quoted odds, with betting duty of 10 pence on each £1 bet.

just over 3 per cent. The model seems to perform best during the middle of the season, and less well near the beginning (September) and at the end (April/May), though bets placed at the very beginning of the season (August) do generate a positive return. Overall, however, the positive average return under $R1$ is insufficient to prevent losses from being realised under both $R2$ and $R3$.

Betting on the forecasting model's predicted outcomes does not represent the most effective use of the information the model generates, because it does not take advantage of perceived inefficiencies in the bookmaker's prices. Table 8.9 shows the average returns obtained from betting on the outcome of each match for which, according to the forecasting model, the bookmaker's odds generate the highest expected return. Overall, this strategy generates a much higher average return than betting on the model's predicted result. Under $R1$, there is a positive average return of more than 12 per cent. The average return under $R2$ is close to zero, while $R3$ still produces an average loss of -9 per cent. This strategy appears to perform better at the start and at the end of the season than it does in the middle. It seems likely that it is more difficult to formulate reliable assessments of the match outcome probabilities at the start of the season (when there is little or no present-season evidence on team qualities) and at the end (when results are heavily influenced by incentive effects) than in the middle of the season.

Finally, table 8.10 shows the average returns from all 4,704 possible bets (3 bets on each of 1,568 matches), ranked in descending order of their expected return according to the forecasting model. All of the bets included in table 8.9 are assessed by the model to represent relatively good value for money (since only the bet with the highest expected return for each match is included). In contrast, by including all available bets table 8.10 provides a better impression of the model's capacity to distinguish between bets which represent good or poor value. The 900 bets assessed by the model as offering the highest expected return produce an actual average return of 7 per cent under $R1$, whereas the next 900 generate an actual return of 15 per cent. The average return then decreases across the remaining three groups, with average losses of -11 per cent realised on the 1,800 bets assessed by the model to offer the poorest expected returns, under $R1$. Of course, the fact that the actual returns correlate with the rankings by expected return produced by the model constitutes further evidence of weak-form inefficiency in the bookmaker's prices. Unfortunately, however, the inefficiencies do not appear to be sufficiently large to create profitable betting strategies after allowing for the bookmaker's margin and for betting duty.

An illustration: bets on the results of Premier League matches played on 24 April 1999

Table 8.11 shows the complete Premier League fixture list for Saturday 24 April 1999. Columns (1)–(3) show the bookmaker's fixed odds for each possible outcome. Columns (4)–(6) show the bookmaker's implicit probabilities, $\phi_{i,j}^r$, and columns (7)–(9) show the probabilities generated by the match results forecasting model, $p_{i,j}^r$, for $r = H,D,A$. Column (10) shows the forecasting model's predicted result, obtained (as before) using the procedure described in section 3.3. Column (11) shows the actual match result.

Columns (4)–(6) and (7)–(9) show that there was a reasonable measure of agreement between the bookmaker's and forecasting model's assessments of the probabilities for different match results. For four of the eight matches (Aston Villa v. Nottingham Forest, Blackburn Rovers v. Liverpool, Tottenham Hotspur v. West Ham United and Wimbledon v. Newcastle United) the respective probabilities for any result were never more than 0.05 apart. But for Derby County v. Southampton, Leicester City v. Coventry City and Middlesbrough v. Arsenal, the model's home win probability was significantly higher than the bookmaker's, while for Everton v. Charlton Athletic the bookmaker's home win probability was significantly higher than the model's.

Columns (10) and (11) of table 8.11 show what would have happened if individual bets had been placed on each of the forecasting model's predicted outcomes on 24 April 1999. In practice, bookmakers do not accept individual bets, except on televised matches. For all other matches, bettors must place combination bets. The requirement to place bets on several matches simultaneously does not affect the expected return on any bet, though it does affect the variance. The variance in the bettor's overall return is reduced or eliminated, however, over a large number of combination bets. Since the purpose of this section is to investigate betting strategies capable of generating a positive expected return, the analysis will proceed by calculating expected and actual returns on (hypothetical) individual bets.

Columns (10) and (11) of table 8.11 show that individual bets on the model's predicted outcomes on 24th April 1999 would have produced four winning and four losing bets. Before payment of betting duty, £1 placed on Aston Villa to beat Nottingham Forest would have yielded 40p. £1 bets placed on Leicester City to beat Coventry City, Arsenal to win at Middlesbrough and Wimbledon to draw with Newcastle United would have yielded £1.10, 80p and £2.25, respectively. The overall gross profit, allowing for the other four losing bets, would have been 55p. But

Table 8.11. *Fixed-odds betting on Premier League fixtures, 24th April 1999*

| Fixture list | Bookmaker's odds | | | Bookmaker's probabilities | | | Forecasting model's probabilities | | | Model's prediction | Match result |
	H (1)	D (2)	A (3)	H (4)	D (5)	A (6)	H (7)	D (8)	A (9)	(10)	(11)
Aston Villa v. Nottm Forest	2/5	3/1	11/2	0.639	0.224	0.138	0.633	0.232	0.135	H	2-0
Blackburn v. Liverpool	4/5	12/5	11/4	0.498	0.263	0.239	0.467	0.285	0.249	D	1-3
Derby v. Southampton	Evens	5/2	2/1	0.447	0.255	0.298	0.577	0.254	0.170	H	0-0
Everton v. Charlton	8/11	5/2	3/1	0.519	0.256	0.224	0.438	0.290	0.272	D	4-1
Leicester v. Coventry	11/10	12/5	15/8	0.426	0.263	0.311	0.549	0.263	0.188	H	1-0
Middlesbrough v. Arsenal	10/3	2/1	4/5	0.206	0.298	0.496	0.330	0.297	0.374	A	1-6
Tottenham v. West Ham	Evens	9/4	9/4	0.448	0.276	0.276	0.493	0.279	0.229	H	1-2
Wimbledon v. Newcastle	5/4	9/4	7/4	0.398	0.276	0.326	0.425	0.292	0.284	D	1-1

Source: Fixed-odds betting coupons.

unfortunately this translates into a net loss of 25p after payment of 10p duty on each bet. In comparison with table 8.8, 24 April 1999 appears to have been a slightly better-than-average day on which to rely on the model's predictions (for Premier League matches at least). In contrast, the strategy of betting on the outcome of each match with the highest expected return according to the model's probabilities would have produced only one winning bet out of eight, on Leicester to beat Coventry. In comparison with the average performance of this strategy for the 1999 season as a whole shown in table 8.9, a gross loss of £5.90 represents a worse-than-average return.

It is perhaps relevant to note that all four of the matches for which there was relatively large disagreement between the bookmaker's and the forecasting model's probabilities carried significance for championship or relegation outcomes, for either or both of the teams involved. The disagreements between the probabilities may reflect the fact that end-of-season matches in which the two teams have different levels of incentive to win are hard to assess. As suggested by table 8.11, the bookmaker appears to have predicted three of these four matches (Derby County v. Southampton, Everton v. Charlton Athletic and Middlesbrough v. Arsenal) more successfully than the model (the exception being Leicester City v. Coventry City). Without wishing to over-generalise on the basis of a very small number of observations, it does seem possible that the model's championship, promotion or relegation significance dummy variable is insufficiently sensitive to detect all of the incentive effects that various configurations of placings in the late-season league table might throw up. It must also be remembered that the bookmakers are able to incorporate into their prices all kinds of qualitative data (e.g. about suspensions or injuries, or about the quality of recent team performances, match results notwithstanding) which are not used in the forecasting model in its present form. But in principle, there is no reason why the model could not be refined to incorporate any additional relevant information that can be collected and quantified systematically.

8.4 Conclusion

The two empirical investigations reported in chapter 8 are linked by a common theme: both are concerned with the transmission of information to secondary markets, in which trade takes place at prices ultimately contingent on occurrences on football's fields of play. Investigation of the speed and efficiency with which relevant information is impounded into prices is an important and widely researched topic in both economics and finance. Interest in this topic is partly theoretical: rapid and accurate flows of information are an essential prerequisite for the efficient functioning of the price mechanism in a market economy. The same topic is also of major practical importance: if some traders have access to privileged information, then they also enjoy (unfairly in certain circumstances) the opportunity to make gains at the expense of the less well informed.

The event study analysis of the daily returns on the prices of the shares of 13 quoted football clubs shows that prices respond rapidly and systematically to changes in the fortunes of the teams on the field of play. The results of regular league matches exert a clearly identifiable impact on the share price on the next trading day. Using predictions generated by the match results forecasting model, it is possible to test and confirm that the unanticipated component of the match result (rather than the result itself) is of prime importance in determining the direction and size of the share price adjustment. This finding, of course, is compliant with the efficient markets hypothesis, which requires that anticipated information should already be impounded into the share price and should therefore cause no further reaction. As well as regular league match results, sporting outcomes with more substantial financial implications also lead to rapid and sometimes very large share price adjustments. These include (in ascending order of importance) elimination from the FA Cup, elimination from European competition and end-of-season promotion or relegation outcomes. Finally, the extreme sensitivity of football clubs' share prices to major news concerning the 1998 BSkyB takeover bid for Manchester United provides further evidence (if any is needed) of the symbiotic nature of the relationship that now exists between the football and broadcasting sectors.

The investigation of the weak-form efficiency of the odds posted by a leading high-street bookmaker for fixed-odds betting on the outcomes of league matches uncovers some evidence of inefficiency in the transmission of information. The match results forecasting model developed in chapter 3 is able to generate data about the probabilities of match results which supplements the information already impounded into the bookmaker's odds. The latter, therefore, do not make maximum use of all relevant historical data in the public domain, and so fail to satisfy the standard criteria for weak-form efficiency. Unfortunately with regard to the present authors' bank balances, however, the inefficiencies revealed are insufficient to suggest trading strategies that can overcome the margins and tax deductions built into the bookmaker's prices. Refining the forecasting model so that profitable trading strategies can be identified represents an interesting challenge for the future.

Ever since the principle of professionalism first gained official acceptance in English football in the late nineteenth century, the remark that football is as much a business as it is a sport has been something of a cliché. But for the first six decades of the twentieth century football was a business run on commercial principles that seem worlds apart from those that currently prevail among the sport's highest echelons in the Premier League. It is either reassuring or worrying, depending on one's point of view, that at the start of the twenty-first century, one can still find evidence in the lower reaches of the Football League that older practices and attitudes are not yet totally extinct.

With hindsight, the last four decades of the twentieth century can be seen as something of a continuum, during which the trend towards what, for want of a better word we shall call the 'commercialisation' of professional football, was always apparent, even though the process gained and lost momentum at different times within this period. Broadly speaking, the 1960s was a decade of fast transformation, as football's economic structure adapted to changes such as the abolition of the maximum wage and the introduction of freedom-of-contract. During the 1970s and early 1980s the pace of change slowed as the sport's policy agenda became mainly defensive, dominated by issues such as the twin demons of hooliganism and declining spectator interest. In the late 1980s and 1990s the pace of change accelerated again, as club owners and players alike were deluged by an avalanche of new revenue from sources such as television, sponsorship and merchandising.

Most of the major policy issues facing the sport at the start of the twenty-first century stem in large measure from the unequal distribution of these new-found riches between clubs and players at different levels within the league hierarchy. An 'avalanche' may be a suitable metaphor for the recent increases in the cash flows of a number of leading Premier League clubs, but the chairman of a typical Division Three club struggling year-on-year to balance the books might be more inclined to view the present situation as a not entirely convincing demonstration of the efficacy of 'trickle-down' economics: the doctrine that a rise in inequality throughout society provides the rich with wealth-creating incentives that also benefit the poor when some of the proceeds eventually 'trickle down'.

But what is the fundamental cause of the sharp increase in economic inequality between different levels of the football hierarchy over the past 40 years, and the attendant rise in competitive imbalance on the field of play that has occurred over the same period? Public discussion usually tends to focus on the actions of three groups: the club owners, the players and the media. This concluding chapter begins in section 9.1 by considering how the economic analysis presented in the preceding chapters of this volume helps pinpoint more precisely the contributions of each of these three groups to football's present situation. Section 9.2 then goes on to examine a number of current issues concerning football's future development as a sport and as a business.

9.1 Sources of competitive imbalance in English football

Chapter 8 has documented major changes in the ownership structure of English football. 18 clubs floated on the LSE during the 1980s and 1990s, and the financing of many others that have remained privately owned was also transformed, as part of the process of adjustment to the new commercial and financial environment. So has the shift towards a more commercially-oriented and profit-driven business ethos suggested by these changes in ownership and financing made a major contribution towards the apparently inexorable rise in competitive imbalance? Conn (1997) argues that the new breed of businessmen and entrepreneurs attracted into football do indeed have much to answer for:

The profit motive became the defining principle of British life. It is sobering to consider now quite how far it has penetrated, how many areas of life – health, education, sport – have lost their sense of what they are and become ruled according to the dictates of buying and selling . . . Some of the hardest heads of the Eighties, to whom market forces had dealt the riches, took their cold look at the figures and began to profess a sudden desire to be involved in football . . . A new breed of football advisor arrived – accountants, brokers, lawyers schooled in the nihilism of 'market forces' – looking at football in the most superficial of ways. Football, according to the City is an 'entertainment product', the clubs are brands. (Conn, 1997, pp. 152, 154, 157)

Conn's data show that a number of individuals have achieved spectacular capital gains from very modest original investments in football clubs, though in some cases these gains are paper ones that have not yet been realised. Industry-level data, however, suggest that with the partial exception of shareholders of Manchester United, club owners in general are capturing only a very small proportion of the revenues currently flowing into football. According to figures compiled by Deloitte and Touche (2000), the 20 clubs that were members of the Premier League in the 1999 season generated a combined revenue from all sources of £2,310 million over the five-year period from 1994 to 1999. Combined operating profits before transfer expenditure were £315 million, but if net transfer expenditures are also included in the calculation, there was a combined loss of £147 million. Admittedly the combined data mask the fact that several of the best-supported clubs were consistently and highly profitable; besides Manchester United (with profits after net transfer expenditure of £93 million), Aston Villa (£7 million), Tottenham Hotspur (£6 million) and Arsenal (£5 million) all recorded significant profits over the five-year period. But the fact that 15 of the 20 Premier League clubs, and 30 out of 39 Football League clubs for which complete data were available turned in losses suggests that if the profit motive really is paramount, ownership of a football club is not a very effective vehicle for realising this objective.

Economic reasoning also casts doubt on the notion that the pursuit of profit could be responsible for rising competitive imbalance within football. As shown in chapter 3 the pursuit of profit rather than utility maximising objectives by the owners of the stronger clubs should actually tend to enhance competitive balance within the league, as profit considerations tend to moderate the willingness of these clubs to spend heavily on players. If this reasoning is correct, the pecuniary greed of club owners might be blamed for many things, but increasing competitive imbalance is not one of them. This point, of course, has not been lost on the supporters of Manchester United, often critical of the relative conservatism of their club's wage scales which, it is suggested, prevent the club from competing effectively with the giant clubs of Italy and Spain for the services of the best international players (see also section 2.1). Tottenham is another case in which the tension between sporting and commercial objectives has been widely publicised and debated.

Of course it is possible to berate club chairmen for many sins of commission and omission: acceding to the extortionate wage demands of greedy players; imposing totally unrealistic demands on managers and then passing the buck when things go wrong (see chapters 5 and 6); or selling broadcasting and sponsorship rights to the highest bidders regardless of the interests of spectators or the broader public. But it does at least seem plausible to suggest that in taking such decisions, chairmen are generally bowing to economic forces more powerful than their own personal preferences and whims.

If rapacious club owners are not the main driving force behind football's growth in competitive and economic imbalance, then perhaps it is the players who should shoulder most of the responsibility. Chapter 2 has charted a number of institutional changes to the structure of players' employment contracts and the organisation of the transfer market, dating back to the abolition of the maximum wage in 1961, and the reforms to the 'retain-and-transfer' system that followed the Eastham v. Newcastle United case at the High Court in 1963. Clearly much has changed between the early 1960s when Fulham's Johnny Haynes became the first English player to earn £100 per week, and the dawn of the new millennium when Roy Keane's new £52,000-a-week contract with Manchester United made him at that point the English league's highest-paid player, earning more in a week than most UK economics professors make in a year! So is it correct to say that the astronomical wage demands of the top players have created a situation in which only a handful of wealthy clubs can afford to employ them, while at the same time conveniently guaranteeing that the same clubs will dominate the league championship year-in-year-out?

It is certainly true that the tendency for the best players to gravitate to the wealthiest clubs is far more pronounced today than it was, say, 30 or 40 years ago. England's 1966 World Cup-winning team, for example, included players whose careers were spent mostly or entirely with relatively unfashionable clubs: Bobby Moore and Geoff Hurst both played exclusively for West Ham United until they were in their thirties and nearing the end of their careers; George Cohen spent his entire career at Fulham; and Gordon Banks' top-level career was split between Leicester City and Stoke City. But in order to explain why 35 years later such players (or their successors) would have been snapped up by Manchester United, Arsenal, Liverpool or one of a handful of overseas clubs, it is important to separate cause from effect. The players' enhanced bargaining power as free agents does not necessarily provide the ultimate explanation.

It is clear that leading players have been able to increase their remuneration spectacularly because changes to the contractual and transfer systems have eroded the monopsony power of individual clubs as buyers of players' services. Under the pre-1963 retain-and-transfer system a player had no choice other than to abide by the wishes of the club currently holding his registration. Quite literally the clubs held all the cards. In contrast in the post-1995, post-Bosman world of free agency, an out-of-contract player is completely free to sell his services to the highest bidder. Small wonder that players' earnings have rocketed as a result. And, as argued in chapter 4, small wonder that the earnings of the most talented players have rocketed the most, since these are the players with the greatest monopoly power as sellers of services for which few or no direct substitutes exist.

Some caution is needed, however, before attributing the rise in competitive imbalance within the league to the same process. As argued in chapter 3, the economically optimal distribution of a resource such as playing talent should be independent of the ownership of the property rights to that resource. In other words, shifting the property rights or ownership of playing talent from the clubs to the players should not affect the optimal distribution of playing talent between the clubs. Essentially, the question as to whether a player's marginal revenue product (MRP) could be increased by moving from Club B to Club A, and therefore the question as to whether a trade can be arranged that leaves both clubs and the player better off (or at least no worse off) is independent of the player's contractual position. If the player is currently under contract and the trade does take place, Club A pays some portion of the capitalised value of the player's MRP in compensation to Club B. Since Club B (not the player) owns the property rights, the player's reward for the move may be small. If the player is out of contract, he can bargain with Club A to increase his remuneration until he captures the bulk of his own MRP with Club A. Since the player (not Club B) owns the property rights, Club B receives nothing when the player departs. But the question as to whether the gains from trade actually exist is different from the question as to who captures the gains, assuming that they do exist and the move does take place. While the rising level of player earnings can be explained, long-term changes in the equilibrium distribution of playing talent between clubs remain unexplained.

Sceptics may argue that the invariance result is a property of a highly stylised abstract theoretical model, but does not necessarily bear much relation to what is happening in the real world. A fair comment, perhaps, but empirical studies in the USA that have investigated the effect on competitive balance of the change from the reserve clause to free agency in a number of sports do not suggest that the change had any discernible effect on the distribution of performance between teams. Nor does the evidence suggest that other regulatory measures intended to influence competitive balance directly, such as the rookie draft or salary capping, are effective in achieving this aim. Admittedly the top US sports operate within an institutional and competitive framework somewhat different to that which applies in European football. But the US experience does suggest that the invariance result is a powerful one, and that considerable caution should be exercised before attempting to infer any direct causal link between the growth in players' earnings and the rise in competitive imbalance.

This is not to say that spiralling wages for the top players are a good thing, or that they do not have adverse consequences for the financial health of individual football clubs or the sport as a whole. Indeed, to the extent that a steeper earnings–talent gradient tends to raise the stakes which clubs just below the highest echelon must be prepared to place if they wish to gamble on improving their status, it may well have harmful consequences. Division One clubs like Crystal Palace and Wolverhampton Wanderers, for whom high-spending gambles on achieving Premier League status have so far failed to pay off, spring readily to mind. An ambitious attempt by Palace's former owners to spend their way back to Premier League status foundered spectacularly in 1999, bringing the club close to the point of bankruptcy and closure. Wolverhampton have spent heavily on players consistently over a number of years, but have regularly finished tantalisingly short of achieving a promotion berth. Only the willingness of the club's owners to subsidise heavy losses has allowed this strategy to continue.

If owners and players are absolved from ultimate responsibility for the rise in competitive imbalance in football, then where does the blame really lie? The theoretical models discussed in chapters 3 and 4 again provide a strong clue to the answer. Economic models of competitive balance and the distribution of playing talent in sporting leagues suggest that the relative size of each team's actual or potential audience is the final arbiter of the degree of competitive balance or imbalance that exists within the league. Economic models also suggest that the ability of the top performers in certain fields to service vast audiences, with little or no additional costs accruing as the audience size increases, explains not only the high earnings of superstars, but also their tendency to capture very large shares of the markets they serve. One should therefore look to changes in the pattern and composition of demand for the ultimate explanation of changes in the distribution of playing talent between clubs. And what has been the biggest single factor influencing the size and composition of the audience for professional football over the past 40 years? A one-word answer to this question will suffice, and clearly that word is 'television'.

As seen in chapter 2 the regular televised screening of league match highlights dates back to 1964. The direct financial impact of television on football was minimal during the 1960s and 1970s because the fees paid for broadcasting rights were puny. Before the days of pay-television, broadcasters could not charge the audience directly for providing the service. Televised football had many of the hallmarks of a public good: audience members unwilling to pay could not be excluded from obtaining the service, so audience members who would have been willing to pay could not actually be made to do so.

Indirectly, however, television was fuelling changes in the composition of football's audience, the long-term impact of which was no less profound for not being directly visible in the short term. Inevitably the television coverage was skewed in favour of the clubs with the most followers, bringing the exploits and achievements of their leading players to the regular attention of millions who previously would have seen no more than occasional newsreel clips or newspaper photographs of their predecessors. This national exposure, together with other social, economic and demographic changes pushing in the same direction, could only weaken the traditional bonds between the residents and clubs of the smaller towns and cities. Consequently, when the long-term decline in attendances accelerated into a nosedive in the late 1970s and early 1980s, it was the smaller clubs that were hardest hit. The advent of regular live coverage in the early 1980s coincided with the television companies experiencing increased commercial and political pressure to maximise viewing figures. As the implicit BBC–ITV cartel disintegrated under the strain, the fees paid for broadcasting rights rose sharply, as did the proportion of coverage devoted to the big-market teams.

But from football's point of view the arrival on the scene of BSkyB and pay-television at the end of the decade was the crucial development that fundamentally and irreversibly transformed the economics of the industry. For the first time it was possible to charge individual audience members directly for the right to watch football on television. From a commercial perspective, at a stroke effective demand was extended from the several thousands or tens of thousands already known to be willing to turn up to watch each team's matches in person, to the millions more who might be persuaded to subscribe to watch televised matches in the comfort of their living rooms. And inevitably, it was the big-market teams and superstar players that were of greatest interest to the television audience, as well as the sponsors and suppliers of merchandise desperate to jump onto the bandwagon at the earliest available opportunity. Unprecedented expansion of the potential audience concentrated disproportionately on a handful of big-market clubs, achieved at almost zero incremental cost to the clubs and players, combined with acute scarcity in the supply of the very best talent, created ideal conditions for massive wage inflation, and for the employment of the most talented players to become increasingly concentrated with those same big-market clubs. So while it is undoubtedly true that the big-market clubs are the only ones able to afford to pay the most talented players, the ultimate reason for this lies in the changing level and composition of effective demand, which in turn has been driven mainly by technological innovation in broadcasting.

9.2 The future of professional football

Having identified rising competitive imbalance as perhaps the most fundamental problem currently facing professional football, and having pinpointed growth in the market for televised football as its ultimate cause, it is now possible to move on to examine a number of specific policy issues currently facing decision makers, including the sport's governing bodies, club owners, broadcasters, sponsors and legislators. The discussion will be organised into three sub-sections, which consider current proposals for European leagues; the issue of players' wage inflation; and issues of ownership, control and media interest in football.

European leagues

Discussions about the possible creation of a new European Super League competition emanate directly from concerns about competitive imbalance within domestic leagues, and from the desire of the big-market clubs in each country to maximise their television and sponsorship income. Should the leading clubs from each country continue to operate mainly within long-standing domestic league structures? Or should they withdraw to create a new European Super League? Or can they have it both ways, by competing simultaneously at European level in midweek and domestically at weekends?

Speculation that a Super League breakaway was imminent reached a peak in 1998 when discussions between the Milan-based consultancy firm Media Partners and a number of leading European clubs concerning the creation of a midweek league appeared to have reached an advanced stage. According to some reports the proposed league would have had a membership of 36 clubs, with 96 clubs taking part in a parallel cup tournament. It would have operated outside the jurisdiction of UEFA, football's governing body at European level, creating chaos in the administration of the sport at the highest level. The world governing body FIFA's response to the breakaway discussions was to threaten any participating club with suspension, which would have meant immediate ejection from involvement in existing domestic competitions.

By the end of 1998 UEFA had succeeded in heading off the threat, mainly by announcing a hasty reorganisation of its three European club tournaments, effective from the start of the following (2000) season. The Champions League would be expanded from 24 to 32 clubs, with two group stages reducing the number of teams first to 16 and then to eight, before the knock-out stages began. A team reaching the second group stage would be guaranteed 12 matches, while a team reaching the final would play in 17. The Cup Winners and UEFA Cups would be merged into an expanded UEFA Cup competition for clubs failing to qualify for the Champions League, as well as eight of the clubs eliminated from the Champions League in the first group stage.

As the expanded Champions League ran its course for the first time during the 2000 season, many commentators felt that the format had become cumbersome and bloated. Although the knock-out stages (in particular) produced some breathtaking football, many group matches were either sterile or defensive affairs that lacked the excitement of sudden-death competition, or uninteresting because the teams were unequally balanced, or meaningless because teams had already qualified or could not qualify for the next stage. Some were played in front of half-empty stadia which contributed to the lack of atmosphere. On the one hand this may have provided a rather sobering view of a future consisting of regular league competition at European level. But on the other hand television viewing figures throughout Europe remained buoyant, with £334 million raised from the sale of broadcasting rights and sponsorship packages for the 2000 season alone (*Marketing Week*, 25 May 2000). The point at which further expansion of the scale of the tournament starts causing viewers to switch off is unknown, but appears not to have been breached so far.

Although the same format has been retained for the 2001 season, UEFA have decided to look again at the structure of the Champions League, with a reduction in the number of matches one possibility under consideration. Evidently there are conflicting pressures on organisers and clubs, which apply equally to the Champions League and to any hypothetical Super League. A smaller tournament reduces wear-and-tear on players and is more exciting, while a larger tournament enables more clubs to compete and generates more revenue.

It seems likely that advocates of a complete withdrawal from domestic league competition on the part of the leading clubs have under-estimated the importance of domestic history, tradition and continuity as defining characteristics of these clubs' identities. Though Manchester United v. Liverpool and Manchester United v. Real Madrid are more prestigious than Manchester United v. Southampton, the latter is still a bigger event than many fixtures, involving teams like Sturm Graz, Rosenborg and Brondby, that could well be staple fare if an inclusive Super League became a reality; especially if (as is always possible) Manchester United themselves turned out to be no more than a mid-table team in a European setting. Of course the same point applies equally to Real Madrid, Barcelona, Juventus, AC Milan and others.

Even so, wholesale withdrawal by the top clubs from domestic league competition seems a more practical proposition than the alternative of having the top clubs participate simultaneously in domestic and European leagues, for the simple reason that players are physically not capable of participating in even more matches than at present. The suggestion that Super League members could field teams comprising second-string players in domestic matches also seems dubious in view of its damaging implications for the competitive integrity of domestic competition.

If the prospect of a withdrawal from their domestic leagues by the top European clubs seems to have receded temporarily at least, negotiations over a similar move on the part of leading clubs from a number of second-tier European football nations remain in progress at the time of writing, possibly with a greater chance of eventual success. At the time of writing Holland, Belgium, Scotland, Portugal, Norway, Sweden and Denmark were involved in discussions concerning the creation of a new 16-team competition, provisionally termed the Atlantic League. The domestic leagues in all of these countries suffer from a 'minimum efficient scale' problem: national populations are too small to sustain 16 or 18 teams able to employ players of sufficient talent to create a league with standards comparable to those of the big five (England, France, Germany, Italy and Spain) and capable of attracting commensurate spectator and television audiences. As a result competition in most of these leagues is highly unbalanced, and television revenues are modest. Ajax Amsterdam and Celtic both received around £2.5 million from the sale of domestic television rights in the 2000 season, for example, while Manchester United received more than £10 million, and Real Madrid and Barcelona more than £20 million each.

A combined population in the seven Atlantic League countries of 59 million offers the possibility of television audiences and revenues on a par with those attainable in the big five European leagues. Under one set of proposals the League would operate within European football's existing organisational framework. The top teams would qualify for the Champions League and UEFA Cup, all teams would participate in domestic cup tournaments, and play-offs would leave the door open for promotion and relegation between the Atlantic and domestic leagues. The possibility of regular financial subsidy from the Atlantic League to the domestic leagues has also been floated. It has been suggested the teams left behind might even prosper in competitive terms if the obligation to serve as cannon-fodder for the top teams twice (or four times) each season is lifted. On balance the top teams look to have more to gain, and the teams left behind in the domestic leagues less to lose, than seems to have been the case at the equivalent stage of the aborted Super League negotiations. Despite continuing resistance from UEFA, it still looks possible, though by no means certain, that the Atlantic League proposals will eventually materialise in some form.

Wage inflation and football's 'arms race'

Returning to the domestic scene, declining competitive balance raises important policy issues at all levels within the English league hierarchy. The widening financial and competitive gulf between the Premier League and Football League has already been touched upon in this chapter, and has been discussed extensively elsewhere (Deloitte and Touche, 1999, 2000). So is it true to say that the escalating wage settlements of the Premier League stars are creating ripple-like effects throughout the Football League as aspiring lower-division clubs strive to keep pace, and that the resulting wage inflation is threatening the viability and survival of many of the smaller clubs?

It certainly seems to be the case that the degree of intra-league mobility in English football is less than it used to be. And nowhere is this more apparent than at the boundary between the Premier and Football Leagues. Only nine of the 20 teams promoted to the Premier League at the end of its first seven seasons (1993 to 1999 inclusive) avoided relegation in the first season after promotion. In contrast, 17 of the 21 teams promoted to Division 1 in the seven seasons following the introduction of 'three-up three-down' in 1974 avoided immediate relegation. In the reverse direction, however, the figures are much closer. Only seven of the 22 teams relegated to Division One between 1993 and 1999 were promoted the following season, while just five of the 21 relegated to Division 2 between 1974 and 1980 achieved the same feat.

In the 1970s one had the impression that any mid-table Division 2 team could realistically aspire to become a mid-table Division 1 team within a year or two, either by making a couple of good signings or (perhaps more by luck than judgement) hiring a particularly effective manager. Not all such teams did so of course, but the possibility was always there. But by the turn of the century, a serious assault on achieving a (relatively) secure foothold in the Premier League appears to have become an operation requiring millions of pounds of up-front investment with no guaranteed return, and several years of patient and consistent development to build up an adequate playing squad, as well as all the accompanying infrastructure that is now commonplace at the highest level. True, Division One teams can still achieve promotion without making all this investment, but a speedy return via the relegation trapdoor can usually be anticipated in such cases. For clubs such as Leicester City,

Middlesbrough, Sunderland and Charlton Athletic, being promoted a second time, having raised revenue and gained experience during an initial short-lived spell in the top flight, was necessary before a degree of consolidation was eventually achieved.

Uncertainty surrounding the rewards that such efforts will produce is heightened by the fact that if a number of rival clubs pursue similar strategies, not all of them can possibly be successful at the same time. Rosen and Sanderson (2000) have suggested that escalating expenditure on players by competing clubs operating within a league has many of the characteristics of a military arms race between nations. If all parties increase spending at the same rate, then all finish up in the same relative positions at the end of the process that they occupied at the beginning. But for each individual club or nation unable to influence the momentum of the process at the aggregate level, increasing its own private spending may be the only rational course of action to pursue for fear of losing ground in the race if it abstains.

In fact, the 'arms race' analogy leads directly to what seems to be the root cause of the endemic loss making propensities of the large majority of professional football clubs: propensities that are just as evident now in boom conditions as during football's darkest days of penury 15 or 20 years ago. Sporting competition places irresistible pressures on clubs to strive for improvement by whatever means the rules will allow. Seeking to attract the best players by paying them large sums of money is one such method. But within a league competition this is a zero-sum game: one team's ascent up the league must inevitably be accommodated by others shifting down. Likewise in an arms race, one nation's relative strategic gain is invariably another's relative loss.

Accordingly, any spending by one club that achieves a relative improvement in performance immediately imposes a negative externality on the others that fall behind. And when all parties make spending decisions on privately rational criteria, ignoring the negative externalities that the same decisions impose elsewhere, the result is over-spending, or a situation where aggregate or social welfare is lower than it would be if only the individual spending could be constrained. A loss-making football club stranded in mid-table despite having spent beyond its means on players (and having seen others do the same) is very like an impoverished nation that has gained no strategic advantage whatsoever by engaging its neighbours in a tit-for-tat arms race.

The preceding discussion of the barriers to mobility between the Football League and Premier League suggests that the volume of additional expenditure required even to stand a chance of making headway up the league's hierarchy has increased over time. In the arms race, sophisticated electronic missiles systems have replaced shells and rockets. But fundamentally the economics of the situation are the same today as they were 10, 20 or 30 years ago. Clubs under intense competitive pressure to improve performance by spending as much on players as their revenues (or the willingness of their owners to subsidise losses) will allow, will tend to do just that, even though most of the benefits from the extra expenditure are cancelled out by other clubs behaving in exactly the same manner. If revenues grow, players' wages automatically tend to follow suit as a result of competition between clubs for their services. As in earlier parts of the analysis costs are endogenous, driven ultimately by demand. At the aggregate level rising player wages cannot be blamed for football clubs' losses because they are simply a consequence of revenue growth, even though at the micro level individual chairmen may feel that they have no option other than to accede to players' escalating wage demands. If club owners are prepared to tolerate losses in pursuit of improved playing performance, then it is inevitable that losses will follow. This outcome should be seen as an entirely predictable consequence of the economic structures in which the clubs operate.

By increasing the bargaining power of players relative to their employers, the Bosman ruling strengthened the tendency for escalating spending on the part of clubs in pursuit of playing success to feed through directly into players' wages. And the European Commission's determination to allow something approaching complete freedom of movement for in-contract players seems certain to add more fuel to the flames. As the football industry struggles to come to terms with the new arrangements, it is worth commenting briefly on the principles that govern intervention at the European level.

A declaration accompanying the Amsterdam Treaty of 1997 recognised football's unique economic characteristics, which could, under some circumstances, justify exemptions from the automatic application of all aspects of European competition and employment law to football. Nevertheless, freedom of movement for all players and clubs within the EU is a principle that can be over-ridden only if it conflicts with sporting objectives that cannot be achieved by other means. Sports governing bodies have the right to take decisions that restrict economic competition, but again these have to be justified by sporting objectives (Foster, 2000). So in the Jean-Marc Bosman case, the ECJ accepted that it was legitimate for big-market teams to cross-subsidise small-market teams to further the sporting objective of competitive balance, but it did not accept that the transfer system that operated pre-Bosman was the only mechanism capable of delivering this cross-subsidy. Similar reasoning explains the Commission's current determination to reform the transfer system for in-contract players. As suggested in chapter 2, the cross-subsidy the transfer system currently delivers could be achieved by means of direct transfer of revenue (known euphemistically as revenue sharing) from the Premier League to the Football League, on a scale that would be modest relative to the income the Premier League currently generates. But of course it can also be argued that the incentive for small-market teams to discover and develop talented players would be less if the cross-subsidy were automatic, rather than payable only when a player is sold.

Details of the arrangements that will replace the transfer system are unclear at the time of writing. Early speculation suggested that something similar to a spot market in playing talent could emerge. Under the latest proposals, players will only be allowed to change clubs during two 'transfer windows' during the summer and winter, each of which will last for a few weeks. No player will be allowed to change clubs more than once in any twelve-month period. In-contract players will be permitted to break their contracts unilaterally, subject to a period of notice of a few months' duration. Such players would be banned from playing for other clubs during the period of notice. Compensation arrangements will still apply for moves involving in-contract players. This system will give players who are in form and in demand massively enhanced bargaining power in wage negotiations. It will also make the manager's tasks of team building and long-term planning more difficult than under existing arrangements.

Predictions made in 1995 that the Bosman ruling would spell the end for the transfer market, resulting in wholesale chaos, were clearly wide of the mark. One of the main reasons is that clubs and players both saw clear benefits in the security that long-term contracts could provide. Securing the services of a star player for several years gives time for a manager to build a successful team, or for a club to exploit fully the player's merchandising potential. A long-term contract provides a player with insurance against loss of form or injury. Consequently clubs were keen to tie their best players in long-term arrangements, and many players were keen to extend contracts before they expired, without reaching the stage of becoming free agents. At present, one can only wonder how these mutual interests in stability and security would be served if European law does eventually dictate that something similar to that a spot market in playing talent must operate in football. Experience suggests, however, that if a need is sufficiently strong, new forms of contractual arrangement will develop capable of satisfying that need within whatever parameters the law imposes.

Meanwhile lower-division clubs (in particular) will worry about the implications of the possible loss of transfer income, especially if the

Premier League proves unwilling to put in place alternative mechanisms for cross-subsidy. Although many club owners may be justified in claiming that they could not continue to operate *as at present* without transfer income, economic reasoning does not necessarily imply that lower-division clubs are collectively approaching the point of financial collapse. The suggestion that in the long term, wage inflation tends to follow revenue growth applies to big-market and small-market clubs alike, and in both cases is supported by the data. Eliminate a key source of income, and wage spending will tend to adjust accordingly. The survival of the small-market clubs in aggregate is jeopardised only if players' wages start to fall to near or below their reservation levels, at which players would switch to alternative occupations rather than remain employed in football. The evidence suggests that for most lower-division clubs, this situation is currently some way off. According to data compiled by Deloitte and Touche (see also chapter 2), total wages and salaries expenditure increased by 160 per cent in Division Two and by 75 per cent in Division Three between the 1994 and 1999 seasons. A recent survey of the wages of players over the age of 20 found that the average Division Two player was earning £52,000 per year, and the average Division Three player £37,000 in 2000 (*The Independent*, 18 April 2000). Although these totals and averages may mask considerable variations between clubs and between individuals, they do suggest there is some slack in the system. Warnings of the imminent financial demise of lower-division football may therefore be somewhat exaggerated.

Does all this mean we should not worry at all about loss making football clubs? Definitely not. From an individual club's perspective there is nothing deterministic in the previous analysis: some clubs may spend wisely and succeed in making progress relative to their peers, while others may over-commit and be faced with financial ruin. What constitutes 'wise spending' is of course a matter of debate: evidence as to whether clubs concentrating on worthy projects such as youth development outperform those spending heavily on wages and transfers is inconclusive. But pursuing the 'jointness of production' argument of chapter 1, if a club does get into financial difficulties this is a matter of general concern. Returning to the Crystal Palace example (see p. 423), this club's identity is obviously a cherished and enriching part of the lives of its own supporters, who can hardly be blamed for the club's financial difficulties. But it goes further than that: rivalry with Palace is also an integral part of the identities of Charlton Athletic, West Ham United, Millwall, Brighton and Hove Albion and many others as well. If Crystal Palace had gone under in 1999 or 2000, all others would have been diminished to some extent. The general point, however, is that clubs encountering grave financial problems are sending signals mainly about the shortcomings of their own management (in the broad sense) rather than signals that the sector as a whole is facing imminent ruin.

What about spiralling player wages? Should nothing at all be done to bring these under control? For reasons that are not entirely clear the inflated earnings of football's top performers do seem to rankle with the public to a greater extent than those of comparable groups such as pop musicians and film stars. The economic analysis, however, regards spiralling wages very much as a consequence rather than a cause of the football sector's changing economic structure. This means that at the aggregate level there *is* a good deal of economic determinism in what is happening. Ultimately the top players are the monopoly suppliers of the performances the public most wants to see and is willing to pay to see. If restrictions on the players' ownership of the property rights to their own performances are removed, and if intermediate links in the supply chain (such as clubs and broadcasters) are subject to the full rigours of competition, then it is inevitable that most of the rent generated by the sale of the rights to view these performances will eventually accrue to the players.

Could a salary cap be used to impose some restraint on wage inflation? Such a measure would presumably have to operate along the lines currently employed in basketball and football in the USA, limiting clubs' total wages expenditure to a set percentage of designated revenues, and not on the lines of English football's original maximum wage that capped the wage payable to any individual player. As already seen, in the USA such restrictions are designed primarily to influence the distribution of playing talent so as to enhance competitive balance, rather than to restrain growth in wages directly (though this may also be a consequence). In the USA there are serious doubts about the effectiveness of salary capping. But in Europe it appears even less likely that similar measures could work in practice. Quite apart from the obvious incentives for clubs and players to cheat, and the probable extreme scepticism of the European courts, the openness of the players' labour market means a cap would need to apply throughout Europe to be acceptable or effective. Clearly it would be difficult or impossible to achieve agreement, let alone monitor compliance, given the sheer number of parties and disparate range of interests involved.

In any case, economic reasoning suggests that achieving restraint over player wage inflation is not necessary in order to secure the financial survival of the football industry. If the stratospheric earnings of icons such as Keane, Beckham, Figo and del Piero are really so distasteful or socially divisive that they demand some form of intervention, that is a different matter, and one that should ultimately be addressed through the tax system. But since there is no sign of any public or political appetite for the reinstatement of fiscal regimes significantly more egalitarian than those in force at present, it seems a little disingenuous to castigate players and clubs for simply acting rationally in pursuit of their private interests within the confines of existing, democratically sanctioned structures.

In view of the previous analysis, the emergence in recent years of a consistent pattern of profitability among a handful of leading English clubs requires some further comment. In theoretical terms, it can be explained by qualifying slightly the conclusion that market power on the supply side of the football industry rests predominantly with the players as monopoly sellers in the labour market. Manchester United in particular, as well as a handful of other clubs, obviously have highly marketable 'brand' identities themselves, that exist irrespective of the identities of the players currently appearing in their first teams. As monopoly owners of the merchandising rights to these identities embodied in club insignia and logos, the clubs can appropriate monopoly rents from the public through the sale of these property rights. Lower down the league's hierarchy, however, although club 'brand' loyalties among their own supporters are just as strong (if not stronger), they are too localised to be of much value to merchandisers reliant on economies of scale. Manchester United has obviously been more successful than any other club worldwide in exploiting merchandising as a source of revenue. In view of the adulation the club apparently attracts in countries such as China and Malaysia, the future commercial potential of global merchandising may be very great indeed, if still largely unquantified and untapped.

The top clubs' 'brand' identities may also help to counter-balance some of the monopoly power enjoyed by the top players as sellers in the labour market. Apart from the pecuniary rewards, the offer of a contract to play for Manchester United (or Juventus, Real Madrid or Barcelona) has intangible value, in terms of the prestige or the sense of having reached the pinnacle of one's career, that it confers upon even the most highly paid superstars. At the very top of the profession, just as the number of individuals that compete directly with the likes of Zidane, Figo and Beckham as suppliers of playing talent is strictly finite, so too is the number of clubs that compete directly with Juventus, Real Madrid and Manchester United as buyers. As there are limits to competition on both sides of the labour market, both players and clubs can expect to earn monopoly rents. Moving down the league hierarchy, the numbers of clubs of similar status and players of similar ability both increase rapidly, but the intensity of 'arms race' competition between clubs as buyers in the labour market appears to increase faster than the intensity of economic competition between players as sellers. Consequently lower-level players still tend to enjoy monopoly rents (earnings above their reservation levels) while the clubs that employ them consistently turn in losses.

Ownership, control and media interests in football

As noted previously, the high profitability of Manchester United is a matter of some controversy among its own supporters, and one that also raises more general questions about the suitability of alternative models of ownership, financial management and corporate governance for football clubs. Manchester United's 1999 season turnover of £111 million was larger than that of any other club in the world. Yet partly because of the club's duty to control its expenditure so as to fulfil its responsibilities to its shareholders, United experiences difficulties in competing with the leading Italian and Spanish clubs to attract the world's top players.

At the close of the 2000 season the contrasting styles of financial management of Manchester United and Real Madrid attracted attention in several articles in the UK financial press (*Financial Times*, 22 July 2000, 18 August 2000; *Scotland on Sunday*, 30 July 2000; *The Independent*, 5 August 2000). In contrast to United's status as a publicly limited company, Real is mutually owned by around 50,000 members, mostly ordinary supporters, who elect a president to run the club. A promise to sign Portuguese star Luis Figo from Barcelona, fulfilled for a world record transfer fee of £37 million in the summer of 2000, was one of the key pledges of recently installed Real president Florentino Lopez's election campaign. Despite having a 1999 season budget of around £72 million, Real earns little or no profit, and has reported debts anywhere between £75 million and £180 million. The club maintains close links with its bankers, however, who are unlikely to withhold access to further lending owing to Real's status as a national institution.

From the supporters' perspective, the most telling comparisons concern expenditures on players. In a survey of the wages of the world's highest paid players (*World Soccer*, November 1999) Real's three highest earners were McManaman (£65,000 per week), Anelka (£56,000) and Roberto Carlos (£40,000). United's three highest were Beckham, Keane and Giggs (all on £17,500 per week). The survey was carried out shortly before Keane's new contract was concluded, but the contrast is plain enough. At the start of the 2000 season, only five of Real's 27 first-team squad members were home-grown; the rest had been signed from other clubs. United had 16 home-grown players in a squad of 34 (Macías, 2000). In the summer of 2000, Real's record transfer signings were Figo (for £37 million from Barcelona) in 2000 and Anelka (£22.5 million from Arsenal) in 1999. United's record signings were Yorke (for a relatively modest £12.6 million from Aston Villa) and Stam (£10 million from PSV Eindhoven) both in 1998.

Nevertheless, both models of ownership and financial management are subject to pressures for change within a rapidly changing commercial environment. Under their new presidency, Real Madrid is seeking to reduce losses and to develop previously under-exploited sources of revenue such as merchandising. The idea of stock exchange flotation has already been mooted by rivals Barcelona. In England, it is significant that BSkyB have now replaced the Edwards family as the largest single shareholders in Manchester United. Media group interests in English football clubs are constrained by an FA regulation restricting any party with interests in more than one club to shareholdings below 10 per cent in each case. Nevertheless BSkyB has acquired shareholdings up to the 10 per cent limit in Manchester United, Leeds United, Chelsea, Sunderland and Manchester City. Granada Media has acquired a similar stake in Liverpool, while cable operator NTL has investments in Newcastle United, Middlesbrough, Aston Villa and Leicester City. It is easy to predict that further vertical integration and joint ventures between broadcasters and football clubs will take place in the future, and that the interface between football and television will continue to be a major battleground in which many of the issues influencing football's future development will be fought out and decided.

As already seen, the role played by technological innovation, diffusion and competition in broadcasting in determining the size and structure of professional football's effective audience cannot be emphasised too strongly. Highly significant for the future is the fact that while BSkyB enjoyed considerable monopoly power as the dominant supplier of pay-television services through most of the 1990s, at the time of writing this phase seems to be drawing rapidly to a close. Soon after the 1992–7 and 1997–2001 television contracts were signed, each providing huge windfall gains to the football industry, analysts were suggesting that relative to the amounts that could theoretically have been raised, both deals might actually have been under-priced. In large measure this was because BSkyB was the only bidder with the necessary pay-television technology and infrastructure in position on both occasions. The outcome of the third sale of televised broadcasting rights since the formation of the Premier League covering the 2002, 2003 and 2004 seasons, which was announced in June 2000, demonstrated that BSkyB's monopoly position has already been considerably eroded.

For a total fee of £1.1 billion BSkyB did succeed in ensuring the continuation of its contract to screen 66 live Premier League matches per season. It was initially intended, however, that the exclusivity of BSkyB's live coverage would not continue, however. Originally the cable operator NTL secured a contract to screen another 40 matches on a pay-per-view basis for £328 million. Under the agreement, the two companies would not screen the same match simultaneously, and BSkyB would have priority in selecting its fixtures. A feeling among commentators that the demand for pay-per-view football in Britain might not be sufficient to sustain the NTL contract appeared to be confirmed several weeks after the initial announcement, when NTL gave notice of its withdrawal. An alternative buyer for pay-per-view had not emerged at the time of writing, and it remains to be seen whether any further components of the June 2000 package will also unravel. For £183 million ITV secured the rights to screen the Saturday evening highlights package. BBC's consolation was a contract with the Football Association for joint coverage of the FA Cup and England internationals shared with BSkyB, for which the joint fee was £340 million. Finally for £315 million the terrestrial digital broadcaster ONdigital secured the rights to screen live Football League matches.

The 2001–4 contracts undoubtedly point towards a future in which heightened competition between broadcasters will reduce the returns to the television companies, and raise the football industry's proceeds from the sale of broadcasting rights, perhaps far beyond even the levels attained during the 1990s. From the television companies' perspective, the winner's curse in sealed-bid auctions of the kind that operated in 2000 has been widely debated. By definition, the successful bidder is the company that made the highest assessment of the value of the package under auction. Given that such assessments are uncertain and prone to error, the successful bidder is the one most likely to have over-estimated the true value, and consequently faces a high risk of realising a loss on the transaction. Certainly the City's reaction to BSkyB's success, reflected in the company's share price, was less than euphoric. Just before the June 2000 announcement, with speculation mounting that BSkyB might lose the Premier League contract altogether, BSkyB shares were trading more than 20 per cent below than their mid-April value. Most of this loss was recovered immediately after the announcement, but by mid-August the price had drifted down again, to around 15 per cent below the mid-April value. Anguish at the BBC over the demise of its *Match of the Day* highlights programme may have been tempered slightly by the knowledge that ITV's expenditure was far too high ever to be recouped directly via increased advertising revenues on Saturday evenings.

Beyond 2004 Internet broadcasting seems likely to play a significant role in the relationship between football clubs and broadcasting companies. Although the technology was not in place to permit transmission of pictures of sufficiently high definition in time for Internet broadcasting to claim a share in the 2001–4 packages, this situation is likely to be resolved in time for the next set of contracts. Already clubs and broadcasters are manoeuvring into positions that will enable them to take advantage. In March 2000 it was announced that BSkyB would invest £50 million in a 30 per cent stake in an operating company being formed jointly with Chelsea to develop Internet broadcasting, with flotation planned within two years. In July existing shareholders Granada Media paid Liverpool a further £20 million for a 50 per cent stake in a similar company, known as Liverpool FC Broadband. NTL have invested £21 million and £6 million in joint ventures with Rangers and Leicester City, respectively. Manchester United's existing links with 9.9 per cent shareholders BSkyB and sponsors Vodafone are likely to be central to its Internet broadcasting strategy.

One predictable consequence of these developments is that the debate which took place in the Restrictive Practices Court (RPC) in 1999 concerning the relative merits of the collective and individual sale of broadcasting rights will eventually be overtaken by future events. Despite the RPC's ruling in favour of the collective sale by the leagues on behalf of their member clubs, it seems clear that the top clubs are positioning themselves so as to be ready to take matters into their own hands and strike out independently with their respective media partners. It is unlikely that the huge increases in broadcasting fees achieved by the leading Italian and Spanish clubs after collective selling was abandoned in both countries in 1999 will have gone unnoticed in many UK football boardrooms.

Nevertheless, broadcasters and football clubs alike will need to exercise due caution in their pursuit of new sources of revenue, as the rapid revision of some of the initially hyperbolic mid-1990s estimates of the revenue potential of pay-per-view has already demonstrated. An initial experiment by BSkyB in screening a limited number of Football League matches on a pay-per-view basis towards the end of the 1999 season is reported to have generated audiences of no more than 25,000 per match (*The Independent*, 16 June 2000). The response of the viewing audience to increasing fragmentation in the provision of televised football is largely unknown. So too is the audience's response to the probable hike in subscription charges that will be required to cover the increased fees. It does seem possible that the television schedules are finally approaching saturation point. And returning to the underlying theme of increasing competitive imbalance, the procession-like character of the 2000 and 2001 Premier League championship races, both won with consumate ease by Manchester United, has surely done little to enhance the attractiveness of the product on offer to the broader television-viewing public.

9.3 Conclusion

The main implications of the arguments developed in this concluding chapter are that in the future, broadcasting companies will tend to act increasingly as a conduit through which revenues are channelled from the public as final consumers to the football clubs. In turn, fierce competition between the clubs as employers in a world of player free agency will ensure, as is already happening today, that most of the proceeds are passed on directly to the players, as the ultimate monopoly suppliers of the performing services the public wishes to view. As monopoly owners themselves of the property rights in marketable 'brand' identities that exist independently of the players they employ, the top clubs will be able to generate sufficient profits at least to satisfy the requirements of their shareholders and other investors. Lower down the league hierarchy, where the sizes of the markets in club 'brand' identities are too small for merchandisers and others to realise economies of scale, any rents accruing from the sale of broadcasting rights will be tend to be dissipated and passed on to players as a result of the impact of 'arms race' competition. At this level, most clubs will continue to realise whatever losses their owners are prepared to tolerate, as has typically been the case in the past.

From an economist's perspective all of this is entirely consistent with the predictions of theoretical models of optimising behaviour on the part of individuals, participating socially as buyers and sellers in markets. Whether the kinds of changes unleashed by market forces in the highly-charged world of modern-day professional football are good or bad is a normative question, of a kind that economists are usually ill-equipped or unwilling to address; indeed, many economists would not even accept that the question is meaningful. Once the genie of market forces has escaped from the bottle, economists may be as powerless as anyone else to do much to influence the consequences, in sports as in other walks of life. But if economists can help clarify the distinction between the underlying causes of human actions and the intended or unintended consequences that follow, they will at least have made some contribution to our understanding.

References

Aigner, D.J., Lovell, C.A.K. and Schmidt, P.J. (1977) Formulation and estimation of stochastic frontier models, *Journal of Econometrics*, 6, 21–37

Alchian, A.A. and Demsetz H. (1972) Production, information costs and economic organisation, *American Economic Review*, 62, 777–95

Ali, M.M. (1977) Probability and utility estimates for racetrack bettors, *Journal of Political Economy*, 85, 803–15

Allen, M.P., Panian, S.K. and Lotz, R.E. (1979) Managerial succession and organizational performance: a recalcitrant problem revisited, *Administrative Science Quarterly*, 24, 167–80

Atkinson, S.E., Stanley, L.R. and Tschirhart, J. (1988) Revenue sharing as an incentive in an agency problem: an example from the National Football League, *RAND Journal of Economics*, 19, 27–43

Audas, R., Dobson, S.M. and Goddard, J.A. (1997) Team performance and managerial change in the English Football League, *Economic Affairs*, 17, 30–6
  (1999) Organizational performance and managerial turnover, *Managerial and Decision Economics*, 20, 305–18

Baade, R. (1996) Professional sports as catalysts for metropolitan economic development, *Journal of Urban Affairs*, 18, 1–17

Baade, R. and Dye, R. (1990) The impact of stadiums and professional sports on metropolitan area development, *Growth and Change*, 21, 1–17

Badarinathi, R. and Kochman, L. (1996) Football betting and the efficient market hypothesis, *American Economist*, 40, 52–5

Baimbridge, M., Cameron, S. and Dawson, P.M. (1996) Satellite television and the demand for football: a whole new ball game?, *Scottish Journal of Political Economy*, 43, 317–33

Bale, J. (1993) *Sport, Space and the City*, London: Routledge

Ball, R. and Brown, P. (1968) An empirical evaluation of accounting income numbers, *Journal of Accounting Research*, 159–78

Barnett, V. and Hilditch, S. (1993) The effect of an artificial pitch surface on home team perfromance in football (soccer), *Journal of the Royal Statistical Society Series A*, 156, 39–50

Barro, R.J. (1991) Economic growth in a cross section of countries, *Quarterly Journal of Economics*, 104, 407–44

Baumol, W.J. (1959) *Business Behaviour, Value and Growth*, New York: Macmillan
  (1986) Productivity growth, convergence and welfare: what the long-run data show, *American Economic Review*, 76, 1072–85

Becker, G.S. (1971) *The Economics of Discrimination*, 2nd edn., Chicago: University of Chicago Press

Becker, M.A. and Suls, J. (1983) Take me out to the ballgame: the effects of objective, social and temporal performance information on attendance at Major League baseball games, *Journal of Sport Psychology*, 5, 302–13

Bennett, R.W. and Fizel, J.L. (1995) Telecast deregulation and competitive balance, *American Journal of Economics and Sociology*, 54, 183–99

Berle, A.A. and Means, G.C. (1932) *The Modern Corporation and Private Property*, New York: Macmillan

Binder, J.J. (1998) The event study methodology since 1969, *Review of Quantitative Finance and Accounting*, 11, 111–37

Birchall, J. (2000) *Ultra Nippon: How Japan Reinvented Football*, London: Headline

Bird, P. (1982) The demand for league football, *Applied Economics*, 14, 637–49

Bodvarsson, O.B. and Brastow, R.T. (1999) A test of employer discrimination in the NBA, *Contemporary Economic Policy*, 17, 243–55

Borland, J. (1987) The demand for Australian rules football, *Economic Record*, 63, 220–30

Bourdieu, P. (1999) The state, economics and sport, in H. Dauncey and G. Hare (eds.), *France and the 1998 World Cup*, London: Frank Cass

Bradley, J.M. (1995) *Ethnic and Religious Identity in Modern Scotland: Culture, Politics and Football*, Aldershot: Avebury

Brown, A. (ed.) (1998) *Fanatics! Power, Identity and Fandom in Football*, London: Routledge

Brown, M. (1982) Administrative succession and organizational performance: the succession effect, *Administrative Science Quarterly*, 27, 1–16

Burkitt, B. and Cameron, S. (1992) Impact of league restructring on team sport attendances: the case of rugby league, *Applied Economics*, 24, 265–71

Burns, J. (1999) *Barça: A People's Passion*, London: Bloomsbury

Butler, B. (1987) *The Official Illustrated History of the Football League*, London: Macdonald Queen Anne Press

Cain, M., Law, D. and Peel, D. (2000) The favourite-longshot bias and market efficiency in UK football betting, *Scottish Journal of Political Economy*, 47, 25–36

Cairns, J.A. (1987) Evaluating changes in league structure: the reorganisation of the Scottish Football League, *Applied Economics*, 19, 259–75

  (1990) The demand for professional team sports, *British Review of Economic Issues*, 12, 1–20

Cairns, J.A., Jennett, N. and Sloane, P.J. (1986) The economics of professional team sports: a survey of theory and evidence, *Journal of Economic Studies*, 13, 1–80

Cameron, S. (1997) Regulation of the broadcasting of sporting events, *Economic Affairs*, 17, 37–41

Campbell, D. and Shields, A. (1993) *Soccer City: The Future of Football in London*, London: Mandarin

Campbell, J. Lo, A. and MacKinlay, A.C. (1997) *The Econometrics of Financial Markets*, Princeton: Princeton University Press

Carling Opta (1999) *Football Yearbook 1999–2000*, London: Carlton

  (2000) *Football Yearbook 2000–2001*, London: Carlton

Carmichael, F., Forrest, D. and Simmons, R. (1999) The labour market in Association Football: who gets transferred and for how much?, *Bulletin of Economic Research*, 51, 125–52

Carmichael, F. and Thomas, D. (1993) Bargaining in the transfer market: theory and evidence, *Applied Economics*, 25, 1467–76

(1995) Production and efficiency in team sports: an investigation of rugby league football, *Applied Economics*, 27, 859–69

Carmichael, F., Thomas, D. and Ward, R. (2000) Team performance: the case of English Premiership football, *Managerial and Decision Economics*, 21, 31–45

Cave, M. (2000) Football rights and competition in broadcasting, in S. Hamil, J. Michie, C. Oughton and S. Warby (eds.), *Football in the Digital Age: Whose Game is it Anyway?*, Edinburgh: Mainstream

Central Statistical Office (CSO) (various years) *Regional Trends*, London C: HMSO

Clarke, S.R. and Norman, J.M. (1995) Home ground advantage of individual clubs in English soccer, *The Statistician*, 44, 509–21

Clement, R.C. and McCormick, R.E. (1989) Coaching team production, *Economic Inquiry*, 27, 287–304

Coase, R.H. (1937) The nature of the firm, *Economica*, 4, 386–405

(1960) The problem of social cost, *Journal of Law and Economics*, 3, 1–44

Colomé, G. (1997) Football and national identity in Catalonia: FC Barcelona and Español, in S. Gehrmann (ed.), *Football and Regional Identity in Europe*, Munster: Lit Verlag

Conn, D. (1997) *The Football Business – Fair Game in the 90s?*, Edinburgh: Mainstream

(1999) The new commercialism, in S. Hamil, J. Mitchie and C. Oughton (eds.), *The Business of Football: A Game of Two Halves*, Edinburgh: Mainstream

Cox, D.R. (1972) Regression models and life tables, *Journal of the Royal Statistical Society Series B*, 34, 187–202

Crafts, N.F.R. (1985) Some evidence of insider knowledge in horse racing betting in Britain, *Economica*, 52, 295–304

Cyert, R.M. and March, J.G. (1963) *A Behavioural Theory of the Firm*, New York: Prentice-Hall

Dare, W.H. and MacDonald, S. (1996) A generalized model for testing the home and favorite team advantage in point spread markets, *Journal of Financial Economics*, 40, 295–318

Davies, B., Downward, P. and Jackson, I. (1995) The demand for rugby league: evidence from causality tests, *Applied Economics*, 27, 1003–7

Dawson, P.M. (2000) *Measurement and Evaluation of Managerial Efficiency in English League Football: A Stochastic Frontier Analysis*, unpublished PhD thesis, University of Hull

Dawson, P.M., Dobson, S.M. and Gerrard, B. (2000a) Estimating coaching efficiency in professional team sports: evidence from English association football, *Scottish Journal of Political Economy*, 47, 399–421

(2000b) Stochastic frontiers and the temporal structure of managerial efficiency in English soccer, *Journal of Sports Economics*, 1, 341–62

Deloitte and Touche (1998) *Annual Review of Football Finance*, Manchester: Deloitte and Touche

(1999) *Annual Review of Football Finance*, Manchester: Deloitte and Touche

(2000) *Annual Review of Football Finance*, Manchester: Deloitte and Touche

Demmert, H.H. (1973) *The Economics of Professional Team Sports*, Lexington: D.C. Heath

Department of Labour and Productivity (1971) *British Labour Statistics, Historical Abstract 1886–1968*, London: Department of Labour and Productivity

Dixon, M.J. and Coles, S.C. (1997) Modelling association football scores and inefficiencies in the football betting market, *Applied Statistics*, 46, 265–80

Dixon, M.J. and Robinson, M.E. (1998) A birth process model for association football managers, *The Statistician*, 47, 523–38

Dobson, S.M. and Gerrard, B. (1999) The determination of player transfer fees in English professional soccer, *Journal of Sport Management*, 13, 259–79

(2000) Testing for monopoly rents in the market for playing talent: evidence from English professional football, *Journal of Economic Studies*, 27, 142–64

Dobson, S.M. and Goddard, J.A. (1992) The demand for standing and seating viewing accommodation in the English Football League, *Applied Economics*, 24, 1155–63

(1995) The demand for professional league football in England and Wales 1925–1992, *The Statistician*, 44, 259–77

(1996) The demand for football in the regions of England and Wales, *Regional Studies*, 30, 443–53

(1998a) Performance and revenue in professional league football: evidence from Granger causality tests, *Applied Economics*, 30, 1641–51

(1998b) Performance, revenue and cross subsidisation in the English Football League, 1927–94, *Economic History Review*, 51, 763–85

Dobson, S.M., Goddard, J.A. and Wilson, J.O.S. (2001) League structure and match attendances in English rugby league, *International Review of Applied Economics*, forthcoming

Dolley, J. (1933) Characteristics and procedure of common stock splits, *Harvard Business Review*, 11, 316–26

Dowie, J. (1976) On the efficiency and equity of betting markets, *Economica*, 43, 139–50

Downward, P. and Dawson, A. (1999) The demand for professional team sports: traditional findings and new developments, *Working Paper*, 99.7, Staffordshire University Business School

Duke, V. and Crolley, L. (1996) *Football, Nationality and the State*, Harlow: Longman

Dunning, E., Murphy, P. and Williams, J. (1988) *The Roots of Football Hooliganism: An Historical and Sociological Study*, London and New York: Routledge & Kegan Paul

Eastham, J. (1999) The organisation of French football today, in H. Dauncey and G. Hare (eds.), *France and the 1998 World Cup*, London: Frank Cass

Eckard, E.W. (1998) The NCAA cartel and competitive balance in college football, *Review of Economic Organization*, 13, 347–69

El-Hodiri, M. and Quirk, J. (1971) An economic model of a professional sports league, *Journal of Political Economy*, 79, 1302–19

Fama, E. (1970) Efficient capital markets: a review of theory and empirical work, *Journal of Finance*, 25, 383–423

Fama, E., Fisher, L., Jensen, M. and Roll, R. (1969) The adjustment of stock prices to new information, *International Economic Review*, 10, 1–21

Ferguson, D.G., Stewart, K.G., Jones, J.C.H. and le Drassay, A. (1991) The pricing of sports events: do teams maximize profit?, *Journal of Industrial Economics*, 39, 297–310

Ferrall, A. and Smith, A.A. Jr. (1999) A sequential game model of sports championship series: theory and estimation, *Review of Economics and Statistics*, 81, 704–19

Finn, G.P.T. (2000) Scottish myopia and global prejudices, in G.P.T. Finn and R. Giulianotti (eds.), *Football Culture: Local Contests, Global Visions*, London: Frank Cass

Fishwick, N. (1989) *English Football and Society, 1910–1950*, Manchester: Manchester University Press

Fizel, J.L. and D'Itri, M. (1996) Estimating managerial efficiency: the case of college basketball coaches, *Journal of Sport Management*, 10, 435–45

    (1997) Managerial efficiency, managerial succession and organizational performance, *Managerial and Decision Economics*, 18, 295–308

Football Association (1991) *The Blueprint for the Future of Football*, London: Football Association

Football Trust (various issues) *Digest of Football Statistics*, Leicester: University of Leicester

Fort, R. (2000) European and North American sports differences(?), *Scottish Journal of Political Economy*, 47, 431–55

Fort, R. and Quirk, J. (1995) Cross-subsidization, incentives and outcomes in professional team sports leagues, *Journal of Economic Literature*, 33, 1265–99

Foster, K. (2000) European law and football: who's in charge? in J. Garland, D. Malcolm and M. Rowe (eds.), *The Future of Football: Challenges for the Twenty-first Century*, London: Frank Cass

Fynn, A. and Guest, L. (1994) *Out of Time: Why Football isn't Working*, London: Simon & Schuster

Gamson, W.A. and Scotch, N.A. (1964) Scapegoating in baseball, *American Journal of Sociology*, 70, 69–72

Gandar, J.M., Dare, W.H., Brown, C.R. and Zuber, R.A. (1998) Informed traders and price variations in the betting market for professional basketball games, *Journal of Finance*, 53, 385–401

Gandar, J.M., Zuber, R.A., O'Brien, T. and Russo, B. (1988) Testing rationality in the point spread betting market, *Journal of Finance*, 43, 995–1008

Gibrat, R. (1931) *Les inégalités économiques*, Paris: Librairie du Recueil Sirey

Goldberg, A. and Wragg, S. (1991) It's not a knock-out: English football and globalisation, in J. Williams and S. Wragg (eds.), *British Football and Social Change: Getting Into Europe*, Leicester: Leicester University Press

Golec, J. and Tamarkin, M. (1991) The degree of inefficiency in the football betting market: statistical tests, *Journal of Financial Economics*, 30, 311–23

    (1998) Bettors love skewness, not risk, at the horse track, *Journal of Political Economy*, 106, 205–25

    (1999) *Econometric Analysis*, 4th edn., Englewood Cliffs, New Jersey: Prentice-Hall

Grier, K.B. and Tollison, R.D. (1994) The rookie draft and competitive balance: the case of professional football, *Journal of Economic Behaviour and Organization*, 25, 293–8

Grusky, O. (1963) Managerial succession and organizational effectiveness, *American Journal of Sociology*, 69, 21–31

(1964) Reply to scapegoating in baseball, *American Journal of Sociology*, 70, 72–6

Guilianotti, R. (1999) *Football: A Sociology of the Global Game*, Cambridge: Polity

Gujarati, D.N. (1995) *Basic Econometrics*, 3rd edn., New York: McGraw-Hill

Hallam, D. and Machado, F. (1996) Efficiency analysis with panel data: a study of Portuguese dairy farms, *European Review of Agricultural Economics*, 23, 79–93

Hamilton, B.H. (1997) Racial discrimination and professional basketball salaries in the 1990s, *Applied Economics*, 29, 287–96

Hart, P.E. and Prais, S.J. (1956) The analysis of business concentration: a statistical approach, *Journal of the Royal Statistical Society Series A*, 119, 150–91

Hart, R.A., Hutton, J. and Sharot, T. (1975) A statistical analysis of association football attendances, *Applied Statistics*, 24, 17–27

Hatanaka, M. (1974) An efficient estimator for the dynamic adjustment model with autocorrelated errors, *Journal of Econometrics*, 2, 199–220

Hausman, J.A. and Leonard, G.K. (1997) Superstars in the National Basketball Association: economic value and policy, *Journal of Labour Economics*, 15, 586–624

Henerey, R.J. (1985) On the average probability of losing bets on horses with given starting price odds, *Journal of the Royal Statistical Society Series A*, 148, 342–9

Hill, I.D. (1974). Association football and statistical inference, *Applied Statistics*, 23, 203–8

Hill, J.R., Madura, J. and Zuber, R.A. (1982) The short run demand for major league baseball, *Atlantic Economic Journal*, 10, 31–5

Hoehn, T. and Szymanski S. (1999) The Americanization of European football, *Economic Policy*, 28, 205–40

Hofler, R.A. and Payne, J.E. (1996) How close to their offensive potential do National Football League teams play?, *Applied Economics Letters*, 3, 743–7

(1997) Measuring efficiency in the National Basketball Association, *Economics Letters*, 55, 293–9

Horne, J. (1996) 'Sakka' in Japan, *Media, Culture and Society*, 18, 527–47

(2000) Soccer in Japan: is wa all you need? in G.P.T. Finn and R. Giulianotti (eds.), *Football Culture: Local Contests, Global Visions*, London: Frank Cass

Horowitz, I. (1994) On the manager as principal clerk, *Managerial and Decision Economics*, 15, 413–19

Horton, E. (1997) *Moving the Goalposts: Football's Exploitation*, Edinburgh: Mainstream

Hugman, B.J. (1998) *The PFA Premier and Football League Players' Records 1946–1998*, Harpenden: Queen Anne Press

Hunt, J. and Lewis, K. (1976) Dominance, recontracting and the reserve clause: major league baseball, *American Economic Review*, 66, 936–43

Jacobs, D. and Singell, L. (1993) Leadership and organizational performance: isolating links between managers and collective success, *Social Science Research*, 22 165–89

Jennett, N. (1984) Attendances, uncertainty of outcome and policy in Scottish League Football, *Scottish Journal of Political Economy*, 31, 176–98

Jensen, M.C. and Meckling, W.H. (1976) Theory of the firm: managerial behaviour, agency costs and ownership structure, *Journal of Financial Economics*, 3, 305–60

Jondrow, J., Lovell, C.A.K., Materov, I. and Schmidt, P. (1982) On the estimation of technical inefficiency in the stochastic frontier production function model, *Journal of Econometrics*, 19, 233–8

Kahn, L.M. (1991) Discrimination in professional sports: a survey of the literature, *Industrial and Labor Relations Review*, 44, 395–418

(1993) Free agency, long term contracts and compensation in major league baseball, *Review of Economics and Statistics* 75, 157–64

(2000) The sports business as a labor market laboratory, *Journal of Economic Perspectives*, 14, 75–94

Kahn, L.M. and Sherer, P.O. (1988) Racial differences in professional basketball players' compensation, *Journal of Labour Economics*, 6, 40–61

Keegan, K. (1999) *My Autobiography*, London: Hodder & Stoughton

Keifer, N.M. (1988) Economic duration data and hazard functions, *Journal of Economic Literature*, 26, 646–79

Kennedy, P. (1998) *A Guide to Econometrics*, 4th edn., Oxford: Blackwell

Késenne, S. (1996) League management in professional team sports with win maximising clubs, *European Journal for Sports Management*, 2, 14–22

(2000a) Revenue sharing and competitive balance in professional team sports, *Journal of Sports Economics*, 1, 56–65

(2000b) The impact of salary caps in professional team sports, *Scottish Journal of Political Economy*, 47, 422–30

King, J. (2000) *FC Barcelona: Tales from the Nou Camp*, London: Macmillan

King, J. and Kelly, D. (1997) *The Cult of the Manager: Do they Really Make a Difference?*, London: Virgin Books

Kirzner, I.M. (1973) *Competition and Entrepreneurship*, Chicago: Chicago University Press

König, R.H. (2000) Balance in competition in Dutch soccer, *The Statistician*, 49, 419–31

Kuypers, T. (2000) Information and efficiency: an empirical study of a fixed odds betting marker, *Applied Economics*, 32, 1353–63

Lambert, C. (1997) *The Boss*, London: Vista

Lanfranchi, P. (1994) The migration of footballers: the case of France, 1932–1982, in J. Bale and J. Maguire (eds.), *The Global Sports Arena: Athletic Talent Migration in an Interdependent World*, London: Frank Cass

Lazear, E.P. and Rosen, S. (1981) Rank-order tournaments as optimum labor contracts, *Journal of Political Economy*, 89, 841–64

Lee, S. (1999) The BSkyB bid for Manchester United PLC, in S. Hamil, J. Michie and C. Oughton (eds.), *The Business of Football: A Game of Two Halves*, Edinburgh: Mainstream

Lehn, K. (1990a) Property rights, risk sharing and player disability in major league baseball, in B. Goff and R. Tollison (eds.), *Sportometrics*, College Station, Tx: A & M Press

(1990b) Information asymmetries in baseball's free agent market, in B. Goff and R. Tollison (eds.), *Sportometrics*, College Station, Tex.: A & M Press

MacDonald, D.N. and Reynolds, M.O. (1994) Are baseball players paid their marginal products? *Managerial and Decision Economics*, 15, 443–57

MacDonald, G. (1988) The economics of rising stars, *American Economic Review*, 78, 155–66

MacKinlay, A.C. (1997) Event studies in economics and finance, *Journal of Economic Literature*, 35, 13–39

Macías, P. (2000) *A–Z of European Football*, Cáceres: Copegraf, S.L.

Maguire, J. (1994) Preliminary observations on globalisation and the migration of sport labour, *Sociological Review*, 42, 452–80

Maguire, J. and Pearton, R. (2000) Global sport and the migration patterns of France '98 World Cup finals players: some preliminary observations, in J. Garland, D. Malcolm and M. Rowe (eds.), *The Future of Football: Challenges for the Twenty-first Century*, London: Frank Cass

Maguire, J. and Stead, D. (1998) Border crossings: soccer labour migration and the European Union, *International Review for the Sociology of Sport*, 33, 59–73

Maher, M.J. (1982) Modelling association football scores, *Statistica Neerlandica*, 36, 109–18

Malcolm, D., Jones, I. and Waddington, I. (2000) The people's game? Football spectatorship and demographic change, in J. Garland, D. Malcolm and M. Rowe (eds.), *The Future of Football: Challenges for the Twenty-first Century*, London: Frank Cass

Marris, R.L. (1964) *The Economic Theory of Managerial Capitalism*, London: Macmillan

Michie, J. and Oughton, C. (1999) Football and broadcasting and the MMC case, in S. Hamil, J. Michie and C. Oughton (eds.), *The Business of Football: A Game of Two Halves*, Edinburgh: Mainstream

Mignon, P. (2000) French football after the 1998 World Cup: the state and the modernity of football, in G.P.T. Finn and R. Giulianotti (eds.), *Football Culture: Local Contests, Global Visions*, London: Frank Cass

Mintzberg, H. (1973) *The Nature of Managerial Work*, New York: Prentice-Hall

Mises, L. von (1966) *Human Action*, 3rd edn., Chicago: Contemporary Books

Monopolies and Mergers Commission (1999) *British Sky Broadcasting Group PLC and Manchester United PLC: A Report on the Proposed Merger*, London: TSO, Cm 4305

Moorhouse, H.F. (1984) Professional football and working class culture: English theories and Scottish evidence, *The Sociological Review*, 32, 285–315

Moran, R. (2000) Racism in football: a victim's perspective, in J. Garland, D. Malcolm and M. Rowe (eds.), *The Future of Football: Challenges for the Twenty-first Century*, London: Frank Cass

Moroney, M.J. (1956) *Facts from Figures*, 3rd edn., London: Penguin

Morrow, S. (1999) *The New Business of Football: Accountability and Finance in Football*, London: Macmillan

Murray, B. (1984) *The Old Firm: Sectarianism, Sport and Society in Scotland*, Edinburgh, John Donald
(1998) *The Old Firm in the New Age: Celtic and Rangers since the Souness Revolution*, Edinburgh, Mainstream

Neale, W.C. (1964) The peculiar economics of professional sports, *Quarterly Journal of Economics*, 78, 1–14

Nogawa, H. and Maeda, H. (1999) The Japanese dream: soccer culture towards the new millennium, in G. Armstrong and R. Giulianotti (eds.), *Football Cultures and Identities*, Basingstoke: Macmillan

Noll, R.G. (1974) Attendance and price setting, in R.G. Noll (ed.), *Government and the Sports Business*, Washington, DC: Brookings Institution

Noll, R.G. and Zimbalist, A. (1997) *Sport, Jobs and Taxes*, Washington, DC: Brookings Institution

Pankoff, L.D. (1968) Market efficiency and football betting, *Journal of Business*, 41, 203–14

Peel, D.A. and Thomas, D. (1988) Outcome uncertainty and the demand for football, *Scottish Journal of Political Economy*, 35, 242–9

(1992) The demand for football: some evidence on outcome uncertainty, *Empirical Economics*, 17, 323–31

PEP (1966) English professional football, *Planning*, 32 (496)

Pickup, I. (1999) French football from its origins to 1984, in H. Dauncey and G. Hare (eds.), *France and the 1998 World Cup*, London: Frank Cass

Pindyck, R.S. and Rubinfeld, D.L. (1998) *Econometric Models and Economic Forecasts*, 4th edn., Boston: McGraw-Hill

Pope, P.F. and Peel, D.A. (1989) Information, prices and efficiency in a fixed odds betting market, *Economica*, 56, 323–41

Porter, R. and Scully, G.W. (1982) Measuring managerial efficiency: the case of baseball, *Southern Economic Journal*, 48, 642–50

Preston, I. and Szymanski, S. (2000) Racial discrimination in English football, *Scottish Journal of Political Economy*, 47, 341–63

Quirk, J. and El-Hodiri, M. (1974) The economic theory of a professional league, in R.G. Noll (ed.), *Government and the Sports Business*, Washington, DC: Brookings Institution

Quirk, J. and Fort, R. (1992) *Pay Dirt: The Business of Professional Team Sports*, Princeton: Princeton University Press

(1999) *Hard Ball: The Abuse of Power in Pro Team Sports*, Princeton: Princeton University Press

Rascher, D.A. (1997) A model of a professional sports league, in W. Hendricks (ed.), *Advances in the Economics of Sport*, 2, Greenwich: JAI Press

Reep, C., Pollard, R. and Benjamin, B. (1971) Skill and chance in ball games, *Journal of the Royal Statistical Society Series A*, 131, 581–5

Reilly, B. and Witt, R. (1995) English league transfer prices: is there a racial dimension?, *Applied Economics Letters*, 2, 220–2

Richards, D.G. and Guell, R.C. (1998) Baseball success and the structure of salaries, *Applied Economics Letters*, 5, 291–6

Ridder, G., Cramer, J.S. and Hopstaken, P. (1994) Estimating the effect of a red card in soccer, *Journal of the American Statistical Association*, 89, 1124–7

Robbins, S.P. (1994) *Management*, 4th edn., Englefield Cliffs, New Jersey: Prentice-Hall

Rosen, S. (1981) The economics of superstars, *American Economic Review*, 71, 845–58

Rosen, S. and Sanderson, A. (2000) Labour markets in professional sports, *National Bureau of Economic Research, Working Paper*, 7573, Cambridge, Mass.: National Bureau of Economic Research

Rothmans (various years), *Rothmans FootballYearbook*, London: Headline

Rottenberg, S. (1956) The baseball player's labor market, *Journal of Political Economy*, 64, 242–58

Rue, H. and Salveson, O. (2000) Pediction and retrospective analysis of soccer matches in a league, *The Statistician*, 49, 399–418

Ruggerio, J., Hadley, L. and Gustafson, E. (1996) Technical efficiency in Major League Baseball, in J. Fizel, E. Gustafson and L. Hadley (eds.), *Baseball Economics: Current Research*, Westport: Praeger

Ruggerio, J., Hadley, L., Ruggerio, G. and Knowles, S. (1997) A note on the Pythagorean theory of baseball production, *Managerial and Decision Economics*, 18, 335–42

Russell, D. (1997) *Football and the English: A Social History of Association Football in England, 1863–1995*, Preston: Carnegie

    (1999) Associating with football: social identity in England 1863–1998, in G. Armstrong and R. Giulianotti (eds.), *Football Cultures and Identities*, London: Macmillan

Saxonhouse, G.R. (1976) Estimated parameters as dependent variables, *American Economic Review*, 66, 178–83

Schofield, J.A. (1988) Production functions in the sports industry: an empirical analysis of professional cricket, *Applied Economics*, 20, 177–93

Schollaert, P.T. and Smith, D.H. (1987) Team racial composition and sports attendance, *Sociological Quarterly*, 28, 71–87

Scott, F.A., Long, J.E. and Somppi, K. (1985) Salary vs marginal revenue product under monopsony and competition: the case of professional basketball, *Atlantic Economic Journal*, 13, 50–9

Scully, G.W. (1974) Pay and performance in Major League Baseball, *American Economic Review*, 64, 915–30

    (1992) Is managerial turnover rational? Evidence from professional team sports, in G.W. Scully (ed.), *Advances in the Economics of Sport*, Greenwich: JAI Press

    (1994) Managerial efficiency and survivability in professional team sports, *Managerial and Decision Economics*, 15, 403–11

    (1995) *The Market Structure of Sports*, Chicago: University of Chicago Press

Shin, H.S. (1991) Optimal betting odds against insider traders, *Economic Journal*, 101, 1179–85

    (1992) Prices of state contingent claims with insider traders and the favourite-longshot bias, *Economic Journal*, 102, 426–35

    (1993) Measuring the incidence of insider trading in a market for state-contingent claims, *Economic Journal*, 103, 1141–53

Siegfried, J.J. and Eisenberg, J.D. (1980) The demand for minor league baseball, *Atlantic Economic Journal*, 8, 59–69

Siegfried, J.J. and Zimbalist, A. (2000) The economics of sports facilities and their communities, *Journal of Economic Perspectives*, 14, 95–114

Simmons, R. (1996) The demand for English league football: a club level analysis, *Applied Economics*, 28, 139–55

    (1997) Implications of the Bosman ruling for football transfer markets, *Economic Affairs*, 17, 13–18

Simon, H. (1959) Theories of decision making in economics and behavioural science, *American Economic Review*, 253–83

Singell, L.D. (1993) Managers, specific human capital and productivity in Major League Baseball, *Atlantic Economic Journal*, 21, 47–59

Sloane, P. (1969) The labour market in professional football, *British Journal of Industrial Relations*, 7, 181–99

(1971) The economics of professional football: the football club as utility maximiser, *Scottish Journal of Political Economy*, 17, 121–46

Smailes, G. (1992) *The Breedon Book of Football League Records*, Derby: Breedon

Solow, R.M. (1956) A contribution to the theory of economic growth, *Quarterly Journal of Economics*, 70, 65–94

Speight, A. and Thomas, D. (1997) Arbitrator decision-making in the transfer market: an empirical analysis, *Scottish Journal of Political Economy*, 44, 198–215

Sugden, J. and Tomlinson, A. (1998) *FIFA and the Contest for World Football*, Cambridge: Polity

Sutton, J. (1997) Gibrat's legacy, *Journal of Economic Literature*, 35, 40–59

Szymanski, S. (2000a) Hearts, minds and the Restrictive Practices Court case, in S. Hamil, J. Michie, C. Oughton and S. Warby (eds.), *Football in the Digital Age: Whose Game is it Anyway?*, Edinburgh: Mainstream

(2000b) A market test for discrimination in the English professional soccer leagues, *Journal of Political Economy*, 108, 590–603

Szymanski, S. and Kuypers, T. (1999) *Winners and Losers: The Business Strategy of Football*, London: Viking

Szymanski, S. and Smith, R. (1997) The English football industry: profit, performance and industrial structure, *International Review of Applied Economics*, 11, 135–53

Tabner, B. (1992) *Through the Turnstiles*, Harefield: Yore

Taylor, A.J.P. (1965) *English History: 1914–1945*, Oxford: Oxford University Press

Taylor, Lord Justice (1990) The Hillsborough stadium disaster (15 April 1989), inquiry by the Rt. Hon. Lord Justice Taylor, Final Report, Cm. 962, London: HMSO

Taylor, R. and Ward, A. (1995) *Kicking and Screaming: An Oral History of Football in England*, London: Robson

Temple, J. (1999) The new growth evidence, *Journal of Economic Literature*, 37, 112–56

Terrell, D. and Farmer, A. (1996) Optimal betting and efficiency in parimutuél betting markets with information costs, *Economic Journal*, 106, 846–68

Turner, D. and White, A. (1993) *The Breedon Book of Football Managers*, Derby: Breedon Books

Vaughan Williams, L. and Paton, D. (1997) Why is there a favourite longshot bias in British racetrack betting markets?, *Economic Journal*, 107, 150–8

Vrooman, J. (1995) A general theory of professional sports leagues, *Southern Economic Journal*, 61, 971–90

(1996) The baseball players' marker reconsidered, *Southern Economic Journal*, 63, 339–60

(1997) A unified theory of capital and labour markets in major league baseball, *Southern Economic Journal* 63, 594–619

(2000) The economics of American Sports leagues, *Scottish Journal of Political Economy*, 47, 364–98

Waddington, I. and Malcolm, D. (1998) The social composition of football crowds in Western Europe, *International Review for the Sociology of Sport*, 33, 155–69

Walker, B. (1986) The demand for professional league football and the success of football league teams: some city size effects, *Urban Studies*, 23, 209–19

Walvin, J. (1975) *The People's Game; A Social History of British Football*, London: Allen Lane

(1994) *The People's Game: The History of Football Revisited*, Edinburgh, Mainstream

Weitzman, M. (1965) Utility analysis and group behaviour: an empirical study, *Journal of Political Economy*, 73, 18–26

White, H. (1980) A heteroscedasticity-consistent covariance matrix estimator and a direct test for heteroscedasticity, *Econometrica*, 48, 817–38

Whiting, R. (1977) *The Chrysanthemum and the Bat*, New York: Avon

Williams, J. (1997) The 'new football' in England and Sir John Hall's 'new Geordie nation', in S. Gehrmann (ed.), *Football and Regional Identity in Europe*, Münster: Lit Verlag

Williamson, O.E. (1963) Managerial discretion and business behavior, *American Economic Review*, 53, 1032–57

Wilson, P. and Sim, B. (1995) The demand for semi-pro league football in Malaysia 1989–91: a panel data approach, *Applied Economics*, 27, 131–8

Zak, T.A., Huang, C.J. and Siegfried, J.J. (1979) Production efficiency: the case of professional basketball, *Journal of Business*, 52, 379–92

Zech, C.E. (1981) An empirical estimation of a production function: the case of Major League baseball, *American Economist*, 25, 19–23

Zellner, A. (1962) An efficient method of estimating seemingly unrelated regressions and tests for aggregation bias, *Journal of the American Statistical Association*, 57, 348–68

Index